The History of Long Melford
- Primary Source Edition

William Parker

THE HISTORY

OF

LONG MELFORD

BY

SIR WILLIAM PARKER, Bart.

PRINTED FOR THE AUTHOR BY 1133
WYMAN & SONS, 74-75, GREAT QUEEN STREET,
LINCOLN'S INN FIELDS, LONDON. W.C.

1873

THE HISTORY

OF

LONG MELFORD.

INTRODUCTION.

HE early history of Melford lies buried deep under the accumulated dust of ages, and grubbing therein for the first tangible knowledge of the far past is but a dry research. Conjecture, often vague, must be coupled with fragmentary records and inferences, in order to reunite the few scattered and severed threads of its old-world story before the Conquest.

The Romans form a slight starting-point in our annals, for it appears plain, from the Roman remains found here, that at least one particular spot in this parish was in their occupation; viz., at the junction of the rivers, on or about the present Stoneylands; and perhaps there was another on Westgate Hill. How long they were here is uncertain, as also whether they were settlers but few in number, or as a small military force, possibly an outpost from the camps of Clare or Cockfield. Perhaps, looking strategically at the position in the fork formed by the Melford river, at its junction with the larger stream of the Stour, a very favourite sort of post in those days,—this latter supposition might seem probable; as they would thus maintain the chain of defence of the great camps of Wixoe and Clare, and thence along the Stour eastward; and at the same time would keep open the communication with the northern camps through those of Lavenham and Cockfield.

Among the Roman remains found here, such as coins of various sorts and dates, urns, pottery, and portions of tesselated pavements, there was excavated from a gravel-pit on Stoneylands, about forty-five years ago, a fine and perfect large glass urn of a rare and valuable shape and quality, which was presented to the British Museum by the late Sir WILLIAM PARKER.

From the time when the Romans evacuated Britain till the reign of Edward the Confessor, the history of Melford is a long blank. We may perhaps fancy that our remote forefathers sent their little quota hence to take part in the lost battles in Suffolk against Sweyn and his Danish marauders; and half a century later, those of a succeeding generation were wistfully scanning the appearance of yet another race of foreign invaders, some of whose nobles may have looked with greedy, longing eyes at the goodly manor of Melford, which, happily for its inhabitants, was beyond the grasp of the Normans, being already an appanage of the Abbey of St. Edmund, which cast the protecting ægis of the Church over the villeins, serfs, and socmen of Melford.

Passing to times later on, its population stood at their doors on a November day in 1214, to see King John pass by on his way to Bury; and though the Melford folk were indebted to him for the boon, important in those times, of the grant of a weekly market and of an annual fair, yet, as probably their feelings towards him were the same as those of the neighbouring people of Clare, of whom it is recorded that "he was so ill received that he quitted the town the same day," so Melford, though usually loyal, may have greeted the unpopular king on this occasion with but cold welcome, and scant applause.*

And besides the known visits of King John, and in after-days of Queen Elizabeth, it is most probable that as Melford lies on the direct road between London and Bury, many other crowned heads may have passed through its long street; for no less than sixteen sovereigns personally offered at the famous shrine of St. Edmund before the dissolution of the Abbey. Their names are thus handed down to us :—Canute, Edward the Confessor, William I., Henry I., Henry II., Richard I., John (twice), Henry III. (twice), Edward I. (twice, or more), Queen Eleanor, Edward II., Edward III., Richard II., Henry VI. (four times), Edward IV., Henry VII.

---

* King John was at Melford 4th November, 1214.—(Archæologia.)

LORD ARTHUR HERVEY, Bishop of Bath and Wells, in his address to the members of the Archæological Society of Great Britain, on their visit to Bury in 1854, is reported to have said that Edward I. was at Bury thirteen times.

Pentlow, the reputed home of "John Wraw," is so near this place that it is very probable that some few of the more discontented and reckless inhabitants of Melford may have been induced to join that ruffian's formidable mob in the insurrection of 1381, and have witnessed the atrocities committed in Bury and its vicinity; and if so, it is to be hoped also shared their punishment at Barton Mills.

In the rising for Lady Jane Grey, on the death of King Edward VI., the men of Suffolk showed themselves strong partisans in favour of the rival claim; and Melford may, not improbably, have been represented by some supporters of Queen Mary, among the garrison of Framlingham Castle, or who may have joined the pursuing force of Lord Arundel for the capture at Cambridge, of the Earl of Northumberland, who was an object of special hatred to the people of the Eastern counties.

Much of this is of course conjecture; but anyhow it is certain that for nearly five centuries the rich and powerful Abbey of St. Edmund held possession of the manor and church of Melford; and its vassals and serfs, generation after generation, saw a succession of thirty-three mitred Abbots of Bury, who took their seats in the House of Peers, tenth in order among the twenty-four abbots who ranked as barons, princes almost in wealth and power, constantly coming with their retinues to and fro between Bury and their country seat at Melford Hall, for pleasure or relaxation from the cares and business of the great religious house.

Whether they were good or bad, easy or tyrannical landlords to their Melford tenants, who can now say; but as they exacted from all officers connected with their estates, methodical habits of business, they eventually left behind them many plain records of their dealings with this manor. So far as their chartularies, terriers, and rentals may be taken as inferences, they were not hard masters; and their vassals enjoyed the advantage, inestimable in days of lawless violence, of the full and unfailing protection of the Church against the strong arm of those powerful barons and their turbulent followers, whose creed was that might constituted right.

Furthermore, whatever the eventual corruption and failure of the old religious system, all must admit that the great conventual houses, in their early days of purity, were grand examples of the sublime force of pious, self-denying devotion. In those days their inmates prayed, taught, and laboured unselfishly; for though wealth and possessions flowed in upon them, the harvest they mainly reaped therefrom was an increase of toil in administering their property for the public advantage, in the maintenance of education, hospitality, and comprehensive charity; and none can deny that in those times the Abbeys and other great religious houses were oases of learning, education, science, and art in the then universal desert of ignorance and barbarism. And so it would seem that Melford and its people, loved and favoured by the successive monastic rulers of the Abbey of St. Edmund, down to the last Abbot, who, as a *native of Melford*, must have held it dear, may perhaps have received from these old pioneers of learning, a ray of enlightenment and civilization in advance of the age in which they lived. And they in turn seem to have striven, so far as they could, to repay to their foster-mother, the Church, some of the obligations and benefits they had received from her, while also caring for the interests of their own place and people; and so one after another, while leaving bequests of lands, money, and goods for charitable purposes, generally apportioned some share thereof to the Church; and when in the 15th century the time came that, either from decay, or from want of space to accommodate the growing population, it became necessary to rebuild the old parish church, the advowson and endowment of which Earl Alfric, the son of Widgar, had given to St. Edmund's Abbey in the 11th century, the people of Melford seem readily and willingly to have contributed their full quota towards rearing and embellishing the present beautiful edifice, on the stones of which are still recorded the names of some of those long bygone worthies, who then vied with each other in this great work of love and piety.

Peace to their manes; but if they could have foreseen the fate that was to befall their work before it had stood a century, they would surely have gone in disquiet to their last narrow resting-places. Even the most Protestant among us must admit that the great Reformation was ushered in, particularly as regards the churches, with unnecessary spoliation, and ignorant, vulgar vandalism. In their bitter religious zeal, the now predominant Reformers could not tolerate or spare the most harmless symbols and decorations, however beautiful, if only they had been used or regarded by Romish worshippers; and it was the "GODLY" who now "brake down the carved work of the temples with axes and hammers." The religious cry was war to the knife; and it was "Væ victis." But could it have been necessary that this puritanical horror of all ornament and fine art should be shown by such gross and wanton destruction as recorded in the case of Melford Church.

Three times was it wrecked and plundered. First by the early Reformers; again, when, after the Marian return to Popery, an attempt had been made to restore to it some little portion of its shorn splendour,—a short-lived effort, entailing yet more complete and sweeping reform of "cleansing from superstition"; and lastly, by the snuffling, canting, roundhead scum of the Rebellion, who, though they could find but little left on which to vent their pseudo-religious spleen, yet added the last touch that was wanting to the work of destruction before it should be "Ichabod," and its glory (morally faulty though it may have been) have finally departed.

They spared nothing, and were probably among the worst and bitterest of the spoliators, having come here expressly to plunder and persecute the Countess of Rivers, then residing at Melford Hall, who was of the most obnoxious class of malignants, being a stanch Royalist and a Roman Catholic. What befell her will appear later in these pages; but doubtless we owe to this ungodly company of "Praise God Barebones" the destruction of the old Market Cross on the Green, and with sundry other mischief of those evil days, the removing of many of the monumental brasses of the church, which had escaped the barbarous rage of the Reformed Commissioners, "the antichristian tomb-breakers," as old *Weever* calls them, or that had been saved by the proclamation of the second year of Queen Elizabeth, which forbade the destruction of the monuments and effigies of the dead.

So, the purification being quite complete, and after the legitimate

Rector, Doctor Wareyn, in 1643, was ejected from his benefice, and for many years the living of Melford had been occupied by a succession of six Puritan ministers, when the Restoration at length came, and not only the king, but the sequestrated clergy enjoyed their own again, this church, in common with most others, had already assumed that deplorable aspect of whitewash, high pews, hat-pegs, bricked-up windows, mouldiness, and general desecration, which continued increasing in degree, with the careless irreverence, not only of the clergy, but of society in general, through the last century down to our own times.

With the educational change that has now come over social feeling, evinced by a growing appreciation of things beautiful, and an improved taste in art, there has arisen, as a natural consequence, a general desire for the restoration of churches, based on a double ground of admiration of the glories of architecture and of a higher sense of reverence and respect. So, here, as in most places, those of the present generation have sought partially to restore, in a mode befitting the altered circumstances of the times, this grand old parish church, in which, with a friendly tolerance most exemplary, all denominations in Melford now take a common pride.

A share in this feeling, and a fond home-love for the old place, has led to this poor attempt to compile some records of Melford, in the hope that thus the history of its bygone times may be in a measure preserved, and that the long chain of historical interest and association which firmly binds Melford past to Melford present, may connect both also with the future.

LIST of SOME of the BOOKS
Which have been quoted from or referred to.

Battely's Antiquitates Sancti Edmundi
 Burgi.

Chronica Jocelini de Brakelonda.

Cox's Magna Britannia [Suffolk].

Haydn's Dictionary of Dates.

Shipley's Ecclesiastical Glossary.

Wright's Essex.

East Anglian.

Cullum's Hawstead.

Gage's Thingoe Hundred.

Almack's Account of Melford Church.

——Suffolk Archæological Society.

Ruggle's History of the Poor.

Burke's Extinct Peerages.

Antiquarian Repertory.

Collings's Gothic Architecture.

Badham's History of All Saints, Sudbury.

Neale's Views of Churches.

Howell's Letters.

Weever's Ancient Monuments.

Peck's Desiderata Curiosa.

Holinshed's Chronicles.

Mercurius Rusticus.

Kirby's Suffolk Traveller.

Proceedings of the Suffolk Institute of Archæology.

Suffolk Churches.

Camden's Britannia.

MSS.

Dr. Bisbie's Records from 1660 to 1685.

Melford Parish Documents, and the Black Book.

Abbot John de Norwold's Melford Chartulary.

Abbot John de Tymworth's Melford Chartulary.

Abbot William Curteys's Melford Chartulary.

THE HISTORY OF LONG MELFORD.

CHAPTER I.

THAT Melford derived its name from the Mill ford there can be but little doubt. From a very remote date there existed a mill near the ford, where the main bridge now stands, being one of the water-mills mentioned in the survey of this parish in Domesday Book.

Starting from the time of Edward the Confessor, it appears that Melford then formed part of the great possessions in Suffolk and Essex of Earl Alfric, the son of Withgar. His name is also called Wisgar in the Domesday Book of Suffolk, but in the Abbot's Chartulary it is throughout spelt Widgar. This great thane, who was styled "the famous Earl," had the custody for Queen Emma, the mother of the Confessor, of the franchise of the eight hundreds and a half, since known as the Liberty of St. Edmund. In the time of Leofstan, who was abbot of Bury from A.D. 1044 to 1065, Earl Alfric gave the manor of Melford to the Abbey of St. Edmund. The Chartulary of Abbot John de Norwold, made in the year 1287, and which is written on parchment in the old monkish abbreviated Latin, recites the original grant of the time of Edward the Confessor, as follows :—

Translation.

"Earl Alfric, son of Widgar, presented Melford to St. Edmund, as stated in the Register [of the Abbey] S.P., folio 32, in these words :—'In the time of St. Edward, King and Confessor, and of Leofstan the abbot, Alfric, the son of Widgar, the famous Earl, gave Melford to St. Edmund, and gave a manor to this church and to St. Edmund, and to Leofstan the abbot; and he conveyed to them the induction to this church in perpetuity, and bound his son Withgar to the same, so that their charter then came into the hands of the monks.'

B

"It was of itself a leta* before the time of the said Alfric, in the reigns of Etheldred, Canute, Harold, Hardicanute, and St. Edward, kings of England, and it is part of the letes of the hundred of Babber,† as is before named in the Abbot's Register, in folio 2 and folio e e, in these words, viz. :—

"'Melford and Aketune [Acton] are seven ferdingas, and tenants de aulâ of Melford are equal : they pay to the sheriff every year three shillings, and the reckoning of the service to the lord remains unaltered. Acton formerly gave the services which they now reckon upon Melford, and six shillings : and there are in it [Melford] various tenants holding in chief of the said king; to wit, the land of Radulphus de Hodeboville, lands of Hanus and Hervey de Clerbec. A secta‡ and two sectæ are due to the same hundred ; viz., one from the land of Gilbert, son of Paganus, and the two others from the land of Aelmus [? Anselm] Ernoldbug.'

"Of Hidagium§ and Warpeny the records appeared formerly in the Abbot's Register, intituled Cu. folio 2, folio E 2, and E 3 ; but whether through unfair means they were erased, or whether, from the age of the material, they became obliterated, cannot now be known. They give aid to the sheriff, and pay to the sheriff three shillings a year.

"[The Abbey of] St. Edmund had this also in the time of William the Conqueror, and had also here XII. carucates of land, and XVII. villeins, and XXX. bordarii, and II. socmen holding 80 acres of land."

A little later on in this century than the date of Alfric's grant the Normans had landed, and there had been subsequently compiled that minute and curious survey of England, called the Domesday Book, perhaps the most valuable ancient record of its kind possessed by any nation. According to the "Red Book" of the Exchequer, the Domesday Survey was commenced by order of William the Conqueror, with the advice of his Parliament, in the year 1080, and completed in 1086. Stowe says that the title, Domesday Book, is a corruption of Domus Dei Book, it having received that name because it was deposited in the King's Treasury in part of the Church of Westminster called Domus Dei. The two original volumes of the Domesday Book are now under a thick glass case in the Record Office. The following transcript of the text relates to Melford ; and a rough translation of the abbreviated Latin is appended.

* A leta, or township, was the twelfth part of a hundred.
† The present hundred of Babergh.
‡ Suit or service at the court of the hundred, or at the court of a manor.
§ Warpeny was payable for military service to the Castle of Norwich. Hidagium was the personal and carriage service of the socoage vassals. (Millar.)

DOMESDAY BOOK, A.D. 1086.
" Sudfolc. Baberhga H.

"Melaforda. t. r. e. ten. S. e. p. man. XII c. tre. Ex hac tra. ten. Galt. XL ac. de Abbate. Sep. XXXVII vill. et tc. XXIV bord. et m. X tc. VIII car, in dnio. m. VI tc. XX car. hou. m. XIII. Sep. XVI ser. et L ac. pti. Silv. LX Porc. et II Molin. m. III r. Sep. XXX an. m. CCC ovs. Sep. CXL porc. m. XII uasa et XL æq. sil. et m. et II soc. de LXXX ac. tre. I. de Galterus ten. I de XL ac. de abb. Sep. II c. sup. hos. ht. Scs. comd. et sac. et soc. et om. csuet necuq. pot. dare a. vend. tras. suas absq. pleno. csensu. abbis. Ecla de II. car. tre. IIII vill. IX bord. sep. II car. eccliæ. semp. II car. hou. tc. hoc. man. val. XX lib. m. XXX ht in long. XVIII qr. et I leug. in lat. et in Gelt. XX d. et obol. qcq. ibi. ten."

DOMESDAY BOOK, A.D. 1086.

The following is a literal rough translation :—

" Suffolk—Babergh Hundred.

" In the time of King Edward [the Confessor] the [Abbey of] St. Edmund held Melford as a manor, there being 12 carucates of land.* Of this land Gualterus holds 40 acres from the Abbot. There have always been 40 villeins,† and at that time there were 35 bordarii ;‡ there are now 10. There were then 8 ploughs in the demesne; there are now 6. There were then 20 ploughs belonging to the homagers, of which there remain 13. There have always been 16 serfs,§ and 50 acres of meadow land; wood sufficient for depasturing 60 hogs, and 2 water-mills. There are now 3 hackneys. There have always been 30 plough oxen. There are now 300 sheep. There have always been 140 pigs. There are now 12 hives of bees, and now 40 husbandry horses ; and 2 socmen ‖ holding 80 acres of land. The said Gualterus holds here of the Abbot 40 acres of land. There were always 2 ploughs on this. The Saint [Abbey of St. Edmund] has over these protection, and sac and soc ¶ and all accustomed rights. No one can give or sell their land without the full consent of the Abbot. The Church [of Melford] holds 2 carucates of land with 4 villeins and

* The extent of a carucate is very uncertain. Perhaps the 12 carucates may be reckoned as 1,440 acres.

† Villani were irremovable from a manor, and of the lowest servile condition.

‡ Bordarii were cottagers holding a small parcel of land, and of a class superior to the servi and villani. They were to supply to the lord a certain quantity of poultry and eggs, but they, with their lands, were the property of the lord.

§ Servi, feudatory vassals, subject to the will of the lord.

‖ Socmen, husbandry tenants holding of the manor, from whom military service was not required.

¶ Sac and Soc right of courts, and other rights.

9 bordarii. There were always 2 ploughs belonging to the Church, and always 2 ploughs belonging to the homagers of the Church. At that time this manor was worth £20; it is now worth £30.* It is 18 furlongs in length, and one leuga † in breadth, and its gelt ‡ is 20 pence and a halfpenny, whosoever may hold here."

From this survey it appears that the size of the manor, and the quantity of land held by the two socmen, or principal husbandry tenants, remained unaltered from the time of the grant by Earl Alfric; and allowing for the rude measurement of those days, the acreage nearly tallies with that of the survey of the 14th and 15th of Edward I.—A.D. 1287. Again the Domesday Book assigns roughly as the property of the Church of Melford two carucates, or about 240 acres of land. The grant of Earl Alfric does not specify the amount of land with which he endowed this church, but the survey of 1287, though separating the descriptive lands into arable, meadow, pasture, and wood, makes the total amount 261¼ acres, which, it also adds, were derived "from Alfric son of Widgar, formerly the lord of the said barony."

Authorities differ however so widely as to the contents of the carucate of land, that its conversion into acres of the present day must be but hypothetical. According to one form of computation, the Abbot's Manor would have been about 1,440 acres, and the Manor of the Church 240 acres. But if the size of the manor is tried by the vague measure of length and breadth given in Domesday, viz. 18 furlongs by a mile and a half broad, the result would be 2,160 acres. From this uncertainty it is difficult to compare minutely the land measurements of that day; but the 261¼ acres recorded in the survey of A.D. 1287 (probably then but roughly measured) as the size of the Rectory Manor approaches very nearly the two carucates mentioned in Domesday, and comprised in the original gift to the Church of Melford.

Thus, from the grant of Earl Alfric about the year 1050, confirmed as it is by the survey of the Domesday Book, we start with a record of Melford more than 800 years ago, and can now attach link after link to its long historical chain down to the present time.

* The pound, in Domesday time, contained three times the weight of silver it now does, irrespective of value.
† Leuga was nearly a mile and a half.
‡ Gelt, the Crown land-tax.

CHAPTER II.

IT is somewhat difficult to separate completely any part of the account
of Melford in early times from that of the Church, the details
of both being often closely interwoven; and inseparable from the
history of this Church is not only much that relates to its foster parent
and patron, the great Abbey, but also the record existing of the Hospital
of St. Saviour, Bury; for this religious foundation, besides affecting
and altering the original endowment of Melford Church, for ever deprived it of a large portion of its inheritance. It becomes, therefore,
necessary to commence by explaining briefly the history of St.
Saviour's Hospital. And although the following Bull of Pope Eugenius III., granting to the Abbey of Bury a *tithe from Melford*, does
not immediately relate to the endowment of St. Saviour's, yet it is
in a manner connected with it, as well as with this place, with reference
to the parent establishment. Its date is probably of 1146 or 1147,
as Pope Lucius II., therein alluded to, was killed by an accident at the
close of 1144, when Eugenius III. succeeded him in the Papacy in
1145; and Anselm, to whom the Bull is addressed, and who in addition
to his office of Abbot of Bury was for some time Apostolic Legate in
England, died in 1148. (*11 January*)

There is no date to this Bull, but, as already stated, it is clear that
it must have been given between the years 1145 and 1148.† In the
Abbey Chartulary of the Melford property and manor (a parchment
book, of course written in Latin) the copy of this Bull is headed thus:
"The Grant to Abbot Anselm, whereby there was a due payable to
the Abbey from Melford of 20 shillings, and from the land
of Galeus there 10 shillings, according to the Bull of Pope Eugenius III." What the land of Galeus in Melford was at this
date there is no evidence to show. Could it have been the separate
Manor of Kentwell afterwards held by de Valence? Or was Galeus
one of the first descendants or successors of Frodo in the Manor of
Kentwell? There is no other mention of this Galeus, though he must
have been a person of some consideration. The said Bull is quoted in
the Register Pinchbeck, fol. 8, 6.

This Bull of Pope Eugenius III., who was Pope from A.D. 1145 to
1153 (and who was canonized), to Abbot Anselm, who was Abbot of

† *Reg. Sacrista.*
July 1147.

Bury from A.D. 1119 to 1148, translated from the Latin text, runs as follows :—

"Eugenius the Bishop, servant of the servants of God, to his beloved son Anselm, Abbot of the Monastery of St. Edmund, these presents, for the security of the better provision for your successors for ever. We are instructed by the Divine precepts and taught by the Apostolic example, that with steadfast affection we are to watch over the state of the Churches. We therefore desire in the first place to support and uphold men of religious orders for the care of the Churches and of the servants of God, that thus through us God should be honoured, and the liberties of the Church be fully maintained. Wherefore, beloved son in Christ, Anselm the Abbot, we, knowing thy fidelity to God and thy signal obedience to the Apostolic Roman Church, have favourably received thy petition, and in accordance with the example of our predecessor Pope Lucius, of happy memory, who gave liberty to the monastery of the blessed Edmund, the glorious Martyr and King, freely to enjoy all gifts it had acquired by royal grants; we hereby decree that the said place shall within its liberty be exempt from payment of all secular dues for ever, as was set forth in the record of King William, and had been settled from his time. And further by this our present writing, we confirm to the uses of the brethren of the Monastery those possessions which thou, beloved son in the Lord, Anselm the Abbot, hast by indenture assigned for this purpose; viz. Harwich, paying 15 marcs in money; Norwich, 2 marcs; land in Beccles, 5 marcs and 8 shillings; the town of St. Edmund, 10 marcs; [Srabensam ?], 10 marcs; Tivetshall, 7 marcs and a half; a mill in Norfolk, 20 shillings; a mill at Sicklesmere, 2 marcs; Rushbrook, 3 marcs; three mills in the town of St. Edmund, 8 marcs; Woolpit, 10 marcs; Semer, 20 shillings; Hengrave, 10 shillings; Cambridge, 20 shillings; [Chellenorda ?], 10 shillings; Brook, 20 shillings; Rutham [? Rougham], 20 shillings; *Melford, 20 shillings; and the land of Galeus (there)* 10 *shillings.*

"Also whatever possessions this Monastery may lawfully claim to possess, whether in churches, tithes, lands, rents, mills, or any other known rights or customs, we fully confirm to you and your successors, and sanction their retention for the use of the said Monastery. We grant to your Church the consecration of chrism, the holy oil, consecration of altars, ordination of your monks, and clergy admitted to holy orders, and other ancient episcopal privileges pertaining to your Church, from whatever Catholic Bishop they may in past times have been received. By the authority of our Apostolic throne, we decree that you shall be permitted freely to appeal to us in matters relating to your Church; and that it shall be unlawful for any person to disturb or to threaten the said Monastery, or to take from it any of its possessions or belongings, or to withhold from it or diminish any of the offerings due to it, or to disquiet it by any vexation. All that now appertains thereto, or which may accrue to it by future grants or gifts, shall remain to it for its use, support, and supply; always saving the authority of the Apostolic See. If any person shall dare to violate any of these our grants, he shall incur the anger of the Holy Spirit, and shall lie under the ban of the Apostolic See.

"We commend you to the Omnipotence of God, and to the protection of his blessed Apostles Peter and Paul. AMEN."[*]

In or about the year 1184, Sampson, tenth Abbot of Bury, commenced to build there, near to the Abbey, beyond the North Gate of Bury, the Hospital of St. Saviour's, at first called Babwell, the foundation of which was intended to consist of a warden, 12 chaplains, 6 clerks, 12 poor men, and 12 poor women. For the endowment of this hospital, which was finally settled in the reign of King John, A.D. 1200, Abbot Sampson gave to it a charter, which received the royal sanction of King John, and was approved by a Bull of Pope Celestine III., and by the confirmations of John, Bishop of Norwich, and of Hubert, Archbishop of Canterbury, whereby certain places were to contribute stated revenues, tithes, and produce; and among them was *Melford*, which was ordered to have alienated from its church property two-thirds of all appertaining thereto, to the use of St. Saviour's. This became in various ways a matter of considerable moment in the future history of Melford, besides creating therein another ruling power. The Abbot had his manor and held his courts. The Rector did the same. There was also another manor here, apparently that of Kentwell, which manor we find a little later held by Sir William de Valence from the king by a knight's service, for 438 acres of land, a windmill, and a free warren. Now there was added the Warden, or, as afterwards styled, the Master of the Hospital of St. Saviour, who had also here his manor and held his courts, and which manor remains to the present day, as the *Manor of the Monks in Melford*.

Before entering upon the detail of the property which then, and subsequently accrued to the Hospital of St. Saviour, it is necessary to give here translations of the original grants and confirmations of the endowments of this charity. The originals were recorded in a folio register book of vellum, enclosed in a wooden cover, with black calf-skin, stated in the leaf in the beginning of it to be "Album Registrum, sive vetus Registrum," formerly belonging to the Abbey of Bury, and which book, in 1690, came into the possession of Sir Robert Bacon, of Redgrave, Suffolk. It is written in old abbreviated monkish Latin.

---

[*] In the Harleian MSS. there is a curious picture of an archbishop reading a Papal Bull to an assembly in the year 1319.

The following description of St. Saviour's may appropriately form the heading to these grants, although taken from a rather less ancient MS.; viz. from " Folio 51 e cartâ Edwardi primi, de divisione bonorum Abbatis et Conventus," 1272—1307.

Rough Translation.

" The Hospital of St. Saviour, which is situated below the four crosses of the town of St. Edmund, beyond the North Gate, with all its goods and possessions, spiritual and temporal, is acknowledged to be assigned for the maintenance of certain chaplains, brethren and sisters, and of other poor people of the same place, in God's service.

" A monk of the Abbey, appointed by a full chapter, is to have the charge of this hospital, in so far as he has hitherto been accustomed to have it.

" Neither the said monk in charge, nor any other secular or ecclesiastical person, shall receive or admit into the said Hospital any brother or sister without the approbation of the Lord Abbot; no question of money payment, however, hindering the reception or admission of any person.

" Also there shall be assigned a sum to be received from the town of St. Edmund, and from other places, of fourteen shillings a year, for the repair of the necessary utensils for food and other purposes of the refectory.

" There shall also remain to the brethren of this Hospital and to their successors the full and peaceable enjoyment of all properties and appurtenances, besides the above, whether apportioned by royal license, and belonging to the convent [monastery] or afterwards by their consent to be acquired, without claim thereto or obstacle on the part of the said Lord Abbot or his successors."

This Hospital, dedicated to St. Saviour, was one of the 540 eleemosynary foundations in England in the Middle Ages. It appears by the terms of Abbot Sampson's charter to have been only intended for the indigent and infirm of Bury, and for pilgrims and poor way-farers; but not for leprous persons, for whose relief, so common was leprosy in those days, no less than 117 out of the 540 hospitals, were founded. And it is noticeable that if the number of hospitals set apart for leprosy may be taken as a proof of the prevalence of this loathsome disease in each of the various counties of England, Suffolk had the unenviable rank of being the fourth highest in order; for only Devonshire, Kent, and Norfolk had a greater number of leper hospitals.

The next document relating to St. Saviour's is Abbot Sampson's foundation charter, though, as will be seen, it is probable that this was not the original grant, but that Abbot Sampson had given to St. Saviour's a previous endowment-deed, which was subsequently amplified by this one of the first year of King John. In the Nigrum Registrum, folio 73, there is mention of a Bull addressed to Abbot Sampson by Pope Urban III., dated from Verona, 4th January, 1186, taking under his protection the *newly-erected* Hospital of St. Saviour, and ratifying to its use Abbot Sampson's grant of the tithes of land newly converted into tillage in Redgrave and Rickinghall. This Bull evidently points to an early charter of Sampson. The other confirmatory bulls and grants are of prior date to King John's ratification-deed of A.D. 1200.

ROUGH TRANSLATION of the Charter of Abbot Sampson of the foundation of the Hospital of St. Saviour.

"About A.D. 1199 to 1200.—To all sons of Holy Mother Church to whom this present writing shall come, Sampson, D.G. Abbot of St. Edmund, and the whole convent of the same place, send eternal greeting in the Lord.

"Know all of you that we, with unanimous consent, and of our free will, for the welfare of our sovereign lord John, the illustrious King of England, and for the redemption of the souls of his predecessors, kings of England, have granted and given in pure and perpetual charity to the Holy Father, and to St. Saviour's, that ground on which the Hospital named St. Saviour's is situated, with its appurtenances, on the north side of the town of Bury, for the support of the poor in Christ and the relief of the necessities of the feeble and indigent of this place, or coming thereto. We further give and grant to the said Hospital of St. Saviour for the maintenance of the poor folk £12 in money from our town of Icklingham, to be annually received through our sacristan.—Also, *two portions* [*thirds*] *of our Church of Melford, with all appertaining to the two said portions.* Further we give and grant to the same, two-thirds of the demesne tithes of Wirlingworth, Saham, Tyleneye, Elmeswell, Elveden, Herringswell, Newton, Cokefelde, and in the same town of Cokefelde 8 acres of produce annually; namely, 2 of grain, 2 of light white wheat [Siligo], 2 of barley, 2 of oats. And in these following towns of ours, one-third of the demesne tithes; viz., in Pakenham, Bungeton, Tiversall, Culford, Horningsherd, and Chelsworth. We also grant to them all tithes of the newly-stubbed-up woodlands in our towns of Redgrave and Rickinghall, and a third of the acquired tithe over meadows in Tylney, and of the houses and meadows in Thetford, with appurtenances, excepting the annual service of the monks there of 2s., and 12d. of the canons. And that this our gift may be for ever valid and lasting, we have set forth this deed, and have thereunto affixed our seal.

"These being witnesses :—

"HEREBERT, the Prior of St. Edmund's.
HERMEUS, the Sub-Prior.
WALTER, the Sacrist.

c

GOCELINUS, the Cellarist.
ROBERT, the Camerarius.
GOSCELINUS, the Almoner.
    (He was Joceline de Brakelond, the Chronicler.)
RICHARD, the Chaplain.
WILLIAM DE GRETINGHAM, the Steward.
RICHARD, the Constable.
Master STEPHEN.
Master ROGER.
Master HERVEUS.
Master ALEXANDER.
"And others."

(Gage says that Sir Richard Ickworth was a witness to the foundation charter of the 1st year of King John.)

Between these two first witnesses, there was a short time before this date, a great contest for the office of Prior; the monks being divided into two parties, intriguing for the appointment of their respective favourites, while the Abbot favoured a third candidate. Herebert was very young, and had been only four years a cloistered monk; while Hermeus was a man of mature age and learning, had been fourteen years a monk, and some time Sub-Prior; he was, however, somewhat ill-tempered and hasty, and not popular. Herebert is thus described (of course in Latin) by Jocelin de Brakelond, the Almoner, who also attests this deed:—"A man of fair stature and personable appearance, handsome and amiable-looking in face, always cheerful and smiling from morn to night, and kind to all; facetious in speech, with a sweet voice in singing, and an easy reader; young, strong, and healthy in body, and always ready for the work of the Church; able always to suit himself to time and place, as well as to every class of person; liberal and sociable, not stingy or avaricious; sober, and speaking French well, being a Norman by birth. But on the other hand a man of shallow intelligence, of whom it certainly could not be said that much learning had made him mad!"

Herebert was however elected Prior, and Hermeus remained as before, Sub-Prior.

Sampson de Botington was Abbot of Bury from the year 1182 to 1211. The Abbot's name is here spelt as commonly received, and as recorded by Battely and other subsequent writers: but John de Taxster calls him "de Tottigtune." He was 47 years of age when he became Abbot, and had been seventeen years a monk. He is so greatly connected with Melford, that his personal appearance and character, as recorded in the Latin Chronicle of Jocelin de Brakelond, are interesting to us. "Abbot Sampson was a man of middle height, very bald; with a prominent aquiline nose, full lips, bright piercing eyes, arched eyebrows and bushy, but constantly shorn or clipped, and very quick of hearing. His voice became hoarse from the slightest cold. He had a few grey hairs in his red beard, and among the small amount of hair on his head, which was dark and inclined to curl; but within fourteen years after his election to the abbacy his hair and beard became quite white as snow. He was a most temperate man; active and never idle; riding and walking much; and thus counteracting the effects of age. When he heard of the fall of Jerusalem (Friday, 2nd October, 1187), he took to wearing hair-cloth on the lower part of his body, and also hair-cloth instead of linen, and he abstained from all meat. He preferred sweetened milk and honey, and sweet things, to other food. Liars, drunkards, flatterers, and coarse speakers he held in abhorrence. He was an eloquent man, conversant both with French and Latin; more an acute reasoner than an ornate speaker; a good English scholar, and he used to preach in English to the people, but with somewhat of a Norfolk dialect, the county wherein he was born and bred."

This descriptive photograph of an Abbot of Bury, still clear and life-like though taken 700 years ago, not only portrays to us the man in his outward semblance, but also makes us acquainted in some measure with his personal character. The reader of Jocelin de Brakelond's Chronicle who becomes more intimate with this great and good Abbot, will better understand the struggles and mortifications which soon turned white the hair of the vigorous, bright-eyed, energetic ruler of the Abbey of St. Edmund. The flickering light which is thrown by the monk's record upon this picture of the far past, brings out also a curious background of the great Abbey, and its condition before, and for a while after Sampson became its Abbot. Under his predecessor, old Abbot Hugh, who had become infirm, purblind, and indolent from age, the affairs and discipline of the monastery had lapsed into an almost hopeless state. The conventual buildings were becoming rapidly ruinous, and their thatch and other coverings were no longer even weathertight, and through gross corruption and mismanagement there were no available means for their repair. The revenues were always pledged or forestalled, and recourse was had to incessant borrowing from the Jews for every trifle of ready money, even the vestments and sacred vessels being pawned. Thus, when William the Sacristan was called upon to make an absolutely necessary repair to save a building of the Abbey from impending ruin, there being no money in the coffers, he borrowed from Benedict the Jew (son of Deodate),* 40 marcs (£26. 13s. 4d.). This debt at compound interest soon ran up to £100; and Abbot Hugh also owing him a private debt of another £100, then gave the Jew a bond for £400, payable in four

---

* In 1171, this same Benedict was fined £40 for taking certain sacred vestments in pawn.

c 2

years. At the end of that time the Abbey being yet more bankrupt, the Jew pressing for payment, obtained a bond for £880, till at last his modest claim amounted to £1,200.

When Sampson became Abbot he was driven to his wits' end how to redeem the Monastery from the chaotic state into which it had been reduced by unthrift, mismanagement, and every sort of abuse. For the first four years of his abbacy, the new Abbot could never stir abroad without being pounced upon both by Jew and Christian usurers, clamouring for their unsettled bonds; but with inflexible will, iron energy, continued vigilance, and rigorous method, Sampson at last created a new life in the Abbey, and among many other old abuses, the great incubus of debt at last rolled away.

Jocelin de Brakelond's Chronicle terminates very suddenly, and gives us no account of the final ending of the career of the great self-sacrificing Abbot; but we know from other sources, that his life of unceasing labour came to a close *at twilight* on the 3rd January, A.D. 1211.

The preceding charter of Abbot Sampson is recorded also in the same words in "Nigro Registro de Vestiario," folio 14, which in 1690 was in the possession of Mr. Cradock, of Rickinghall, Suffolk, but is now in the public library in Cambridge.

Also, in the same words in the Register of Walter Pinchbeck (or Pyncebec), folio 221, in the same person's possession as above in 1690, but now likewise at Cambridge.

This charter bears no date upon it, but being dedicatory to King John, and that king's ratification of it being dated 15th March, 1200, it is clear that this Endowment Charter of Abbot Sampson was dated between 6th April, 1199 (the date of the death of Richard I.), and the 15th March, 1200. Now, as the building of St. Saviour's Hospital commenced in 1184, and the confirmatory Bull of Pope Urban III. being dated 4th January, 1186; the confirmation of John, Bishop of Norwich, 1190; and the Bull of Pope Celestine III., 6th May, 1192, it appears probable that this Endowment Charter of Abbot Sampson was an amplification of a former one, given at the time of the original grant to the Hospital, and which was perhaps cancelled by this latter one.

Here follows the confirmation of the original endowment, by the Diocesan of Melford, John, Bishop of Norwich, a prelate of considerable distinction. He was John of Oxford, formerly Dean of Salisbury, and chaplain to King Henry II. Weever, in his book of Ancient Monuments, describes him thus:—"A man, who in the soliditie of good doctrine, in the maturitie of judgemente, and in alle the graces of rhetoricall specche, did wondrouslie abounde." He was employed at divers times in embassies to Rome, France, and Sicily; and he wrote a History of the Kings of Britain, and a treatise of his journey into

Sicily, with other literary works. He took the cross and became a Crusader 31st January, 1188; but he opposed and prevented Abbot Sampson's doing the same on the ground that the counties of Norfolk and Suffolk would not be left in safety, if they were both absent abroad at the same time. Bishop John greatly repaired Norwich Cathedral in 1197.

TRANSLATION of the Confirmation of John, Bishop of Norwich, of the Endowment of the Hospital of St. Saviour's, Bury, A.D. 1190.

"To all sons of Holy Mother Church, John, D. G. Bishop of Norwich, sends greeting in the Lord. We will that all should know that we, in piety and for the service of God, on the petition and representation of the venerable brother in Christ Sampson, D. G. Abbot of St. Edmund, do grant that the poor and infirm of the Hospital without the town of St. Edmund's, which the said Sampson has established there, shall receive for their use in perpetuity *two-thirds of the Church [possessions] in Melford*, except and reserved all honours, reverence, and dignity due to the Church of Norwich; *and one-third portion of the said Church [possessions] of Melford shall be reserved for the support of a vicar, who shall minister in the same;* and further, that whoever shall be instituted to the said third portion shall be responsible for all the episcopal burdens, whether synodals or others, and whether for the brethren's portions or for his own, and reserving to us and to our successors for ever all pontifical and parochial rights.

"These being witnesses :—
"The ARCHDEACON.
MASTER ROBERT, of Gloucester.
UMFREDUS, the Chaplain.
MASTER ROBERT DE TYWA.
ALAN DE GREY.

"Given at Gypuwic [Ipswich] by the hand of Master de Verham, in the fifth [? 15th] year of our pontificate."

In the Latin text of this date there is evidently a word omitted, or a clerical error made; for the year named stands as "quinto" instead of "decimo quinto." The fifth year of the pontificate of John of Norwich would have been A.D. 1180, which was before Sampson became Abbot, and before St. Saviour's Hospital was built. The fifteenth year of John of Norwich would have been 1190, which is probably the correct date.

In the Bishop's Registry at Norwich, the book called the Norwich Domesday Book, which commences about the year 1400 or soon after, contains a survey of all the parishes whose temporalities and spiritualities belonged to that see, in which Melford was then comprised. This book has an alphabetical index prefixed of "Nomina Villarum."

ROUGH TRANSLATION of the Confirmation of the Endowment of St. Saviour's Hospital, by Hubert, Archbishop of Canterbury.[*]

"Hubert, D. G. Archbishop of Canterbury and Primate of all England, to all the faithful in Christ to whom this present writing shall come, greeting in the Lord. We desire to make known to all of you, that whereas we are bound to provide for the well-being and security of poor and religious men : now by the authority vested in us for the discharge and administration of like duties, we grant in perpetuity and confirm to the Hospital of St. Saviour, without the North Gate of St. Edmund's, *two-thirds of the Church [possessions] of Melford,* in like manner as John of *pious memory, late* Bishop of Norwich, had reasonably granted to the said Hospital, and having perused its charter, we confirm the same; and that this our confirmation should be valid and binding, we have set our seal in witness thereof to this present writing."

There is no date to this, but it is probably of the latter half of the year 1200, as from the above text it appears that John, Bishop of Norwich, was then dead; and he died on the 2nd June, 1200.

ROUGH TRANSLATION of the Bull of Pope Cælestine III. [†]

"A.D. 1192.—Cælestine the Bishop, servant of the servants of God, to his beloved sons the present Master and the Brethren of the Hospital of St. Saviour of St. Edmund's, and their successors for ever. Deeming it well that their request should be freely complied with, and that the sincerity of their devotion therein should duly shine forth, and that the work should unfailingly acquire due weight and power: for all these reasons we lovingly and tenderly attend to the petition of our beloved sons in the Lord, and in so far as the support of the sick and poor of the said Hospital of St. Saviour may be assigned, we by the Divine office transfer the same to you. We take you under the protection of the Blessed Peter and of ourselves, and confirm the same by these presents, decreeing further, that whatever possessions or goods this Hospital justly and canonically now possesses, or by future pontifical grant, kingly munificence, or offerings of pious

---

[*] Hubert Walter, Archbishop of Canterbury, was the predecessor of Cardinal Langton in that see. He crowned King John, and was long his adviser, though the king rejoiced at the death of his wise counsellor, which occurred in July, 1205, when John seized upon his possessions for his own use, although they had been otherwise bequeathed by the prelate's will. His arms were az. and arg., a cross or. ; in first and fourth quarters, five mullets of the first, in saltire ; in the second and third, an eagle displayed sable.—(Magna Charta.)

[†] Cælestine III. was Cardinal Hyacinthus Bubo. His arms were—argent, a cross azure ; in the second and third quarters, a star of eight points of the second, all surmounted by a bend gules.

princes, or in any other mode by God's help may in the future acquire, shall remain full and unimpaired to you and your successors for ever.

"Given and conveyed by the hand of Egidius, Deacon, in Arce Tulliana of St. Nicholas, the 6th of May, Anno Domini 1192, and in the second year of our pontificate."

In this Bull of Pope Cælestine III. there is no mention of the details of the endowment, or of the grant of Melford Church lands and tithes; but all these seem to be included in the general terms of "quascunque possessiones, &c." This Cælestine III. was Pope from A.D. 1191 to 1198.

There are three charters of King John relating to the Hospital of St. Saviour, Bury. They bear the dates of 15th and 16th March, 1200, and were all attested by the same great persons as witnesses. The first relates only to Mildenhall, and refers back to the charter of Richard I. relative thereto. The second also is concerning Mildenhall. The third, which has reference to *Melford*, is here given at length; the numbers in the heading are the references to the old rolls of the Records formerly in the Tower of London. This charter contains some added words, which are in none of the other grants or deeds of this charity, as well as some omissions, and which, therefore, may have been the error of a careless scribe, otherwise they would have greatly altered the alienation of tithes as regards Melford; and in later days they did evidently lead to some misunderstanding on this subject.

TRANSLATION of the Third Charter of the first year of King John, concerning the Hospital of St. Saviour: Nos. 121, 115, and 174 (in the Rolls, formerly in the Tower of London).

"A.D. 1200. John, D.G., &c.—Know that we have granted and by this our charter do confirm the following gifts which Abbot Sampson and the Convent of St. Edmund gave to God the Father and to St. Saviour in pure charity for ever, for our good estate and for the redemption of the souls of our predecessors the kings of England, and for their own souls: viz., that land on which the Hospital called St. Saviour's is situated, on the north side without the town of St. Edmund's, with its appurtenances, for the maintenance of the poor in Christ, and of sick persons, and for the necessities of the indigent coming to the said place. We further grant to the said Hospital of St. Saviour for the support of the poor £12 in money of their town of Icklingham, besides *two-thirds of their Church* [*property*] *of Melford, with all appertaining to the said two portions*, and a third part of the demesne tithes of Wirlingwood, and of Saham and Pakenham, *and of Melford*. Tithes also of the land formerly woods, newly stubbed up for tillage, in the towns of Redgrave and Rickinghall, and eight acres in the town of Cockfield annually (of produce): namely, two of corn, two of light white wheat (called 'Siligo'), two of barley, and two of oats, and a third part of their demesne tithes in the town of Ormingesden, as set forth in the charter of the said Abbot and Convent.

" Witnesses hereto :—

" WILLIAM MARESC (Mareschal or Marshall), *Earl of Pembroke.*

[This was the famous earl who died in 1219. He was one of the executors of King John's will.]

" WILLIAM, *Earl of Salisbury.*

[This was the great William Longespée, son of King Henry II by Fair Rosamond. He was a Crusader in 1219, and died 1226.]

" ROGER LE BIGOD, *Earl of Norfolk.*

[He was one of the twenty-five securities for the performance of Magna Charta. He died 1220–1221. His son Hugh, who succeeded him, married Maud, eldest daughter of the above Earl of Pembroke.]

" ROBERT, son of the above Roger le Bigod.

[Query : was he a natural son ; for Roger le Bigod had no legitimate son of the name of Robert ?]

" WILLIAM DE STUTEVILLE.

[He had a memorable dispute with another great Baron, William de Mowbray, concerning the Barony of Fronteboeuf, which was claimed by both. Mowbray gave King John 1,000 marks (£666. 13s. 4d.) to determine the case, when the barony was awarded to Mowbray, Stuteville receiving nine knights' fees, and £12 yearly rent, and the claimants were reconciled on Septuagesima Sunday, 21st January, 1201. A knight's fee was estimated at 12 plough lands, or carucates, and valued at £20 a year.]

[There is also further mention of this William de Stuteville in 1202, by Jocelin de Brakelond, who relates that on St. Agnes's day, the king's messenger came to Abbot Sampson, bringing a Papal brief, directing that the Bishop of Ely and the Abbot of St. Edmund should examine Geoffry, son of Peter, and William de Stuteville, and certain other English nobles, who had taken the cross, for whom the king sought absolution from their vow, alleging their bodily infirmity and that their counsel was of importance to the safety of the kingdom.]

" ROBERT DE TURNHAM.

" HUGO DE NEVILLE.

[He was one of the advisers of the Crown who is named in Magna Charta, and he was a witness thereto. He was probably the Hugh de Nevill who in the 8th of Henry III. was made principal warden of the king's forests in England, and was ancestor of the Barons Nevill of Essex.]

"Given by the hand of S. Wellen, Archdeacon [of Wells], and John de Gray, Archdeacon [of Cleveland], at Silveston, the 15th of March, in the first year of our reign."*

This document must have been dated in the year 1200, as Richard I. did not die till 6th *April*, 1199. Silveston is presumably the place of that name near Towcester, and one of these three charters was signed on the following day, 16th March, at Northampton.

There is a copy of these charters in the Register of Walter Pyncebec, folio 222; and also in the Black Register de Vestiario, folio 14. There was also a further confirmation in 1222 by Stephen, Archbishop of Canterbury, but on what grounds does not appear.

On comparing this charter of King John with Abbot Sampson's endowment charter, there are many discrepancies observable: towards the end the scribe has endeavoured to curtail the text to shorten the deed, and has transcribed it hastily, and in so doing has made a complete jumble of the original. For instance, after the mention of the two-thirds of the Church of Melford, he names *one-third of the tithes* of Wirlingworth, which he calls Wirlingwood, and of Haham, of which places the original grant had apportioned *two-thirds*; with six other places, which he omits altogether; and he names *one-third of the demesne tithe of Melford*, which Abbot Sampson never gave at all; and he again omits five other places which were to give one-third, and he names a place, "Ormingseeden," which is not named in the original grant, thereby completely confusing the sense of Abbot Sampson's endowment. It is evidently the work of a careless or ignorant writer.

A composition as to the share of the tithes from Melford to the Hospital of St. Saviour was made at a later date, whereby for a long period the Rector paid annually to the hospital £2 for tithes. When the Abbey lands came into the hands of Henry VIII., by a survey then made, this proportion of the tithes was valued at £5. 13s. 4d., as it had been since 5th ... 1501.

In 1239 to 1240 there was a dispute between the Hospital of St. Saviour and the then Vicar (as he was called) of Melford, Master Enever, as to the division and apportionment to each of certain lands in Melford, near Cranmoor, of which a portion is still part of Melford glebe, and on which there arose a suit. It appears that the land in question did not form part of the original grant to the Church by Roe Suffin, but had been given by one Juliana, wife of Richard de Bonard before the above date, to the Church of Melford, subject seemingly to certain rights of her daughters, Adelina le Bonard ... probably died single, and certainly without children if married; and Juliana, who married Walter de Bononia. Although in the due course of record

3

the results of the suit must be first shown, yet the agreement which afterwards follows between the Abbot of Bury for the Hospital of St. Saviour, and Master Hervey, the Vicar of Melford, better explains the issue.

The first suit relates to the claim of Adelina, the elder daughter. It is headed thus:—

"Inter Recorda Regis receptæ Scaccarii sui, sub custodia Dominorum Commissionariorum per Thesaurios et Camerarios ibidem remanentes: viz. inter pedes finium tempore Regis Johannis inter alia sic continetur ut sequitur.

"Ligula prima finium Regis Johannis. Comitatu Suffolciæ numero 10."

TRANSLATION.—"Among the Records in the King's Exchequer, in the keeping of the Lords Commissioners, &c., in the Fines Roll, in the reign of King John, &c.

"County of Suffolk. No. 10.

"This is the final agreement made in the King's Court of Westminster, within one month after Easter, in the first year of King John's reign, before Gilbert son of Peter, Richard de Herry, Simon de Patishul, Osbert son of Hervey, John de Gestling, Hugo de Boby, Henry de Wichington, Eustace de Fauconberg,* judges, and other lieges of the king there present; between Walter, the Master of the Hospital of St. Saviour beyond the South Gate† of the Abbey of St. Edmund Bury, and Master Hervey,‡ of the Abbey of St. Edmund, appellants; and Adelina, daughter of Richard [de Bonard§], holding half a carucate of land [she held about 56 acres] with appurtenances, in Cranmoor, of which the matter at issue between them was whether it was the lay feoff of the aforesaid Adelina, which she claimed to hold of the Abbot of St. Edmund, or whether it was of free bounty, as belonging to the Church of Melford: now whereas the said Adelina admitted the whole of the said land to be held, with its appurtenances, of the free bounty of the said Church; in return for this recognition and determination, and with the consent of the aforesaid Walter, Master of the Hospital, and of Master Hervey, Sampson, Abbot of St. Edmund, patron of the said Church of Melford, being present and consenting thereto, they granted to the said Adelina and the heirs of her body all the said land, with its appurtenances, to be held by her and her heirs from the said Church, free of service, by

* Eustace de Fauconberg became the first Chancellor of the Exchequer, about 1221.
† This is evidently a clerical error for "North Gate."
‡ Master Hervey, who was now vicar of the church of Melford, had been one of the witnesses of Abbot Sampson's grant of land from Melford Church to St. Saviour's Hospital.
§ He was the husband of Juliana de Bonard, Adelina's mother.

payment of forty pence a year, to be paid to the said Church at four terms: viz., at the feast of St. Michael, ten pence; at Christmas, ten pence; at Easter, ten pence; and at the feast of the Nativity of St. John the Baptist, ten pence; in lieu of all service, except extraneous service, and except the services of these persons: viz., Fulco le Newman; Mabel, daughter of Robert; and William Boniface, with their holdings and their tenants; and except as regards 22 acres and a half, of which five acres and a rood are in the capital messuage of Cranmoor, and in Stoneyland, both arable and pasture, and lying along the bank of the river from *Glemsford-bridge* to the messuage; and fifteen acres and three roods, and also an acre, and a half acre are in Tumane field. And if it should happen that the said Adelina should die without heirs of her body, then the whole of the aforesaid hereditament shall revert to the said Church without let or default."

This deed was examined by John Lowe and Peter Leneve, Vice-Chancellors of the Exchequer, the 9th of February, 1693, and was endorsed thus:—"A copy of landes in Cranmere, belonging to the Church of Melford, Suffolk." *Peter Leneve.*

This deed is also recorded in the Abbey Black Register de Vestiario, page 188.

The next following agreement to the above is between Juliana, wife of Walter de Bolonia, daughter of Juliana de Bonard, and younger sister of the aforesaid Adelina, and the Hospital of St. Saviour, and the Vicar of Melford. It is in identical terms with the foregoing one, except in the change of names from Adelina to Walter, and Juliana his wife, and as reserving to the Church of Melford a yearly rent of 32 pence, by four payments of 18 pence each, &c., and except the services of these persons, Ankotill, Mabilla, Robert Curez, Gilbert Winefer, and Agnes his wife, and excepting 22 acres and a half lying next to the land called Kingstons on the north. And if it should happen that the said Juliana should die without heirs of her body, then the said Walter was to hold for his life the lands which she held; and after the death of the said Walter, it was all to revert to the aforesaid Church.

Then follows the agreement before alluded to between the Abbot and Convent of Bury, for St. Saviour's Hospital, on the one part, and Master Walter Hervey, Vicar of the Church of Melford, on the other part.

TRANSLATION of this Agreement of apportionment between St. Saviour's Hospital and Melford Church, A.D. about 1200.

"Agreement entered into between the Abbot and Convent on the one part, and Master Walter Hervey, of St. Edmund's, Vicar of the

Church of Melford, on the other part, before A. B. C., upon the question between them as to certain lands which had belonged to Juliana de Bonard, in the town of Melford : viz., that the said Abbot and Convent shall have for the endowment of the Hospital of St. Saviour the messuage with the adjoining wood, and all the arable demesne land which had belonged to the aforesaid Juliana on the day she died.   But the remainder, whether of free tenants or of servi, with such holdings as they had in fee from Juliana at the day of her death, with whatever meadow there was lying beside the river bank between Glemsford and Cranmoor, that had belonged to the said Juliana, they give for the endowment of the above-mentioned Vicar.   Nevertheless, it is agreed between the brethren of the Hospital and Master Hervey. that the said brethren shall have two parts of all the lands and serfs [servi] of Walter de Bolonia and Juliana his wife, and of Adelina her sister, after their death, if the said sisters should die without heirs of their bodies, as mentioned in the chirographs made in the king's court between them, and that Master Hervey shall have the other third portion.   But if they have heirs of their bodies, then the said brethren shall have two-thirds of the rent which they pay to the Church of Melford for their holding in the said township, as set forth in the aforesaid syrographs."

Originally these syrographs, or chirographs, were a duplicate deed, written on one piece of parchment ; and in the middle between the two copies, were the letters of the alphabet, or sometimes the word *syngraphus* ; and the two copies being then cut through these letters, or the word, in an indented manner, one was delivered to each party concerned, and their authenticity was proved by their matching exactly in the divided portion.

In Abbot John de Norwold's Chartulary of the Abbey lands, of the date of A.D. 1287, among the entries of the free tenants who held lands in Melford, which were not of the demesne, is included "the Master of the Hospital of St. Saviour's of St. Edmund's," as holding a manor with its court appertaining to this charity.   From the following copy of the said register it would appear that other land in Melford, independently of the two-thirds of the alienated church lands, had come by gift of certain persons to St. Saviour's, as in the case of the land of Giles de Wachesham, &c.   In comparing with other entries in this terrier, the quantities at the above date belonging to the Hospital, and stated to be parts of the tenure with which the Church was endowed, it appears that previously to the alienation, as well as subsequently thereto, other land besides Earl Afric's original grant had been settled on the Church of Melford by Abbot Sampson, independently of the acquired land of Juliana de Bonard.   For St. Saviour's endowment here is said to have consisted in 1287 of 150 acres in manor, together with 73¼ acres held of it by its villeins : total 223 acres, as two-thirds of the original church land ; which would have made Earl Alfric's original grant to the Church 334¼ acres, whereas it was really only 261¼ acres. And although, perhaps, the larger quantity may include also ⅓ of the De Bonard's lands, even that supposition would not account for the increase. And again, the other ⅓ of Alfric's grant remaining to the Church after the alienation to St. Saviour's would have been only 87 acres ; and if with ⅓ of the De Bonard's land added, 106 acres ; whereas in this very terrier of A.D. 1287 it appears that the parson of Melford held 111 acres of land, besides 60 additional acres, with certain rights *which came of the gift and charity of Abbot Sampson ;* and although, after the lapse of nearly 600 years, it is difficult accurately to reconcile such details as these, yet it is evident that Abbot Sampson, while endowing his charity of St. Saviour's, apparently at the expense and to the great detriment of Melford Church, had partly made up the loss to the latter by some other gifts of property.

EXTRACT from the Register of Abbot John de Norwold " de Itinere Salamonis de Roff, et Sociorum suorum," in the 14th and beginning of 15th year of the reign of King Edward [I.], son of King Henry [III.], A.D. 1287, as in the 247th page of the Register of Walter Pinchbeck, and in folios 174 and 234, and in the Abbot's Register (*now at Melford Hall*).*

" Magister Hospitalis Sancti Salvatoris de Sancto Edmundo holds a manor in the town of Melford with CXXXVI. acres of arable land, VII. acres of mowing meadow, III. acres and a half of pasture, and IV. acres of wood, all parts of the tenure from whence the aforesaid church was endowed ; and is of the gift in charity of Sampson, formerly Abbot of St. Edmund.

"Also the same holds IV. acres of land of the feoff of Dominus Gerardus de Wachesham, as a perpetual gift in charity from Egidius de Wachesham, and the said Sir Gerard is bound to defend the right of this gift against Dominus Peter de Calesworth [Chelsworth], and the said Sir Peter against the King, with his other holdings.

" The same Magister holds II. acres of wood of Radulphus de Elmeswell, and the said Radulphus holds of the Abbot of St. Edmund, and the said Abbot as from the King.

" The same Magister holds III. acres of wood and IV. acres of arable

* The justiciaries itinerant, from whose report this survey was compiled, were Salomon of Rochester, Thomas de Sudington, Richard de Boiland, and Walter de Hopton. They were punished for malpractices in 1289 (see Holinshed's Chronicles). These justiciaries were charged with the superintendence of the national survey.

land from John de Cramawell, and the said John holds of Gerard de Wachesham, and the said Gerard holds as is before mentioned.

"He also has the right of regulating and setting the price of milling and grinding flour, and of selling ale by his homagers; and these rights were given to the Hospital by Sampson, Abbot of St. Edmund, in perpetual charity.

"The Hospital has also LXXII. acres of arable land, I. acre of mowing meadow, and III. roods of wood, which the villeins hold with their messuages from this said manor.

"It has also II. cottars, who hold of this manor a rood and a half of land with their houses.

"GALFRIDUS DE PALESHAM holds of the said Hospital a messuage and VIII. acres of land for 5s. a year.

"FAREMAN DE HUNDENETYM holds from Alan Boydyn v. acres of arable land and I. rood of pasture; and the said Alan holds from Galfridus, son of Thomas; and the said Galfridus from the Hospital for 20d. a year.

"The same FAREMAN holds III. acres of arable land from Adam Thurgor; and the said Adam holds from Galfridus, son of Thomas; and the said Galfridus from the Hospital for 13¼d. and III. suits a year to the general court.

"REGINALDUS DE GUNTON and RADULPHUS his brother hold II. acres and a half of land from Sarra de Wyches; and the said Sarra from Galfridus son of Thomas; and the said Galfridus, from the Hospital for 10½d. a year.

"STEPHANUS DE CARNENDE holds I. acre of land of the said Hospital for 4d., and III. suits a year to the general court.

"The same STEPHANUS holds II. acres of arable land of Isabella de Ash, and the said Isabella from the aforesaid Hospital for 10d. a year; and the said Stephanus holds a messuage and an acre of arable land from Walterus Wythune, and the said Walter from the Hospital for 8d. a year.

"THOMAS MOYSENT holds of the said Hospital II. acres of land for 12d., and III. suits a year to the general court.

"WALTERUS LE POER holds of the said Hospital half an acre and half a rood of land for 5d. a year.

"WILLELMUS filius Hugonis holds of the said Hospital a messuage and XXXI. acres of arable land, III. acres of pasture, and I. acre and a half of meadow for 18s., and III. suits a year to the Court.

"ISABELL LE FORESTER holds of the said Wm. VI. acres of land for 3s. a year.

"JOHANNES PEYTENYN holds of the said Wm. II. acres and a half of land for 6d. a year.

"JOHANNES DE LAUSELE holds of the said Wm. II. acres of land for 1¼d. a year.

"RICHARDUS DE SOLIO holds of the said John a messuage and II. acres of land for 1¼d. a year.

"THOMAS WYOT holds of the said Richardus half an acre of land for 4d. a year.

"JOHANNES MERCATOR holds from Willelmus, son of Hugo, II. acres and III. roods of land for 9d. a year.

"RICHARDUS COLE holds of the feoff of the Hospital a messuage and an acre of land for 5d., and III. suits a year to the General Court.

"JOHANNES filius Hugonis hold from Galfridus, son of Alanus, a messuage and IV. acres of land for 13d. a year. The same has II. cottars who hold a rood and a half of land for 5¼d. a year.

"ROBERTUS ALWAN holds of the said Hospital II. acres and a half of land for 13d. a year.

"GILBERTUS filius Roberti Folk holds of the said Hospital a messuage and an acre of land for 5d., and III. suits a year to the Court.

"JOHANNES MERCATOR holds of Willelmus Sweyn an acre and a half of land for 6d., and the said Wm. holds of the Hospital.

"WILLELMUS SENNAS holds from the said Hospital a messuage and an acre and a half of land for 9d. a year.

"JOHANNES MERCATOR holds of the said Wm. an acre of wood for 1d. a year.

"The same JOHANNES holds of Thomas Wyot a rood of land for 1d. a year.

"RICHARDUS DE SOLIO holds from the said Hospital VI. acres of land for 10d. a year."

After this time the manor belonging to the Hospital of St. Saviour's became known by the name it still bears, of the "*Manor of the Monks in Melford;*" and though after the dissolution of the Monastery the property became somewhat divided, the bulk, which was granted to the then owners of Kentwell Hall, retained that name, as it does to the present time.

Tracing on the history of this Manor of Monks (independently of the chronological record of the rest of the parish), it appears to have been commonly farmed out, and the following lease, of the early date of 137⅞, is particularly noticeable, as well from its antiquity as also from the fact that by it, not only was the Manor of Monks then let to a tenant, but there also appears in this instance to have been included with it, what is called in this lease, the Rectory of Melford, for the sum of £13. 6s. 8d. (twenty marcs), for which the tenant was to have the use of all the live and dead stock, the personal and other services of the manorial villeins and freemen, and he was to take all the manor dues. These concessions, with the addition of the Rectory, may perhaps account for the rent being a high one of 1s. 2¼d. per acre, at a time when arable land here was let at an average of about 7d. to 10d. per acre. It is, however, difficult to understand how the Rectory of

Melford came to be let in this instance with the Manor of Monks, for three years, to a layman. In the Institution record of the Rectors of Melford, there occurs under the date of 1372, a presentation of a Priest (Thomas de Grynesby) to the living, by "*the King of England on a recovery in his Royal Court against the Abbot of Saint Edmund, through the default of the said Abbot, the real Patron of this Church.*" But whether this entry may point to any solution explanatory of the lease of the Rectory, is a difficult question.

In the original Latin deed a portion had become obliterated and undecipherable so long ago as 1680. The part that remained, translated into English, runs as follows:—

"A.D. 1372-3.

"This indenture witnesseth that we, Brother John [*de Brinkale*], by Divine permission Abbot of St. Edmund, and the convent of the said place, have granted and to farm let to John Roughend* of Melford, the Manor belonging to the Hospital of St. Saviour in Melford, with the Rectory of Melford, and with all demesne tithes, and tenths, and all lands, tenements, woods, meadows, grazing grounds, pastures, sheep-walks, dues, and services, whether of freemen or customary services, and all else belonging to the said Manor called the Monks, and the live and dead stock in the said Manor: To have and to hold the said Manor and the Rectory, with all its appurtenances aforesaid, to the said John and his executors, from the Feast of St. Michael in the 46th year of King Edward, the third after the Conquest, unto the end of three years next following and fully ended: paying annually for the said term to the Hospital of St. Saviour of St. Edmund, £13. 6s. 8d. by equal portions, at the Feast of the Purification of the Blessed Mary, Easter, the Nativity of St. John the Baptist, and St. Peter ad Vincula; except that in the last year of the said term the said John Roughend shall pay £12 at the above-named terms.   *   *   *   *
*   *   *   [part obliterated].   *   *   *   *

"In witness whereof, to the one part, remaining with the said Lord Abbot and Convent, the said John Roughend has placed his seal; and to the other part, in keeping of the said John, the common seal of the chapter was affixed.

"Given at St. Edmund's the 8th day of October."

There were many other leases of the Manor of Monks; and among them was the following one of a part of this manor, with the tithes

---

* In Abbot John Tymworth's Chartulary of Melford, in 1386, John Roughend's name occurs as holding two acres, formerly held by the Prior of St. Bartholomew, and which had belonged to Alan Boydyn. In a copy of the lease in the text, the sums given are liii. and lii. pounds: sums out of the question, the l being probably an error for the old long-tailed x, which often resembled an L.

belonging thereto in the year 1501.   This lease was copied and translated into English in the 17th century, from a great vellum book, consisting of 139 large leaves, and which was the chartulary of John Reeves, *alias* John de Melford, the last Abbot of Bury.   It was generally made up of leases commencing the 9th year of Henry VIII., to the 30th year of the same king; but it also contained this lease and another dated the same year.   The book was afterwards in the possession of Sir Willoughby d'Ewes, and the original of this document was long in the possession of the owners of Kentwell Hall.

"LEASE made by the Abbot and Convent of Bury to Sir Wm. Clopton, of Melford, concerning the lands and tithes within Melford aforesaid, belonging to the Hospital of St. Saviour's without the North Gate of Bury. Given and granted in our Chapter-house, the 23rd day of the month of December, the year of the reign of King Henry VII. the 17th, and the year of our Lord 1501. [The spelling of the old translation has been modernized.]

"This indenture witnesseth that the Lord William [Codenham], Abbot of the Monastery of St. Edmund of Bury, and the Convent of the same place, with one assent and consent have granted and to farm let to Sir William Clopton, of Melford, in the county of Suffolk, knight, all the lands, pastures, and meadows belonging to our manor called the 'Monks,' appertaining to the office of the custody of the Hospital of St. Saviour's, without the North Gate of Bury St. Edmund's, as they lie between the said manor called the Monks and the dwelling-place* of the said William Clopton, where numbered to the sum of 258 acres or thereabouts, and lie in four fields; the one called Bargate Field, the second Crow Meadow, the third Middle Field, and the fourth called Prestly Field, with a little angle of meadow called the Marsh, and it containeth half an acre parcel of the said sum.   And also we have granted to the said William Clopton certain lands lying by the Parsonage Mere, during his life and no longer, containing in two pieces to the sum of 12 acres and 1 rood.   Also we have granted to the said William a pasture lying at Kentwell Down, by the Park of the said William Clopton, containing 4 acres 2 roods and 27 perches.   Also we have granted to the said William Clopton five other pastures, as they lie from the place of the said William unto the Cross, called Clopton's Cross; and the said five pastures contain—the one, 2 acres 1 rood and 30 perches; the second, 4 acres 2 roods and 18 perches; the third, 1 acre 1 rood and 24 perches; the fourth, 2 acres 1 rood and 12

---

* The older house of Kentwell, before the erection of the present Kentwell Hall, was called "Lutons." From the acreage above named, it would appear that the extent of the manor of Monks had been augmented since the year 1287.

E

perches; and the fifth, half an acre. Also we have granted to the said William Clopton two groves, as they lie between the said William Clopton's place and the highway leading to Bury, with all manner of tithes of the said lands; and except alonely the said William Clopton nor his assigns shall fell no timber growing in the said woods or hedgerows belonging to the said lands to him letten. But it is agreed that, the woods to him letten are with cropping and shredding in seasonable time in all the woods and hedgerows, such as before have been cropped and shred. And also it is agreed and covenanted that the said William Clopton shall fell no timber growing in the woods or hedgerows; and also at every time the said William shall fell any underwood in the said two groves, he shall lawfully defend the same from hurting the new slop, and shall leave standing in every acre with the old trees and stallings that were there before, 40 of the best stallings. And also it is covenanted and agreed that if the said Hospitaller or his successors fell any timber, the said William Clopton shall have the toon [?] half of the offal of the trees, as well of wood as of bark, and the Hospitaller for the time being the other half, save each of the parties shall equally pay for the making of the wood, and the pilling of the bark. And also we the said Abbot and Convent have granted to the said William Clopton all the tithes to us belonging as to the said place called the Monks, from a tenement called Boohers, lying of the east side of the way leading to Bury, unto the furthest end of the Park of Melford, except alonely such tithes as belong to the demesnes of the chief manor of Melford, with a barn called the Tiled Barn, lying within the manor of Monks aforesaid, with free going and coming to the same, so that no great hurt nor noyance be done to him that shall dwell and be fermor in the said place; and also we have granted to the said William Clopton a garden plot called Monk's Garden,* and it is paled about and lies for an acre and a half, with free going and coming to the said garden, as there is a cast gate made at the end of the said pale standing next the garden of the parsons of Melford, for term of the life of the said William Clopton; and after his decease the said garden plot of an acre and a half to be again in our hands to let at our pleasure; this indenture notwithstanding. And also it is covenanted and agreed that if the said William Clopton will cherish any young stallings in the hedgerows, that it shall be lawful to the said William Clopton to shred and crop at his pleasure in lawful time. To have and to hold all the aforesaid lands, meadows, pastures, woods, and tithes (except before excepted) to the said William Clopton, his heirs and assigns, from the Feast of St. Michael the Archangel last past, unto the end and term

---

* This garden was near the north-east end of the churchyard, and the parson's garden here named was that belonging to the priest's house or college, not rectory, which will be afterwards alluded to. The site of the manor-house of Monks was at the north side of the churchyard, one part abutting on Melford Green.

of four-score years next following and fully ended; yielding therefore to us and our successors by the hands of the Hospitaller, or keeper of the Hospital aforesaid, which shall be for that time, or his certain attorney, vi$^{li.}$ xiii$^{s.}$ iiii$^{d.}$ [£6. 13s. 4d.], of good and lawful money of England at the feasts of Easter and Michaelmas. And also it is agreed that the said William Clopton, his heirs and assigns, shall yearly to the Hospitaller *for a day and a night, find to him with four men and five horses, meat, drink, and horse meat.* Also we have granted to the said William Clopton yearly during the said term, *a gown*, being to the value of xv$^{s.}$ [15s.] or else 15s. therefore; and if it fortune the said farm of vi$^{li.}$ xiii$^{s.}$ iiii$^{d.}$ to be behind or not paid in part or in the whole by the space of two months after any of the feasts aforesaid, so that it be lawfully asked of the said William Clopton within the town of Melford, that then it shall be lawful to the said Abbot, convent, or their successors, or their certain attorneys, to enter and distrain, and the distress so taken to drive away and keep unto the time that the said farm be fully contented and paid, with the cost and charges of the same therefore had. And if it fortune that the said farm of vi$^{li.}$ xiii$^{s.}$ iiii$^{d.}$ to be behind in part or in all, by the space of vi. months after any of the feasts aforesaid, so that the said William Clopton or his assigns be warned ten days before, and not paid; that then it shall be lawful to the foresaid Abbot, convent, and their successors, or their certain attorneys, in the premises to re-enter and distrain, and the distress so taken to lead away and keep, and the aforesaid William Clopton, his heirs and assigns, from the said farm to put for ever, these indentures notwithstanding. And also it is covenanted and agreed that if it fortune, after the decease of the said William Clopton, that none of his children, nor none of the children of them coming, being heirs male, have the *place called Lutons wherein the said William Clopton now dwelleth,* that then the said Abbot and his successors and assigns shall take all the said lands, woods, meadows, pastures and tithes, into their hands again, and them let at their pleasure to whom they will, these indentures notwithstanding. In witness whereof unto the one part of this indenture, as anenst the aforesaid William Clopton remaining, the aforesaid Abbot and convent their common seal have set. To the other part, as anenst the aforesaid Abbot and convent remaining, the aforesaid William Clopton, knight, his seal hath put to. Given and granted in our Chapter-house, the 23rd day of the month of December, the year of the reign of King Henry VII. the 17th, and the year of our Lord 1501."

In the above lease the whole of St. Saviour's lands were not included, but only such as lay conveniently for Sir William Clopton; and comparing the rentals, it would appear that he had made a very favourable bargain, as he rented the bulk of the property at £6. 13s. 4d., though it was in truth the least valuable part, whereas the small remainder let for £16. 3s. 9½d. The following is the lease of the other part, dated 1516. There is a note to the copy of it, that in 1674 it was, with the lease which follows it, among the bundle of leases formerly belonging to the Abbot of Bury in the Court of Augmentation at Westminster. To the second lease the seal was at that time firm and entire.

EXTRACT from the Lease from Robert Shuleham, Hospitaller of Bury, of Lands and Tithes in Melford, to Richard Hoo, of Melford, A.D. 1516.

"Master Robert Shuleham, Hospitaller of the Monastery of St. Edmund's, by indenture under his seal bearing date the 20th July, in the 7th year of King Henry VIII., leaseth out to Richard Hoo, of Melford, all manner of lands and tenements, rents, alterages and tithes, which the said Hospitaller hath in the town of Melford, except such lands, tenements, and tithes which the said Hospitaller had letten to Sir William Clopton, of Melford, Knight, and to one George Dix, of Melford aforesaid, for the term of ten years, paying yearly xvi^{l} iii^{s} ix^{d} ob. [£16. 3s. 9½d.]; and by the said indenture the Hospitaller aforesaid granteth to discharge the said Richard and his assigns during the said term, against the *Parson of Melford*, for all tithes due to the said parson, of and for such ground as the said Richard or his assigns occupy of the said Hospitaller for this said lease."

(It does not however mention what these said grounds are.)

EXTRACT of Lease from Thomas Geale, Hospitaller of Bury St. Edmund's, of lands and tithe in Melford, to Robert Coleman.

"The 16th March in the 22nd year of King Henry VIII., A.D. 1531, Master Thomas Geale, Hospitaller of the Monastery of Bury St. Edmund's, by indenture leased out to Robert Coleman, of Melford, clothier, [the same lands as mentioned in the last lease,] for the term of ten years."

EXTRACT of Lease made the 8th day of February, 1539, between John, Abbot of Bury, and Robert, Simon, and James Coleman, of Melford.

(This Lease is of the lands of St. Saviour's Hospital, including some of those which had been leased to Sir Wm. Clopton.)

"Lease made the 8th of February, in the 30th year of King Henry VIII., 1539, between the Right Reverend Father in God John

[Reeve, alias de Melford], Abbot of the Monastery of Bury St. Edmund's, the Prior and Convent of the said place, and Robert, Simon, and James Coleman, of Melford, clothiers,—of lands and tithes at Melford belonging to the Hospital of St. Saviour's, Bury, for 30 years, at xxxvi^{li} ii^s v^d [£36. 2s. 5d.] rent."

(The covenants are exactly similar to the former leases.)

At the dissolution of the Abbey of Bury the Hospital of St. Saviour, with all its possessions, came into the hands of the Crown, and part of the lands and tithes which had been leased to the Cloptons, of Kentwell, were granted by King Henry VIII. to William Clopton, of Kentwell Hall; and other parts and tithes leased to the Colemans, became by the grant of Queen Mary the property of William Cordell, of Melford Hall, together with a portion of tithes, formerly of the possession in Melford of the College of Stoke by Clare, which had been in the tenure of William Clopton. The tithes of St. Saviour's, which were granted to William Cordell, were afterwards settled by him as part of the endowment for ever of the "Hospital of the Holy Trinity," in Melford, which he founded; and these were finally adjusted and apportioned by the Tithe Commutation Commissioners under the Act of 1839, and commuted at an annual value of £380. 17s. 4d. The commuted tithes, now impropriate to Melford Hall, were purchased from the owners of Kentwell; but originally, with the Kentwell impropriate tithes, formed part of the grant from the Crown to the Cloptons from the dissolved Hospital of St. Saviour.

CHAPTER III.

MELFORD CHURCH.

AS before recounted, the Church of Melford was endowed in the eleventh century with a manor and about 261 acres of land. Of the ancient fabric itself there are no descriptive records, though the roll of its clergy, and the history of its property, and the changes which occurred therein, already related, go back to the twelfth century. If only two churches have been successively erected here, the old church undoubtedly stood on or about the site of the present one. Presumably its style of architecture was Saxon, for Earl Alfric gave and endowed it, and established here clergy some years before the Norman conquest. Whether this same structure stood till the fifteenth century, or whether there was one of intermediate construction, is now unknown. There are in some of the ancient wills relating to this place, bequests for the church and its furniture, many for the bells, and some for its Lady Chapel, which refer to a date prior to the construction of the present edifice, and are connected with that which immediately preceded it.

The present noble church is one of the three hundred and ten mediæval churches of England which were dedicated to the Holy and undivided Trinity, and, like the great mass of Suffolk churches, is Perpendicular, and some part of it late in that style. As generally the case throughout the eastern counties, it is built of flint and stone, in the manner called "flush work," dressed flint forming the panels, and the stone on the same face not raised from the surface marking the divisions of the panels. The great variety of the work on this church and its Lady Chapel is surprising. Below the base moulding round the church is a pedimental range of richly-carved stone panels; and on the north side there still remain some very good grotesque stone gurgoyles.

Before, however, entering upon the further history of the existing church, the following lists, showing the patrons of the church and living of Melford, and the successive rectors thereof from very early times, are here recorded :—

Patrons of the Church and Living of Melford.

1. EARL ALFRIC, who first endowed this church and gave the patronage of it to the respective Abbots of Bury St.

Edmund's for ever, together with his manor of Melford Hall.

2 to 33. LEOFSTAN, the second Abbot, A.D. 1044 to 1065; and the thirty-one succeeding abbots of Bury down to the year 1539, when the Abbey was dissolved.

34. HENRY VIII., King of England, into whose hands the said Abbey of Bury, and therewith the manor of Melford and the advowson were resigned by John Reeve, alias John de Melford, 4th November, 1539. King Henry does not appear to have actually presented to the living, but perhaps he confirmed therein William Newton, who was rector from 1534-5 to 1548.

King Edward VI. did not present to this living, but he seems to have resigned his right to do so to his sister Queen Mary, as shown in the presentation of Henry Mallet, her chaplain.

35. QUEEN MARY.

36. Sir WILLIAM CORDELL, Knight, Master of the Rolls, a Privy Counsellor, and Speaker of the House of Commons, 1st and 2nd of Philip and Mary.

37. Mistress JANE ALLINGTON, sister and heir of Sir William Cordell, and wife of Richard Allington, Esq., second son of Sir Giles Allington.

Queen Elizabeth presented the Rev. WM. GILBERT, *failing a presentation by the rightful patron.*

38. Sir THOMAS SAVAGE, who became Viscount Savage of Rocksavage, son of Sir John Savage, who had married the daughter and heiress of Jane Allington.

His son became the second Earl Rivers, but did not present to the living. (He was a Roman Catholic.) There is also here the hiatus of the Rebellion, when Puritan ministers were appointed by the Parliament.

39. Sir ROBERT CORDELL, Bart., who bought the estate and advowson from John, Earl Rivers, and the countess his mother.

40. Sir JOHN CORDELL, Bart., his son.

41. Sir JOHN CORDELL (the second of the name).

42. MARGARET CORDELL, his sister and heiress, who married Sir Charles Firebrace, Bart. (She did not present.)

43. Sir CORDELL FIREBRACE, Bart., their son.

44. Lady FIREBRACE, his widow, who married Mr. Campbell, of Lyston Hall, Essex.

45. The Rev. JOHN LEEDS.[*]

* He is said to have bought the living for £2,400, and to have insured the life of the then incumbent, the Rev. E. Butts, for that sum; and that, as the latter only lived two years afterwards, the advowson only actually cost Mr. Leeds the two years' insurance premiums.

46. The Rev. WILLIAM TYLNEY SPURDENS.*

47. JOHN COBBOLD, Esq.

48. JOHN COBBOLD, son of the above.

49. JOHN CHEVALIER COBBOLD, Esq., M.P., half-brother of the above.

50. The Rev. CHARLES JOHN MARTYN.

List of the Rectors of Melford.

N.B.—The Institution books in the Bishop's Registry at Norwich commence only from 1299, John Salmon being then bishop.

A.D. 1198 (et ante).—HUGH, the Clerk, was Rector of Melford before the appropriation of part of Melford Church property to the Hospital of St. Saviour at Bury. The appropriation was not to take effect until after the death of Hugh, the Clerk, *then parson.* He died in that year or the following one.

1199–1200 (et post).—WALTER HERVEY was at that time (as then called) Vicar of Melford.

Here occurs a lapse of nearly a century of which there is no record, till the commencement of the Bishop's books.

10th October, 1309.—Dominus SIMON DE CLAYBER, Priest, on the presentation of Abbot Thomas de Tottington.

5th December, 1311.—HENRY DE STANTON, presented by the same abbot for a short term. This was made a matter of certain conditions, as shown in an agreement among the Abbots' grants (Chapter IX.).

9th October, 1312.—Dominus ALLANUS DE ELY, Priest, on the presentation of the same abbot.

[No date.]—Dominus . . . . DE WELBORNE.

9th December, 1326.—Dominus THOMAS DE CHEDWORTH, Priest, on the resignation of . . . . de Welborne (ex causa permutationis), on the presentation of Abbot Richard de Draughton.

3rd April, 1333.—Magister SIMON DE DRAUGHTON, Priest, on the resignation of Thomas de Chedworth, on the presentation of the same abbot.

7th June, 1334.—RICHARD DE HARLINGE, Priest, on the presentation of the same abbot,

6th February, 1364.—Magister THEODORUS DE OTLANIA, Priest, on the presentation of John de Brinkale, Abbot of St. Edmund's.

30th July, 1371.—THOMAS DE GRYNESBY (or Grymesby), *primam habens tonsuram clericalem,* on the presentation of the same abbot.

* He is stated to have purchased the living for a considerable sum, and to have sold it for a smaller price to the Cobbold family.

10th February, 1372.—THOMAS DE GRYNESBY, Priest, on the presentation of "*the King of England, on a recovery in his royal Court against the Abbot of St. Edmund, through the default of the said Abbot, the real Patron of this Church.*" (The Abbot at this period was John de Brinkale.)

25th August, 1410.—Magister WILLIAM WYGOR DE CAVENDISH, Priest, on the resignation of Thomas Grynesby, on the presentation of Abbot William Cratfield.

1st April, 1417.—NICHOLAUS MANSEL, Priest, "*on the presentation of Brother Robert, Prior of the Monastery of St. Edmund of Bury, and of the venerable and religious man, Brother William, of the said Monastery; the Abbot being absent in foreign parts, and they being, as his Vicars in general spiritual matters, the patrons of this Church.*" (*William Exeter was the Abbot.*)

2nd February, 1419.—Magister THOMAS BARNSLEY, Priest, on the presentation of William Exeter, Abbot of St. Edmund's.

6th December, 1429.—STEPHANUS WILTON, in Doctor's orders, on the resignation of Thomas Barnesley, on the presentation of William Curteys, Abbot of St. Edmund's.

In a very large vellum folio book, with whitish leaves and leather straps, indited "Registrum Will: Curteys, Abbatis," folio 30, anciently belonging to the Abbey of Bury, and which came into the possession of Sir Robert Bacon, of Redgrave, Suffolk, it is stated thus:—

"Memorandum, quod Magister Stephanus Wilton, decretorum Doctor, præsentatus fuit ad ecclesiam parochialem de Melford, per liberam resignationem Magistri Thomæ Barnesley, ultimi Rectoris ejusdem, sexto die mensis Decembris, Anno Domini MCCCC. nono, et W. Abbatis, anno primo." (*It is evident the word vicesimo is here omitted accidentally before the word nono, as William Curteys became abbot in the year 1429.*)

Translation.

"Memorandum,—That Master Stephen Wilton, in Doctor's orders, was presented to the parish church of Melford, on the voluntary resignation thereof of Master Thomas Barnesley, the former rector of the same, on the 6th day of December, A.D. 1409 and in the first year of William [Curteys] the Abbot."

The 1409, as before mentioned, should be 1429.

7th February, 1433.—The Venerable Father in God, JOHANNES, ENACHDUNENSIS EPISCOPUS, was presented by Abbot William Curteys, to the living of Melford, on the voluntary resignation of Stephanus Wilton, on the 12th January, 1433, and in the 4th year of William, Abbot of Bury.

In folio 43 of the above-mentioned book, "Registrum Will: Curteys, Abbatis," will also be found an entry to this effect.

F

(The Prelate above-named was John, Lord Bishop of Enachdun or Enaghdun (now Annadown), in the Irish province of Tuam, a little see, maintained apparently to give a title to a suffragan. Six bishops of this see were at various periods English suffragans. Bishop John of Enaghdun, who was "provided" by the Pope to his see on the 9th of June, 1421, was in that year also suffragan of Salisbury; and of Exeter in 1438. He was also Provost of St. Elizabeth's, Winchester, and Rector of Cheddington. He was certainly a friar, though there is a doubt to what order he belonged; but as he was presented to the living of Melford by the Abbot of Bury, who was a Benedictine, it is probable that he may have been of that order. His family name was Boner, or Bonere; but according to some authorities, Camere.)

3rd August, 1439.—Dominus THOMAS LEWYSHAM, presented by Abbot William Curteys :—

> "I, WILLIAM, Dei gratia, Roffensis [Rochester] Episcopus, in the matter of the exchange of benefices between John, Lord Bishop of Enaghdun, and Rector of the parish church of Melford, and Dominus Thomas Lewysham, Rector of the parish church of Bromlegh, in the diocese of Rochester, by my own authority as Ordinary, as well as by the authority of Magister John Wigenhall, of the degree of Doctor, Vicar-general in matters spiritual of the Reverend Father in Christ Thomas, Dei gratia, Lord Bishop of Norwich, coming as Commissary in this spiritual matter to me, the said Lord Bishop of Rochester, and I, having heard, examined, and fully discussed this exchange, have permitted the removal of the said Thomas Lewysham to the said church of Melford."

(The Latin text of this entry is somewhat difficult to decipher, but the above appears to be the meaning thereof.)

19th July, 1441.—THOMAS CRAMEWORTH, Priest, on the presentation of Abbot William Curteys.

5th March, 1446.—WILLIAM HANNIBALD, on the presentation of the above-named abbot.

21st June, 1454.—WILLIAM COXE, Bachelor of Laws, Priest, on the presentation of Abbot John Boone (or Bohun).

21st December, 1456.—JOHN MYDWELL, on the presentation of the same abbot.

21st April, 1460.—THOMAS WARDEN, Professor of Theology, on the presentation of the same abbot.

25th July, 1470.—JOHN STORY, Clerk, on the presentation of Abbot Robert Coote.

8th (or 18th) April, 1474.—ÆGIDIUS DENT, Bachelor of Theoogy, on the presentation of Abbot Richard Hengham.

14th September, 1484.—THOMAS ALEYN, *alias* CARVER, Priest, on the presentation of Abbot Thomas Racclesden.

9th March, 1504.—WILLIAM SKEEN or SKEYNE, on the presentation of William Codenham, Abbot of St. Edmund's.

5th March, 1514.—Magister ROBERT STOURTON, Professor of Theology, on the presentation of Abbot John Reeve, *alias* de Melford. (The last Abbot of Bury.)

21st July, 1514.—Magister JOHANNES MALTBY, on the presentation of the same abbot.

About the year 1534.—WILLIAM NEWTON, presented by the same abbot. (He held his first court for the manor of the Rectory of Melford, 1534.)

In 1539 the Abbey was dissolved.

20th July, 1548.—HENRY MALLET, Clerk, on the presentation of " The most excellent Mary, patron of this church, sister of the most illustrious King Edward VI., and daughter of her well beloved father Henry VIII., of pious memory." (So that, as before remarked, Edward VI. had delegated to her his patronage of this church. Henry Mallet was the Princess Mary's chaplain.)

30th March, 1558.—Magister CHRISTOPHERUS HILL, Bachelor of Theology, on the presentation of Sir William Cordell, knight, Master of the Court of Chancery of King Philip and Queen Mary.

About 1560.—EDMUND HUMPHREY. (The record of the date of his presentation is wanting; but he held his first manor court for the Rectory of Melford, 17th July, 1560.)

6th February, 1583.—RALPH JONES, Professor of Theology, on the presentation of Dame Mary Cordell, widow of Sir William Cordell, knight, deceased, the late patron.

28th November, 1590.—PETER WENTWORTH, Clerk, on the presentation of Jane Allington, widow, patron in her own right. (She was the sister and heiress of Sir William Cordell.)

4th September, 1599.—WILLIAM GILBERT, Clerk, Master of Arts, was presented to the Rectory and Church of Melford, then vacant, on the right of presentation belonging to Queen Elizabeth, failing other legal mode of presenting. (The aforesaid William Gilbert was buried the 7th August, 1618. He was chaplain to Gilbert Talbot, 7th Earl of Shrewsbury, and held his first court of the manor of the Rectory on the 18th September, 1600.)

23rd September, 1618.—ROBERT WAREYN, Clerk, Master of Arts, on the presentation of Thomas Savage, knight and baron (*sic*). (Doctor Wareyn in October, 1643, during the Rebellion, he being a Royalist, was turned out of the living. On the Restoration, in 1660, he was again restored to the benefice; but on the 24th November, 1660, he resigned: it is stated "he being then 96 years old." He died the following year.)

1643—1660.—Six Puritan Ministers.—Seth Wood, Samuel Boardman, Ralph Brideoak, Seth Wood, Peter Sainthill, Claudius Salmasius Gilbert.

12th November, 1660.—NATHANIEL BISBIE, Priest, Master of Arts, on the presentation of Sir Robert Cordell, Bart., on the resignation of Robert Warren. (In 1689, Nathaniel Bisbie was deprived of the Rectory of Melford, for refusing to take the oath of allegiance to William III. He himself expresses it thus : " At which time the foresayd Nath. Bisbie, being then in the 55th year of his age, and 30th year of his incumbency, by vertue of an unrighteous Act of a factious and rebellious convention, was deprived of the Rectory of Melford for not withgoing his faith and sworn allegiance to King James the Second, and transferring it to William, Prince of Aurange, and was succeeded by Henry Felton, LL.D. Deus dabit his quoque finem.")

26th July, 1689.—HENRY FELTON, LL.D., Fellow of St. Peter's College, Cambridge, on the deprivation of Nathaniel Bisbie. (It does not appear whether he was presented by Sir John Cordell (2nd bart.) or by the Crown.)

1701.—JAMES JOHNSON. His son became Bishop of Worcester, and was killed at Bath by a fall from his horse. Presented by Sir John Cordell (3rd bart.), (who also was killed by a fall from his horse in 1704).

1741.—ABRAHAM OAKES, LL.D. Presented by Sir Cordell Firebrace, Bart. (Abraham Oakes married the daughter of Sir John Jacob, Bart., and died in 1756. From his second son descends the present representative of the Oakes baronetcy.)

1758.—JOHN JACOB OAKES, eldest son of the above, presented by Sir Cordell Firebrace, Bart.

1771.—ROBERT BUTTS, son of the Bishop of Ely. (The Register of the parish of Lackford, Suffolk, has the entry of the Bishop's marriage as Bishop of Norwich to Mrs. Anne Reynolds, daughter of the Rector of Lackford, 4th December, 1735; and in the year 1738 there is an entry in the Register of Burials of the same parish, of the burial of their infant son, James. In this entry the Bishop is called " Bishop of Ely.")

1790.—JOHN LEROO, on his own presentation, having purchased the advowson,

1819.—BRANSBY FRANCIS. Presented by the Rev. William Tylney Spurdens.

1830.—EDWARD COBBOLD. (The living was for many years in se-

questration for his debts.   He committed suicide in London.)
Presented by his father, John Cobbold.

1862.—WILLIAM WALLIS, M.A., on the presentation of John Chevalier
Cobbold, M.P.

1869.—CHARLES JOHN MARTYN, M.A., Christchurch, Oxford, on his
own presentation, having purchased the advowson.

Making a total number of 47 rectors in the course of 570
years, giving an average of about 12 years' incumbency to each
rector.   Besides 6 Puritan ministers during the Rebellion.

On the chancel wall is a board painted a few years ago, which
purports to record some of the benefactions, and also the names of
the rectors to 1590.   It commences with Symon Clayber, and ends
with Peter Wentworth, but is very erroneous and imperfect.   Three
rectors' names during that period are omitted, and the order of their
succession is in several cases wrong, and the spelling of the names
often incorrect.

From the detail of the church property, as stated by the Abbot's
Register of A.D. 1287 (which is recorded in the 6th chapter), until the
rebuilding of the old church, we have no other particulars connected
with it, save the list of its patrons, Abbots of Bury, and of the various
rectors.   Its appearance, size, and style of architecture are all uncertain; but it may be fairly presumed that the early church of the
eleventh century, if it had not been rebuilt, was but small, for two
hundred years afterwards the population of Melford may be roughly
guessed by estimation from the various Chartularies of the Abbey, as
being in round numbers from about 550 to 650 inhabitants.   This, however, can only be taken as an approximation, and this estimate of the
population from A.D. 1250 to 1300 is given with much diffidence; for
it is a matter of considerable difficulty to arrive at any definite conclu-
sion from the small known data on this subject.   If only the messuages
and the cottages named in the Chartularies are to be taken as the
total number of dwellings, and the standard rule of five to a household be applied thereto, the population would only amount to about
400.   Every dwelling may be fairly considered to have contained a
family, for a person living alone was at that date a very rare exception.
But the estimate of population on the above basis seems fallacious for
several reasons: such as, that on some of the larger holdings, cottars
are mentioned, but no number of their cottages given; and the above
calculation only includes those actually stated, namely, about twenty-six,
which is probably much below the real number of cottages.   Further
it must be borne in mind, that at that period early marriages being
greatly discouraged, the households of the larger yeomen and other
owners generally included under their roof, besides their own families,
most of the persons whom they employed.   After weighing these

points and comparing them with other evidences, the number of the
population of Melford has been estimated, as named above, to have
been not less than from 550 to 650 inhabitants in the year 1287.   If,
therefore, the original church was still standing and continued to exist
till the 15th century, it was probably then too small to accommodate
the increased population, and moreover must have been suffering from
the inevitable decay of four centuries; and its restoration in part, or
its entire reconstruction, may have become inevitable.

From a comparison of various small details, there appears reason
to believe that at first there was either an attempted restoration or
rebuilding of a portion of the old edifice, or perhaps a new structure
was built on a small scale with a tower, in the early part of the 15th
century; and that some years later it had either become absolutely
necessary to entirely rebuild the remainder of the church, or if it had
been partially rebuilt, it was so small that it required to be added to.
Though part of the present south aisle is said to be the newest (latest)
erection of the nave and aisles, it appears that the 5th window from
the east in that aisle was glazed by the family of Roger Bee (or Ibe,
as sometimes spelt), in 1460.   In the 7th window on the same side
occurs the expression that Abigail Felt was a great benefactress to
the *new structure* of the church (*ad novam fabricam*).   Robert Sparrow,
whose name is on the north wall of the church, made his will in
1468.

The supposition of a prior rebuilding is partly founded on some of
the expressions in the following narrative, written by a rector of this
church, who not only had the opportunity of access to then existing
records and local traditions now lost or forgotten, but he had also the
further advantage of viewing the past from an intermediate stand-
point, 200 years earlier than our own time:—and with his account
must be compared the dates connected with the names, histories, and
wills of certain persons who are identified with the work; and perhaps also in a measure by a careful consideration of some of the details
of the existing building.

The MS. from which this is transcribed, was at at one time in
the possession of the Rev. William Tylney Spurdens, of North Walsham, Norfolk.   It is dated August, 1688, and was written by the
Rev. Nathaniel Bisbie, Rector of Melford, and runs thus:—

"Much about the middle of the parish of Melford, alias Long
Melford, in Suffolk, upon an hill most pleasant for air and prospect, here
standeth a large and beautiful church called Trinity Church, because
dedicated to the Holy and Undivided Trinity.   It hath three iles, which
from the north to the south wall contain together in breadth 61 feet
6 inches.   Part of it was of an old erection: viz., the whole north ile,
the steeple, a great part of the porch, and perhaps the east end of the
south ile.   All the other parts are of a much later erection, as by the

different sort of building and the several inscriptions still extant in and about the said church, may most evidently appear."

Here then are named certain portions of an older structure than the remainder of the present church, but it is beyond question not only that no part of the work is of earlier date than the 15th century, but that the style of the oldest part is of the same century as all the rest of the building, though perhaps somewhat earlier. Again, when in 1867-8 the church was entirely gutted for its recent restoration, much earth had to be removed from the interior. On the north side there was no trace of any foundation within the present north wall, but on the south side, some feet within the present south wall, there stood the foundation several yards in length of an old flint wall: this extended eastward from opposite the porch about halfway along the church. As to the steeple or tower (since destroyed), which Dr. Bisbie says was of an old erection, it is impossible to say whether it was part of the original church or of a later rebuilding. Apparently it was not round, but was a square tower, and is so shown on the parchment map of the Manor of Melford, designed by Israel Amyce, of Barking, Essex, in 1580, and also in the better-drawn map of 1613 by Samuel Pearse, of Maidstone. This tower was destroyed by fire caused by lightning, about 1709-10—certainly not later than 1711, as in that year contributions were solicited to rebuild it.

Continuing Dr. Bisbie's account, with the inscriptions visible in his day, more light will yet be thrown on this subject. His MS. goes on thus, speaking of the present church:—

"The middle ile from the steeple, exclusive to the east end of the chancel, hath one entire advanced roofe, in length 152 feet and 6 inches; distant from the pavement beneath, 41 feet and 6 inches; supported on each side with 10 arched pillars, separating the said middle ile from the 2 other iles, which are in height 24 feet, and in length 135 feet and 4 inches.

"The pious benefactours concerned in the building of the advanced ile may be known [and let their memories never perish] by the inscriptions under the battlements without the church, and by like inscriptions in the windows undemolished within the church.

"From the inscriptions under the battlements of the advanced ile without the church, beginning on the north side, here John Clopton, Esq., worthily deserved to have his memory preserved; a zealous and eminent promoter of the new erection. He built the 4 first pillars and arches on the north side counting from east to west, whereof one of them is in the nave of the church; though his name be now obliterated and by time and weather quite eaten out. Though the aforesaid inscription be now obliterated, yet several persons have read the same, the obliteration being but of very late date, and particularly the present Rector of the church [Dr. Nath. Bisbie], who hereby sacredly and solemnly affirms that the merit of the action was ascribed to one or more of the family of the Cloptons; and as he remembereth and verily believeth, to John Clopton, in memory and good of him, his wife, his children, and his ancestors. Nay, to this very day [1688], though the rest be obliterated and worn out, * * * * ton is plain to be espied, which insinuates that Clopton was the benefactor for the building of those arches and pillars. After him this inscription follows :—

" ' *Pray for the sowlis of Roberd Spar'we and Marion his wife, and for Thom' Cowper and Ma'el his wif, of quos goodis Mast Gilis Dent, John Clopton, Jon Smyth, and Roger Smyth, wyth y help of y weel disposyd me' of this [town]* dede these se'on archis new repare anno domini milesimo cccc * * * * [I'].'*

"Whereas the full account of the annus D be defaced, yet by reason of the mention of Giles Dent in the inscription and the I at the end of the said account, it is, ought, and can be no otherwise than Anno D 1481, for Mr. Giles Dent was instituted into the Rectory of Melford ♃ Aprilis, 1474. He made his will ♃ April, 1484, nominating Robert Cutler and Thomas Ellis his executors, and John Clopton his supervisor. On ♃ July following he adds a codicil to it, bequeathing all the grain of his glebe and his tithes to be disposed of in charitable uses. Thomas Aleyn† his successor was instituted ♃ Sept 1484 into the said Parsonage; and, therefore, there being I to end the annus wherein the north side of that advanced ile was finished, it could be no other, as before is hinted, than A.D. 1481.

" The inscriptions under the battlements on the south side are as followeth :—

" ' *Pray for the sowles of Rogere Moryell, Margarete and Kateryn his wyffis, of whos goodis the seyd Kateryn, John Clopton, Mast Wyllem Qwaytis and John Smyth, dede these VI archis new repare: and ded make the tabill at the hye awtere, anno domini millesimo quadringentesimo octogesi p'm°. Pray for y sowl of Thomas Couper y wych y II arche dede repare. Pray for y sowl of Law. Martyn and Marion hys wyf,*

---

* The word and number bracketed in this inscription are now no longer visible, and had ceased to be so before 1831.

This Robert Spar'we, or Sparrow, was descended from William Sparrow, of West Harling, in Norfolk. Robert Sparrow, of Melford, had by his wife Marion two sons, Robert and William. Robert was the first of his name who held Combewells, afterwards called Sparrow's Hall, in Sible Hedingham. He is said to have married Agnes, a sister of Roger Martyn, of Melford, by whom he had Thomas, who lived to a very great age, and died about the year 1595, at Bocking, leaving two sons, the eldest of whom, John Sparrow, was steward to John de Vere, Earl of Oxford, and is said to be the ancestor of the present family of the Sparrows of Gosfield, in Essex. The ancient arms of Sparrow were Vert, a stag trippant, or.; but they were subsequently altered to Or., three roses, proper.

Robert Sparrow, named in the inscription, made his will 1468.

† He also went by the name of " alias Thomas Carver."

and for Rychard Martyn, and Elizabeth and Jhone hys wyvis and frendis, thyat thys chawncel repared, a° d°¹ M°ccccLxxⁱˣᵉ."

In the case of the first-named person in this inscription, Roger Moryell, it is plain that he was dead at this date of 1481, for the building was done at the cost of his goods by his second wife Katherine and the other persons named, who were probably his executors. Now we know, from the list of free tenants of the Manor of Melford in the 20th year of the reign of King Henry VI., and in the 14th year of William Curteys, Abbot of St. Edmund's, A.D. 1442, that Roger Moryell then held of the Manor, lands adjoining to, or forming part of, . the present Mr. William Mills's farm at Rodbridge, and adjoining the lands called " Nelys," which were bequeathed in charity to the parish ; and also adjoining the lands of Roger, sometimes called Ibe and some-times Bee, whose family glazed the 5th window from the east, south side, in 1460. Roger Moryell also kept one of the only two mentioned taverns (the inns of the period) in " Halle Strete, on the east side in Melford, near to the olde market* [*on or about Chapel Green*], and held therewith a piece of the waste land of the Manor in front of the tavern gate."

Probably this piece of the waste was for the erection of his sign-post, for in the case of the other tavern, which was held by William Martyn at this same date, it is expressly stated that he held a piece of the waste of the Manor, by the street, in front of the gateway into his tavern, " *and erected there a pole for a sign, at the gate of his said tavern.*"

There were two John Smyths holding lands in Melford in 1442 ; one in High Street, holding Harefield, &c. ; the other was a locksmith, who lived in a messuage on the east side of the Hall Street, which formerly belonged to Roger Dyster.

Lawrence Martyn was dead at the time of this inscription. He lived at Melford Place. He also held many copyholds of the Manor in 1442, and he had also land beyond Bridge Street. He died 1460. Richard Martyn died 1463 ; so that perhaps the date of 1479 refers to the work of his second wife and friends, through his benefactions.

Of the following inscription, as given by Dr. Bisbie, part is now gone, having been damaged in the fall of the tower. In his day, however, it ran thus :—

" *Pray for yᵉ sowl of Mastᵉ Giles Dent, late parson of Melford, of whose goodis, John Clopton, Maist.ᵉ Robtᵉ Coteler and Thomas Elys dede yᵉ arch make and glase, and yᵉ ruf over yᵉ Porch.*"

As before mentioned, Robert Cutler and Thomas Elys were the executors, and John Clopton the supervisor of Mr. Giles Dent's will,

---

* The new market was opposite the Bull Inn. The old butchers' stalls existed there till within a comparatively recent date.

who died 1484; therefore this window and the roof of the porch were not built till soon after that date. Thomas Elys, in the list of manorial free tenants of 1442, is described as a clothier, holding property in several detached portions, and living nearly opposite to the present "High Street Farm," on land now belonging to Kentwell Hall, the site now occupied by John Lilly, the woodman, forming part thereof. Thomas Elys had also lands at Breggestrete (Bridge Street): some of that which he then held continued to belong to persons of the name of Elys or Ellys down to the year 1580 and afterwards.

As to John Clopton, he will be further noticed in his place; as also will be William Clopton his father, who is named in the next inscription.

From the inscription over the porch it appears that John Clopton was the builder thereof, excepting the roof:—

"*Pray for yᵉ sowlis of William Clopton, Margᵗ and Margᵗ his wifis, and for yᵉ sowle of Alice Clopton and for John Cloptoʼ, and for alle thoo sowlisʼ yᵗ yᵉ seyd John is boʼnde to prey for.*"

Over the lower windows from the porch to the east end of the said south aisle is inscribed as follows :—

"*Pray for yᵉ sowle of Rog: Moriell of whoᵗ goodᵗ yᵉ arch was made. Pray for yᵉ sowle of John Keche, and for his Fadʼ and Modʼ of whoᵗ goodᵗ yᵉ arche was made.—Pray for yᵉ sowl of Thomʼ Elys and Jone his wife, and for yᵉ good sped of Jone Elys makᵗ hʼof.—Pray for yᵉ sowl of John Pie and Alys his wife, of whoᵗ goodᵗ yᵉ arch was made and yᵉ twey wyʼdowys glasid. Pray for yᵉ sowlis of John Distᵗ and Alis, and for yᵉ good sped of John Distᵗ and Xʼpian makᵗ hʼof.*"

John Dister was a wealthy clothier of Melford, and who also carried on a branch of his trade at Glemsford. He had land around Bridge Street, Melford, and also at Belchamp Otten, where he owned 295a. 1r. 24p. He was a person of some importance, for he was entitled to bear arms, which were gules, a chevron, or, between three eagles with two heads displayed, argent. Crest: on a wreath and helmet, a paschal lamb passant. Other members of this family had part of the Bulney lands; and John Dister and Alice held some land south of Hall Street, abutting on Broadmeadow.

Over the lower windows of the Martyn Chapel, on the south side, is inscribed :—

"*Pray for yᵉ soulis of Lawrens Martyn and Marion his wyffe, Elysabeth Martyn aʼd Jone, and for yᵉ good estat of Richard Martyn and Roger Martyn and yᵉ wyvis, and alle yᵉ childri of whose goodis . . . . made anno Dᵒⁱ millesimo CCCCLXXXIIII.*"

Richard Martyn, son of Lawrence, died 1463; his wife was Elizabeth Mundeford. The inscription round the Lady Chapel runs thus :—

"*Pray for yᵉ sowle of John Hyll, and for the sowle of John Clopton, Esqᵗoyer, and pray for the sowle of Rychard Loveday, boteler wyth John*

Clopton, of whos godys thys Chappell ye imbaytylled by his excewtors.—
Pray for the soulis of William Clopto', Esquyer, Margery and Marg'y
his wifis, and for all ther parentis and childri', and for ye sowle of Alice
Clopton,' and for John Clopton and for all his childri', and for all y^e
soulis that the said John is bonde to p'y for, which dede y^u Chapel new
repare a' dom' MᵒCCCCLXXXXVI. Crist' sit testis heo me no' exhibuisse ut
merear laudes, sed ut spiritus memoretur. Roger Smyth and Robert
Smyth.''

The William Clopton here called Esquire was William Clopton of
Kentwell, generally styled as a knight, who died in 1446. He had
two wives of the name of Margery. The first was the daughter of Sir
Roger Drury, of Rougham, knight: she died 1420. The second was
the daughter of Helias Francys, or Francis, of Norfolk: she died 1424.
Sir William Clopton's recessed mural tomb, with his effigy in armour
much disfigured, is near the north-eastern entrance door in the
Clopton Chapel. There is a brass thereon (the inscription on which
is given in Chapter V.), and four coats of arms : first, Clopton ; second,
Myld, the mother of Sir William, who brought Kentwell to the family ;
third and fourth, Clopton impaling his two wives. Margery Francys,
the second wife, is buried near, and her effigy in brass remains in a
stone in the floor.

John Clopton, whose name is also recorded on the foregoing inscription, was the son of the above Sir William by Margery Francys,
the second wife, and was born 1423. He was sheriff of Norfolk and
Suffolk, 30th of Henry VI. (1452-1453) ; he married Alice, daughter
of Robert Darcy, of Malden, in Essex, and died in 1497. His is the
Easter Tomb, between the chancel and the Clopton mortuary chapel,
and open to both. On the sides of the arch over the tomb are portraits
of his wife and children in fresco, now, alas, almost obliterated by
neglect and ill-usage.

By the following extract from the will of John Clopton it would
seem that the inscription round the Lady Chapel was placed there after
his death. His will, which is dated 4th November, 1494 (proved 16th
November, 1497), contains the following entry.

"Memorandum that I, John Clopton, red over this my testament
the xxii. day of February, the xii. yere of Kyng Henry the VII. [1497],
which I will shal stonde in everye poynte.—Also the saide John
Clopton wole that whereas by the jugement of the parsonne of
Melford, and by thassent of thexecutours of John Hille the saide John
Clopton shal have c. marcs [C66. 13s. 4d.] for to relese his interest
that he and his feoffes have in the Maner of Bowre Hall, in Pentley,
the saide John Clopton will that the saide c. marke be spent on the
garnysshyng of oure Lady Chapell, and of the cloister ther abowte
that the saide John Clopton hathe done new made in Melford Churchyard, and that there bee made a speciall remembraunce for to pray for

the sowle of the saide John Hille, and for the sowle of the saide John Clopton, and for the sowles that bothe the saide Hill and John Clopton ar mooste bounde to pray for."

He also directs, " my body to be buried in the lytell Chapell in Melforde Churche, there my grave is redy made, even by my wif."

His description of the surrounding aisles of the Lady Chapel, as *the cloister there about*, or round it, is noticeable.

John Clopton was the principal restorer or rebuilder of the church, and in his old age he filled many of the windows with portraits of his connections by blood, marriage, or politically. Being of the Lancastrian party, he was arrested and sent to the Tower of London, with John, Earl of Oxford, Aubrey de Vere his son, Sir John Montgomery, Sir Thomas Tuddenham, and William Tyrell, on the charge of corresponding treasonably with Margaret of Anjou. All of these were beheaded on Tower Hill, 22nd February, 1461, except John Clopton, who somehow made his peace, and lived to see the Lancastrian party dominant. He was a man of great consequence, and much esteemed and trusted during a long and eventful life. He was executor to many great persons ; viz. with Lord Dynham, Sir Thomas Bouchier and others, to the will of Ann, Duchess Dowager of Buckingham, who died 1480. Also to the will of Thomas Darcy in 1486 ; to the will of Sir Thomas Montgomery, Knight of the Garter, 1489 ; also to the will of Lady Darcy, 1489 ; and in 1478 to that of Dame Annes Say, widow of Lord Wenlock, killed at the battle of Tewkesbury, 1471.

Of the other persons mentioned in the inscription, the name of Richard Loveday, butler to John Clopton, is noticeable.

The foregoing mural inscriptions on the battlements of the church, together with some old wills, form the basis of the information we possess as to the final rebuilding. The painted glass, which had escaped destruction, and still existed in 1688, adds further to the knowledge of the names of the benefactors ; but stained glass had continued to be placed in memorial windows up to a time subsequent to the last date of the mural inscription over the Lady Chapel, which appears to have been the final erection. So little by little, during the latter half of the fifteenth century, the rebuilding and ornamentation of this grand old church steadily progressed ; the labour of love of the many pious benefactors whose names we can still read upon their glorious work, aided by many others whose means did not permit them to contribute so largely as their more favoured neighbours ; and though the names of some of these humbler assistants are now lost to us, we can yet gratefully appreciate the services of those " *well-disposyd men of this towne*," who were zealous for the honour of God's house, and of whom, though there be now no worldly knowledge, doubtless there remains the undying record, " they have done what they could." Some officer of the great Abbey of Bury, one of those best and most tasteful of architects, the monks, was probably the designer of the fine fabric of the church as it yet partially remains to us; but now, how shorn of many of its fair ornaments, and how marred in its outward appearance by the hideous tower of last century's erection. Still enough remains to enable us to picture to ourselves this church in its pristine glory, before it had lost its pinnacles from the battlements, and the many figures from the now empty niches, and when it yet retained its tower, doubtless then in perfect character with all the rest; and if so, a noble specimen of architecture, when the stonework was all still sharp and perfect; for though that has become more venerable from the mellowing effect of time, the added beauty has been more than counterbalanced by the damages of mischief and neglect. And in the interior also, when not only the walls and roofs were bright with paint and gilding, and the great carved reredos, representing the Crucifixion, was resplendent with gold and colours; the high altar glittering with a profusion of plate, jewels, embroidery, and precious hangings : when also, before the great rood, the several minor altars, and the many images of saints, there hung brilliant costly draperies; and the officiating priests shone in rich vestments of silk, satin, velvet, and cloth of gold (of all which the inventories still exist), although these accessories belonged to a form of religion opposed to our feelings, and to a ceremonial of which we of the Reformed faith must disapprove, yet we may well imagine how grand must have been here the effect, and how dazzling the brilliancy of colour lighting up this noble church, when in the sunshine, combined with the gorgeous reflected hues of the stained glass with which its 72 windows were then filled.[*] And when we thus picture to ourselves the great churches, such as this one, in their original splendour, we can better understand and realize what charms such a system must have had for the minds of many whose hearts were reached through the external senses; and before they could even legally conform, what a bitter struggle must have been undergone by those Roman Catholics whose imaginations were too warm, and whose admiration for external ceremony and order was too high, to rest content with the change from brilliant decoration to the now bare and whitewashed walls of the churches, and to descend to the comparatively cold and austere simplicity which formed the standard of the Reformation ceremonial.

One part of this church appears to be an addition of a rather later date than the adjoining structure, and bears no outward inscription. From alterations made in the vestry in 1870 by the Rector, the Rev. Charles Martyn, it became evident that this portion between the Martyn Chapel and the south-west end of the Lady Chapel had been built subsequently to the main edifice. For when the interior walls

---

[*] In the church, Lady Chapel, vestry, and chantries, there are altogether 91 windows.

adjoining the church and Lady Chapel were stripped of their plaster, they proved to have been at one time the outer walls of the church; their dressed flint-work having been preserved by the mortar with which they had been afterwards covered, as fresh as the day it was laid. And further, the lower part of the south-east window had been filled in, as still visible, to allow of the roof of this vestry. Presumably this portion had been added after the completion of the church, to supplement the small space allotted as a vestry between the back of the High Altar and the Lady Chapel, and which appears to have been used also as a basement chamber by the Chantry Priest, who had a combined sleeping and living chamber as well, above it. Until the late improvements and alterations made by the Rector, this part was in a ruinous state, only a few of the upper floor joists remained, and the lower portion had been for years used as a rubbish-place and coal-store. Some of the features of these chambers have been now carefully preserved. One of the old principal floor-girders remains, as well as the recessed sedile. The stonework of the south window has been renewed, but its position and character is the same. The northern window has been added to obtain sufficient light. On the basement story is the stone frame of a door leading immediately into the chancel by the side of the High Altar, with another side-door adjoining it, which probably led into the open air where the added vestry now is, going behind the main buttress in the thickness of the wall; for the opening, on being partially cleared, showed a winding passage; or it may have led by a small corner of cloistered covering into the Martyn Chapel for access to the priest's door on the south side thereof. In the east wall of the chamber was a stone mullioned window open to the Lady Chapel, now converted into a door; and there was a squint in the wall, now closed, through which the High Altar therein could be seen; and another door in the south wall opening into the added vestry. In the east wall was also the flue of a chimney from the basement story, the fireplace of which had been bricked up. In examining this flue during the alterations, there was found therein the skeleton of a goose! How did it come there? What was the goose's history? Had some *bon vivant* chantry-priest been purposing to convert a fast into a feast-day; and being somehow interrupted, had he been unable to cook his goose, and had he stuffed his goose up the chimney, and for some reason, perhaps his sudden departure, never been able to extract it? Who can now say? Doubtless this goose opens a wide field for inquiry and sage reflection on the part of ecclesiastical archaeologists!

Before adding any description of the church in its present altered condition, its former history will be better traced by such of its older records as remain, and perhaps the best connecting link, with the already mentioned mural inscriptions, will be the painted glass, in so far as the history remains to us subsequently to the Reformation, and again after the Rebellion.

It will be seen that in 1688 the great east window was quite bare of painted glass; so no doubt its designs had been saints and sacred subjects, which had been probably the most beautiful in the whole church, and had been utterly destroyed, as "*superstitious imagery.*" In 1828 the inhabitants of Melford determined to collect into the east window (which was then partly filled up with brickwork) some of the principal remaining figures from other parts of the church, which had been spared by the former iconoclasts, and had since, with some other small remnants, escaped the barbarous ill-treatment and neglect of subsequent generations. To Mr. Almack all here owe a debt of gratitude, not only for urging this restoration of the glass, but also for the great personal care and trouble which he bestowed on the super-intendence of the work; and when again, in 1862–3, all the further remains of the old glass were collected to fill the two west windows, he again took upon himself the onerous task of the arrangement and repair, a labour involving such archæological knowledge as few but himself could bring to bear upon it. These three windows in their present state will be afterwards described, but here must follow the description given in the MS. of about 1688, which appears to have been, like the former one, the work of Dr. Nathaniel Bisbie, and is headed thus :—

"BENEFACTORS, as by the inscriptions in the windows undemolished, within the Church of Melford,—circa 1688.

"EAST WINDOW.

"The east window, *celebrated formerly for its imagery and painted glass,* hath nothing in it now but white glass.

"I^st Window on the South Side from the East.

"This likewise lyeth under the same defacement.

"IInd Window, South Side from the East,

"Hath at the very top in one light **J. h. s.,** *i.e.* Jesus Hominum Sal-vator, and in another **M.,** *i.e.* Maria. Under the aforesayd upper lesser lights, in the first pane [compartment] nothing but white glass : in the other two panes thereof, two Kings with crowns on their heads, encircled with glory, having globes in their hands. In the lower parts of the said window nothing but white glass.

"IIIrd Window, South Side from the East,

" On the very top of it hath **I. H. S.** ; in another light **M E R C Y** ; in the next light thereunto the Martyns' cloth-mark, which is a globe with a cross and streamer on the top, with **R** on the one side and **M** on the other ; and in next light **M**, pro Maria, ut prius. In the upper part of the window beneath these lights there are three imageries all in glory, the middle whereof is supposed to be the Blessed Virgin ; and all of them encompassed with flower de luces.—The first whereof hath a sword in his right hand and a book in his left—the other a long and profuse Beard. All three sitting in chairs as at rest in glory.

"IV^a Window, South Side from the East,

" On the very top of it hath in one light, **I. H. S.**, in another light **M E R C Y**, in another **M**, ut prius.—In the upper part of the said window beneath these lights there are three imageries in glory, in each pane one, sitting in their chairs as at rest ; the 3rd whereof hath a black cap on his head, a blue wardrobe [dress], and seemingly two pencils in his hands.—In the three panes of the lower part of the said window nothing but white glass.

" V^a Window, South Side from ye East,

"Hath on the top of it in the lesser lights, **I. H. S.**—**M E R C Y.**— **R. M.** with his cloth-mark, and **M** pro Maria, ut prius.—In the upper part of the said window, beneath these 3 lights, an Abbot or Bishop in the first pane thereof with a mitre on his head—a Pope with his triple crown in the second—a Cardinal with his hat and scarlet in the next, all encircled with glory, and sitting in chairs as at rest.—In the lower part of the said window, and in the first pane thereof, a Priest, as is supposed, with the Tabernacle in his hand ;[*] in the second pane Mary Magdalene, with her hair disshevel'd, and her box of spikenard in her hand.—In the third pane the imagery not known.— Under the imagery of the four last mentioned windows in the upper part there are these words remaining written as followeth :—

' . . . . KATARINE MARGARETE *uxorem ejus & pro a'iabus o'ium hujus . . . . . eccle'iæ in Melford, memoriam de bonis præfati Rogeri Bee fene ritriate Anno D'ni M·CCCCLX·.'*

"And in the lower part of the fourth window last mentioned, under the imagery thereof, there is written, ' . . . . *Rector hujus Eccle'iæ necnon MATILDI HYNE, in D'ni Bon-fact.'* "

---

[*] This might be St. Jerome, or St. Nicholas, or indeed any ecclesiastic who was notable as a rebuilder or restorer of a church. There are many such instances.

The figure of the priest recorded in the foregoing description was perhaps the rector in whose memory this window was partly glazed. Thomas Warden was the rector of this parish from 1460 to 1470.

A Robert Hyne, of Sudbury, held lands in Melford, of the Abbey of Bury, in 1442 and afterwards. Perhaps the Matilda Hyne mentioned above was his widow.

Roger Bee is also mentioned as a tenant of Abbey lands in Melford, abutting on the north on lands of St. Gregory's College, Sudbury, and south on lands of Sir James Ormond, Knt., whose lands were between St. Bartholomew's Priory, Rodbridge, and Stalis Tye.

"VIth Window South Side from ye East,

"Which is the *first in the Church*, all the former being in the chancell, hath in the lesser lights on the top of it, I. H. S.—M E R C Y. —R. M. with the Martins' clothmark between, and M pro Maria, ut prius.—Underneath these lights, and in the upper part of the said window in the first pane nothing but white glass :—the second pane mostly white glass.—The third pane *St. Vincent* standing with a book in his hand and his head encircled with glory: having on one side of his face SANCTÆ, and on the other VINCENTI.—Under the aforesaid 3 panes this inscription remains: '(? ROGER) COUPER AND MARY HIS WIFE.' In the lower part of the said window, and in the first pane thereof, a *King* with a crown on his head and a sceptre in his hand, and a flower de luce on each side of his head.—In the second pane *St. Christopher* as is supposed, sed quære.—In the third *Mary Magdalene* with her hair disshevel'd and a box of spikenard in her hand, under which three pictures there is written, 'ORATE PRO ANIMABVS . . . . RE MARIONE ISTA ECC'SIA MULTIPLICITER DECORATA EST & ORNATA.'

"VIIth Window South Side from the East,

"Hath in the lesser lights atop of it, the same as in the last window; underneath in the three upper panes, there are three several pictures of the *Blessed Virgin* alike in face and wardrobe [dress].—By the face of the first is written MARIA, by the face of the second ALMA. DEI. GENITRIX, by the face of the third SANCTA,—the rest broken; with this subscription: '[? Giles] *Dent, John Clopton, Esq., John Smith and Roger Smith this arch did repare of new.*' In the lower part of the said window, and in the first pane thereof, supposed to be *Joseph*, ye spoused husband of the Blessed Virgin.—In the second the *Virgin* herself with the new born babe in one hand, a sceptre in the other, and a crown upon her head.—In the third, supposed to be one of the *Wise men*, having a golden cup in one hand full of burning incense, and in the other a bundle of myrrh: Sed de his quære.—Subscribed: 'ORATE PRO A'I'ABUS JOANNIS WAINS, JOHANNIS FELT ET ABIGAIL UXOR EORUM—FUIT OPTIMA ADJUTRIX . . . . NOVAM FABRICAM HUJUS ECC'SIAE.'"

Query—Is this name of Wains abbreviated from Warins or Waryn, who was a

H

benefactor to the Church! A John Waryn, by his will in 1448, left, besides other charities, 40 shillings for the repairs of the Lady Chapel.

" VIII^a Window South Side from the East.

"In the lesser lights nothing—underneath, in the first pane of the upper great lights towards the top, HIC JOHANNIS, under which is *Herod and his wife.* Under Herod a woman with an infant in her arms; under his wife *St. John* laid along. Historia quære? Under the said prostrated St. John is written S^{CTUS} JOHANNES, and under that the soldiers arresting him.—In the second pane *St. John* in the wilderness, having over his head these letters ECCE ANGUM, which should have been ECCE AGNUM.—In the third pane *St. John baptizing the Holy Jesus.*—In the lower part in the first pane thereof, a *soldier* with a sword in his hand and *John the Baptist* lying in the prison with his head off: underwritten, •••^{CTUS} JOHANNES. In the second pane *Herod the Tetrarch,* and *Herodias* his wife, with their servants about them, their *daughter kneeling by,* presenting a charger with the Baptist's head in it,—underwritten S^{TUS} JOHANNES BAPTISTA.—In the third pane *St. John Baptist's disciples* standing about the trunk of his body, in order to their having been to his burial—in the middle whereof is written in letters reversed, S^{TUS} JOHANNES BAPTISTA, and at the bottom of the said window, 'ORATE PRO ANIMABUS JOHANNIS SMITH ET MARGARET ET AGNETE UX. . . . . . .'

"IX^a Window South Side from the East.

"In the lesser lights in the top nothing. In the first pane of the upper part underneath, *St. Peter* with his key. In the second *St. Paul,* with his sword. In the third *St. Andrew** with his cross, and underneath them, '*Pray for ye soules of Robt Colet,*† *Marion and Margarete his wives.*' In the first pane of the lower part *St. John* with a cup in his left hand.—In the second *St. James the Great,* with staff and scrip.—In the third *St. Simon the Zealot,* with his spectacles on his nose and a book in his hand; underneath whom there is written, '*Of whose goods John Clopton, Thomas Elys, and John Haugh did this window glass.*'

" X^a Window South Side from the East.

"In the lesser lights nothing.—In the three upper panes, three imageries supposed to be apostles: sed de his quære.—In the lower panes three imageries, the first and last almost defaced, one wholly

* This is now in the great east window.
† Robert Colet, in 1442, held a tenement and various parcels of land, adjoining Richard Waryn's lands. *See* Window XL.

remaining; supposed to be all Apostles.—Under the upper lights is inscribed, ' *Pray for ye Soules of Roger Hoo,* Alson, and Elizabeth his wives.*' Under the lower panes is inscribed, ' *Of whose goods John Clopton, M*ʳ *Giles Dent, and Thomas Elys did this window glass.*'

" XIᵗʰ Window South Side from the East.

"In the lesser lights atop, I. H. S., and on each side W.† In the first upper pane *St. Katherine* crowned, with Sᵀᴬ on one side of her face, and KATHERINA on the other.—Second pane defaced.—Third pane a man holding in one hand a book open, in the other a staff, with a cross on the top of it, by which there is written Mᶜᴬ. The inscription underneath these is all defaced, except ' *Pray for the soul of* . . . . . .*'' In the first pane of the lower part, *St. Peter* with a key.— In the second and third, in each a *mitred Bishop* with a crozier, the inscription under them all defaced.

" XIIᵗʰ Window South Side from the East.

"In the lesser upper lights I. H. S., and HELP. The first upper pane is defaced.—In the second pane the *Blessed Virgin* with a crown on her head, with a sceptre in her right hand, and the Holy Babe on her left arm.—In the third pane a *Bishop,* with mitre and crozier.—In the first pane of the lower part is *St. Edmund,* crowned, with sceptre in one hand and an arrow in the other.—In the second pane *St. Cytha,* her head encircled with glory; on one side of her face is inscribed Sᵀᴬ, and on the other CYTHA.—In the third pane *a Priest,* with a wand in his hand, on the left side of whose face is written RO'K, and just above his knee are written other letters, supposed to be KAPBALL.

" XIIIᵗʰ Window South Side from the East.

"In the upper lesser lights is inscribed 'Sɪᴛ Dɴ'ɪ Noᴍᴇɴ ʙᴇɴᴇᴅɪᴄᴛᴜᴍ.' In the first upper pane *Moses* with horns on his head—In the second *Aaron* in priestly vestments—In the third *Saul* in his mantle—sed de his omnibus quære.—In the first lower pane, *St. John the Evangelist,* and

---

* Roger Howe (here spelt Hoo) left by his will, dated 1481, the sum of 26s. 8d. to the " *church work,*" besides other bequests. Part of his will is given in the chapter of Melford charities.

† From these W.'s and from the St. Katherine, it is probable that this window was of the goods of Richard Waryn and his wife Katherine, who held lands, in 1442, south of Hall Street, about Broadmeadow, Smaleybridge, Nether Bulney, and near the church gate. John Waryn, who lived in 1442, near the church gate, and had property near there, was a stonemason; and he therefore probably worked in the rebuilding of the church. He made his will 1448.

by him is written S^{TUS} JOHANNES EVANGELISTA.—In the second, *St. Peter*, and by him is written S^{TUS} PETRUS.—In the third, *St. James*, and by him is written S^{TUS} JACOBUS. The remaining inscription under these in the lower part is, ' *Orate* . . . . . . *his Horset* . . . . . . *et pro a'abus* . . . . *Johannis* . . . . . . *Roberti* . . . . *Agnete uxoris.*' "

This Horset's name is spelt in his will Harset. He was *Robert Harset*, clothmaker, of Melford, who, by his will of 1484, left large bequests for the service of the church of Melford, and legacies to his wife *Agnes*, and to *John*, his brother, and to *Robert*, the son of John.

" XIV^a *Window on the South Side from the East.*

"Lesser lights nothing.—First upper pane a man, whose hands, thighs, and legs naked, still remain—the upper part of him defaced. Second pane, a figure supposed to be *King David;* and in the third pane another supposed to be *King Solomon*, sed de his quære.—The inscription under them is all defaced.—In the first lower pane, *The Blessed Virgin Mary* with *Our Saviour* in her lap, as taken down from the Cross, with the Crown of thorns upon his head. In the second pane, *Mary Magdalene* weeping: sed quære.—In the third pane *Our Blessed Saviour*, naked, with his Crown of Thorns upon his head. —The inscription under these all defaced.

" XV^a *Window on the South Side from the East.*

"In the lesser lights be four coats of arms, de quibus quære.—Beneath these in the first upper pane, *St. Bernard* with his crozier, and by him is written S^{TUS} BERNARDUS. In the second pane, *Our Blessed Saviour* with the scarlet robe and the thorny crown.—In the third pane, only white glass.—At the foot of these is this inscription : ' *Orate pro bono statu Johannis Pie et Alicie* . . . . . . *et* . . . . . . *statu Johannis Firmin et* . . . . *uxoris ejus.*'—In the first lower pane *Mary Magdalene*.—In the second pane only white glass.—In the third pane a *Priest.*—At the bottom of all is the remains of an inscription '. . . . . *pro Vivis et Mortuis* . . . . '

" XVI^a *Window on the South Side from the East.*

"In the lesser lights on the top, NOMEN D^{NI} EST BENEDICTUM.—In the first upper pane only white glass—In the second pane, a *Flower Pot* beset with flowers, imitating such a picture as in the 32nd page of the Virgin Marie's Office, set forth by Pope Pius V., the book printed at Antwerp in the year 1598.—In the third pane the Blessed Virgin sitting in a chair and encircled with this inscription : ' ECCE ANCILLA D^{NI} FIAT MIHI.'—In the first and lower panes only white glass.

—In the third pane, a man somewhat defaced, holding in his right hand a book, and in his left a staff with a cross on the top—by his head is written S^ctus Barthol. Sed de illo quære. Underneath is subscribed '. . . . . *Isabella* uxor ejus . . . .'

"XVII^a *Window on the South Side from the East.*

"Lesser lights nothing.—First upper pane, St. *Edmund* the king with his crown on his head; a sceptre in his right hand and arrow in his left—under his feet written S^ctus Edmundus.*—Second pane, part of an imagery defaced, subscribed S^ctus Antonius.—Third pane, defaced. -—First lower pane only white glass.—Second pane, St. *Katherine* with her wheel; on the one side of her face written S^cta, and on the side Catharina.—Third pane, supposed to be St. *Barnabas*; on one side of his face is B, and on the other B A S—sed de illo quære, and underneath is written '. . . . . est mor . . et pro bono statu Agnet: uxor ejus . . . . Johannis et Marione uxor ejus.'

"XVIII^a *Window South Side from the East.*

"In the lesser lights at the top, two Priests. All the rest of the window white glass, save the first lower pane, which hath St. *Dennis* habited, with a crozier in his hand; on one side of his head is written Sanctus, and on the other Dionis.

"XIX^a *Window South Side from the East,* which is the window on the south side next to the steeple.

"In the lesser lights at the top be two coats of arms.—In the remainder of the window nothing.

————

"Now proceed we to the North side, commencing from the steeple, and going towards the east, the numbers of the panes being therefore reversed.

"I^st *Window North Side, next the Steeple.*

"In the upper lesser lights a coat of arms.—In the third pane of the upper part, the head and part of the body of a woman.—All the rest white glass.

"IInd *Window North Side from the West.*

"In the lesser lights a coat of arms,† *Azure a fess between three*

* This fine portrait is now in the great east window.
† This is now in the great east window.

leopards' faces, or, for *De la Pole*, impaling *France and England.*—In the first and third panes of the upper part, nothing. In the second upper pane a woman, and under these is subscribed, ' *Orate pro a'i̇'a Honorabilis Principissæ Dom. Elizab. Duciessæ Suffolc.*' In the first lower pane, white glass.—In the second pane, a woman with her face turned backwards and upward.—In the third pane, *Howard* in his coat armour, kneeling, under whom is written, ' *Johannis Howard, Miles.*'

" IIIrd Window North Side from the West.

" Lesser lights nothing.—Upper lights also nothing, but under them is written, ' *Orate pro bono statu Dⁿⁱ Druris. . . . . ac pro . . . . Domini . . . .*' In the three lower panes, *William Clopton* between his two wives, *Juditha* [?], daughter of Grey of Bockenham, and —— *Cockwell*, subscribed under them '. . . . . *Juditæ Clopton fil . . . . Mar. Clopton fil . . . . Cockwell ux . . . .*' "

This Sir William Clopton, Knight, son of Walter Clopton and Alice FitzHugh, married Ivetta (not Juditha, as above), daughter of Sir Thomas de Grey, Knt., of Buckenham Castle, Norfolk, as second wife. His first wife was Mary, daughter of Sir William Cockerel, Knt. (not Cockwell, as above). Sir William Clopton died 1376: his will is dated that year, and was proved 14th January, 1377.

" IV^a Window North Side from the West.

" In the upper parts, the glass of which is much defaced, is John, *Lord Dynham, K.G.* and *his wife*, in their coat armour, having this subscription '. . . . . . . Pro bono statu Dⁿⁱ Denham . . . . Domina Uxore suæ.' In the first pane, lower part, *Sir William Clopton*, kneeling, subscribed ' *Wm. Clopton, miles.*' In the second pane, *Dame Frances Trussell*, his wife, underwritten ' *Francisca Clopton.*' In the third pane, the glass much defaced, but apparently *Sir William Clopton*, kneeling (*ut prius*) subscribed ' *Willielmus Clopton, miles.*' "

John Lord Dynham, Knight of the Garter, married Elizabeth, daughter and heiress of Lord Fitzwalter. She survived him, and afterwards married Sir John Ratcliffe. There is a faded coat of arms of theirs which was placed in the north-east window in 1832. The Sir William Clopton here represented, who died childless, probably at the commencement of the fifteenth century, and who was grandson of the Sir William in the third window, married Frances, daughter of William Trussell, and widow of Sir Robert de Salle, Knt., who was murdered by insurgents in a rising at Norwich, in 1381. There was, as named in the text above, another Sir William Clopton in this window; and as it is unlikely that there would be two portraits of the same person, it is probable that the other was his father, who was also Sir William Clopton, and who is recorded as having sold his Hawstead property in 1415.

" V^a Window North Side from the West.

" In the upper part *Howard* impaling *Oxford*, in their coat armour, under which is written, '*Orate pro bono statu D⁻ᵃ Howard, ac pro Domina uxore sua.*' In the lower parts thereof three Cloptons kneeling, subscribed, '*Walterius Clopton, Miles.—Thomas Clopton, Miles.—Will⁻ᵐ Clopton de Ashendon, Armiger.*'"

The portrait of Elizabeth Howard, who married the Earl of Oxford, is now in the east window, and will be noticed in its place. Her husband's portrait is lost. The three Clopton portraits are probably Walter Clopton, who married Alice FitzHugh and Ivetta de Weyland, and who died 1325-6; and his sons, Sir William Clopton, who married Mary Cockerel and Ivetta Grey, and who died 1376-7 (he bought Newenham Manor, in Ashdon, Essex); and Sir Thomas Clopton, who married Katherine Mylde, and who died 1383. The line of Sir William, the elder brother, became extinct in his grandchildren.

"VIᵃ *Window North Side from the West.*"

"In the upper parts, in coat armour, kneeling, three effigies, whereof two are supposed to be the same man, and in the middle of them his wife, under them is written '*Orate pro bono statu D⁻ᵃ Thomas Montgomery, Militis, ac pro D⁻ᵃ Dame Phillippe uxore sua.*' In the underpart is *Sir Thomas Clopton* between his two wives, one the daughter of *Walter Clopton* and the other the daughter of — *Mylde.*"

The portrait of Sir Thomas Montgomery is now in the east window. Sir Thomas Clopton, of Kentwell and Lutons, was twice married. The first wife, who was buried in Chipley Priory, cannot be identified, but that she was a daughter of any *Walter* Clopton is improbable. The second wife, whose portrait is now in the east window, was Katherine Mylde, who brought Kentwell to her husband.

"VIIᵃ *Window North Side from the West.*"

"In the upper parts are the effigies of three judges, thus subscribed: '*Pray for the good state of William Howard, Chief Justice of England, and for Richard Picot and John Haugh, Justices of the Law.*'

"In the lower parts are *Sir William Clopton* between his two wives, *Margery Drury* and *Margery Francis.*—Under the said William is written '*W⁻ Clopton, Arm. filius et hæres Thomæ Clopton, Militis;*' and under the first wife is written, '*Uxor W⁻ Clopton, Filia Drury,*' and under the second, *Uxor W⁻ Clopton, Filia et hæres Eliæ Francis.*'"

The portraits of William Howard and Richard Pygot are now in the east window. John Haugh, or Hawte, is now in the south-west window. This Sir William Clopton is the person whose recumbent effigy is in the recessed mural tomb by the north chancel door. He died August, 1446. His first wife was Margery, daughter of Sir Roger Drury, of Rougham, Knight: she died 1420. The second wife was Margery, daughter of Helias Francis, of Norfolk: she died 1434.

"VIIIᵃ *Window North Side from the West.*"

"In the upper panes, *Reinsforth* between his two wives, under whom is written, '*Orate pro bono statu Laurentii Reinsforth militis et D⁻ᵃ*

Hungerford, et Elysabethæ Reinsforth, uxor. suaru', et filioru' suor' et filioru' suaru'.' In the lower panes nothing."

This Lady Hungerford was Lady Ann Percy, daughter of that Earl of Northumberland who was killed at the battle of St. Albans, 1455. She married, first, Sir Thomas Hungerford, Knight; secondly, Sir Laurence Reinsforth, Knight; and thirdly, Sir Hugh Vaughan, Knight.

"IXᵃ Window North Side from the West.

"In the upper part, three women in their coats of arms, having the following inscription, viz.: ' *Pray for the soul of Dame Annes Frey, and specially for Dame Margaret Leynam, and for the good state of Elysabeth Walgrave.*' In the lower parts are *two Cloptons*, and the wife of one of them, *Joane Marrow.*"

Dame Annes Fray's portrait, together with those of her daughters, Leynham and Waldegrave, are now in the south-west window: her maiden name was Danvers, and she married three times. First, Sir John Fray, Lord Chief Baron of the Exchequer from 1436 to 1448, by whom she had two daughters,—Margaret, married to Sir John Leynham, Knight: she founded a chantry in the church of St. Bartholomew-the-Less (near the Exchange), London, 1481-2. The second daughter, Elizabeth, married Sir Thomas Waldegrave, who was knighted by King Edward IV. at the battle of Towton, 1461. Lady Fray married, secondly, John, Lord Wenlock, who was slain at the battle of Tewkesbury, 1471. Her third husband was Sir John Say, Knight. By her will, of which John Clopton is one of the executors, she directs that a "priest shall sing for the souls of my Lord Wenlock, Sir John Fray, and Sir John Say, my husbands." Of the two Cloptons in the lower part, one is Sir William Clopton, of Kentwell, Knight, who married twice, his first wife being Joane, daughter of William Marrow, of Stepney, in the county of Middlesex, citizen and alderman of London, and Lord Mayor 1455. The large monumental slab, with one shield remaining, bearing the arms of Clopton impaling Marrow, used to be in the floor of the chancel, in front of the tomb of his father, John Clopton; but in the restoration of the church this slab was moved to the north aisle (towards the west end thereof). There is a brass of one of their children still in the floor of the Clopton chancel, viz. their third son, Robert, a priest, who died 1530-1. Sir William Clopton's second wife was Thomazine, eldest daughter of Thomas Knevet, and sister and heiress to Edward Knevet, of Stanwey, Essex. In the Clopton chancel there is a very perfect brass of the second son by this wife Thomazine Knevet, Francis Clopton, with his arms impaling those of his wife Bridget, daughter of Sir Robert Crane. Francis Clopton, who was of Groton, Suffolk, made a will dated 2nd February, 1558.

"Xᵃ Window North Side from West.

"In the upper parts *Ralph Joslin* in his Lord Mayor's habit, with *Clifford* and *his wife* in their coat armour, and under them is written, ' *Pray for the soul of Ralf Joslin, twice Mayor of London: and for the good estate of Robert Clifford and Dame Elizabeth his wife.*'—In the lower parts, *Elizabeth Clopton*, between her two husbands, *John Gedney*, Mayor of London, and *Robert Cavendish*, sergeant-at-law.—Under them is written, ' *Orate p' a'i'a' Joannis Gedney, Mayoris Civitatis Londinensis . . . . . . Roberti Cavendish . . . . . . et Elyzabethe uxoris ejus ac . . . . . . armig.'* "

Ralph Joslin was Lord Mayor of London in the year 1462 or 1464, and again in 1476. He married Elizabeth Barley, who afterwards remarried Sir Robert Clifford. She and Ralph Joslin are now in the north-west window. Sir Robert Clifford is in the east window. Elizabeth Clopton, daughter of Sir William Clopton, by Margery Francis, was born 1423-4. For her mother married 1420-2, and had two children, John, born 1422-3, and this daughter Elizabeth, in childbirth with whom she perhaps died, as she was buried in 1424.

"XIª Window North Side from the West.

"In the upper parts *Montgomery* and *Darcy*, and the effigies of two females in their coat armour; viz. *Tyrell*, Argent two chrevrons azure within a border engrailed, impaling Darcy, under whom is written,. '*Orate p' bono statu Annæ Montgomerie et p' a'i'abus D'næ Elinore Tyrell, et Margarette Tyrell de . . . . . . orum amicorum suorum.*' Lower part three effigies; *John Harliston* and *Alice* his wife, and a Clopton, [?] under whom is written, '*Orate pro a'i'abus Joannis Harlistoni senioris, et Aliciæ uxoris ejus, filiæ Wm Clopton, et pro a'i'a Joannis Harlistoni filius et hæres.*'"

The shields of Montgomery and Darcy and Tyrell and Darcy are now in the east window. Anne Montgomery is now in the south-west window.

Dame Margaret Tyrell was a daughter of Robert Darcy, and Dame Elinore Tyrell was her sister. They married uncle and nephew. They were sisters of John Clopton's wife, Alice Darcy. Margaret's name only is written under the figure of Elinor, now in the north-west window, in the lower part. Alice Harleston was daughter of Sir William Clopton and Margery Drury, and was probably born about 1410. From the inscription under them, it appears likely that the third person with them is wrongly described as a Clopton, but was intended for the son, John Harleston, junior.

"XIIª Window North Side from the West.

"In the small upper parts are coats of arms; Azure an estoile with six points argent for *Ogard*, impaling Argent on a fess between three cross crosslets fitched gules, an escallop of the field, for *Crane*, and a coat of *Drury* impaling Crane. Under them in the upper panes are three effigies, viz. *Robert Crane*, between his wife *Ann Ogard* and another woman.—In the lower panes are three effigies, viz. *John Denston* and *Catherine* his wife, and their only daughter *Dame Ann Broughton*. On Denston's coat is, Argent on a chevron sable a cross crosslet of the field, for *Denston*, quartering Azure, two lions passant, gardant, Or, for *Wauton*.—On the first woman, Catherine Denston, the same arms impaling Clopton—on the second woman, Ann Broughton, the same impaling, Argent a chevron gules, on the upper part two torteauxes, on the lower part a mullet gules for Broughton, under whom is written, '*Orate pro a'i'ma Joannis Denston et pro bono statu Catherinæ uxor ejus filiæ . . . . . . Clopton arm. ac Annæ Broughton filiæ et hæredis p'fat' Joannis et Catherinæ.*'"

The arms of Ogard and Crane, and the portraits of Crane and his wife, are now in the east window.

Catherine, the wife of John Denston, of Denston Hall, Suffolk, was the daughter of Sir William Clopton and sister of John Clopton, and her only daughter, Ann, married Sir John Broughton, Knight. The portrait of John Denston is now in the east window.

"XIII⁰ Window North Side from the West.

"In the upper panes, *Peyton* between his two wives, *Margaret Bernard* and *Margaret Franceys*, under whom is written, ' *Orate pro a'i'abus Thomæ Peyton, Armig. Senior ; et Margarettæ et Margarettæ uxor' suarum.*' In the under panes are *Rookwood* between his two wives, *Hilton* and *Clopton*, in their coat armour; under them is written, ' *Uxor Willi Rookwood, Thomæ Rookwood, uxor Thomæ Rookwood fil. de Hilton, filiæ Willi Rookwood, filiæ Joannis Clopton.*'"

Sir Thomas Peyton is in the great east window.

Thomas Rookwood is now in the south-west window. The above transcript of the inscription under him appears to be a jumble, and is probably incorrect. Ann Clopton, daughter of John Clopton, married Thomas Rookwood of Stanningfield, who was living in 1475.

"XIV⁰ Window North Side from the West.

"In the upper panes three Archangels, *St. Gabriel, St. Michael,* and *St. Raphael.* In the lower panes, *Thomas Curson,* of Billingford, between his two wives in coat armour, and under them is written, ' *Uxor Thomæ Curson. Thomas Curson Armiger, uxor Thomæ Curson Arm. filius Joannis Scoynford, filius et hæres Joannis Curson—Joannis Clopton Arm.*'"

Two of the archangels are now in the west windows.

As to the inscription it appears all jumbled, and should read thus. Under one wife, "Uxor Thomas Curson, Arm., filia Joannis Scoynford ;" under Thomas Curson of Billingford, who died 1511, should be, "Thomas Curson, Armiger, filius et hæres Joannis Curson ;" and under the other wife, "filia Joannis Clopton, Armiger." She was Dorothy, daughter of John Clopton, and sister of Ann Rookwood, of the previous window.

"XV⁰ Window North Side from the West.

"In the upper panes are *Saint Ducius* with his left hand lifted up—*Saint Franciscus* holding with both hands a book open, and in the bend of his right arm a staff advanced with a cross on the top.—*Petrus Mille.*—Under them is written, ' *Orate pro anima Elizabethæ Drury et Henrici Hardman . . . . . . et Willi Twaytes . . . . .*' In the lower panes are, *Saint George* with his red cross on his right arm and on his armour.—*A Priest* with censer in his right hand and taper in his left; and under is written, ' *Orate pro bono statu Joannis Story, et Joannis Stannard, Clericorum et Benefactorum.*'"

John Story was rector from 1470 to 1474.

"XVI⁰ Window North Side from the West.

"In the upper panes *Saint Andreas* with his cross—the *Blessed*

Virgin, with our Saviour in her lap as taken from the Cross with the Crown of Thorns on his head, and the print of the nails in his feet.—*Saint Gyles* with a crozier on his hand, and at his feet, *Saint Ægidius*, and under that is written, ' *Laudes D'ni in Æternum cantabo*—*Orate pro anima magistri Egidii Dent, quondam Rectoris hujus Ecclesiæ.*' In the lower parts only white glass."

Egidius, or Giles Dent, was presented to the living of Melford by Abbot Richard Hengham of Bury, 8th April, 1474. He died as rector, 1484.

" *XVII*ᵃ *Window North Side from the West.*

" In the upper panes are *Saint Oswoldus*, and under his feet a shaven monk.—*Saint Edmundus*—*Saint Edwardus*; and under these two are two mitred Abbots, viz. Hengham and Rawlesdon, Abbots of Bury; and under them is written, ' *Orate pro anima Edwardi* [?] *Hengham nuper Abbatis de Bury : et pro bono statu R. Rawlesdon Abbatis : et R'ci Norton.*' In the lower parts only white glass."

The monk under St. Oswald was Richard Norton.
The effigy of St. Edmund, with Abbot *Richard* Hengham (not Edward, as in the text) under him, is now in the east window. Abbot Richard Hengham died 1479, and was succeeded by Abbot Robert Racclesden, as usually spelt, though here called Rawlesdon.

" *XVIII*ᵃ *Window North Side from the West.*

" In the upper part, *Saint Anna* with a child in her hand supposed to be the Blessed Virgin, her daughter—The *Virgin Mary* with Crown and Sceptre and her son the blessed Jesus in her arms—At their feet, under three coats of arms, is written, ' *Elizabethæ Ducissæ Suffolciæ.*' "

Having thus described the windows as they were recorded to remain in 1688, notice must now be taken of the present east window, and of the two west windows, into the former of which in 1828, and the latter in 1862, all that remained of the old glass in the church was collected and arranged. Of the glorious old glass in the east window, which Dr. Bisbie says was famous for its imagery, none remained even in his time. Whether it succumbed to the iconoclastic zeal of the early Reformers, or was destroyed by the Puritans, there is no certain knowledge ; but William Dowsing, the parliamentary visitor appointed for demolishing the superstitious pictures and ornaments of churches in Suffolk in 1643, 1644, makes no mention of Melford in his journal of his sweeping destruction of church glass and other memorials around here ; though, as regards many neighbouring parishes, he records works of demolition, as in Sudbury, Cornard, Glemsford,

Clare, and others.   He had, however, several deputies under him, and ·
possibly they may have visited Melford : perhaps the visitor here may
have been Mr. Westthorp, of Hunden, *a godly man*, who was appointed
a deputy.

Dowsing, in his Diary, records, as to parishes immediately adjoining and near this place, as follows :—

Dowsing's Diary, 1643.

"We brake down at *Sudbury, Peter's Parish,* a picture of God
the Father, 2 crucifixes, and pictures of Christ, about an hundred in
all, and divers angels, 20 at least, on the roof of the church.

"*Gregory Parish, Sudbury.*—We brake down 10 mighty great
angels in glass : in all 80.

"*Allhallows (All Saints) Sudbury.*—We brake about 20 superstitious pictures, and took up 30 brazen superstitious inscriptions,
' ora pro nobis,' and ' pray for the soul.'

"*Haverhill*—1643.—We brake down about an hundred superstitious pictures : and one of seven Fryars hugging a Nunn : and
divers others very superstitious ; and 200 others had been broke
down before we came.

"*Clare.*—We brake down 1000 pictures superstitious :—I brake
down 200 : 3 of God the Father, and 3 of Christ and the Holy Lamb,
and 3 of the Holy Ghost like a Dove with wings.   And the 12 Apostles
were carved in wood on the top of the Roof, and 20 Cherubims, which
we gave order to take down.   And the sun and moon in the east
window by the King's arms to be taken down.

"*Cornard Magna.*—I took up 2 inscriptions ' pray for our souls,'
&c.   John Pain, churchwarden, for not paying nor doing his duty, I
charged Henry Turner, the constable, to carry him before the Earl of
Manchester.

"*Glemsford.*—We brake down many pictures, one of God the
Father, and a picture of God the Holy Ghost in brass."

Altogether he records, in only a part of Suffolk, the destruction
of nearly 7,000 pictures in stained glass, besides many broken before
his visit to the churches by Puritans of the parishes.

It seems, however, unlikely that Dowsing, if he had visited Melford and destroyed glass therein, would have omitted the mention of so
important a church in his elaborate diary : and yet we know that
many pictures of saints and other sacred subjects (some of which still
exist), besides the historical portraits, had survived the wreck of the
Rebellion.

Perhaps those deemed the most superstitious, including the whole
of the east window, were defaced in 1579, by Firmin of Sudbury, who

*was employed for the purpose, or had been already destroyed by the earlier Reformers, of whom Weever thus speaks : —

"Towards the end of the reigne of Henry VIII. and throughout the whole reigne of Edward VI., and in the beginning of Queene Elizabeth, certaine persons of every county were put in authority to pull downe, and cast out of all churches, roodes, graven images, shrines with their reliques, to which the ignorant people came flocking in adoration : or any thing else which tended to idolatry or superstition.— Under color of their Commission, and in their too forward zeale, they rooted up and battered downe crosses in churches and churchyards, as also in other public places,* they defaced and brake downe the images of Kings, Princes, and Noble estates, erected, set up, or portraied for the only memory of them to Posterity, and not for any religious honor ; they crackt a-pieces the glass windows wherein the effigies of our blessed Savior hanging on the Cross, or any one of his saints was depictured ; or otherwise turned up their heels into the place where their heads used to be fixed : as I have seen in the windows of some of our country churches. They despoiled churches of their copes, vestments, amices, rich hangings, and all other ornaments whereupon the story or the portraiture of Christ himself, or of any saint or martyr was delineated, wrought, or embroidered : leaving Religion naked, bare, and unclad.

"But the foulest and most inhuman action of those times was the violation of funeralle monuments. Marbles which covered the dead were digged up, and put to other uses ; tombs hackt and hewne a-pieces : images or representations of the defunct, broken, erased, cut, or dismembered, inscriptions or epitaphs, especially if they began with an *Orate pro anima*, or concluded with *cujus animæ propitietur Deus*. Sepulchres for greediness of the brass despoiled, notwithstanding this request cut or engraven upon them, *propter misericordiam Jesu requiescat in Pace*."

Deplorable as had thus been the loss of beautiful glass before Dr. Bisbie catalogued the figures still existing in his day, it will be seen to what a small remnant this church glass had been further reduced by carelessness and wanton destruction in the subsequent 150 years. It will hardly be credited that even towards the middle of the present century, these treasures of art were not only taken out and thrown away as old rubbish, but that during repairs scaffold-poles were pushed through them, in order that what was called the *dirty old glass* might be replaced with new white common glazing.

Among the figures saved are some probably of as great interest as can be found in England.

* It was the Parliamentary Puritans, however, who destroyed the cross on Melford Green, for it was standing later than the year 1615. But the Reformers destroyed our churchyard cross, and sold its fragments in 1547.

The East Window, in its present restored state, is full of stained glass, and the portraits in it are of great value. All the secular figures kneel, and face towards the middle light, as if in adoration of the central figure of the Virgin and our Saviour.

In the lesser lights at the top are small figures, and several coats of arms of distinguished personages.

There are shields of arms of Tyrell and Darcy; of Montgomery and Darcy; of Clifford and Barley; of Edward the Confessor; of Stafford and Beaufort (being the arms of the Lady Margaret, Countess of Richmond, and her second husband, Sir Harry Stafford—she married thirdly Thomas Lord Stanley); of Sulyard quartering Gude and impaling Andrews, for Sir John Sulyard, Lord Chief Justice, who died 1516, and Ann his wife, daughter of John Andrews, of Bailham; De la Pole impaling Plantagenet, for John de la Pole, Duke of Suffolk, who died 1491, and his wife, sister of the kings Edward IV. and Richard III.; of Crane and Ogard; of Josceline and Barley.

The small figures in the upper lights are an abbot or bishop mitred—probably one of the abbots of Bury; St. Osyth with her head in her hand; St. Etheldreda, or St. Osyth; an angel with a cross on his head; an abbot or bishop (probably an abbot of Bury); Edward the Confessor; an abbot (probably of Bury); a female saint (perhaps St. Osyth); St. Mary Magdalene; St. John the Evangelist, with a cup; the Virgin and Child; St. Andrew; St. Peter; an angel.

In the greater lights, commencing on the south side, at top, is Robert Crane of Chilton, near Sudbury, in his coat armour; under him is John Denston, of Denston Hall, Suffolk, with the arms of Denston quartering Wanton on his coat. He married Catherine, daughter of Sir William Clopton, and sister of old John Clopton.

At the bottom of this compartment is Richard Pygot, a judge. He was made Serjeant-at-law the 4th of Edward IV. This portrait formerly stood with Howard and Hawte, in one of the north windows, where they were described in the old inscription under them as "Judges of the Law." Howard is now in this east window; Hawte is in the north-west window. Sir Wm. Dugdale says, in his diary, 3rd February, 1664, "Paid to Mr Hollar, for the pictures of the judges at Long Melford 4ᴸ" (This was for his "*Origines Juridiciales*," of which almost all the copies were destroyed in the great fire of London.)

In the next compartment, the upper figure is Anne, the wife of Robert Crane, and daughter of Sir Andrew Ogard, Knight, of Buckenham, in Norfolk, in her surcoat of arms.

Under her is Sir Thomas Montgomery, Knight of the Garter, of Faulkbourne Hall, Essex, a person of great importance in his day. By his will, dated 1489, he directs his body to be buried in the Abbey of the Tower-hill, and that the body of Dame Philippa, his wife, shall be removed from Faulkbourne to the Tower-hill, to be laid by him; and he appoints John Clopton one of his executors. He is dressed in his coat armour.

Under him, at the bottom of this compartment, is the standing figure of a saint, armed with a sword and dagger. The only remains of inscription about him is Pet. Mille., with a small figure of a nun kneeling at his feet. In the record of 1688 there are named in three compartments of one window, St. Ducius, St. Franciscus, and Petrus Mille. In the upper part of the next, which is the centre compartment, is St. Andrew with his cross.

Under him is the central figure of the window—the Virgin Mary, with our Saviour, as taken down from the cross, lying on her lap, while awaiting interment. This subject, commonly called our Lady of Pity, is often to be found in 15th century glass. At Woolpit there is a somewhat similar painting which may indicate the date and cost of this one; for in 1477 Amy Fen bequeathed 20 shillings and 20 pence, and two bushels of malt, to make the painting in glass of our Lady of Pity for the east window of the church of Woolpit. The picture in Melford Church is a curious one, and is of very coarse and rude execution, as compared with the rest of the glass. The countenance of the Saviour is very repulsive, and his disproportionate figure is altogether hideous. His body is speckled all over with once red, but now black, triple drops of blood, emblematic of the Trinity in the bloody sweat; and though the wounds of the nails in his feet, and of the spear in his side, are duly represented, the artist appears to have omitted the wounds in the hands. At his feet kneels a small figure of a man in a furred blue gown, with a ring on each of his thumbs, but with no other distinctive mark, and under him is the inscription,— "Nomen Domini benedicatur." From his dress and rings he was apparently a person of some consideration, and possibly the giver of the glass.

Under this is a noble and very finely-drawn standing figure of St. Edmund, crowned, with sceptre in one hand, and an arrow in the other, and with a small figure of a mitred Abbot of Bury (perhaps Richard Hengham, who died 1479) kneeling at his feet; and under the Abbot the inscription, "Orate p. a. Abbatis de Buri."

In the next compartment towards the north, at the top, is Elizabeth, daughter of Sir John Howard, Knight, and wife of John, 12th Earl of Oxford. In 1425 her husband, being then a ward, and having married her without license, was obliged to pay £2,000 into the Exchequer to obtain pardon for the marriage. On the accession of Edward IV., in 1461, her husband, and their son Aubrey de Vere, were beheaded with others on Tower Hill, on the charge of corresponding with Margaret of Anjou; but their friend in trouble, John Clopton, escaped their fate, and included them in his memorial windows. But, alas! only the portrait of the lady now remains.

Next under her is Sir Robert Clifford, Knight of the Body to Henry VII., son of Thomas, Lord Clifford, ancestor of the Earls of Cumberland, by Joanna, daughter of Thomas, Lord Dacre, of Gillesland. Sir Robert Clifford was the first person of any importance who appeared in support of Perkin Warbeck. In the north-west window is his wife, Elizabeth Barley, near her first husband, Sir Ralph Joscelyn, Lord Mayor of London.

Under Clifford is a standing figure of a saint, who may be St. Ægidius, with a small figure, perhaps of Giles Dent, once parson of Melford, and one of the active restorers of the church (whose name is inscribed on the battlements), kneeling at his feet. But the identity of these two figures seems uncertain. Perhaps this figure may be St. Oswold, with Richard Norton under him.

In the next compartment, which is that on the north side, the upper figure is Thomas Peyton, High Sheriff of Cambridge and Huntingdon, 21st and 31st Henry VI., and 17th Edward IV. He married Margaret, daughter of Sir John Barnard, of Isleham, in Cambridgeshire, by which match the Isleham estate was acquired by the Peyton family. He rebuilt the church of Isleham. Her portrait is in the south-west window.

Under him is Catherine Mylde, wife of Sir Thomas Clopton, and grandmother of old John Clopton, by whom the Clopton family acquired the Kentwell estate. She was also the ancestress of a much greater family; for her second husband was Sir William Tendring, of Tendring Hall, in Stoke by Nayland, Suffolk, by whom she had one child, Alice Tendring, who married Sir John Howard, Knight. Alice Tendring was a great heiress, and her grandson, John Howard, was the first Duke of Norfolk of that family, who was killed at the battle of Bosworth, 1485.

Under her is Sir William Howard, described in the ancient inscription as " Cheff Justis of Englond." From him the Howards of the present day are descended. This portrait has been engraved.

In the north-east window a few fragments of old glass have been placed, consisting of small figures and coats of arms, one of which is D'Ewes impaling Clopton.*

The two *west windows* were filled in 1862-3 with all that remained of the old painted glass in the church, some of which was much broken. In their present state they are once again not only beautiful, but, like the east window, most valuable as a splendid collection of historical portraits. They contain as follows :—

* The descriptions of these figures and those in the west windows have been mainly extracted from the account published by Mr. Almack, F.S.A., in 1853.

West Window, South Side.

All the minor tracery at the top is filled with small figures and saints, angels, and some coats of arms.

In the first large light on the *south* side of the window there is at top a small figure of a saint over the portrait of Anna, wife of Sir John Broughton. She was the only daughter of John Denston and Catherine his wife, who was daughter of Sir William, and sister of John Clopton. She is dressed in her coat of arms, and is described more fully in the 12th north window from the west.

Next under is a small figure, and arms of Clopton and others.

Next under is John Haugh, justice of the law, in his robes. He was formerly kneeling with Howard and Pygot, also judges, who are now in the east window.

In the next light, at top, an angel.

Next under is Margaret, wife of Thomas Peyton (who is in the east window). She was the daughter of Sir John Bernard, Knight, of Isleham, in Cambridgeshire, which estate came to the Peyton family by this marriage. She has on her surcoat the arms of Bernard quartering Lilling. Part of her head was missing and was repaired, but it appears that the part of a lady's head in the bottom north corner of this window belonged originally to this portrait.

Next under are the arms of East Anglia, the monogram of L. H. S., and other fragments.

Next under is Lady Howard.

The centre light has at the a very fine large figure of St. Michael the Archangel, with a sword. He is winged, and all portions of his limbs which are shown, except face, hands, and feet, are feathered. This was originally, with the figures of the other two archangels, St. Gabriel and St. Raphael, in the 14th window from the west, on the north side.

Next under is Thomas Rookwood (Rokewode) in armour, with his shield of arms over him. He was living in 1475, and married Ann, daughter of John Clopton, and also —— Hilton. The wives' portraits are lost. They, with him, were originally in the 13th window from the west, on the north side.

Next under is a lady, with the inscription beneath her of "Orate pro bono statu Annæ Montgomere." She is dressed in her surcoat of arms. She was Anne Darcy, sister of John Clopton's wife, and married John Montgomery. She was buried in the Nuns' Choir of the Minories, without Aldgate, as will be noticed by the will of the Duchess of Norfolk, mentioned in the next window.

In the next light, at top, there is an angel.

Next under is a lady, with the inscription under her, "Pray for

K

D^m Annes Fray." She is dressed in her surcoat of arms. A full description of her has already been given in the account of the 9th window from the west, on the north side.

Next under are sundry emblems of the Trinity, a small figure of the Resurrection, and badge of the White Rose.

Next under is Lady Elizabeth Walgrave (Waldegrave), the daughter of the above Dame Annes Fray by her first husband, Sir John Fray; she married Sir Thomas Waldegrave, who was knighted by King Edward IV. at the battle of Towton, 1461. She is dressed in her surcoat of arms.

In the next light, at top, there is an angel.

Next under is a man in his surcoat of arms (?), but without inscription under him.

Next under are coats of arms and small figures, &c.

Next under is Dame Margaret Leynam (Leynham), daughter of Sir John and Lady Fray, who married Sir John Leynham, Knight, and founded a chantry in the church of St. Bartholomew-the-Less, in London. She is dressed in her surcoat of arms.

Next under, among other fragments, is the fine head of a lady in a large horned coif (this appears to have been part of the head of Margaret Lady Peyton), and a small head of a man crowned.

North-west Window.

In all the lesser lights in the upper tracery of the window are small figures of saints and various coats of arms.

In the first large light on the south side of the window there is at top an angel.

Next under is John Gedney, Lord Mayor of London, in his robes. He married Elizabeth, sister of John Clopton. His portrait, with hers and her second husband's, Robert Cavendish, was originally in the 10th window from the west, on the north side.

Next under are various arms and other fragments.

Next under, the wife of Thomas Sulyard, dressed in her surcoat of arms.

Next under, a small figure and other fragments.

Next Light.—At the top are coats of arms, &c.

Next under is Dame Elinor Tyrell, and under her inscription is also the name of Margaret. These two ladies were daughters of Robert Darcy, and were John Clopton's sisters-in-law. They married uncle and nephew. This portrait, with that of Dame Margaret Tyrell, which is now lost, was originally in the 11th window from the west, on the north side. Dame Margaret married William Tyrell, of Gipping, who was Sheriff of Suffolk 24th of Henry VI., 1445-6, and she was the mother of Sir James Tyrell, Knight, Master of the Horse to Richard III., who was beheaded 17th of Henry VII., 1501-2. On the ancient chapel of Gipping, in Suffolk, are Sir James's arms, with those of his wife, daughter of Sir John Arundell, of Cornwall; and there is also an inscription on the chancel arch, "Pray for the soules of Sir James Tirell and Dame Ann, his wyf." He was supposed to have been the chief agent in the murder of the young princes in the Tower. Dame Elinor was the wife of Sir William Tyrell, Knight (nephew of her sister's husband), by whom she had Sir Thomas Tyrell, Knight Banneret, Sheriff of Essex 1482. She is dressed in her surcoat of arms.

Next under are arms, the monogram M, and part of a small figure of Jesus wearing the crown of thorns.

Next under is a lady, dressed in her surcoat of arms, under whom is inscribed, "Orate pro D⁼ Denham." She was Elizabeth, daughter and heiress of Lord Fitzwalter, and married John, Lord Dynham, Knight of the Garter, whom she survived, marrying secondly Sir John Ratcliffe. Her portrait was originally, with Lord Dynham's, in the 4th window from the west on the north side. His is lost; it is described as being much defaced in 1688. Lord Dynham, by his will, dated 7th January, 1505, desires his body to be buried in the Abbey of Hartland, which he founded, if he died within 100 miles thereof; or otherwise in the Grey Friars, London. He gives to Elizabeth, his wife, 1,690 ounces of plate.

Centre light, at the top, is an angel and emblem of the Trinity.

Next under is, a very fine large figure of St. Gabriel the Archangel, feathered similarly to that of St. Michael in the south-west window, with a trumpet in his hand.

Next under is a fine portrait of Sir Thomas Clopton, Knight, in surcoat of arms.

Next under is a fine fragment of a crowned head, and a coat of royal arms.

Next under are two ladies, kneeling at one desk, facing one another; and under them is inscribed:—

ELIZABETA	ELIZABETA
NAT: TALBOT	NAT: TILNEY
DUCISSA NORFOLCIÆ:	UX: THOMÆ HOWARD.

These portraits have been in Melford Church since about 1490; the inscriptions are modern, replacing the old ones, which were much broken; but the arms on their dresses are entirely ancient, and are of importance to explain the confusion which has long continued respecting their identity.

The second-named lady was Elizabeth Tilney, daughter and heir of Sir Frederick Tilney, and wife of Thomas Howard, Earl of Surrey, who commanded at the battle of Flodden, and was restored, in 1514, to the dukedom of Norfolk.

Sir Harris Nicolas, in his "Testamenta Vestusta" (vol. ii. p. 482), gives the wills of this Elizabeth, (so-called) Duchess of Norfolk. He says they are three in number. The first one of the 28th February, 1472, was made when she was the widow of Sir Humphrey Bouchier. It begins, "I Elizabeth, daughter and heir of Frederick Tilney, &c." Her second will, of 8th May, 1472, adds to her description thus: "Dame Elizabeth Howard, daughter and heir of Frederick Tilney, and now wife of Thomas Howard, son and heir of John, Lord Howard, &c." The third will *attributed to her*, of the 6th November, 1506, proved 28th June, 1507, was made, as was said, after her husband became Duke of Norfolk. She calls herself therein " Elizabeth, Duchess of Norfolk," and directs that she is to be buried as near as possible to the resting-place of her dearest friend in life : thus, she says, "My body to be buried in the Nuns' quire of the Minories without Aldgate, nigh unto the place where Anne Montgomery is buried." On this third will the difficulty seems to hinge, as it was asserted that this lady never became Duchess of Norfolk, but she was Countess of Surrey. The confusion arises from the fact that her husband's second wife was Agnes, daughter of Sir Hugh Tilney, of Boston, who proved her husband's will in 1524. It seems never to have appeared to the different antiquaries that the Elizabeth, Duchess of Norfolk, who made her will in 1506, was not Elizabeth Tilney, but was Elizabeth Talbot, widow of the last Mowbray, Duke of Norfolk, who died 1475 ; and the arms on her dress in the portrait in Melford Church confirm this view. The arms of Talbot and Fitzalan are the same, gules, a lion rampant, or ; except that Talbot has a border engrailed. This border is apparent in the picture. The cloak of Elizabeth Talbot, Duchess of Norfolk, has on it the coat of arms of *Brotherton* (the three lions of England, with a file of three points for difference), which were generally used as the first quarter by both Mowbrays and Howards descended from Thomas of Brotherton, son of King Edward I. In this instance it is the only coat given for the husband of this duchess, and would equally apply to a Mowbray married to Talbot, or a Howard married to Fitzalan ; but the small *border engrailed* proves that this lady was a Talbot.

Sir Humphrey Talbot, in his will dated 18th February, 1492, says : "I will that a priest shall pray for my father and mother, and for the prosperity of my sister Elizabeth, Duchess of Norfolk."

Jane Talbot, widow of Sir Humphrey, in her will of the 10th January, 1505, says, "My body to be buried in the Church of the Friars Minors, without Aldgate, London, near to the place where Anne, late wife of John Montgomery, Esquire, is buried. I will that a priest pray continually for the souls of me, my husband [other relations also mentioned], and of Elizabeth, Duchess of Norfolk."

Anne Montgomery, as already mentioned, was a Darcy, and there-fore akin to John Clopton. She was the wife of John Montgomery, brother to Sir Thomas Montgomery, of Falkbourne Hall, Essex. This

Sir Thomas, in his will of the 28th July, 1489, mentions John, his brother, and says, " I will that a priest be found to pray in the Abbey of Tower Hill, for the souls of my father and mother, and of my sister Anne Montgomery." He also appoints John Clopton one of his executors.[*]

In the next light there are an angel and various fragments and coats of arms, and among them, Clopton impaling Barnardiston.

Next under is Elizabeth, wife of Sir Robert Clifford, Knight, in her surcoat of arms. He is in the east window. He was her second husband, for her maiden name was Elizabeth Barley, and she married, first, Sir Ralph Joscelyn (whose portrait is in the next light of this window), who was twice Lord Mayor of London—1462 or 1464, and in 1476.

Next under are shields of arms, &c.

Next under is Elizabeth Lady Reinsforth, with inscription under her (referring to her husband), " Orate pro bono statu Laurentii Reinsforth ;" and under this another inscription, " et Dominæ Hungerford, filia Comitis Northumberland." Lady Hungerford was Lady Ann Percy, daughter of the Earl of Northumberland killed at the battle of St. Albans, 1455. Her second husband was Sir Lawrence Reinsforth, Knight. (The original full inscription is given in the 8th window, north side.)

Next under is a lady dressed in a surcoat of the arms of Clopton.

Next light.—In the upper part, St. Katherine.

Next under is Ralf Josselyn, Lord Mayor of London (mentioned in the last light), in his robes.

Next under are arms and other fragments.

Next under is a lady, with the inscription under her of " Uxor Walteri Clopton, filia Johēs Picot, miles." She was Elizabeth, daughter of Sir John Pygot, and married Sir Walter Clopton, of Topsfield Hall, Hadleigh, third son of Sir William Clopton, Knight (who died 1376), by his wife, Ivetta Grey.

Next under is a small figure and other fragments.

Beautiful facsimiles, both in size and colour, were taken with much care and labour from the portraits in these west windows, as well as from those in the east window, in 1869–70, by Mr. Charles Bailey,[†] which, it is to be hoped, may some day be published, though it will probably be necessary to greatly diminish their size.

[*] To Mr. Almack's heraldic genealogical research this correction of the errors as to the duchesses of Norfolk is due.

[†] The author of an interesting work on Ancient Timber Houses, and other archæological publications.

From this account of the east and west windows it will be observed that the number of large figures remaining is now reduced to 45. The church contains 72 windows, and the Lady Chapel, vestry, and Kentwell Chapel, 19 more, making a total of 91 windows in this grand building; and when they were all filled with stained glass, the larger subjects in them alone must have numbered between 500 and 600 figures, besides an immense number more in the smaller traceries.

The following account of the state of the interior of the church before the Reformation was written by Mr. Roger Martyn, of Melford Place, who described it as he personally remembered it, and also recorded some of the pre-Reformation ceremonials. The account was transcribed in 1692 from Mr. Martyn's old manuscript, by Mr. Jonathan Moor (schoolmaster of Melford), by order of Dr. Bisbie. In Dr. Bisbie's observations on this matter, he states his belief that Mr. Roger Martyn died about the 23rd of Elizabeth, and that he, Dr. Bisbie, had shown the transcript to Mr. Valentine Martyn. This mention of the supposed date of Mr. Roger Martyn's death raises an apparent difficulty, for in the verified Martyn pedigrees there is no mention of a Roger who died about the 23rd of Elizabeth, 158$\frac{0}{1}$. Which Mr. Roger Martyn, then, was it who wrote the account? Old Roger, the Bencher, died in 1542, and as the writer of the reminiscences mentions his grandfather (the Squire at Melford Place) being then living, who, in this Roger's case, would have been Laurence Martyn, who died in 1460, he clearly was not the author of the account. The next of the name was that Roger's grandson and godson, Roger the Recusant, who died 3rd August, 1615, aged 89, as inscribed on his brass; so that he would have been quite of an age in 1541–2 (the last years of his grandfather's life) to remember the events of that period, which must have been of the deepest interest to such stanch adherents of the old faith as the Martyns. During the short return to Popery during the Marian period, this Roger was churchwarden from 1554 to 155$\frac{0}{1}$, and it is probable that to him is to be attributed the account. The Mr. Valentine Martyn to whom Dr. Bisbie showed the transcript was born 1644, and died 1711, and was the great-great grandson of old Roger the Recusant.

"THE STATE OF MELFORD CHURCHE and of our LADIE's CHAPPEL at the Easte end, as I, ROGER MARTYN, did know it.

"*Memorand :*—At the back of the High Altar in the said Church there was a goodly mount, made of one great Tree, and set up to the foot of the Window there,* carved very artificially with the Story of Christ's

---

* There is still in the centre of the east wall, behind the present modern hideous reredos, a recess which reaches up to the foot of the east window, in which probably the centre part of this carving and the Saviour's cross were fitted and fixed.

The old spelling of this document has been modified throughout.

passion; representing the horsemen with their swords, and the footmen, &c., as they used Christ on the Mount of Calvary, all being fair gilt, and lively and beautifully set forth.   To cover, and keep clean all the which, there were very fair and painted boards, made to shut to, which were opened upon high and solemn Feast days, which then was a very beautiful show.   Which painted Boards were set up again in Queen Mary's time.   At the North end of the same altar, there was a goodly tilt Tabernacle, reaching up to the roof of the chancel, in the which there was one large fair gilt image of the *Holy Trinity,* being Patron of the Church; besides other fair images.—The like Tabernacle was at the South end.

"There was also in my Ile called 'Jesus Ile,' at the back of the altar,* a table with a crucifix on it, with the two thieves hanging, on every side one, which is in my house decayed, and the same I hope my heires will repaire, and restore again one day.—There was also two fair tilt tabernacles from the ground up to the roofe, with a fair image of Jesus in the tabernacle at the North end of the Altar,† holding a round bawle in his hand, signifying I think that he containeth the whole round world: and in the tabernacle at the South End there was a fair image of our Blessed Lady having the afflicted body of her dear Son, as he was taken down off the Cross lying along on her lap, the tears as it were running down pitifully upon her beautiful cheeks, as it seemed bedewing the said sweet body of her Son, and therefore named the *Image of our Lady of Pity.*

"There was a fair Rood Loft with the Rood;‡ Mary and John of every side, and with a fair pair§ of organs standing thereby; which Loft extended all the breadth of the Church, and on Good Friday a Priest then standing by the Rood, sang the Passion.   The side thereof towards the body of the Church, in 12 partitions in boards, was fair painted with the images of the 12 Apostles.   All the roof of the Church was beautified with fair gilt stars.   Finally in the vestry where there

* This refers to the altar in the Martyn Chapel.   The table here spoken of was probably a carved and painted wooden altar-piece, or reredos.

† There were several altars in the church; viz, the High Altar, the above-named Jesus Altar, St. Edmund's Altar, John Hill's Altar, Mr. Clopton's Altar, St. Anne's Altar, and perhaps others.

‡ Fuller thus describes the ancient roods :—"The Rood was an image of Christ on the Cross, made generally of wood, and erected in a loft for that purpose, just over the passage out of the church into the chancel.   And wot you what spiritual mystery was couched in this position thereof?   The church, forsooth, typified the Church militant; the chancel represents the Church triumphant; and all who will pass out of the former into the latter must go under the rood-loft; that is, carry the cross, and be acquainted with affliction.   I add this the rather, because Harpsfield, that great scholar, who might be presumed knowing in his own art of superstition, confesseth himself ignorant of the reason of the rood situation."

§ Old organs were generally portable, and for this reason were constructed divisible in two parts : hence called a pair of organs.

were many rich Copes and Suits of Vestments, there was a fair press with fair large doors to shut to, wherein there were made devices to hang on all the Copes, without folding or frumpling of them, with a convenient distance the one from the other. In the Quire was a fair painted frame of Timber, to be set up about Maunday Thursday, with holes for a number of fair tapers to stand in before the Sepulchre, and to be lighted in Service time. Sometimes it was set overthwart the Quire before the Altar. The Sepulchre being always placed and finally garnished at the North End of the High Altar, between that and Mr. Clopton's little Chappel there, in a vacant place of the wall, I think upon a tomb of one of his ancestors: the said frame with the tapers was set near the steps going up to the said altar. Lastly it was used to be set up, all along by Mr. Clopton's Ile, with a door made to go out of the Rood loft into it.

"Upon Palm Sunday the Blessed Sacrament was carryed in procession about the Churchyard under a fair canopy borne by 4 yeomen. The Procession coming to the churchgate went westward, and they with the Blessed Sacrament went eastward: and when the Procession came against the door of Mr. Clopton's Ile, they with the Blessed Sacrament, and with a little bell and singing, approached at the East end of our Ladie's Chapel, at which time a boy with a thing in his hand pointed to it, signifying a prophet as I think, sang standing on the tyrett,* that is on the said Mr. Clopton's Ile door, *Ecce Rex tuus venit*, &c., and then all did kneel down, and then rising up went and met the Sacrament, and so then went singing together into the Church, and coming near the Porch a boy or one of the Clerks, did cast over among the boys, flowers, and singing cakes, &c.†

"On Corpus Christi day they went likewise with the blessed Sacrament in procession about the Church green in Copes, and I think also they went in Procession on Saint Mark's day about the said green, with hand bells ringing before them, as they did about the bounds of the town in Rogation week, on the Monday one way; on the Tuesday another way, on the Wednesday another way, praying for rain or fair weather as the time required; having a drinking and a dinner there upon Monday, being fast day: and Tuesday being a fish day they had a breakfast with butter and cheese, &c., at the Parsonage,‡ and a

---

* The brick tower of the rood-loft, which is of later date than the rest of the church.

† This was also called houselling bread. Somers, in his Tracts, says that singing cakes also served for the use of private mass, as mentioned in one of Queen Elizabeth's proclamations, which directed that Eucharistic bread was to be made in larger form than the singing cakes which were formerly used for private mass. They derived their name from the fact that their making was generally accompanied by singing of a religious character.

‡ The old parsonage by Cranmoor.

drinking at Mr. Clopton's by Kentwell, at his manor of Lutons,* near the Ponds in the Park, where there was a little Chappel, I think of Saint Anne, for that was their longest perambulacion. Upon Wednesday being fasting day they had a drinking at Melford Hall. All the Quire dined there, three times in the year at least; viz. Saint Stephen's day, Midlent Sunday, and I think upon Easter Monday.—On Saint James's day, Mass being sung then by note, and the organs going in *Saint James's Chappel*, (which were brought into my house with the Clock and bell that stood there, and the organs that stood upon the Rood Loft,) *that was then a little from the road*,† which Chappel had been maintained by my ancestors : and therefore I will that my heires *when time serve*, shall repair, place there, and maintain all these things again. There were also fair stooles on either side, such as are in the Church, which were had away by John King's means, who was Sir William Cordell's Bailiff; *about which Chappel there was paled in round about a convenient piece of the green for one to walk in.*

"On Saint James's even there was a bonefire, and a tub of ale and bread then given to the poor, and before my doore there was made three other bonefires, viz. on Midsummer even, on the even of Saint Peter and Saint Paul, when they had the like drinkings, and on Saint Thomas's even, on which, if it fell not on the fish day, they had some long pies of mutton, and Pease Cods, set out upon boards, with the aforesayd quantity of Bread and Ale. And in all these bonefires, some of the friends and more civil poor neighbours were called in, and sat at the board with my grandfather, who had at the lighting of the bone-fires wax tapers with balls of wax, yellow and green, set up all the breadth of the Hall, lighted then and burning there before the image of Saint John the Baptist, and after they were put out, a watch candle was lighted, and set in the midst of the said Hall upon the pavement, burning all night."

Mr. Martyn mentions in his narrative a good many festivals and saints' days, and alludes in general terms to more. When this country was still under the papal rule, there were 95 festival days and 30 pro-festi, besides the Sundays.‡

* This description shows where the old manor-house stood, then called Lutons, not Kentwell. Kentwell Hall was not built till after the Reformation. (See Chapter VII.)

† This St. James's Chapel was a small church which anciently stood on Chapel Green. It was nearly opposite Mr. Martyn's house. It was, no doubt, dismantled at the Reformation, when Mr. Martyn removed, as he states, the organs, &c. Whether it was used at all as a church subsequently to the Reformation does not clearly appear, but it is depicted as a church, with a steeple, on the manor map of 1580, and it has a cross on the gable of the east end. This fact is, however, of no importance, as other churches on this map have also this symbol. In the maps of 1613 and 1615, a building is still shown on the same site, but it seems to be purely a secular one. This building no longer exists, but there is no record of when it was pulled down. There were many bequests to this chapel, mentioned in various old wills up to the year 1538.

‡ Cullum's "History of Hawstead."

L

The following extracts from the churchwardens' accounts continue to throw light upon the past state of Melford Church, and further furnish the history of its gradual decadence. These curious inventories set forth the furniture and ornaments of the church; and the different accounts show how at various times all these things were either sold or delivered up to the King's commissioners: then replaced partially during the short return to Popery in the reign of Queen Mary, when we find the stanch old Papist Roger Martyn one of the churchwardens; and afterwards again sold and scattered, and the purification of the church finally accomplished. Among many other persons employed as despoilers, we read of one *Prime*, the painter, being paid, in 1562, the sum of 16 pence for " ye scrapeinge owt of the payntinges all ye lengthe of ye quire;" and in 1579, "Payde to Fyrmyn, ye glasyer of Sudburye, for defaceinge of ye sentences and imagerye in ye glasse wyndowes, 2 shillings." They both earned their money, and swept away many works of art of infinite value. Fortunately the area of the work being large and the pay small, they did not take the trouble to make a clean sweep of the whole. Fyrmyn left behind him much glass which he either did not consider superstitious, or which, being out of his reach, was troublesome to get at; and though Prime had thoroughly scraped out the paintings on the choir walls, those in the body of the church had only been whitewashed over. On the accumulated coats of whitewash being scraped off in 1830, the old paintings were perceptible, though, alas! too much defaced to be copied or retained. Over each pillar was represented an angel or saint, standing on a pedestal, with labels of religious Latin sentences issuing from each one's mouth. The church had also been ornamented with a running border of vine-leaves and grapes painted in red ochre around the windows; the effect of which must have been somewhat questionable. Some faint painting was lately still discernible opposite the porch door, and some still exists in the Clopton Chapel.

Probably soon after the rood-loft was finally taken down, about 1562, a new screen across the choir was erected, which was brought to view in 1858, as follows:—

In the choir of the church there stood, on the north and south sides, large square high pews, leaving between them a narrow passage to the altar. These belonged to Melford Hall, and were erected in the 17th century. About fourteen years ago these pews were reduced in size and height, and during the progress of the work the remains of a choir-screen became exposed to view. Only the solid base portions were extant, from which the mullions which had supported the upper tracery had been sawn off. The parts which remained and which had been built into and cased up in the pews, and cut away to fit into them, were rather heavy and plain, and not very ornamental; the mouldings coarse, with solid panels supported by small buttresses; all of which had been very gaudily painted in red, green, and white; and on them were the remains of two inscriptions, of which the only parts still legible ran thus; the date being 1575 :—

(On North Side.) {
" Bothe in welth and also in wooe
Date Gloriam . . . . Deo.
Pray for the soules of John Smythe
. . . .
}

(On South Side.) {
" . . . . Foote wyth whoose goodys Jone
his executryce dede do thys arche to be peynted, .
anno Dⁿⁱ M^oDLXXV."
}

At the same time there was found under the floor of these pews a tradesman's token, nearly new, of " Nicholas Dansie of Lavenham, 1667." He was a man of substance, and a woolcomber by trade, and was alive in 1686. Mr. Thomas Cordell, merchant of London, son of the first baronet of that name, and who died at Zante in 1686, owed to this Nicholas Dansie the sum of £12. Perhaps the two were connected in business, for Thomas Cordell was a merchant dealing in hosiery and woollen goods abroad, and mentioned this debt in his will as due by him. So Dansie may have been at times a visitor to Melford Hall, and, sitting in the Hall pews, had dropped a piece of coin out of his pocket, which had fallen between the boards, not to come to light again for 200 years.

CHAPTER IV.

RECORD OF THE ANCIENT PLATE, FURNITURE, VESTMENTS, AND UTENSILS IN LONG MELFORD CHURCH, PRIOR TO, AND AFTER, THE REFORMATION.

THIS note of the furniture belonging to Melford Church and the Lady Chapel was taken A.D. 1529, and was transcribed by Dr. Bisbie, Rector of Melford, the 30th September, 1686, from a paper book belonging to Sir Roger Martyn, Bart. The spelling has been partially modernized. The various things which were entered in the churchwardens' records as having been afterwards sold or delivered up to the King's commissioners in 1558, and subsequently to that date, are distinguished in this list by an asterisk against them. In this account are entered many items which do not afterwards appear in the churchwardens' books and inventories. Some probably were lost when the church was broken into and robbed, the great iron chest being forced and the locks broken on the 13th January, 1531. Again, the visitors appointed for the examination and suppression of the monasteries not only inspected the religious houses, but also the larger churches. Whether Dr. Ap Rice, who took in his circuit the eastern counties and the Abbey of Bury, visited Melford, there is no record; but if, as is likely, he did so, the loss of some of these church goods might thus be accounted for. We are told that these visitors did their work roughly and coarsely, and with much peculation, and that their servants and followers imitated them with overbearing insolence and profanity. In the large churches they stripped the rich dresses from off the principal images, and desecrated the sacred symbols openly, often riding along the highways, using copes as mock doublets, and tunicles and other vestments for saddle-cloths.

It is possible also, that some of the sacred relics may have been hidden or conveyed away after the visitations commenced, as was done in many known instances elsewhere, and as shown in the case here of the sculptured tablet of the Adoration of the Magi sold to Mr. Clopton, and by him buried for many years. We read that at Northampton a finger of St. Andrew was pawned for £40, in order to preserve the precious relic. It was, however, discovered, and one of the visitors drily reported that "he did not intend to redeem it at the price, unless so commanded." Judging by after-events, we may imagine that the pawnbroker must in the end have been obliged to dispose of this unredeemed relic pledge, which had become a drug in the market, at *a most alarming sacrifice!*

The persons by whom the following account was made, John Dyke and Robert Cawston, were probably related, for the family of Dyke appears to have inherited from the Cawstons land now in the "Burton's farm." John Dyke's name appears in the Rectory Manor in 1505 and in 1533, as also the names of many Cawstons, to the end of that century.

The ACCOUNT made by JOHN DYKE and ROBERT CAWSTON, Wardens of the Church of Melford, the 11th day of December, in the 21st year of the reign of King Henry VIII., and of our Lord God 1529.

First.—Of the Plate belonging to the said Church.

A Chalice, parcel gilt, weighing 13 oz.

A Chalice, whole gilt, the gift of Mr. Kerver, late Parson of Melford, 31 oz. 1 dwt.

A Chalice, parcel gilt, three of the feet broken, belonging to Mr. Clopton's altar, 10 oz.

A Chalice, the gift of Sir Thomas Turret, late Priest of Melford, parcel gilt, 9 oz. 3 dwt.

A Chalice, the gift of Mawt Barker, belonging to Jesus Altar, parcel gilt, 21 oz. 3 dwt.

A Chalice belonging to Jesus Altar, the gift of Miriam Coort, 22 oz.

A Chalice, the gift of Jone Ellis, belonging to John Hill's altar, parcel gilt, 15 oz.

A Chalice, double gilt, with a quadrant crucifix upon the foot, 41½ oz.

A Chalice, the gift of Mr. John Clopton, double gilt, with his arms upon the foot of the backside, 22½ oz.

A Chalice, the gift of John Mason, parcel gilt, 18 oz.

A Chalice, the gift of John Hill, gilt, 20 oz.

The best Chalice, gilt, 133½ oz.

A Chalice, parcel gilt, which was sometime in the keeping of Jeffrey Foot, 20 oz.

A Monstrar to bear in the blessed Sacrament, the gift of Mr. John Clopton and Sir John Lanham, Knight,† and their wives, of silver and gilt, with a crucifix of gold, 13 oz.

A Relique of the Pillar that our Saviour Christ was bound to, the gift of Sir William Clopton, Knight, inclosed with silver.

Two Basons of Silver, and parcel gilt, the gift of John Hill, 107 oz.

A silver Pot, the gift of Mother Barrell, 32 oz.

† Sir John Leynham and his wife Margaret, daughter of Sir John Fray.

A Pax† of silver, parcel gilt, with a crucifix of iron, 10½ oz.

* A Pax, the gift of Robert Jermyn, parcel gilt, 8¼ oz.

* A Pax, the gift of Isabel Boolington, parcel gilt, 8¾ oz.

* A Cross with Mary and John, clean gilt, 69½ oz.

A Cross, the gift of Robert Dyster, silver and gilt, 53½ oz.

A Pix‡ of silver and parcel gilt, 21¾ oz.

A Chrysmatory§ of silver, parcel gilt, for oil and cream, 22 oz.

A little Chrysmatory of silver, and enamelled, to bear in the holy Oil of Extreme Unction, which cost 10s. 1d., above one ounce.

A Ship‖ of silver and parcel gilt, the gift of Foot, 9¼ oz.

* Another Ship of silver, parcel gilt, the Batchelors' gift, 13¼ oz. The said ship was given anno 1517.

* Two silver Candlesticks, parcel gilt, the gift of old John Smith, 56 oz.

* Two Cruetts of silver, parcel gilt, the gift of young John Deek [*Query Dyke*], 10¼ oz.

* Other two Cruetts of silver, parcel gilt, the gift of Mr. Roger Smith, 13¼ oz.

¶ These cruets stood on the altar, and contained water and wine for mass.

* A Censer, the gift of Trinity Guild, parcel gilt, 28 oz.

Another Censer, the gift of our Lady's Guild, parcel gilt, 31¼ oz.

The ancient guilds date from Anglo-Saxon times : they were finally suppressed in the reign of Edward VI. These guilds were formed for the joint advancement of charity, religion, and trade. Every member contributed towards the support of the brotherhood to which he belonged. The parson of the parish and the leading persons were generally members, besides the ordinary community. The guild frequently met for business, but their grand assembly was on the day of their patron saint, when they went in procession to church, and offered up their prayers at his special altar for all the members of the society, both living and dead. The following guilds are mentioned as having existed in Melford ; viz, Trinity Guild, the Batchelors' Guild, Corpus Christi Guild, Our Lady's Guild, St. Peter's Guild, and Jesus Guild. There was also a guildhall here, with a member's cross opposite, which is named in old wills of persons of this place, who left legacies for the support of their guilds.

Hereafter specifieth of all such Jewels, with other Ornaments, pertaining to Our Lady's Chapel in Melford aforesaid.

First, a Girdle, the gift of Madam Brooke, of silver, and enamelled with 10 bars, and the Corse is green, weighing, with the Corse, 12¼ oz. *Now it is stolen.*

---

† The Pax is the instrument with which the priest gives the kiss of peace at mass, which is then conveyed to the people to kiss in turn. It is a small tablet of metal, and generally has the Crucifixion engraved on it.

‡ The Pix or Pyx, in which the Host was kept, was generally in the Middle Ages in the form of a dove : it afterwards took the shape of a cup.

§ Here is an example of vessels set apart for distinct forms of chrism, or holy oil.

‖ These ships were vessels shaped like a boat, for holding incense.

Query: Should the word "corse" be "cross," as in the description of the next girdle? These girdles were narrow bands, generally of silk, and of all colours, to keep the alb in its place. The one above mentioned seems to have been made entirely of metal.

A Red Girdle, the gift of Madam Tye, weighing, with the Cross, 4 oz.; *now stolen.*

Ten Langets of silver, the gift of the said Alice Tye, weighing 1¼ oz. with the strings.

RINGS OF SILVER, AND SOME GILT.

Three Rings upon the Apron of our Lady.

Two little Rings, one shelling another.

Four little Rings, shelled together, in silver.

Upon the said Apron a Spon of silver, which Spon was broken, to set in the Stones about our Lady.

An Ouch of gold, and enamelled, with one stone in the midst of it, with 8 pearls about it. [*Ouch of Gold, see Exodus xxxix. v. 16.*]

A pair of Beads of Coral, with the Pater Noster of silver; and upon the same beads a piece of Coral closed in silver, and one Buckle of silver.

A Pair of Jett Beads, with a button of silver and gilt, for the Crede; and upon the same beads be twenty-three small round beads of silver.

A Stone enclosed with silver and gilt, with the Trinity graven on the back side.

A Lyon or Lebard, parcel gilt, with a chain to the same.

A Piece of Carall [coral] closed in silver, the gift of Alice Tye.

A Buckle, with ten stones set in the same.

A Buckle of silver and gilt, with 13 square chequers upon it.

A Buckle, with three stones in it, and 3 are out.

An Agnus Dei enclosed in silver and gilt.

Two other like Hoops, with either of them 4 branches upon them of silver.

Ten other like small Buckles, whereof 4 be silver, and I suppose the other is such.

Query: Who was the person who wrote this?

Upon the said Apron [*of our Lady*,] 11 Greens [? Garnets,]
One Stone cross in coral.
I small stone, 21d. etc.
A little stone cross in silver.
Sum of the weight of all these Jewels, weighing, with the apron,
22 oz.

COPES AND VESTMENTS BELONGING TO MELFORD CHURCH.

* First the best Cope of Cloth Tissue, the gift of Simond Smith.
* Another Cope of Cloth of Tissue, the gift of Robert Hayward.
* A Cope of Red Velvet branched with Gold, with the suit of the same, called the best Suit.
* A Cope of Blue Velvet branched with Gold, with a suit of the same.
* A Cope of Red Velvet with a suit of the same, called "Cokket's suit."
* A Cope of Red Silk for Good Friday with the Vestment of the same.
* A Cope of Crimson Velvet, the gift of William Deek and Margery his wife.
* The Suit of the same, of the gift of Mrs. Nonnell's, of London.
* A Suit of white branched Damask with 2 Copes to the same.
* A Suit over-worn of Black Damask.
* Two Quire Copes of Blue Satin.
* A Cope of Blue Velvet with Stars, now black.
* A Vestment of Red Velvet, the gift of John Hill's wife, with the name of Jesus in many places written in gold, of the same, belonging to John Hill's Altar.
* Two old Quire Copes.
* A Vestment of Cloth of Bawdkin, with Birds, called the Sunday Vestment.

Bawdekyn was gold brocade, otherwise called Baldachino, or cloth of gold made at Baldeck.

* A Vestment of Red Sarsnet, the gift of Miriam Court, belonging to Jesus's Altar.
* A red Vestment with green in the midst, the gift of Sir Thomas Turret, Priest, which by his will must be in keeping of Mr. Martyn's Priest, and to be used by his Priest, and kept in the Coffer standing in Jesus's Aisle, which Coffer or hutch was of the said Sir Thomas's gift, belonging to Jesus's Altar.

The name of Sir Thomas Turret, or Tirret, occurs repeatedly in matters relating to Melford. The honorary prefix of "Sir," being a translation of the Latin word Dominus, was applied to priests down to the seventeenth century, certainly till 1662. This Sir Thomas Turret was John Hill's chantry priest, and his stipend was £7. 5s. a year. It appears by the above that he was dead before 1529.

* A Chasuble and two Tunicles of red Silk with Birds, whereof the Albs be in decay. [*In another hand-writing*] "Now amended."
* Eight single Chasubles with some of their Albs in decay.

A Cope of Green Velvet with a suit of the same, the gift of Jone Foot, widow, in the year of our Lord God 1516.

These same names occur as those of a benefactress on the old choir screen; but it can scarcely have been the same person, as the date on the screen is 1575: perhaps, however, they were both widows of the same family.

COATS BELONGING TO OUR LADY.

First a Coat for the Good days of Cloth Tissue, bordered with white: and for her Son, another of the same in like case.

These coats were the mantles on all images.

A Coat of Crimson Velvet, and another for her Son in like case.

A Coat of white Damask, and another for her Son in like case, bordered about with Green Velvet.

An Altar Cloth of white Branched Damask of the same, bordered with Green Velvet.

A Vestment of Green Satin, and another of white Fustian.

The fustian here named was not at this time at all a mean material, and was much used for chasubles: it was made with a warp of linen thread and a woof of thick cotton, twilled and cut, to look like a low pile.

ALTAR CLOTHS.

Two Altar Cloths of Tissue and Crimson Velvet, the gift of John Smith.

An Altar Cloth of white Damask in our Lady's Chapel, of the said John Smith's gift.

* An Altar Cloth the gift of Thomas Ellis and Roger Fuller, of cloth of Bawdkyn.

* An Altar Cloth of Blew Damask with Garters upon the same, the gift of Mr. John Clopton, with all such cloths of silk as belongeth to the Sepulcre.

* An Altar Cloth of Silk, with blew birds bordered with blew velvet and blew worsted, the which was made of the old cloth for to bear over the Sacrament.

OTHER ALTAR CLOTHS.

Three Altar Cloths for every day, the gift of Jone Foot, widow.

Ten good Altar Cloths, whereof the three best be the gift of John Foot.

Twenty-two Altar Cloths which are simple.

Two good Altar Cloths belonging to our Lady Chapel.

One Altar Cloth of Diaper, given to the High Altar by Mrs. Chester, Anno 1544.

This entry is interlined in another handwriting from the rest, and is more than fifteen years later.

M

Ten Towels of Diaper, good.
Four Towels of plain cloth.

COVERLETS.

A Coverlet of linen and woollen for the Herse, the gift of Jone Dent.

A Pall Cloak, very simple.

Four Clothes to lay upon the Altar, of Black Buckram.

An old Coverlet of Linen and Woollen which serves to pluck before the Cross on Palm Sunday.

MASS BOOKS PERTAINING TO THE CHURCH.

A printed Mass Book.

Two Mass Books belonging to the High Altar.

A Mass Book called Jesus Mass Book.

A Mass Book, the gift of John Hill.

A Book, the gift of Mr. Roger Smith and Richard Butler.

A Mass Book, the gift of Mr. Thomas Kerver, late parson of Melford.

Two old Mass Books, one at St. James Chappel [Chapel Green], and the other in the church.

A Mass Book in print belonging to our Lady's Chapel.

* A Mass Book called the *Red Mass Book, with many Relicks on the same, adorned with Jewels and Stones.*

ANTIPHONERS OF THE SAID CHURCH.

A great Cowcher, the gift of Mr. Roger Smith.

A great Cowcher lying before the Parish Priest.

A great Antiphoner lying upon the north side of the Choir before Jesus's Priest, the gift of Sir Thomas Turret, Priest.

Three other Antiphoners lying within the said Choir, with two old Portuasses [*Breviaries*].

Couchers were books lying before the desk. In this case they were evidently, with the Antiphoners, books of psalms and hymns, originally introduced by St. Ambrose.

GRAILS.

Ten Grails with one old grail.

A written Book of Parchment for Priests to study upon, lying in our Lady Chapel, the gift of Sir John Gent, Priest.

Grails, or Graduals, were books containing the introits, kyries, glorias, and, in fact, all the musical portion of the service at Mass.

PROCESSIONERS.

Nine Processioners, all written.

These books contained the services of the processions at Mass and Vespers and special days.

A Processionary, the gift of Sir Robert Barrett, Priest.

Three Manuals, one written and two in print.

Two old Martyrolages.

One Hymnal noted in paper, the gift of Sir Richard Dodington, Priest. [*This priest was living in 1484.*]

An old Ordinal [*Rubrics of the Mass*].

One Hymnal printed, the gift of Sir Thomas Turret, John Hill's Priest.

A Processioner, printed, the gift of William King.

CORPORASSES.

Ten principal Corporasses, of five of which one was the gift of Mr. John Clopton, and another the gift of my Lady Clopton; the third, the gift of Mrs. Court; the fourth, the gift of Mrs. Catherine Foxmere;† the fifth, the gift of Mrs. Jane Clopton.

Two Corporasses.

One Corporas belonging to St. Ann's Altar.

Another Corporas to Jesus Altar.

Another Corporas to John Hill's Altar.

Another Corporas to St. Edmund's Altar.

Two Corporasses belonging to the Altar of our Lady's Chapel.

* A Cloth of Blue Silk to bear over the Sacrament, with Chalices of gold embroidered thereon, the gift of Robert Miller.

Two Corporasses with their cloths of crimson velvet, embroidered with gold.

A Corporas Case with the Resurrection upon it, with Images of Gold inwardly.

All these belong to the *High Altar*. Other Corporasses in the custody of the Chantry Priests.

LATTIN‡ PERTAINING TO THE CHURCH.

Two great Candlesticks.

Two second Candlesticks, lately bought, which are called Secondans.

† Dorothy Clopton, grand-daughter of John Clopton, in her will, dated 1508, calls Catherine Foxmere her cousin.

‡ *Latten*, a mixed metal of brass and tin. It was greatly used for monumental brasses as well as for utensils.

Two small Candlesticks to the High Altar.

Two small Candlesticks to Jesus's Altar, both of Lattyn.

A Candlestick of Lattyn, with 10 branches standing before the Image of Jesus.

A Candlestick.

A Candlestick of 10 branches before St. Ann.

A Candlestick with 3 branches belonging to the Trinity, and now the said candlestick standeth before the Image of St. Nicholas.

A Candlestick with 10 branches, standing before the High Altar.

Two little pretty Candlesticks of Lattyn, belonging to John Hill's Altar.

A Candlestick of Lattyn with 10 branches, now in the Vestry.

·A Candlestick of Lattyn with 3 branches, now in the Vestry.

HOLY-WATER PAILS OF LATTYN.

Two Holy-water Pails of Lattyn, with one Holy-water Stick of Lattyn.

BASONS AND EWERS.

Two Basons and one Ewer of Lattyn.

One Ewer of Pewter.

To the Blessed Sacrament belong two Canopy Cloths.

There are two great Lectorns of Lattyn in the Quire, whereof two of the feet be broken.

One Censer of Copper and Gilt.

A Ladder, the gift of Giles Ellis, standing at the Steeple door.

Three Cross Staves, twain good, and one simple.

CHESTS.

A great Chest upon the Vestry Soler,* with two great locks to the same, of iron, the gift of Mr. Clopton : *which two great locks broken by the thieves, January 18, 1531, quá die spoliata fuit ista Ecclesia Melfordiensis.*

Another Chest upon the said Soler, with one lock.

Another plain Hutch there with one lock.

One simple Chest in the *Vestry beneath.*

Another Chest in the said Vestry.

Another Chest in the said Vestry, with an old Chest to lay in Copes, all in the keeping of the Sexton.

---

* *Soler,* the upper story.

At Jesus's Altar a Chest, the gift of Sir Thomas Turret, Priest.
Another Chest at the Quire door, and now in the Vestry.
In our Lady's Chapel two old Chests in decay.
Another Hutch in St. Ann's Chapel.

CROSSES.

A Cross of Copper and Gilt for the week days.
A simple Cross without the feet.

CROSS CLOTHS.

A Cross Cloth of Silk, the gift of Mr. Roger Martyn.
Another Cross Cloth, the gift of Mr. Skern, sometime parson of Melford.
Three other Cloths simple, with one simple Cross Cloth of Silk, with 3 cross staves.
A Cross Cloth of Silk, the Batchelors' gift (1530), which cost 11s. 8d.

These cross cloths were used to cover crosses generally, and the rood in Lent.

Two Streamers of Silk, one the Batchelors' gift, the other of Corpus Christi guild.
Three Banner Cloths, the gifts of the Guilds of Our Lady, Corpus Christi, and St. Peter.

OTHER CLOTHS.

At the High Altar one simple Altar Cloth hanging before the said Altar for every day.
One for Lent with Whips and with Angels.
Before the Image of the Trinity at the High Altar, one white cloth.
A cloth of Adam and Eve to draw before the High Altar in time of Lent, called the Veil.
Before our Lady one cloth of blue.
At Jesus's Altar an Altar Cloth painted, the gift of Maid Aleyn of Bury.
To the said Altar a cloth for Lent painted about with Whips and Angels.
One cloth before the Image of Jesus, white.
Afore our Lady of Pyte [Pity] at the said Altar, a painted cloth.
At St. Ann's Altar a stained altar cloth for every day.
At the said Altar two cloths stained with flowers.
Afore St. Ann one cloth, white.
Afore St. Leonard one cloth, white.

At John Hill's Altar one simple stained cloth.

Over the said Altar is a good stained cloth of the Trinity, the gift of Robert Collett.

At St. Edmund's Altar is a painted cloth of St. Michael and Our Lady.

Three long cloths hanging before the Rood Loft stained or painted with "the dawnce of Powlis" [*elsewhere called daunce of Paule*].

A cloth hanging before the Rood, very simple.

One Cloth with a Vallon, before the image of St. Saviour, white.

A Cloth, the gift of Jone Foot, hanging before the Rood Loft, with 3 small white napkins.

Before St. John Baptist a white Cloth with a Vallon.

Afore St. John the Evangelist a stained Cloth.

Afore St. Peter a new white Cloth.

Afore St. Anthony a stained Cloth with part of the mount.

Two other little Cloths hanging upon two Tabernacles [*Canopies*].

Before St. James a white Cloth.

Before St. Catherine a white Cloth.

Before St. Margaret a stained Cloth.

Before Mary Magdalen a Cloth.

Before St. Edmund a little Cloth.

Before St. Sythe [St. Osyth] a white Cloth.

Before St. George two drawn curtains stained.

Before St. Thomas a simple Cloth.

Before the Image of St. Christopher one cloth, white.

Before the Images of St. Andrew and St. Loy one Cloth, white.

Three other simple cloths to cast about divers Saints in the church, and some stained and some other to the sum of thirteen Cloths.

In our Lady Chapel an Altar Cloth stained.

A Black Buckram Cloth for the Altar.

A stained Cloth hanging before the said Altar.

A Cloth afore our Lady's Tabernacle.

Another Cloth on the other side before the other Tabernacle, white, and both Cloths the gift of John Barker of Acton.

* Altar Cloth of Sattin of Brydges [*Bruges*] in Panes [*squares as in patchwork counterpanes*], and with flowers, and a little Image of Jesus in the midst of the said Cloth, which "Mother Thresser," otherwise called "Clementi Thresso," widow, bequeathed and gave to the said Altar of Jesus, which cost 31s. 8d., Anno D^m 1526.

·In the inventory of 1553 of articles delivered to the Commissioners, this is called, "of Sattyn of Brydgys, with Payrs [pears] and flowers, &c."

Two Altar Cloths, white, the gift of the brothers of our Lady's Guild, in the year of our Lord God 1529.

[The following entry is written in another hand] :—

Mem. 6 April, 1541.—There was given to the Church of Melford, two stained Cloths, whereof the one hangeth towards Mr. Martyn's Ile, and the other to be used about the Sepulchre at Easter time, and also a Red Coverlet for a Forecloth to the High Altar.

A quantity of the cloths in the church and chapel appear to have been sold in one lot in 1547, according to the entries in the Churchwardens' accounts for that year.

OTHER FURNITURE.

A Coffer, the gift of Sir William Hodson.

Two Candlesticks of Lattyn standing at the said Altar.

In the Vestry two short ladders.

In the Church-house a table of beech, the gift of Mr. Roger Martyn.

Two other tables lying in the mole (?) with one forme.

One Forme in our Lady's Chapel, the gift of John Fuller.

In the Church two Lanterns to go with a visitation, and one of them is in decay.

In the Church-house is another Forme.

———

The following inventory was made a year and a half after the dissolution of the Abbey of Bury. Of the two churchwardens of that date, William Smethe was admitted to copyhold land in the Manor of the Rectory (now in the Burton's farm) in the year 1538.

1541.

A REMEMBRAUNCE mayd the fyrst day of Julye, an° D⁰¹ Mᵐcococoᵐxli, then Churchwardens, WYLL™ KYNGE and WYLL™ SMETHE, of the plate belonginge to the Churche.

Fyrst : One Chalys of the gyft of Maister Kerver, layt parson of Mellforde, weying **xxvi** ounces and a quarter, hooll [whole] gylte.

Item : One Chalys belonging to Mr. Clopton's Aulter, parcell gylte, with the feet brokyn, weying **xi** ounce.

Item : One Chalys of the gyfte of Maute Barker, parcell gylte, weying **xxi** ownce and **iii** quarters, longing to Jesus Aulter.

She was probably Margaret, the widow of John Barker, who lived at "the Foste," who, by his will, dated 1513, left gifts to this church. She was Barker's second wife, and she afterwards married Mr. Danyell, of Acton. She gave this chalice to Melford Church before the year 1529, for it is entered in the inventory of that date as her gift at a previous period.

Item : One Chalys of the gyfte of Maryone Cowrte, parcell gylte, weying **xvii** ownces.

Item : One Chalys of the gyfte of John Elys, belonging to John Hyll's Aulter, parcell gylte, weying **xv** ownces.

To this entry there is a note appended in another handwriting : " Delyvred unto the Churchwardens ;" *i. e.* returned to them for the use of the church, when the remainder of the plate, &c. was surrendered to the king's commissioners.

Item : One Chalys percell gylte, weying to the some of **xv** ownces longing to our Lady Aulter.

Item : One Chalys, dowbyll [double] gylte with a quadrante crucyfyx upon the fote, weying to the some of **xli** ownces and a dĩ.

Item : One Chalys of the gyft of John Hyll, gylte, weying **xx** ownces.

Note in another handwriting : " Delyvered unto the Kyng by Mr. Payton, p̃ Kyng's Surveyor."

Item : The best Chalys, gylte, weying **xlviii**. ownces and a dĩ.

Item : One Crysmatory of sylver wych was mayde of the pott of sylver wich was of the gyfte of S̃ʳ Wyll̃ᵐ Clopton.

Item : One Monstre of yᵉ gyft of M̃ʳ John Clopton and Syr John Lavenham, Knyght, and ther wyfes, of sylver and gylte with a crucyfyx of golde, weying **xiii** ownces and therwith a relycke of the pyler [*the pillar that our Saviour was bound to*], of the gyft of Syr Wyll̃ᵐ Clopton, enclosed within Crystall in the custodye of Wyll̃ᵐ Mayre.

The Mayor family lived at " Prowdes," opposite the road to Wissendale Mill.

Query : Is this monstrance the one referred to in John Clopton's will of 1494, thus : " Also I will that the monster that I have made to bere in the Sacrament, be yovene [given] to Melford Churche " ?

The above inventory appears to have been but a very partial one, including only some of the church plate. It was taken during the progress of the Reformation, which, although commenced in 1534, was not finally completed in England till 1547. (Haydn.) The succeeding records up to 1553 show how the church goods were gradually sold and dispersed, but it was not until that year, and just before the Marian return to Popery, that a great quantity of the church plate and vestments were finally delivered up to the Reformation commissioners.

1547 (1st year of Edward VI.).

A copy of the presentment mayd by these men within named the viij daye of November, ye yere within expressed.

The INVETORYE of the Churche Godes of Melforde vewed by Will̃ᵐ Marshall and Will̃ᵐ Dycke, Churchwerdeynes of the same towne the yere of our Lorde God mccccxlvii (1547).

Of Copes.

Item : Two Copes of Clothe of Tyssew.

Item : One Cope of purple velvet with the hole sewt belonginge therto.

Item: One Cope of grene velvet with the hole sewt belonging therto.

Item: One Cope of braunche damaske with a sewt belonging therto of a rede color.

Item: One Cope of blew velvet with a sewt therto.

Item: Two Copes of wyghte damaske with a sewt therto.

Item: One old Cope of purple velvet with a sewt therto.

Item: One old Cope of black velvet with decon and subdecon, wede of blacke damaske [*the gift, by will, of John Clopton, 1494*].

Item: Fowre Copes, two of blew saten and two of sylke braunched.

Item: One olde Cope and one Vestment of rede sylke.

OF VESTMENTS & AWLTRE CLOTHES, AND OTHER FOR THE SEPULCRE.

Item: One Vestment, with decon & subdeacon of sylke with byrdes, and braunches of don sylke.

Item: One Vestment of grene and rede braunches for every day.

Item: One Vestment of blacke worstede.

Item: The best Aulter Clothe of cremesyn velvet and braunched sylke, rede & grene.

Item: One Awltre Clothe of blewe damaske.

Item: One Awltre Clothe of tewke, grene and blacke.

Item: One Awltre Clothe of Don sylke [*Query, yellow*].

Item: One Awltre Clothe of grene sylke and purple, for the syde Awltre.

Item: One Clothe of tewke and three stayned clothes for the other awltres.

Item: XXI Awltre Clothes of lynnyng, whole and broken.

Item: XI Towels of lynning, gode and badde.

Item: Fowre old Vestements and fowre olde lynnyng Albes to them.

Item: VI Corporax Clothes with cases of sylke velvet, and clothe of golde, belonging to them.

The three following items came of the gift of old John Clopton, and formed part of the vestments and altar-cloths which he bequeathed to this church by his will in 1494, wherein he says, "I will that suche clothes of velvet, wyth alle maner braunches, flowres, and alle maner oder stuffe that I have sette abowte the Sepulture at Ester, as well the grene as the red, I yefe and bequeth it alwaye to the same use of the sepulture : and I will that the blacke vestement and that longeth to decone and subdecone, that I have at home, be yovene to Melford Churche, to be kept for obite daies."

Item : Two Clothes of purple velvet for the Sepulcre.

Item: Two Clothes of grene, braunched, for the Sepulcre, of Say.

Item : One halfe yerde of clothe of golde and one yerde of whyte Sypers [? Cyprus, a peculiar embroidery work] braunched, for the Sepulcre.

The following quaint entry carries with it rather a smack of " Old Clo " !

N

Item : Syx peces of blew damaske for the same, *of the gowne of a gentlewoman.*

Item : One old vayle clothe for Lente, of whyte.

Item : Thre crosse clothes of sylke, and two olde.

Item : Two stremers of sylke.

Item : Two herse clothes of dornekyl [*a coarse damask*].

Item : One rede clothe of olde say.

OF BOKES AND CHESTS AND ORGAYNS.

Item : xv gret bokes and xII processyoners.

Item : Of chests and hutches vIII, and two in our Lady Chapell.

Item : Thre payre of Orgayns.

The old organs, for the sake of portability, were made divisible : hence called a *pair* of organs.

OF BELLES AND BRASSE.

Item : In the steple be fyve Belles, and a Sanctus Bell.

Item : Thre belles for processyons.

Item : One bell and one payre of orgaynes that was of late in our Lady Chapell, now in the hondes of Mr Wyllm Clopton.

Item : Two lectorns of brasse, one with fete and the other without fete.

OF JEWELS, CHALICES, & OTHER PLATE.

Item : One Crosse of sylver parcel gylte, weyinge iiij li xiij ownces and a halfe.

Item : One payre of Sencers, weying xxxIII ownces and one halfe.

Item : Crysmatorye weying xIx ownces.

Item : Two Candlestykes weying LxIII ownces.

Item : One Shype weying xIII ownces.

Item : One Pax weying vIII ownces.

Item : One Pax called the " Rede Masse boke," adourned with perles, and crystall stones garnessbed in plate.

The inventory of 1529 adds, " with many reliques on ye same."

Item : One Chalice dooble gylte with a quadrant Crucyfyx, weying xliij (XLIII) ownces.

Note, in another handwriting, "in keping of Willm Maye wyth a noder lesser challys."

Item : One Chalice weying xxvI ownces.

Item : One Chalice weying xv ownces.

Item : One broken Chalice weying xIIII ownces.

Item : One Chalice belonging to John Hyls Awlter, weying XX ownces.

Nota, in another handwriting, "delyved unto Mr Payton pr (ye) Kynges surveyors."

Item : One Chalice weying II ownces, in the honde of Rogare Smythe.

Item : One Chalice broken weying xv ownces, in the honde of Sr Crystopher Deybeck, prest.

Item : Two Basens of sylver in the honde of " Mr. Rogare Martyn "* [*Name erased, and entered in another handwriting, " Sr Wyllm Walde-grave: witnesses Willm Clopton & Francis Clopton, Esquier."*]

Item : One Chalice weying xLVII ownces in the honde of Mr Roger Martyn.

Item : Wyllm Kyng kepeth from the Churche one pix, a monstre for the Sacrament, and two Cruwets of sylver and gylte, sythe he was Churchewardeyne and will not delyver them.

Item : One Chalice in the kepyng of Symon Cawson and sumtyme . . . . in our churche.

In another writing is a note, "Item: owyng to ye same Wyllm Kyng IIII marks" (£2. 13s. 4d.). So he perhaps detained the above-mentioned articles as security for the payment of this balance due to him when churchwarden. Eventually, as appears by his son's statement, the pix of silver was sold to him in payment of the debt, balanced in cash; and his son John finally settled by a balance payment to the churchwardens of 5s. 4d.

Then follows the list of church goods and furniture destroyed or sold in obedience to the Royal Injunctions of Edward VI.

These Injunctions gave great offence in some parts, and especially in the Eastern counties : for they produced a popular rising in Norfolk, when the insurgents were eventually dispersed by a body of troops at Castle Rising, near Lynn, in which engagement Sir William Fermor's brother was killed.

Account of the Sale of Part of the Church Property of Melford after the Reformation.

1517-8.

Thys ys the Reckenyng made by Willm Dyke and Willm Marchall, Churchewardens, from the fest of Sent John Babtyst in the fyrst yere of the reygn of Kyng Edward the VI, unto the Sonday after Sent Lewke, in the second yere of our Soverayn lord Kyng Edward the VI,

* Roger Martyn being a Papist, these church goods, not yet delivered up to the Reformation commissioners, were taken from his charge, and his name was therefore erased as their custodian.

before the Chefeste of the parysshe and inhabytors of the towne of Melford, as well of the gere takyn down by the Kyngs commandement and vysytors, as in the Kyngs Injunccyon doth appere, in the xxviii artykle and other places, as of the other goods longyng unto Melford Churche that was to you delyvered.

Receyvyd.

Thes be the goods takyn and solde by Willm Dyke and Willm Marshall, Churchewardens of Melford, in the seconde yere of the reygn of Kynge Edward the VI, from Sent Mathew day unto that day.

			s.	d.
Item : Sold and recevyd in Brasses $\frac{xx}{xvii}$ li [340 lb.], sold to Thomas Sparpoynt		liii^{s.}	53	0
Item : for $\frac{xx}{iv}$ li. [300 lb.] of wex sold at ii^{d.} a pound, he payd		l^{s.}	50	0
Item : for the Clothes stayned and whyghte in the Churche and Chapell prysed by Thomas Crysall and Thomas Campyon, Roger Coo, Pet. Grenegras, and Mathew Lyes, the stayned		xxv^{s.} viii^{d.}	25	8
Item : for iii belles for prossessyon to answere for ii to the invetory of the Kyng, wayyng xv pound at iii^{d.} a pound,		iii^{s.} ix^{d.}	3	9

The brasses referred to in the above account were probably brasses which had religious inscriptions on them, of a character deemed to be superstitious; such as, "Pray for the soul of," &c.; or the "Bede roll mass" brasses, or such-like.

In the continuation of this account of 1548, it appears evident that the Reformation being now fully completed, and the reformers' powers being no longer questionable, the final stripping of the Church, and the demolition of everything therein considered to be superstitious continued without scruple or hindrance. Every ornament was swept away; not only the rood-loft, the remaining figures of saints, and minor altars, but also all fragments of gilding and colour, even to the stars on the interior of the roof; till the church was left bare to its walls.

Times had indeed changed in a dozen years. For we read that at midnight in 1534, four men of Dovercourt, zealous Reformers, a little too much in advance of the times, had burnt the rood of the church there. This rood was a very celebrated one, and supposed to have miraculous powers. In their case swift retribution followed this sacrilege: three of them being captured red-handed, were forthwith hanged for the offence. The men's names were Robert King, who was taken to Dedham, and immediately hanged as a public example; Nicholas Marsh, hanged in like manner, at Dovercourt; and Robert

Dedham, who was hanged at Cattawade Causeway. The fourth man, Robert Gardiner, contrived to make his escape. Wright's history gives the year of this occurrence as 1532; but Froude, quoting from the State papers, names the above date.

		s.	d.
Item: for yerne [iron] sold unto Humfrey the Smyth at II tymes. Recevyd owte VII greate Doggys of yerne for the Chyrchehowse, and for other gere from the Rode lofte, thys thyng acceptyd, &c . . . . . xxxi vij		31	7
Item: for other yerne lefte of the hygh alter and od gere sold unto Robert Alfownd' for a 1ᵈ a pounde . . ij vij		2	8.
Item: Sold to Mast' Clopton the greateste Image aboute the Churche and Chappell of Alebast' for . . . iijˢ		3	0
Item: Sold to a Goldesmyth of Sudbury the Images and the mownte of the hygh Alter the Image dysvyguryd [*disfigured*]: recevyd the bord and planke dores and yerneworke . . . . xiijˢ		13	0
Item: the gylt of the od gere in the Churche . . iiijˢ		4	0
Item: of parcell of od gere sold to Rafe Borom, one pece of the Candelbeme [on the Rood-loft] . . . xviˢ		1	4
Item: Sold to John Gray ij lytell peces for . . . ijˢ		0	2
Item: Sold to Alyn Barly for the stondyng of the greate Image of Sent Savery [? Saviour] . . . . xijˢ		1	0
Item: to the sayd Barly for iij shorte bord and wall . xijˢ		1	0
Item: Sold to Will'm Warde pecys of bord . . . iiijˢ		0	4
Item: Sold to John Dowty a plancke and halfe the Crosse [probably the cross on the Rood-loft] . . . viijˢ		0	8
Item: Sold to Will'm Mayerl a starr of the Rowell [roof] viijˢ		0	8
Item: Sold to John Grenegras of the small corvyn gere ijˢ		0	2
Item: Sold to Gyles Strachy of Sudbury xxiiii yard of Prest [? What is this] . . . . vijˢ		·7	0
Item: to Mast' Parson for the tabyll of the north syde in the Churche he pavd . . . . . . iiijˢ		8	0
Item: Sold to Gallant, M' Cloptons carpenter vi smale bords . . . . vjˢ		0	6
Item: Sold to Will'm Marshal to mend a lede xi li of lede vjˢ		0	6
Item: Sold to John Sargent all the greate Imagys vjˢ viijˢ		6	8
Item: Sold to John Alheke for ye facion of gylte of ye Rowelle and iiij lytell bedstares . . . . . viijˢ		0	8
Item: Sold to M' Clopton the alt' of Alebast' in our ladys chappell . . . . . . vj vijˢ		6	8

And left unto Mast' Clopton ij stonys at the end of the Alter in Mast' Clopton's yelde and the tup' of Alebaster in the sayde yelde and a lytel tabyll in Sent

Annys Chappell, and all the gere therin, to dres up the Chappell and dyscharge the Churchwardens, and to do yt at hys plesur.

This is further described in the notice of the monuments in the church.

		s.	d.
Item : Sold to Mast' Clopton the *brokyn Crosse in the Churche yard wyth all the stonys therewith as they be* . ij*. iiij.*ᵈ.**		2	4
Item : for the II syde of the Rowell and the flore of the syde ij*.		2	0
Item : Sold v plancke & iiij staves . . . . ij*.		2	0
Item : Delyverd to Mast' Clopton to make up a marke . iiijᵈ		0	4
Item : Sold Sent Nycholas' cote and woode [coat and hood] greatly eatyn wyth moth . . . . iij*. iiijᵈ		3	4
Item : Sold the bare myt (?) unto a paynter of Sudbury hall . . . . xxᵈ		1	8
Item : Receyvyd of Rudlond and Sparpoynt at owr lady's day in Lent and before . . . . . iij*. iiijᵈ		3	4
Item : to Robert Alefound' for a cloth in ye lady's chappell that was pryce xxᵈ and a stayned cloth was callyd the vayl sumwhat peryshyd in sum placys—pryce . . xviᵈ		1	8
		1	4

EXPENDITURE of the Churchwardens DYKE and MARSHALL.

1547–8.

Thes be the coste and chargys payd.

Imprimis : Payd for our chargys to Bury on Sent Matthew daye, the fyrste yere of the reygn of Kynge Edwarde the VI unto the vysytors . . . xviᵈ

Item : To the Kyngs Commyshoners the XIII daye of Marche and the seconde yere of Kynge Edwarde the VI : payde . . . . ii*. iiᵈ

Item : Payd at another Commyshon where Maister Bedo dyd set another to make an inventorie of the Churche goods. Payd for the makyng of the inventorie to M' John Gayton (*a priest*) . . . . . viiiᵈ

And for to receyve of gyfte mony . . . . xiiᵈ

And for our costes . . . . . . i*. viᵈ

* These churchyard crosses (but few of which now remain in England) generally stood south of the church, that being the side at which the congregation most commonly enters. Originally they were erected for a double object; one being, that all persons passing through the churchyard on their way to divine service, on looking at the sacred symbol, should be reminded to pray for the souls there interred. And these crosses also frequently denoted the bounds of sanctuary or space of refuge which in certain cases extended beyond the walls of the church into its precincts of consecrated ground.

Item : Payd for the havyng downe of the *Imagys* and
    Tabernacles and oder *Tabylls.* Rafe Borom and hys
    lad, Robert Alefounder and hys lad, Gregory Cosyn,
    Nycholas Corder, hered by the daye : besyde oder
    helpe not payde, but drynke dyd geve unto .   .   vij^{s.} j^{d.}

Item : For the takynge downe of the Funt and Hyghe
    Awlter wyth ther helpe .   .   .   .   .   j^{s.} ij^{d.}

    Query : What was this font ? Was it an ancient piscina for priests to wash their
hands in before Mass ; or was it one of the many chancel holy-water fonts of all of which
the Reformers ordered the removal ? Yet many remained in Dowsing's time, 1643.

Item : Payd for 2 seme (16 bushels) of lime and a lode
    of sonde .   .   .   .   iij^{s.} iij^{d.}
    [*There is something else obliterated in this entry.*]

    In the next entry appears the first application of that terrible whitewash, which
continued to disfigure the church for more than 300 years.

Item : Payd to John Kendall for the whytyng of the
    Churche and Chappell above and beneth .   xxiiij^{s.} viij^{d.}

Item : Payd to John Lyteman for the Desk, fonte, and
    candelbeme .   .   .   .   xiv^{s.}

    Query : Was this desk a pulpit ? It is noticeable that among all the other church
furniture there is no mention of a pulpit ; and it is said that pulpits were not commonly
to be found in country churches before the sixteenth century.

		s.	*d.*
Item : payd to Rafe Borom for takyng downe of the volte and settyng up agayne . . . . . x^{s.}		10	0
Item : payd for forlocks and byndes of yerne and in-gayles . . . . xvj^{d.} ob.		1	4¼
Item : payd for helpe and other thyngs . . . hys bargayne x^{d.}		0	10
Item : payd for the bordyng of the candelbeme, and for nayles to Borom . . . . . . iiij^{s.} iiij^{d.}		4	4

    Query : Was this the Altar candle-beam or the Rood-beam ?

		s.	*d.*
Item : payd to Borom growncellyng [*ground cilling*] of the stoles [*stools* or *benches*] of the northe syde of churche xx^{d.}		1	8
Item : payd to the scyd Borom for makyng of the churche gate, and for mendyng of the pales aboughte the churche gate, and for nayles & for yerne worke aboughte the churche gate . . . . iij^{s.} iiij^{d.}		3	4
Item : for mendyng of the Churche howse [*the sum erased*].			
Item : for makyng of the stagys for the paynter and wryter, & for other helpe . . . . vij^{s.} iiij^{d.}		7	4
Item : payd to John Hall the paynter of Sudbury for the worke done in the Churche & Chappell & Rodelofte & candelbeme, & makyng of the Kyngs harmys [arms] xxviij^{s.} iiij^{d.}		28	4

		s.	d.
Item: payd unto Stayworth for wrytyng of the churche & chappell [? commandments] . . . xxxiij⁴ iiij⁴		33	4
Item: payd for ij quayers of paper and for makyng of *iiij bokes for the Regester* & iij bokes for the pore peple and hyghe wayes. . . . . ij⁴ iiij⁴		2	4
Item: payd to M⁴ John Gayton for *wrytyng of the coppy in the Regester* of the invetory . . . . . viij⁴		0	8
Item: payde for a new locke to set on the cheste . iiij⁴		0	4
Item: payde to Dyster for mendyng of iij lockes . v⁴		0	5
Item: payd for yerne . . . . . . i⁴		0	1
Item: payd for washyng of the churche gere . iij⁴ iiij⁴		3	4
Item: payd to the plummer of Sudbury and hys man ij dayes worke and for vij li. of sowdyer & ther borde iiij⁴ viij⁴		4	8
Item: payde for drynke at ye helpe . . . j⁴ ob.		0	1½

The overplus that was solde of the lynen cloth of stayned and whyght more, and that was prysyd by Thomas Crysall & Thomas Campyon, & Pet⁴ Grenegras, Rog⁴ Coo, & Matthew Lyes, was spent in stayyng of the ij sylver basyns longyng to Melford Church, gyvyn by John Hyll by hys lyves tyme, & they remayn by the commandyment of my Lord Protector unto a furder tryall, in the charge of Sir Will⁴ Drury, Mast⁴ Danyell, & Sir Will⁴ Walgrave.

And beside that payd for a byll of complaynte and other charge for commyshone in Sir Will⁴ Druryes and Mast⁴ Danyell's hands, for the poore people, hyghe wages & churche goods . . . . v⁴		5	0

Item: for horse labor & mans labor, & paynes of thys sewte and for all paynes and lete of worke not rekened but carry on your good rewarde.

Also leyd oughte for the coste of Sur Edward Tyrell, Wyll⁴ Marshall, Thomas Sparpoynt, & John Aldrede, to goo to my Lord Protector and other of the Kyngs Councell to have had the gyfte of Bower Hall to Melford for a scole, as the Kyngs Commyshoners dyd wyll us to doo . . . . xx⁴		20	0
Item: to Rafe Borom for mendyng of the churche ladder & tumberl . . . . xi⁴		0	11
Item: to *John Cordell** for a copy makyng of the byll of compleynt of Thomas Berker and commyshon of the same for the ij Sylver Basyns . . . . . . xij⁴		1	0
Item: payd for wrytyng of ij bokes of Thomas Hardy . ij⁴		2	0

* Was this John Cordell the person of that name who married Emma Webbe, of Kimbolton, Hunts, and who was buried at Melford 7th January, 1564, and whose son was Sir Wm. Cordell, Knight, of Melford Hall? Or it may have been the third son of the above John, and who died *s. p.*

The seyd Willm Dyke & Willm Marshall, Churchewardens, dyd not receyve, dyscharge nor acquytt none of thys folowyng— .

Item : Sir Willm Clopton's gyft.
    „   The gyft of Thos. Smyth and hys wyff, & John Smyth hys son.
    „   John Barker at the Feaste.
    „   Owyn of Robert Colman.
    „   of Robert Gager & other unknown.
    „   of olde Mr Smyth for led.
    „   of now lent by us.

[The following are only partial extracts] :—

1549—1550.

Churchwardens ; SYMON COLMAN and JOHN GAGER.

Receipts.

Receved of Wolbard of London, Merchant taylor, for a sylver
    basyn .   .   .   .   XIII^{li} v^{s.}
Solde to oder men of Sudberye 35^{li} of brasse   .   .   VI^{li} IX^{d.}

Expences.

At Sudberye at the delyvery of the invetory of their stuffe . VIII^{d.}
Agayn at Burye for lyk businys .   .   .   .   .   IX^{d.}
For the Kyng's booke sette forthe by Parlamente .   . IV^{d.}

1551—1553.

Churchwardens ; PETER GRENEGRAS and WILLIAM SPONER.

Expences.

For the churche servyce bokes and sendyng to Burye and
    other placys to serch for the same .   .   . XVII^{d.} ob:
For our expensys at Sudburye when we went fyrst before my
    Lorde Wentford for Churche goodds .   .   . XII^{d.}
Payd for the movyng of the great orgaynes .   .   . XII^{d.}
Item : for mendyng the key of the orgayne .   .   . I^{d.}
For makyng IIII surplosses .   .   .   .   . VIII^{d.}
Payd to my Lorde Wentworth and other the Kynge's .   .
    .   .   . [*The rest of this entry is obliterated*]. . XX^{s.}

1553.

Thes delyvyryd to my Lord Wentford, Sir William Walgrave, and other Commissioncrs at Witsenstyde, in the yere of our Lord God MCCCCCLIII [1553], wherof they resurved to the use of the towne II payre of Chalice.

o

Two basons of sylver and parcell gylt of the gyft of John Hyll, weying $\frac{xx}{v}$ ownces and VII [107 *ounces*].

One Pax of the gyft of Robert German, parcell gylte, weying VIII ounce and a quarter.

One Crosse with Mary and John, clean gylte, weying $\frac{xx}{iii}$ ownce and IX and di. [69$\frac{1}{2}$ ounces].

One Pax of ye gyfte of Isabell Bolington, parcell gylte, weying VIII ownces III qrs.

One Shype [ship] of sylver and parcell gylte of the Bachelors gyfte, weying XIII ounces and a quarter. Anno D⁰ Mill⁰ oooco and XVII [1517].

Two Sylver Candelstycke of ye gyfte of olde John Smyth, parcell gylte, weying LVI ownce.

One Censure of the gyfte of Trynyte Gylde, parcell gylte, weying XXVIII ownce and a quarter good.

Two Cruett of ye gyfte of yong John Dycke, parcell gylte, weying X ownce and one halfe.

Two Cruett of ye gyfte of M⁰ Roger Smyth, parcell gylte, weying VII ownce and a di [7$\frac{1}{2}$ ounces].

The Rede Masse Boke adorned with jewels and stones. [*The inventory of* 1529 *says, "with many Relics on the same."*]

VESTMENTS, &c.

Thes parcelles war delyveryd also to the Comishioners at Sudburye at the tyme before wrytten and the same yere.

Mem. that certeyn paynted clothes was delyveryd to Will⁰ Kyng & Will⁰ Smeth, then Churchwardens, by S⁰ John Cavendysh, Prest, to contynew to the use of the Churche duryng hys plesure, & ys now gyfn from them: the wyche clothes was sold by Will⁰ Marshall and Will⁰ Dycke, Churchewardens, as many other thynge war for nowght, as yt apperyth (althowghe not trulye) in their accownte wyche ys before wrytten. [*Sir John Cavendish made his will in* 1544.]

Thys specyfyeth as herafter followeth of the COPES and VESTMENTS belongyng to thys CHURCHE of MELFORDE.

Fyrst one best cope of clothe of tyssew of the gyfte of Symon Smythe.

Item: one other cope of clothe of tyssew, of the gyfte of Robert Heywarde.

Item: one cope of rede vellvet braunched with golde, with the sewte of the same called the best sewte.

Item: one cope of blew welvet braunched with golde, with a sewte to the same.

Item: one cope of rede welvet with the sewte of the same called Cokets sewte.

Item : one cope of rede sylke for good Fryday, with the vestment to the same.

Item : one cope of crymesyn velvet of the gyfte of Willm Dycke and Margery hys wyfe.

Item : the sewte of the same of the gyfte of Mystres Nonneley of London.

Item : one sewte of whygte braunched damaske, with two copes to the same.

Item : one sewt overworne of blake damaske.

Item : two quere copes of blew satten.

Item : one cope of blew welvet with starres, now blake.

Item : one vestment of rede welvet, of the gyft of John Hyl's wyfe, with the name of Jesus wryten in many places in golde, belongyng to John Hyls awlter.

Item : two old quere copes.

Item : one vestment of cloth of bawdkyn [cloth of gold] with byrds, called Sonday vestment.

Item : one vestment of rede sarsnet longyng to Jesus Awlter.

Item : one vestment of grene, of the gyft of Syr Thos. Tyrett, Prest, longyng to Jesus Aulter.

Item : VIII Syngull Chesabulls, with some of ther albes in dekay.

Item : one Chesabull and two tunykylle [tunicles] of rede sylke wyth byrds, whereof the albes be now amendyd.

Item : one cope of grene velvet of the gyft of Jone Foot, widow, in ye yere of owre lorde God MCCCCC and XVI [1516], with a sewte of the same.

Item : one aulter clothe of the gyfte of Thos. Elys and Roger Fuller, of the clothe of Bawdekyn.

Item : one aulter clothe of blew damaske, with garters upon the same, of the gyft of Mayster John Clopton, with all such clothes of sylke as longeth to the sepulcure.

Item : one aulter cloth of rede sylke, with byrds, bordered with blew welvet and worsted, the wich was borne over the Sacrament.

Item : one Aulter clothe in satyn of brydgys with payrs and flowers of the gyft of Clement Thresher to the hye alter.

This is meant for satin of Bruges with a pattern of pears and flowers. The giver's name is recorded in a former inventory as " Clementi Thresso, widow." She made her will in 1525.

Item : thre albes now with ther pavytors for the blacke sewt.

Item : one clothe of blew sylke to bere over the sacrament, with Chalyces of golde embroyded, of the gyft of Robt Myller.

Item : one goode vestment and one foreclothe of whyte damaske payned with grene velvet in our Ladye Chapell.

Item: one coverlet of lynse wolse for the herse, of the gyft of Margaret Dyster.

The Dister family were clothiers of Melford, and helped to rebuild the south-west end of the church.

A change now comes over the scene, and the work of spoliation is for a time checked. Queen Mary had come to the throne, and the religion of the country became again Roman Catholic. The Melford Papists, now once more in the ascendant, with Roger Martyn at their head, made an effort to re-embellish the church according to their form of worship; but the attempt must have been at best a sorry one, for all that was handsome and valuable had been already seized by the Reformers, and sold or delivered up to the Royal Commissioners.

1553.

Memorandum that thys ys the Specyalte of the Boke belonging to the Church of Melforde.

The following note is in a different handwriting; probably Roger Martyn's :—

The premyssis scateryd abrode and delyveryd to sacrewlydge persons wyche payd lytle or nothyng for them, war many of them spoyld and mangelyd, and some of them that war savyd we broaght agayne as yt apperyth afterward in the yere of our Lord God xv°LIII [1558].

Fyrst, two messe boke belonging to the hyghe aulter.
Item: one messe boke called Jesus Messe boke.
Item: one booke of the gyft of John Hyll.
Item: one booke of the gyfte of Mayster Roger Smyth and Richard Boteler.
Item: one booke of the gyft of Mayster Thos. Kerver, layt parson of the sayd churche.
Item: two old messe books, one at Saynt James Chappell and the other in the churche.
Item: one messe booke in prynte belonging to our Lady Chapell decayed.

Thes be ANTIPHONARS of the sayd Church.

Fyrst, one gret cowcher of the gyfte of Mayster Roger Smythe.
Item: one cowcher lying befor the parysho prest.
Item: fowre antyphonars lying within the sayd quere, of the wych one of ye gyft of S' Thos. Tyret.
Item: fyve grales with one olde grayll [*gradual*].
Item: one booke of Syr John Gent, gyfn to the prest to study upon, lying in our lady's chapell.
Item: XII processyoners.

Item : iij manuels, one wryten & two in prynte.

Item : one Hymnall prynted, of the gyft of Sir Edward Tyrrett, John Hyll's prest.

Item : one Hymnal wryten & noted, of the gyft of Mayster Rychard Dodyngton. [*He was living in* 1484.]

Item : one ordynall [*the forms for ordination and consecration*].

Item : one processyoner prynted, of the gyfte of Willm Kynge.

Hereafter foloweth the AULTER CLOTHES longing to the CHURCHE of MELLFORDE, and also the Towells and Crosse Clothes and Baner - [banner] Clothes with Stremars [streamers].

Inprimis, ten aulter clothes good, wherof thre of the best be of the gyft of John Fote and other twayne be in the chapell of them.

Item : eyght other aulter clothes which are sympull.

Item : two canape clothes longing to the Sacrament.

Item : one crosse clothe of sylke of the gyfte of Mr Roger Martyn.

Item : one crosse clothe of Mr Skyrn, somtyme parson of Melforde.

Item : fyve pryncypall towells of great length.

Item : one aulter clothe of dyaper gyfn to ye hyghe aulter by Maystres Chester, A° D^m MCCCCXLIV [1544].

Item : fowre menar [*meaner*] towells for other mynystracyon.

Item : one crosse clothe of sylke of the Bachelor's gyft, wich cost vj^s viij^d [6s. 8d.], An° D^m M^m quin^mo trice^mo [1530].

Item : two stremers of sylke, the one of the Bachelors gyft; the other of Corpus Christi gyld.

Item : thre baner clothes of the gyfte of the gyldes of our Lady, Corpus Christi, & Saynt Peter.

Thes be the CORPORAXES belonging to the CHURCH of MELFORDE.

Item : two Corporaxes with ther clothes of crymasyn velvet embroyded with golde.

Item : thre other good with theyr clothes.

Item : one *Corporaxes Case* with the **resurrection upon yt embroyded wyth ymages of golde inwardly** : all these belong to the hyghe aulter.

Item : other Corporaxes in the Custodye of the Chauntre prests.

Thes be the CROSSES, CANDELSTYCKE, and other Parcells of Coper [copper] and LATYN [*mixture of brass and tin*], to the CHURCH of MELFORDE belonging.

Inprimis one crosse of coper & gylte for the weake days.

Item : one sympull cross without the foote.

Item : the ymages of Mary and John, coper and gylte, now in the vestre brokyn from the crosse.

Item : two great candelstyck and two secound candelstycke wich are called secundaryes, the soket of the one lyeth brokyn in the vestre.

Item : two small candelstycke to the hygh aulter and two small candelstycke to Jesus aulter, of lattyn bothe.

Item : two lytyll prety candelstycke of latyn belonging to John Hyll's aulter.

Item : one candelstycke of latyn with fyve braunches, now in the vestre.

Item : one candelstycke of latyn with thre braunches, now in the vestre.

Item : two holy water pales of latyn wyth one holywater stycke of latyn [*holy-water sprinkle*].

Item : two great lectorns of latyn in the quere, wherof the one, thre of the feet be brokyn and be in the vestre.

Item : one coper censure and gylte.

Item : one basyn of latyn and another of pewder.

Item : one ure [ewer] of pewder.

Item : thre crosse staves, twayn good and one sympull.

Note, in another handwriting (? Roger Martyn's): "Thes premisses lykewyse usyd as before ye sayd" (referring to the former note of 1553). In the same writing, as follows.

Item : bequethd by Robert Gager of Melford to Melford
Churche . . . . vᵈ

Mem. that I John Gager payd for the shetyng of the Sancts
bell of the gyfte of my fathers Robᵗ Gagers goods the   £. s. d.
yere of our Lorde God ᴍᴄᴄᴄᴄxʟɪɪɪɪ [1544] . ixˢ viijᵈ   9 8

Item : by the same J. Gager of the sayd bequest . xiiijᵈ   1 2

Item : by the same at an other tyme . . . xixˢ   19 0

Item : at another tyme to the mendyng of ye crosse, vjˢ viijᵈ   6 8

Item : xvˢ   Item xɪɪɪɪᵈ
              Summa . . . . lijˢ viijᵈ   2 12 8
So ther remaynyth yet . . . . xʟⱽɪɪˢ ɪɪɪɪᵈ [2 7 4]

Thes be the CLOTHES hanging and being aboute the Ymages in the CHURCH and also Hutches, Cofers, Tressells, Tables, Formes, Ladders, & such other Utensyls and Necessaryes to the Church of Melford belonging.

Item : one sympull aulter clothe for evry day to the hygh aulter.

Item : one clothe to the sayd aulter for *Lent*, with *wyps* [*whips*] *aboute with aungels.*

Item : at the Aulter of Jesus one fore cloth paynted, of the gyft of Mayd Alan of Bury, and one clothe for Lente with wyps aboute and aungels.

Item : at Saynt Jamies aulter one forecloth for evry day.

Item : one forecloth to John Hyls aulter stayned of Saynt Myghell & our Ladye.

Item : two foreclothes in our Lady Chappel, one of whyte damaske with paynes of blake velvet, the other stayned in the kepyng of our Ladyes prest.

Item : before the *ymage of the trynyte* at the Hygh Aulter one whyte clothe.

Item : thre before the ymage of our Ladye, one clothe blew.

Item : before the hyghe aulter one clothe with Adam and Eve for Lent called the vayle.

Item : one clothe before the ymage of Jesus, whyte.

Item : thre before the ymage of our lady, one clothe whyte.

Item : before the ymage of Saynt Anne·one clothe whyte.

Item : before the ymage of Saynt Leonarde one clothe whyte.

Item : one stayned clothe of the Trynyte hanging before John Hyls aulter paynted, of the gyft of Rob' Colet.

Item : thre long clothes called the *daunce of Paule* hanging befor the Rode lofte, and also the vayll hanging befor the Rode, very sympull.

Item : one clothe with a valaunce before the ymage of Saynt Sayvyour, whyte.

Item : before the ymage of Saynt John Baptyst one clothe whyte with a valaunce.

Item : before the ymage of Saynt John Evangelyst one clothe stayned.

Item : before Saynt Antony one clothe whyte.

Item : before Saynt James one clothe whyte.

Item : before the ymage of Saynt Kateryn one clothe whyte.

Item : before the ymage of Mary Magdalen one clothe whyte.

Item : before the ymage of Saynt Chrystopher one clothe whyte.

Item : before the ymage of Saynt Edmund one lytyll clothe whyte.

Item : before the ymages of Saynt Andro and Saynt Loy one clothe whyte [*St. Eligius or St. Loye*].

Item : two drawn curtayns stayned before the ymage of Saynt George : new.

Item : In our Lady Chapell one clothe before the aulter drawn, with one blacke bukkerond clothe.

Qaery, black buckram cloth.

Item : one clothe before the ymage of our Lady's tabernacle whyte, and another of the other syde whyte, bothe of the gyfte of John Barker of Acton.

Here follows a note in a different handwriting from the rest of the entries in this inventory.

Mem^d that the syxt day of Apryll in the yere of oure Lorde God, MCCCCCXLIIII [1544] ther was gyfn to the churche of Melford two stayned clothes, wherof the one hangeth toward Mr Martyn's Yle, the other to be usyd about the Sepulcre at Ester tyme, and also a rede coverlet for supercllothe to the hygh Altre : by Mayster John Cawndysh [*Cavendish*], prest.

Item : in chests belongyng to the sayd Churche.

Inprimis : One great cheste upon the Vestre with two grete loks brokyn by the theves the XIIII daye of Januarie : qua die Januarii spoliata fuit ista ecclesia Melfordiensis in Anno D¹ M^{mo} Quingent : XXXI [1531].

Item : one other grete cheste bounde with yrons and dyvers stapuls to hange on loks ; being to lay in the evydens and dedes belonging to the churche, and other gode uses within the towne.

Item : one other fayre hutche to lay in the vestments, albes, and towells.

Item : in the Vestre beneth, a grete hutch bounde with yrons, of the gyfte of Sir Willm Clopton.

The vestry beneath means the old vestry at the back of the chancel, under the upper story, which was the priest's chamber, the floor of which is now removed. Sir William Clopton gave this new iron-bound chest to replace the broken one, after the robbery of the church, above mentioned.

Item : two other hutches : thes more sympul.

Item : another olde hutche, to lay in the processyoners.

Item : at Jesus Aulter one hutch of the gyft of Sir Thos: Tyrrett, prest.

Item : one other chest at the Quere dore wherin the Regyster boke, and the churche boke be kept.

Item : in oure Lady Chapell, II chestes in dekay.

Item : one other hutche in Saynt Anne's chapell.

1554–5.

At this date it appears that the churchwardens took some of the fees now paid to the parson, for there often occur such entries as these :—

		s.	*d.*
Of Eustas Strutte, for that hys mother lyethe in the Churche	VI^{s.} VIII^{d.}	6	8
Of Sperpoynt for the hyryng of the churche folde one yere, II^{s.}		2	0

But sometimes what they could not get in money, they were obliged to take in kind, as in the following example, where part of the debt had been owing ten years :—

Received of John Gawger, in partye of payement of ys fathers
    legacye, thre sylke pelowes, two candelstickes, two ymage
    of alibaster, a Booke, and a peynted table, at the pryce of   xv$^{s.}$
[Rather a curious job lot for the 15s. Some of the other part
payments are entered in 1553.]

    Occasionally they got paid by instalments for legacies and be-
quests, thus :—

Recevyd of Richard Smyth for the resydew of hys fathers
    bequeste geven to the steple, the Mondaye after Trynyte
    Sondaye . . . . x^{l} £10
So he hath answeryd the hole bequeste of hys father beyng twentye
    markes [£13. 6s. 8d.]

    At the temporary Marian return to the Roman Catholic religion,
we note a different sort of expences laid out by the Churchwardens,
Mr. Richard Clopton and Mr. Roger Martyn, Papists.

1554–5.

Payd to Hornerd of Glemesford for song Bokes .   .   .   xii$^{d.}$
To the joyner for makyng of the sepulcre and for foure
    standes for to bere upp the canape clothe .   .   .   ii$^{s.}$
For makyng of the case wherin the Sacramente ys .   .   iv$^{d.}$

1555.

Payde to Beryes and others for watchyng of the Sepulcre .   viii$^{d.}$

    Berry was then the church clerk. The sacrament on the sepulchre was watched
from Maundy Thursday till Easter morning.

Layde owte for the gret orgaynes makyng .   .   .   £4 iiii$^{l.}$
Layde owte for a holye water spryncle .   .   .   iii$^{d.}$
For wasshyng of the ymages and mendyng y^{e} churche dore xi$^{d.}$
To John Grys for watchyng uppon Chrystemas nyghte .   ii$^{d.}$
Layde oute for a pewter pyxe. a cope, and a lyttell crosse . viii$^{s.}$ x$^{d.}$
For makyng of the ymages of Marye and John .   .   .   ix$^{s.}$

    They must have been but rude works of art for this price.

To Sparrowe's wyff for makyng of cake and of appulcake
    agenst the Ale keppt in Lent .   .   .   .   .   xi$^{d.}$

    These church ales, whereby money was procured for the use of the church, are
repeatedly mentioned in these accounts, and it appears that people attended them from
considerable distances, for we see in another entry that a person was paid for proclaiming
them in towns as far away from here as Braintree and Ipswich. These ales were held at
various times, such as Lent, Whitsuntide, and the feast of the dedication of the church.

Payde owte for strekyng of the common lyght .   .   .   xx^d

Query: What was this strekyng? The common light was kept burning at the sepulchre from Good Friday to Easter-day.

To John Grys for goyng of errunts, and watchyng the
    Sepulcre .   .   .   .   .   ,   .   .   .   xvi^d
For payntyng and gyldynge of the roode .   .   .   .   x^d
For staynyng of a crosse clothe and for frynge for the same,
    for the hanclothe of the Trynyte, for the han poles,
    and for the hanclothe of Seynt Peter .   .   .   iiii^s viii^d
To Harne the mason, for all hys cherge abowt the grete
    crosse on the Grene .   .   .   .   .   .   viii^s vi^d

There is another date against this of 1556. This was the ancient market cross on the Green; so that perhaps it had been damaged by the Reformers, and required repairs.

To Spon for carrying of the stones for the grete crosse on
    the Grene .   .   .   .   xii^d
For makyng upp of fower nobles, for copes bowght .   .   iii^s iiii^d
For an altar clothe of grene sylke and a hanbell .   .   vii^s iiii^d
To Mr Rycherd Clopton for a seme of malte ageynst the
    gamynge [Church ales—a seme was 8 bushels] .   .   xiii^s x^d
For borrowynge of pottes at the gamynge .   .   .   .   ix^d
To Hammont for proclamyng the Games at Brantre, and to
    Peter for proclamyng them at Ypwyche .   .   .   x^d
Layde owte for pewter for ye orgaynes .   .   .   .   iii^s iiii^d
Layde owte to ye Ryngers when the Busshope came to town   x^d
    [The next entry is a very remarkable one.]
For a cope of blew satten, a cope of wyght wyth the Erle
    of Oxford's armes, and for a frontlet of an altar clothe
    havyng the Lord Chamberlaynes armes .   .   .   xxx^s
Two alter clothes, one of grene sylk wyth geets, and an-
    other of whyte fustian wyth crossys .   .   .   .   vi^s

Query: What were geets? Fustian, as made at that time, was not a mean material.

To Matthew Lyes for a crosse clothe .   .   .   .   .   xx^d
For settyng of xiii settes [seats] in the Churcheyerde .   vii^d
For what was owyng for the games and for fyrynge .   .   xvi^d
For the sante bell rope .   .   .   .   .   .   ix^d ob

Sanctus bell, or mass bell, used at Mass at the elevation of the Host.

Layd oute to the nunnes for mendyng of the vestimentes .   viii^d

What nuns were these? Most of the religious houses had been dissolved long before this date. Perhaps they had been formerly members of some of the ejected communities.

To Harry Boram for makyng of the herse . . . . . iiij^d
To Hernes for storyng of Brassys agaynst Chrystmas . . ij^d
Layde owte to Mr Goldyng for an Antiphoner and a crosse
    clothe . . . . xiij^s iiij^d

*After this there follow many items of labour and material for
mending the steeple.*

It is noticeable that in the next account of 1559, though Queen
Mary was then dead (17th Nov. 1558), the Roman Catholic formulary
yet continued, Mr. Roger Martyn being still churchwarden. After
that time till 1575, the remainder of the proscribed church vestments
and furniture were finally disposed of.

1559.

Churchwardens, ROGER MARTYN and JOHN CLENCHE.

(Expenditure *inter alia*.)

For watchyng of the Sepulcre . . . . xij^d
For mendyng of the Crysematorye . . . . . . vj^d
To Mr Roger Martyn for iiij^{li} waxe . . . . . ij^s iiij^d
For strybyng of the Sepulcre lyght . . . . . ij^d
For xvi yerdes of locern [lawn] for surplysse . . . ij^s
For v yerdes of geyer [gauze, i.e. better quality, but is worth] ij^s j^d
To the Myller of Halle M^rl for the gryndyng of ij somes
    [16 bushels] malt for the Churche Ale . . . . ij^d
For a quayer of paper . . . . j^d
For ix^{li} and ii quarters of waxe for the plowght lyghts . ij^s ij^d
    [Lent between Easter and Twelftide.]
For vj^{li} waxe for ye sepulcre lyghts . . . . . j^s iiij^d
For the makyng of iii surplises . . . . . . j^d
To Berye for wasshyng of the . . . . j^d
To John Greye for caryng . . . . j^d
To Peter Kive for . . . . ij^d
    the sepulcre ryts . . . .

Item iij crosse staves remaynyng in the vestre.

Item j payntyd clothe of the crucyfyx part servyth for the crosse staffe.

Item j sacre bell [*sanctus bell, for the elevation of the Host*].

Item j paxe of wood.

Item a handbell bowght of John Kyng with ye church monyes.

Note [*in another handwriting*]. As for vestments and copes wyche remaynyth in ye churche appereth by bylles indentyd, wherof one remaynyth with Willm Smethe & Thos. Sparpoynt, churchwardens for this yere. A° D^ni 1559. Another with Mr Roger Martyn; and the third with Willm Berye, clerke.

So that within the time from 1554 to 1559 a number of the vestments, &c., had again been dispersed and got rid of, most of them probably after the death of Queen Mary.

CHESTES, HUTCHES & PRESSE, with other such lyke Thynges.

Inprimis a clorse [close] presse the wyche the copes hangyth in.

Item. In the vestre fower great chests bownd with yron.

Item. Another old hutche, with a long cheete of borde.

Item. A table ther with a forme.

Item. Uppon the soler [upper chamber] in the vestre, two hutches well bownde with yerne and fower great locks perteynyng to them.

Item. One other playn hutche ther for to lay in the napre [napery].

Item. A case of borde ther.

Item. A long cheste in the Chauncell.

Item. III formes in the same Chauncell.

Item. III great ladders and thre other lytle ladders wherof one ys in the vestre.

Item. One lytle longe hutche stondyng in Mr Clopton's yeld havyng a locke and keye with yren [iron] particions therin.

Item. One other hutche with a coveryng of olde red canvas.

Item. In our Ladyes Chappell II olde hutches bownde with yerne.

Item. One table with hys frame wyche servyth for to lay copes theron.

Item. One lytle forme wyche was parson Malletts.

Item. A pastall [paschal] standard [*Candlestick for the Gospel side of the Altar.*]

Item. A harrow for the teneble candells.

This was for the service of the Tenebræ on Good Friday. It was a sort of frame or candlestick, holding 14 yellow wax candles and one white one; the yellow ones representing the eleven Apostles, the Virgin Mary, Mary the wife of Cleophas, and Mary Magdalene. Of these candles, one was extinguished after each psalm; but the white one, which was called the Judas candle, was held behind the altar during the Benedictus and then brought back, to typify Christ's resurrection from the dead.

CUSHYNGS, with Corpres [corporas] Cases, and Lynnen Clothes for ye same.

Inprimis: IV cushens wherof two ar of blew sylke storred with down, and two other whyte and red of sattyn of Bryggys [*manufactured at Bruges*].

Item. III olde cushens.

Item. An olde coverlet of dornyxe.

Dornyx was a coarse damask, originally made at Tournai.

In the following accounts only the entries of greater interest have been selected. From the receipt for timber of the Rood-loft and other parts of the Church which had been sold, it is evident that the work of demolition was yet going on.

Extracts from Churchwardens' Accounts.

1562.

THOMAS SPARPOYNT and WILL^M SMYTHE, Churchwardens.

Receipts.

Receyved of Mistres Warbelton of the legases of hir husband Master Francis Clopton . . . . XL^s

Receyved of Pamers of Sudberye for *Gylte of the Rod lofte* and for the *carved tymber* of ye same . . . XXVI^s

Recveyved of Willm Dashe for tymber that ye Rode stode upon * . . . . II^s XI^d

Receyved of Robard Alfunder for a pece of the partycions that was at Mr Clopton's Chappell . . . . XIX^d

Receyved of John and Gylb^t Gringrass for 4 bordes that longed to ye Aulter . . . . XIII^d

Receyved of Gylb^t and John Gringrass and John Humferye for *sertayne trashe whiche cam of the Rode lofte and ye Aulter* . . . . X^s VIII^d

Receyved of *Mistres Clopton for an Aulter stone.* . . VI^s

Payments.

Payde to John Prime for ye mendyng of both ye sydes of ye churche wher ye Rode lofte was: and for ye pavinge of Mistres Smith's grave . . . . . . III^s VIII^d

Item payde to Prime for the whiteing of the Chauncell . IV^s

* Dash was an innkeeper, and lived at the Hart, now Brook House, and also held the Hall mill.

Payde to Nicolas Corder for the takyng down of ye Rode
    [loft] and makyng of ye lectorne .   .   .   .   III^{s.}

Payde to Nicolas Corder and Willm Roper for takyng downe
    of ye Rode . .   .   .   .   .   II^{s.}

"Lofte."—This word is here scratched out, and the word "soller," or upper floor, entered in lieu thereof. The great crucifix had been taken down long before.

Payde to John Sparpoynt for meat and drynke for them
    whiche dyd take downe ye Rode Soller .   .   III^{s.} VIII^{d.}

Payde to Pryme for ye scrapeing owt of the payntinges all ye
    lengthe of ye quire .   .   .   .   .   XVI^{d.}

Payde to Nicolas Corder for ye making of a childe bere and
    for nayles for it . .   .   .   .   .   IV^{d.}

Payde for the injuncions .   .   .   .   .   IV^{d.}

Payde for 2 bokes of Prayer and of fasting that were latlye
    restored .   .   .   .   .   .   VIII^{d.}

Payde to ye Commishyoners and to hir Majesty for ye pre-
    sentment of ye Regester boke .   .   .   XVI^{d.}

Payde for the writyng out of the Regester boke * .   III^{s.} VI^{d.}

Payde for the Charge at Sayn Edmond Bury before the Com-
    mishyoner . .   .   .   .   .   II^{s.} VI^{d.}

Payde for a hors here forthe by Clar † .   .   .   IV^{d.}

Payde for the Commaundemente boke .   .   .   XX^{d.}

Payde to John Smeth for the carying of claye to Glemes-
    ford brege at the commandemente of Mr Martyn . . II^{s.} IV^{d.}

1563.

The same Churchwardens.

The following entries appear to refer to the first adoption in this parish of the system of poor-laws of 1535.

Payde to Symonne Cawsonne out of the monye of the
    pore, which monye Mr Martyn did receyve of the
    sayd Symon Cawsonne, for the howse called
    "*Strangers Howse*" .   .   .   .   .   XXX^{l.} III^{s.} IV^{d.}

Payde to John Flecher for the kepyng of the pore chyld
    called "Bothe," for a year and a q^r and 9 weekes
    at VI^{d.} a week .   .   .   .   .   XXXVII^{s.}

Payde to John Brembele for the bryngyng up of the
    pore chyld called "Bott," as Mr Clopton, M^r

* The first entries in this Register-book date from 1559. Register-books were first ordered to be kept in 1539.

† Horse-hire by the Clare road.

Smyth, Willm Ellis, and Symon Cawsonne, and the
other ye men of the towne ware agreed to give him   xxx^{s.} iv^{d.}

Payde to Edward Haxshall and Manode and hys wyffe
for howse rente for the kepyng of Robart Bent when
he laye bedrede with them to his deth   .   .   .   xxviii^{s.} viii^{d.}

Payde to John Rede for Mother Grengrasse for the tyme
that she was wyth hym   .   .   .   .   vii^{s.} iv^{d.}

Item : Geven in lynnen clothe to the somme of $\frac{xx}{vii}$ and
iii yeards, whiche coste viii^{d.} ob a yarde, that was
geven to the pore in shyrtes and smokkes, whose
names doth followe, the skore and aitetene, and
made of them $\frac{xx}{iii}$ and iii at i^{d.} ob a pece, and xv
gowne was made   .   .   .   .   .   v^{l.} ix^{s.} i^{d.}

This quaint entry of goods supplied to the poor, is of 143 yards of linen at 8½d. a yard, of which were made 63 shirts and shifts, at 1½d. each for making, which were distributed to 38 families. The £5. 9s. 1d. does not seem to include any charge for making the 15 gowns or petticoats.

1563 to 1567.

Thomas Smythe and John Gryngrasse, Churchwardens.

Memo. Nothing received of the Widowe Spowner during the said accomptant time for the landes called "Hopkin Heywardes."

This was the charity land, called the "Organ land," which was somehow lost to the parish before the year 1600.

1567 to 1569.

William Chaplen and John Grocer, Churchwardens.

Expence of the reparacions of the Churche   .   .   .   v^{li.} xi^{s.} x^{d.}

Memo. Nothing aunswered by Mr Francis Clopton, esquier, during the sayd accomptant time : neyther in the time of Tho: Smythe and Jo: Grenegras beinge thon Churchewardens for the landes aforesayd called Hopkin Heywardes, contrary to his agrement as appereth : per añn xxx^{s.}

Yerelye Rentes due to any use wthn the towne of Melford : as
followeth :—

Bower Hall, Pentlowe, per añn to the pore   .   .   .   iv^{li.} iv^{d.}

Thumes in Cranmer Strete, Melford, to the pore   .   xxxvi^{s.} vi^{d.}

Two Croftes geven by Robt. Alfounder to the men-
dynge of the glasse wyndowes of the sowth syde   } iii^{s.} iv^{d.}
of the Churche   .   .   .   .   .

Nelys—Hyeways   .   .   .   .   .   .   iii^{li.} xiii^{s.} iv^{d.}

Hopkyn Heywardes—Churche   .   .   .   .   xxx^{s.}

1569 to 1572.

WILL^M ELLYS and SYMON CAWSTON, Churchwardens.

Owing (inter alia) by Francis Clopton, Esquier, for the
 ferme of londe called "Hopkyn Heywards," geven
 to the Churche, from the tyme that the wedow Spon
 dyd foregoe the same, untyll Mychellmas, 1572 . x^L xi^s i^d

1572 to 1575.

JOHN GROCER and WYLLYAM CHAPELYNE, Churchwardens.

Layde oute for the purchase of the Tenement called
 Osmundes, bowte of Wm Allen, 1575 : and lette
 for iiii^L p : ann. . . . . $\frac{xx}{iiii}$li [£80]
[*This is now let for £35—1873.*]

1575 to 1580.

JOHN GROCER and WILL^M CHAPLEN, Churchwardens : and after the
death of CHAPLEN, ROBERT CRYSALL.

The Rentes of Nelys and Bower Hall are the same as in the
yere 1569, but the rente of Thums is now encreased to xxxvii^s x^d
p : ann.
Resceved for certen tyle and for oulde tymber solde . x^s

Against the following entries of sales of church vestments and furniture there is this
note in the margin, in another handwriting : "Enquirend pro particularibus, et quo
warranto vendita erant et de valore." And there is a further note against the entry of
the cope delivered to Dr. Styll, who was Archdeacon of Sudbury in 1579 : "Recipitur
inde : quo warranto liberatam fuit."

Resceved of Willm Ellys for certen Coopes [copes] and
 Vestments solde to him . . . . . x^s
Item : Of Thomas Dyke for certen Coopes solde to him . vi^s viii^d
Item : One coope delyveryd to Doctor Styll.
Item : For certen caundellstycke and other thyngs solde
 to Symonde Cawston, Smyth of Burtons, John
 Smethe, and to Arethur Younger . . . . iii^s iiii^d

In this account of 1575 to 1580, the last entries occur of the sale
of copes, candlesticks, or other articles pertaining to the service of the
Roman Catholic faith. It is evident by all the previous accounts that
the bulk of the altar-cloths, vestments, all the plate and jewellery, and
most of the gear of any value, had been delivered up to the Royal
Commissioners.

What was eventually sold was mainly material, pulled down and set aside in the progress of demolition. Thus in the accounts of sales we find only realized by copes sold, 16s. 8d.; cloths for images, £1. 5s. 8d.; various materials, £4. 5s. 10d.; materials of the rood-loft, £3. 11s. 2d.; materials of altars, £1. 12s. 5d.; memorial and bederoll brasses, £2. 13s.; one *large alabaster image*, 3s.; others, 1s. 8d; and *several great images*, 6s. 8d.: the total for many images of 11s. 4d., proving that they were clearly at that time a drug in the market; while in 1554 there was paid for the making of two images only, Mary and John, 9s. And, finally, among the sales, the great churchyard stone cross was sold for 2s. 4d.

1575 to 1580.

Payde owte.

Payde : For Bred and wyne for a communion for J. Smethe
    and wedow Alefounder .   .   .   .   .   IIII^d

This is the first entry in the parish accounts of the purchase of sacramental elements.

Payde : To John Gawger for wrytinge of the Regester and
    for suinge and allowynge the same at Sudburye .   .   III^s II^d
  To Mr. Martins man for makinge the lease betweene the
    Towne and Allen for Osmundes .   .   .   .   VI^s
25 Decr 1576. Payde for wyne for the Communyon .   .   VIII^d

The first entry of purchase of sacramental wine for public communion.

To Gawger for wrytinge the Regester, suinge the same,
    and for his paynes .   .   .   .   .   .   III^s VIII^d
26 May 1577. Payde for wine for the Communyon .   .   VI^d
Payde for wrytinge the articles .   .   .   .   .   VIII^d
For mendynge the Communyon clothe that Coppm rent   IIII^d
For x yerdes of Hollund for surples . .   .   .   XIII^s VI^d
1579. Payde to Fyrmyn the Glasyer of Sudburye for de-
    faceinge of the sentences and imagerie in the glasse
    wyndowes .   .   .   .   II^s
Payde to the apparator for the certificat of the visitacon
    made by Doctor Styll, Archdeacon .   .   .   XXI^d
  To the Archdeacon of Sudburye for his cherges .   .   II^s
Payde for bawderyks for the belles the xth of February
    [bellropes]. .   .   .   .   .   .   XVI^d
27 Apryll : Payde to Corder for mendinge of the Churche
    style at Mr. Cloptons beryall .   .   .   .   II^d

Francis Clopton, son of the builder of Kentwell Hall, married Agnes Crane, of Chilton, and died the 5th April, 1578.

Q

Payde : for Bredd and Wine for the Communyon   .   .   XIII^{d.}

First entry of the purchase of bread for public communion.

To Gawger for wrytinge of the Regester of Christeninges
and Buryalls, and for his cherges at the sewall [suing]
at Sudbury.   .   .   .   .   .   .   III^{s.} VIII^{d.}
Washynge of the Communyon clothes and surpleces   .   III^{d.}
Payde for the firste tome of Homylyes   .   .   .   XII^{d.}
13th April 1579.   Payde to John Gawger for wrytinge of
the Regyter of Christeninges, maryedges, and buryalles   III^{s.} VIII^{d.}
For writeing of the verdict at the Busshoppes visitacon   .   XVI^{d.}
For Articles ther, and a benevolens towards Bath
Churche   .   .   .   .   VI^{d.}
To the Ringers when the Busshoppe came throwe Mel-
forde .   .   .   .   III^{s.} IIII^{d.}

Payde oute for the Hye Wayes.

1575.   Hye wayes and Bridges .   .   .   .   .   XXVII^{s.} IIII^{d.}
1577.   .   .   .   .   XXXIIII^{s.} IX^{d.}
1578.   .   .   .   .   XLIII^{s.} VI^{d.}
1579.   Layde oute the III Maye at the Quarter Sessions
at Burye and at the Assizes there the XXIII Julye,
for the traverse of the indictament founde agaynst
the Towne for repayring of Radbridge   .   .   XLIII^{s.} II^{d.}

*The town of Melford had denied their liability to repair the bridge at Rodbridge ;
they were therefore proceeded against by indictment, and a verdict given against them.
Their legal costs of £2. 3s. 2d. were not very large.   Lady Cordell, by her will, a few
years later, left £2 for the repair of Rodbridge.*

1580.   Hyewayes and Bridges .   .   .   .   XLVIII^{s.} X^{d.}

Payde for the Pore.

Payde to Peter Candeler for kepinge of a base childe   LX^{s.}

1581.

ROBERT CRYSALL, Churchwarden.

In this year, and the three years following, only one churchwarden is named.

Payde to Gawger, Clerke, for regysteringe of marradges, christeninges,
and Burryalls   .   .   .   .   .   .   III^{s.} VIII^{d.}
Payde to Darbye the appariter for Doctor Dayes visita-
tion   .   .   .   .   XIII^{d.}
Item : For mallmesey wine for a communyon on Newe
yeres daye   .   .   .   .   VIII^{d.}

Item : For a cote for the boye that Candeler kepes   .   II^s

Item : Payde to Candeler for II sherte for the forsayd
    boye . . . . II^s VIII^{d.}

Payde for the taxe of the Towne oute of Bowerhall rente IIII^{li.}

Item : For the hallf yeres rente of Mother Scryvener her
    howse . . . . II^s

Item : For the buryinge of Mother Spylman . . . XVI^d

Payde oute sy' thence by the sayd accompt to Master
    Skynner for the defence of the suyte of Carter's
    infant agaynst one Fyrmyn . . . . . III^s IIII^d

1582.

JOHN MAYOR, Churchwarden.

The Mayor family owned land now in Melford Place Farm.

Receved one whole yeres rent of the ferme of Osmundes,
    dewe and ended at oure Ladye . . . . V^{li.}

So this rent had been raised from £4, which it was in 1575.

Payde for II newe stoles . . . . . . XL^s

Stoles : probably church benches.

Payde to Cloughe for the Clocke makeinge . . . XL^s VI^d

This must have been a new clock; for there are many small entries before this date for repairing and keeping in order a former clock, which, from the frequency of its repair, appears to have been but an indifferent time-keeper.

1582 to 1584.

HUGH ISACKE, Churchwarden.

Payde for II shurtes for one of Phillippes sunnes . . II^s VI^d

    For one woyte cote for Harry Chamfylde . . II^s VIII^d

    And for him . . . . II^s

Geven by Doctor Jones comandemente to twoo scollers of
    Melforde . . . . II^s

The following expenses relate to the repair of a broken bell, amounting in the total to £5. 2s. 7d.

For takeinge downe the broken Belle . . . V^{s.}

For carryinge the broken belle to Burye . . . V^{s.}

For helpe to loade it . . . . . . II^{d.}

For layde oute at Burye for wayinge the belle . . VIII^d

Two jorneys to Burye . . . . . . XVI^d

For makeinge the wrytinge between the Churchwardens
    and the Bellfounder . . . . . . II^{d.}

To the Bellfounder for castinge of the belle and metalle,   III^{l.} XIIII^{s.} II^{d.}

For hangeinge the belle .   .   .   .   .   .   XI^{s.} VIII^{d.}

1680.

JAMES BASSET, Gent., & ROB^r SPARKE, Churchwardens.

Payments.

	£.	s.	d.
Imp^s There was layd out by them at the Generals at Sudbury on the 8th day of May 1679, and at the Generals at Melford on ye 16th of Octob^r followinge, for the drawinge of their presentments and their charges to the apparitor, sidesmen & themselves .	01	05	11
They spent upon the boys when they went the bounds of the parish.	00	03	02
To a travaileinge stranger	00	00	06
For mending the 4th Bell wheel	00	00	06
For mending the 6th Bell	00	00	06
For ye ringers on Gunpowder treason . . .	00	01	03
For ye ringers on ye kinge's birthday . . .	00	01	00
For mending the Governors *Pewdoor [the Governor of the Hospital]*.	00	00	06
For Bred for ye Comunions	00	01	04
To Thos. Windle for 18 quarts of wine for the Comunions throughout the year	01	00	10

Receipts.

	£.	s.	d.
Of the Feoffees for Thuñis for *halfe* a years rent ending at Lady Day 1679.	05	00	00
Of Mr Witham for the buryal of his child within the church	00	06	08
Of Mr Hobart for the buryall of his father within the church	00	06	08
Of Mr Boston for the buryall of his mother within the church	00	06	08
Of Dr. *Bisbie for the Pigeon dung out of the steeple* .	00	02	06
They received upon Rate	12	02	06

1681.

JAMES BASSET & ROB^r SPARKE, Churchwardens.

Receipts.

	£.	s.	d.
A six months rate	73	10	00
No receipts of charities.			
From Will. Corker, being the remanent of ye money gathered for drums, &c	00	11	00

Payments.

	£.	s.	d.
To the apparitor, for a proclamation, a fast book, & two citations	00	02	00
For a Book of Canons for the use of ye church	00	01	00
Repaires of Roof of south Isle of church, viz.: carpenter, Will Borley	17	12	02
Smith's work, John Maynard	01	16	10 ob.
Plumber Joseph Sawyer (including 10402ᵇˢ old lead 2230ᵇˢ new lead)	41	15	04

	61	04	04 ob.
Repaires done to the Steeple	05	12	06 ob.
Repaires Church Porch, Vestry, Churchyard, including inter alia	06	11	03 ob.
Planck for ye seat in ye Church Porch	00	05	00
For board about the *young men's seat in the North Isle* & fixing	00	01	06
For *an iron chain for ye porch*	00	03	09

General Expenses.

For bread for ye communion for ye year	00	01	02
For wine do. do.	00	19	00
For cutting the bryars about the church, cleaning the churchyard, & mending the old pales against the ecclesiastical visitation*	00	02	06
For cleaning ye church against ye said visitation*	00	02	06
To the visitors of the church being their usual fees	00	02	06
For a bottle of sack to entertain them	00	02	00
To two rogueing travailers [*who cheated the churchwardens*]	00	01	00
For mending ye bruise in one of ye silver flagons	00	00	06

1632.

John Knopp & Thos. Page, Churchwardens.

Receipts (inter alia).

By rate from the several inhabitants of this parish of Melford and the outleets thereunto belonging	73	08	00
By money from the estate in Bower Hall	02	16	04

---

* So the briars were generally allowed to grow up to the church, which was seldom cleaned inside, and only the fear of the visitation produced a little effort of tidying up. Perhaps it was wise to propitiate the visitors, and help to keep them in good humour with a bottle of sack.

Payments (inter alia).

	£.	s.	d.
For the book called " *Ye Reasons for dissolving the last Parliament,*" ordered to be read in church . .	00	00	06
For cleaning ye Church against the Generalls held in the same	00	05	00
For the other charges at the two Visitations . .	01	04	08
For bread & beer at ye perambulation . . .	00	03	00
For bread for the Comunions for the year . .	00	01	02
For wine for the Comunions do . . .	01	15	00
For a Comon Prayer book	00	11	07
Ye Ringers on 29 May & 5 Nov. . . .	01	00	00
To Darson for catching of several foxes . .	00	07	00
For 7 travellers	00	02	06
For ye Apparitor when he brought the Kings declaration	00	00	06
For a warrant to distreyn Eegden concerninge the Wollen Act	00	01	00

29th of Charles II., obliging all persons to be buried in woollen, or the person directing the funeral to forfeit £5.

| Repairs of Church Roof, &c. . . . . . | 64 | 17 | 06 |

1683.

[Same Churchwardens.]

Receipts.

From the tenant of Thumbs (part of £10 rent) . .	06	00	00
From Osmunds by the hands of Mr John Drew at two several times	13	03	09
From Osmunds by the hands of the said Mr Drew at another time	04	19	03

Payments.

For bread for the Comunions	00	00	09
For wine for the Comunions of the year . .	01	01	04
Paid to several passengers	00	01	00
For a book of Articles	00	00	06
For 4 passengers more	00	01	00
To altering the 7th bell clapper . . .	00	05	00
Repaires of the Church	30	16	03

1683.

JOHN KNOPP & THOS. PAGE, Churchwardens.

A CATALOGUE of the severall Utensills belonging to the CHURCH of MELFORD as they were surveighed and accounted for by Mr John Knopp and Mr Thos. Page, Churchwardens, and by them delivered to the following Churchwardens.

In the Vestry.

1. A large ironbound hutch with 3 keys belonging thereunto—the one in the custody of the Rector, the other two in ye hands of the present Churchwardens: and in the said hutch the several writeings and evidences belonging to the parish.

2. A Table, a large Chaire, 2 forms, a large press and shelves, and two charity boxes.

3. A large Surplice and a Divine's Hood.

4. A book of Homilys, a book of Articles, a book of Canons, and a table of Marriage.

5. The Parish Register, an old black Churche Book for fair accounts, another weekly book for accounts, and a third for registring preachers names and briefs.

6. A black herse cloath purchased out of the alter money for the use of the Towne.

In the Chancel.

1. A decent table of wood placed alterwise at the east end of the sayd Chancelle, with pesses thereunto belonging.

2. A green cloath carpet for the same, given by Sir Robert Cordell, Baronet, and Dame Margaret his wife, Anno 1661.

3. A damask table cloath with two damask napkins, given by Nathaniel Bisbie, Rector, Anno 1661.

4. Two silver flagons gilt, each of them weighing sixty-eight ounces at 8s 6d per ounce, with inscriptions setting forth the donors and their Coat of Arms. They cost £57. 1s 10d, and were given by Sir Thomas Darcy then of Kentwell Hall in Melford, and Dame Jone his wife, Anno 1674.

5. Two leather cases for the said flagons given by the afore-mentioned benefactors.

6. One silver Chalice given by Mr William Gilbert, late Rector of this parish, weighing sixteen ounces, with this following inscription— " Gulielmus Gilbert quondam Rector Ecclesiæ Melfordiensis me legavit eidem."—(1600–1618).

7. One silver Chalice weighing fifteen ounces and a halfe, with this inscription, " Deo sacrum et Ecclesiæ parochiali de Melford, Suff.

votivum." Purchased by the sale of a smaller Chalice and Altar money.

8. One large silver Patin with last mentioned inscription, purchased by the sale of a smaller patin and Altar money, and weigheth four ounces and sixteen pennyweight, which said chalices and patin were gilt, at a cost of £5. 1. 6., to suit with the flagons aforesaid.

9. Two large Pewter flagons with this inscription, "Trinity parish, in Long Melford, 1616."

10. One Pewter Chalice and patin, purchased with Alter or offertory money, to be used with the Pewter flagons in the absence or disappoyntment of the aforesaid gilt flagons.

For the Desk and Pulpit.

1. A large green serge Cushion with a silk fringe, formerly belonging to the pulpit, now to the desk.

2. A new large Common Prayer book and two old ones.

3. A large Bible.

4. A large green velvet pulpit cloath fringed, given by Sir Rob' Cordell, Bart. and Dame Margaret his wife, lettered "$_R{}^d{}_M$, Anno 1661."

5. A large green velvet cushion fringed, suitable to the aforesaid pulpit cloath and given by the aforesaid Benefactors.

In the Steeple.

1. Eight well tuned Bells with wheels and ropes, and all other necessarys thereunto belonging.

2. One Saints Bell, upon which the clock striketh.

In the Church.

A spade, a shovell, a mattock, a long iron grave spoon, a dirt skip, a ladder of two and twenty steps, another ladder of twelve steps, two large Biers, one childs Bier, one Cradle for repairs.

Belonging to the Church.

(1.) Twelve leathern Buckets in the Church, twelve more at M' Hobarts house in Hall Street—six more at M' Knopp's house in the said street—six more at Ford Hall in Bridge Street, and two iron Cromes at the Signe of the Black Bull in Hall Street.

[*The entire stock and plant of the Melford Fire Brigade.*]

(2.) Two head pieces, two Breast pieces, two Back pieces, two Gorgets, two Pikes, one old sword; all gathered together by Nich' Steed, and now layed up in the Vestry.

This account of the weapons, both offensive and defensive, in the parish armoury furnishes us with an idea of the Long Melford train-band, or militia company of the period. It is evident that the officer carried the sword as well as a pike; and in addition, there was also a proportionate band, for we find elsewhere a mention of a parish drum: but as there is no record of any accoutrements for the drummer, he was probably a sort of plain-clothes musician, and a non-combatant. It is a matter of deep regret that the name of our gallant townsman, who was the officer commanding the force at this time, has not been handed down to us. We may well picture to ourselves how the ardent military spirit of the people of Melford must have been at times stirred to the utmost pitch of enthusiasm, when the gallant Melford corps, consisting of the one fully-armed private, led by the commanding officer with the old sword, and headed by the plain-clothes drummer with the drum, marched through the street for occasional reviews and manœuvres of the force on the Green. As old Roger Martyn would have expressed it, "A noble sight, and goodly to behold."

GOODS, ORNAMENTS, and UTENSILS belonging to MELFORD CHURCH.

1753.

Two Silver Flagons washed with gold, weighing 65 ounces apiece.
Two Silver Cups washed with gold.
One Silver Salver washed with gold, weighing about 26 ounces.
Two Carpets for the Communion Table, of blue and green cloth.
One Pulpit Cloth and Cushion, of purple velvet.
One fine Damask Cloth and two Napkins for the Communion Table.
Two Surplices of Holland and one black silk Scarf.
Three Common Prayer Books.
One large Bible of the last translation.
A Book of Homilies.
Eight Bells with their frames and appurtenances, as they now hang, containing in weight sixty-seven hundred, which were altered to that weight by a faculty from the Bishop.

BELLS.

Note in Churchwardens' Book, 1775.

8 bells thought to weigh—No. 1, 3 cwt.; No. 2, 4 cwt.; No. 3, 6 cwt.; No. 4, 7 cwt.; No. 5, 9 cwt.; No. 6, 12 cwt.; No. 7, 17 cwt.; tenor, 21 cwt.

In 1791 the tenor is stated to weigh 16 cwt. 1 qr.

Note.—The total of these weights does not agree with the previous entry of 1753.

PLATE.

1775. 2 silver flagons washed with gold	.	.	.	65 oz. each.
2 „ cups „ „				
1 „ salver „ „	.	.	.	26 „

R

At a vestry called for the purpose of replacing the Communion
Plate *lately lost*, it was resolved that 2 flagons, 2 cups, 1
salver, and 1 offering-plate, of silver, be purchased by rate
on the whole parish.   They were accordingly provided in
Oct. 1775, by E. Scales, silversmith, Strand, London.

2 silver flagons, weighing about .   .   . 55 oz. each.
2 ,, cups ,, ,, ...
2 ,, salvers ,, ,, . . . 36 oz. the two.

The church plate had, for the second time, been stolen by thieves.

1777. The Plate was now kept at Melford Hall, and was used for
Communions 19 times in that year.
1778. The same was used 14 times.
1780. 22 times.

The following entries also occur in the Churchwardens' accounts.

1782. Paid for a Bassoon and Reeds for the Church Singers, £2 12ˢ 0ᵈ
1784. Paid for Handel's Oratorio of the Messiah, 10ˢ 6ᵈ

The effect must have been solemn and truly grand when played by the talented
Melford musicians with the new bassoon, reeds, and base viol !

1789. Paid for a form of Prayer of Thanksgiving for his Majesty's
recovery, 1ˢ
1797. Paid for building Churchyard stone wall, £5. 1ˢ 6ᵈ
1799. Paid for 3 volumes of Arnold's music books, 13ˢ 6ᵈ
1800. Paid Ringers on account of peace, £1. 1ˢ 0ᵈ
1809. Paid for a Base Viol and case, £7. 2ˢ 0ᵈ
Paid Mr. Blunden for erecting a gothic gallery, and forming a
gothic window in the tower, with door and staircase,
£124. 4ˢ 0ᵈ

This *early gothic gallery* was presumably yet more unsightly than its successor, for it
was replaced by another *gothic* gallery in 1828, having only stood nineteen years.

Paid for painting the pews, £51. 1ˢ 0ᵈ
1813. Paid Ringers for the battle of Vittoria, £1. 1. 0.
Paid Ringers for the Coronation, £1. 11. 6.
Paid Ringers on news of the war, £1. 11. 6.
Paid for an iron chest for the Registers, £5. 5. 0.
1814. Paid Ringers on peace with America, £1. 11. 6.

In 1850 the plate is entered as

Two silver Flagons, weighing about 55 ounces each.
Two Silver Cups.
Two Silver Salvers, weighing about 36 ounces the pair.
All inscribed " Revᵈ ROBERT BUTTS, Rector."

GEORGE LANGDALE }
JOHN HAYWARD } Churchwardens [in 1775].

1850.   The Registers of Baptisms, Marriages, and Burials, which commence January, 1559, amount at this date to 12 volumes.

In 1853 a new silver salver was purchased at the cost of £10. 7s., whereon is inscribed

DANIEL MILLS ⎫
THOMAS BLUNDEN ⎬ Churchwardens.

1869.   The two silver cups, being of very ugly and inconvenient shape, were altered, and gilt internally.

The weight of the tenor bell is stated in 1850 to be 16 cwt. 1 qr., and it is stated also at that date that "three of the Bells have been recently recast."

Since that period another of the bells, which was broken, has been recast, and machinery for chiming by one person has been adapted to the bells.

The following account of the collection of alms to rebuild the Church Tower, destroyed by lightning, and which in its fall injured some of the adjoining parts of the Church, furnishes the date of the occurrence.

RESTORATION of MELFORD CHURCH TOWER, and part of the Church, after Destruction by Lightning.

19*th May*, 1711.   Queen Ann, by her letters patent, under the Great Seal of Great Britain, granted unto the minister, church-wardens, and inhabitants of the parish of Long Melford, in the county of Suffolk, license to ask and receive the charitable contributions and assistance of all her loving subjects " for the enabling them to repair and rebuild their parish church and steeple": and appointed " Sir Thomas Hanmer & Sir Robert Davers, B^{ts}, John Moor, Ch^s Moor, Chas. Firebrace, John Poley, Geo. Golding, Thos. Williams, John Gurdon, Josh. Alston, Thos. Taylor, & Chr^r Appleby, Esq^{rs}, Francis Hutchinson, & Nich^s Cleggatt D^{rs} in Divin^y, Jas. Johnson, Clerk, Chas. John Drew, & Matt^w Richardson, Gentlemen, Receivers & Trustees."

24*th June*, 1711.   The said John Moor, Chas. Firebrace, J. Gurdon, J. Johnson, and Matt. Richardson, under their hands and seals, appointed Wm. Green, Edw. Ward, and Hen. Walker, all of Stafford, Gent^n, as their deputies to ask, collect, receive, &c.

These three last-mentioned persons appear to have been the common farmers of briefs at that period.   There is no further available record as to what sums were eventually collected, and happily for the fame of the architect who built the present hideous new structure in 1725, his name is buried in oblivion.

CHAPTER V.

MONUMENTS AND BRASSES, &c.

The Martyn Aisle of Long Melford Church.

IN this aisle or chapel there is an ancient altar tomb of green Purbeck marble, of the same description as that of the old church font. The brasses for a husband and two wives are gone from it; but their matrices remain. This is generally said to have been the tomb of *Lawrence Martyn* and his two wives, and to have had the image of St. Lawrence with his gridiron over him. But only the name of one wife, "Marion," appears in the Martyn pedigree, or is recorded on the external mural inscription of this portion of the church, which was completed through his benevolence, though it is doubtful whether this part of the work was begun in his lifetime, for he is said to have died 1460. Here also is buried *Roger Martyn*, Bencher of Lincoln's Inn, who died 1542, and who had two wives, Mary, daughter of Thomas Mountney, of Mountnessing, in Essex, and Alice, daughter of Forde, of Hadleigh. In his will, made the 20th April, 1535 (proved 14th October, 1542), he directs thus:—"My body to be buryed in the South Ile in Melford Churche, which my father caused to be made, before the image of our Blessed Lady of Pyttie, betwixt my *tombe*, and the place where my last wyfe [Alice Forde] lyeth buryed; and sone after my dethe, *I will there be gravyd suerly in brasse, and sett in the valle ageynst my seyd Tombe*, the true entent of this my last wyll, expressing therein the contynuaunce of my father's preest and myne, keeping of our Obytt daye, paying of the por people: and for the bedrowle according after my mynde as more plainly shall appere afterwarde," &c. This plate was no doubt afterwards taken down, as being superstitious, being the roll of dead persons for whom mass was to be said; but in the south wall, near the tomb, there remains the space where this square brass plate was let into the wall; and also an old holy-water stoup, which was probably near the altar of Jesus, on or near which was the image of our Lady of Pity. There are some large slabs in this chapel which have lost their brasses, and it is not known with certainty to which of the family they belonged; but one *Richard Martyn*, by his will, dated 13th June, 1500, and proved 11th September in the same year, directs that his body be "buried in the South Ile of Melford Church, by my wife," to which aisle he also left £40 for reparation; and to St. James's chapel (Melford Chapel Green) 20 shillings. *Laurence Martyn*, by his will, dated 13th November, 1516, proved 16th December, 1518, directs that his body is to be buried " in the Churcheyarde of Melford Church, on the south side, by the windowe of the *VII Sacraments*."

Brass portraits still remain of *Roger* Martyn, Recusant, who died 1615, aged 89, and of his two wives, Ursula, daughter of Sir Thomas Jermyn, of Rushbrooke, Suffolk, buried at Melford, 30th April, 1562; and Margaret, the second wife, daughter of Walter Bowles, of co. Pembroke, Esq., buried at Melford, 16th April, 1578; and two brasses of their children, six sons (two of whom died very young) and four daughters. The inscription on the brass is " Here lyeth Roger Martin of Long Melford, esquier, who dyed the third day of August, in the yeare of our Lord 1615, and in 89th yeare of his age." His son Thomas, by Margaret Bowles, the second wife, went abroad to the wars when 35 years of age, and was never heard of afterwards.

There is also a brass of *Richard Martyn*, son of the above Roger, and of his three wives, Eleanor, daughter of Francis Mannock, Esq., of Gifford's Hall, Suffolk; Barbara, daughter of Thomas Daniel, Esq., of Acton, Suffolk, buried at Melford, 29th July, 1592; and Alice, daughter of Edmund Smith, Esq., of Tuddenham, Suffolk. The inscription is simply " Richard Martin died the 8th of March, 1624, etat. 65 years." There were also four shields of arms, the brass of one of which remains, and three brasses of babies, the brasses of two of which remain. There is also a brass of a young man and a child together, and a square matrix of a brass.

The last Martyn memorial is for *Sir Roger Martyn*, the third baronet, who was born 1689; married 5th June, 1739, Sophia, daughter of Brigadier-General Lewis Mordaunt, brother to the Earl of Peterborough: she died 22nd Dec., 1752. The inscription is, " In memory of Sir Roger Martyn, Bart., who died ye 4th June, 1761, aged 73 years."

Among the other Martyn slabs which have lost their brasses, the following remain in the Martyn chapel with their matrices only, in the stones.

One for a man and his two wives, another for a woman, with four shields of arms.

The following were also in this chapel, but are now in the south aisle.

A slab with the matrices of two women with a scroll over them, and two shields of arms.

A slab with the matrices of a man and two wives, and of two brasses for children.

A slab with the matrices of a man and two wives, with a shield of arms, and of two brasses for sons and daughters.

There was also in this Martyn chapel or chancel an old pew, with much quaint and grotesque carving, and with the arms of Martyn, Eden (1st wife of Richard Martyn, who died 1572), and others. This pew was removed at the last restoration of the church : its panels are now at Melford Place.

The cloth-marks of the Martyns, who were settled at Melford from the time of Richard II., appear on thirteen stone shields outside and above the Martyn chapel, bearing also the initials of Laurence and Roger (or Richard) Martyn.

CLOPTON MONUMENTS.

In the record of the church, notice has already been made of the recessed tomb in the north wall, in which is the effigy in armour of Sir William Clopton, who died in 1446, and who was the father of John Clopton, the great benefactor to the church.

On a brass plate below the figure of Sir William Clopton is an epitaph in queer doggerel Latin, as follows :—

> " Dapsilis et largus, prudens, et in omnibus Argus
> Artibus et gnarus, generoso sanguine clarus,
> Conditur hoc Tumulo Clopton Will'us in arto,
> Sed nimis exiguo, tanto virtutis Amico.
> Hic dum vivebat prudentis nomen habebat
> Juste ; nam cunctis dare suevit sensa salutis ;
> Consiliumque petens fit lecior inde recedens
> Quam veniens : nempe discordes pacis amore
> Nectere gaudebat, dape quos propria refovebat.
> Pauperibus patuit sua janua semper, abivit
> Nullus ab hac vacuus indigena seu peregrin'.
> Quid moror ? heu fera mors . . . . ut rata vult sors
> M. C. quater, sexto Christi quater X simul anno
> Huic mundo rapuit qua Xpo. hoc quievit,
> Augusti mense, post festum virginis alme,
> Quarta nempe die, Bernardi vigiliaq:
> Huic thori socia fuerat Margeria bina :
> Prima fuit nata Darcy, Frauncesq: secunda."

On the recessed sides of the tomb there had been brasses, of which the matrices only remain.

Near his tomb is a fine brass of his second wife, Margery Francys, in her coat of arms. She died 1424.

The name *Darcy* in the last line of the epitaph was a mistake of the engraver of the brass, for *Drury*. His son, John Clopton, who died 1498, is buried near his monument, commonly called the Easter tomb, in the recess of the chancel, which is open also to the Clopton Chapel.

This tomb is of Purbeck marble. The site on which it, like similar Easter tombs, is erected, was in old days esteemed the most holy place of sepulture; and from its use as a table for the sacred vessels and elements on sacramental occasions, it was coveted by the pious for their last resting-place, that when the congregation came to pay their devotions to our Lord's Body at the holy seasons, they might be moved to pray for the repose of the souls of those interred in the Easter tomb, who were generally persons of rank or note. At certain seasons lights were kept burning before it: there were the "Common light;" the "Batchelors' light;" and the "Husbandmen's," or married men's, light.

In the vaulted arch over this tomb there are fresco portraits of John Clopton, his wife, and their children; but they are now, alas! almost obliterated, from neglect and mischief; but a figure of our Saviour is still fairly discernible. He is dressed in a green and red garment, and shows the wounds in his side, feet, and hands, and drops of blood on his forehead, but without a crown of thorns. In his right hand he bears a cross with a small banner attached, with a red cross on it. His left hand is raised in the act of blessing, and over him is the inscription, "Omnis qui vivit et credit in me non morietur in æternum."

Near to this tomb, in the chancel floor, there was a large monumental stone slab to Sir William Clopton, Knight (son of John Clopton), who died 20th February, 1530, aged 80 years. This slab has been removed to the north aisle floor. All the brasses are gone from it, except one shield bearing the arms of Clopton impaling those of Sir William's first wife, Joane, daughter of William Marrow, who was Lord Mayor of London in 1455. His second wife was Thomazine, daughter of Thomas Knevit, of Stanwey, in Essex. There is still remaining in the Clopton or Kentwell Aisle, a very perfect brass effigy of *Francis Clopton* (died 1558), son of the last-named Sir William Clopton by his second wife, Thomazine Knevit, with the arms of Clopton impaling those of Francis Clopton's third wife, Bridget, daughter of Robert Crane, Esq. (His two other wives' names were Nevil and Hasset.) There is also a fine brass of a priest, with four shields of Clopton: this is probably Sir W. Clopton's younger son by Joane Marrow, "Robert Clopton, a Priest, 22 Henry VIII." There is another slab with the brass of a young lady without coat of arms (? circa 1480), and a fine brass portrait of the wife of a Clopton (circa 1430), besides the before-mentioned one of Margery Francys, 1424; and several other slabs which have lost their brasses, and of which only the matrices remain: these following are now in the north aisle; viz.—

Of a man and his two wives.

Of an inscription and a shield, but with no figure.

Of a man and his wife.

Of a man and his two wives—from his mouth had issued a scroll, and there had been an inscription under them—and a small brass above.

Of a man and two shields of arms.

The slab already noticed of Sir William Clopton and his wife, of which only the brass of one shield, Clopton impaling Marrow, remains.

Of a man, and two shields of arms, and of a small brass under.

Of a man and wife.

Of a man, with a legend issuing from his mouth—a shield of arms, and he has had an inscription under him.

Of a man and his two wives, with sons and one daughter.

Of a man and his wife.

It may be incidentally here noted that of 55 portraits in brass which were recorded as in this church, only 24 now remain. Some of the stone slabs were under the pew floors.

In a slab in the floor, near to the door of the Kentwell Chapel, there is a brass plate, which bears the following inscription :—

"Depositum Thomæ Clopton Armiger, sub hoc marmore tumulati filii et hæredis (quatuor grandioribus natu fratribus Thoma, Francisco, Willielmo, et Georgio sine prole extinctis), Willielmi Clopton, Armigeri, et Mariæ filiæ Georgii Perient, generosi, secundæ suæ conjugis. Iste Thomas ex Maria uxore sua filia, Elizabethæ Mildmay consortis suæ duobus susceptis filiis Williellmo Clopton, Milite, et Waltero Clopton, Armigero, et filiabus totidem Elizabetha et Maria nuncupatis placide in Domino obdormuit die xi Feb⁻ A. D⁻ᵈ MDXCVII°, A. xL Regin. Eliz. superstite relicta eadem Maria quæ duobus a viri charissimi morte non exactis annis die xix Decemb⁻ A. D⁻ᵈ MDXCIX° A. xLII Reginæ ejusdem ultimuᵘm natuᵐ debitum persolvit et sepelitur in Ecclesia Sancti Martini Westmonasteriensis."

This Thomas Clopton's will was dated 25th January, 1597, and proved 16th May, 1598; buried 16th February, 1597. He married, in 1591, Mary, daughter of Sir William Waldegrave, of Smalbridge, Knight. She died 1599. Their eldest son, Sir William Clopton, Knight, married, first, Anne, daughter of Sir Thomas Barnardiston; and secondly, Elizabeth, daughter of Sir Giles Allington. The tablet to the first wife is in the Kentwell Chapel.

The Kentwell Chapel, or Clopton Chantry, as it is differently called, had been at one time very richly and elaborately ornamented, though now sadly defaced. Underneath it are the vaults of the Cloptons and subsequent owners of Kentwell. There are two stone sedilia in the side of the chapel, and a holy-water stoup and credence over, so that doubtless there stood an altar under the window at the east end. It was also apparently partially resided in by a chantry priest, for near the entrance-door there still exists a fireplace with a chimney-flue in a recess, which has a beautifully carved stone ceiling over it; and near to this there is a small window opening into the churchyard, now bricked up, through which he could receive supplies and communicate with persons outside, without leaving the church.

In the corner of the west and south walls there is a very perfect double hagioscope or squint, by which the officiating priest and others in the Clopton Aisle of the church, could see the high altar through the corner of this chapel. In the side wall of the larger squint there remains visible a picture of the Virgin and Child in colours: the Virgin is represented standing on a sort of bracket, and the figures had been thrown into relief by a broad side shadow. They are now unfortunately almost obliterated. In the south wall are beautifully carved, recessed, and canopied niches, in stone, for the twelve apostles; and under them is the arch open from this chapel into the chancel, over the tomb of John Clopton. On that wall are also shields with the arms of Clopton, . impaling several marriages; and in addition to others before-named, there are Fitzlangley, Bellhouse, and Cornard or De Grey. In the north wall is part of a Clopton monument, with a shield of twenty quarterings. Also a tablet with Clopton impaling Barnardiston, of the date of 1615, for the first wife of Sir William Clopton of Kentwell, knighted at Newmarket 20th February, 1613, who died March, 1618, aged 27. His two wives were, first, Anne, daughter of Sir Thomas Barnardiston, Knight, of Clare, Suffolk. She was married at Clare, 1st January, 1610, her husband being then only about 19, and she 16 years old. She died 4th February, 1615, aged 20. The second wife was Elizabeth, widow of Sir Henry Pallavicine, and daughter of Sir Giles Allington, of Horseheath, where she was married to Sir William Clopton, 30th October, 1617. She remarried, thirdly, Sir John Tracy, Knight.

There is also here a monumental slab for Dame Sissellia (died 29th May, 1661), wife of Sir Thomas Darcy, Bart., of Kentwell. She was the daughter of Sir Symonds d'Ewes, Bart., by Anne his wife, who was sole daughter and heir of the above-mentioned Sir William Clopton (by his first wife). Dame Anne was baptized at Clare, 2nd March, 1612. Ladies appear to have married young in those days, for she was only 14½ years old when, on the 24th October, 1626, she married Sir Symonds d'Ewes. Another slab in this chapel is of 1701, in memory of Dame Dorothy, wife of Sir Hugh Middelton. She was a daughter of Sir William Oglander, Bart., by Dorothy, daughter of Sir Francis Clarke, Bart. On the slab are the arms of Middelton impaling Oglander. In the south wall there are also the matrices remaining of several small mural brasses of many figures, the brasses of which are gone.

Nearly the whole of the walls of this chapel had in past times been covered with Scriptural legends and prayers in black letter, now covered with whitewash (perhaps by the Reformers), and, with the exception of a few scattered words, no longer decipherable. These inscriptions appear to have been detached subjects, for traces remain of coloured borders to some of them, separating them from others. The ceiling was painted blue, and had on it leaden six-pointed stars, gilt. The moulded rafters were painted red, with white scrolls on them, bearing alternately on each the words "IHU mercy," "And gramercy." Between the feet of each of the rafters there had been filling-in pieces of carved wood gilt, each bearing a coloured shield of arms of Clopton intermarriages, and beneath them, in black letter, the names of the families represented.   Only one of these now remains (which has been removed from its original place), from which all colour is gone.   The arms were those of Walcote, Azure a lion rampant, Or, impaling Clopton. A sister of Sir Thomas Clopton, who died 1383, married a Walcote. In Collings's book on Gothic ornaments, another shield is shown as then existing (it is now lost), which was evidently Clopton and Francis. Collings also copies two of the verses in this chapel.

Another portion of the ornament is of great interest; it consists of a carved scroll which runs round the cornice of the four sides of the chapel, on the face of which are a series of black letter inscriptions, each of eight lines, in verse, of a religious nature, the authorship of which is attributed to John Lydgate, the learned monk of Bury (a disciple of Chaucer), who died 1440, aged 60.[*]   This scroll was once brilliantly painted.   It commences in the S.-E. corner, with a man's hand issuing from a brown garment, holding the end of it.   The back parts of the turns of the scroll had been red on a green background, and throughout these parts was a beautiful carved running pattern of interlaced green stems and foliage with flowers, having a sort of pine-shaped centre, gilt.   The border under the scroll was red, with a carved roll pattern in gold.

---

[*] Whether these verses are really his, might perhaps be verified by some one who could minutely search the MSS. in the Harleian collection.   There seems, however, but little reason to doubt the fact.   Among Lydgate's works, published after his death, are as follows : "The Sege and Dystruccyon of the Worthy City of Thebes," with reprints of 1561 and 1687 ; "The Lyf and Deth of Hector, one of the fyrst and moste puissante, valyant, and renouned Monarches of the World, called the Nyne Worthys," reprinted in 1614 ; "The Lyves and Myracles of the Sayntes," MS. Harl. 2278, fol. 101 : "The Lyf of Oure Ladye," printed by Caxton between 1470 and 1480 ; "Troye Boke : the Hystorie, Sege, and Dystruccyon of Troye," printed 1513 ; and "The Fall of Princes."   One verse of this latter is here given as an example of Lydgate's style in secular writing, for comparison with the verses in the Clopton chantry ; allowing for this distinction :—

> "Oute of the Frenche I drough it of entent
> Not worde by worde, but followyng in substance
> And from Paris to Englande yt sent
> Onlie of purpose to do you pleasance.
> Have me excusid, my name ys John Lydgate
> Rude of langage, I was not born in France
> Her curious metres in Englisshe to translate
> Of other tonge I have no suffisance."

It seems curious that the poem in the church should never have been transcribed ; but all inquiries have failed to discover any copy of the inscriptions in the Clopton chantry chapel, the greater part of which are now unfortunately lost.

This colouring is now all faded and tarnished, and the scroll has been sadly mutilated in past times by ignorant workpeople. Cracks have been filled up with dabs of mortar, and, worse still, several of the inscriptions have had large pieces cut out of them to admit the heads of iron bolts, let in for some repairs. These misusages, combined with the effect of time, have rendered illegible a great part of the poem; but the portion which remains decipherable runs as follows. Commencing from the hand, on the south side (the parts obliterated being marked with asterisks, and the doubtful words bracketed in italics) :—

(1) Now in the name of oure lord IHS
of right hool herte and in our best entent
our lyf remēbryng froward and vicious
ay contrarye to the commandement
of Crist IHU now wyth avisement
the lord beseeching of mercy and pete
our youthe and age that we have myspent
wyth this woord mercy knelyng on our kna.

(2) O IHU mercy wyth support of thy grace
for thy meke passion remēbre our cōplent
durynge our lyf with many gret trespace
by many wrongh path wher we have myswent:
we now purpose by grace influent
[to I] calle to remembraunce of furfetis don to the
* * * * *
wyth I H S mercy knelyng on our kna.

(3) And under support IHS of thyn favour
Or we passe hens this is hooly our entent
to make the IHS to be chef Survicur†
for our laste wyll set in our testament:
weche of ourself be insufficiente
* * * but mercy and pete
be ƥferred or thou do jugement
to us that calle to the I H S on our kna.

(4) Our wretchil lif to amende and correcte
we us ƥpose with support of thy grace
thy deth thy passion thy cros shal us directe
which suffredist deth IHU for our trespace:
we wreechis unworthy to loke on thy face
thy feet embracyng to which we thankful wynne
wyll we have here leiser tyme and space
they requyrenge thus wole begynne.

---

† This word stands for *supervisor*. In all old wills the testator not only named his executors, but also a supervisor to his testament.

(5) O myghty lord of power myghtyest
wyth oute whom al force is febylnesse
bounteous I̅H̅U̅ of goode goodlyest
mercy to graunte or thou thy domys dresse :
delaye rigr to punnishe our wikkednesse
(*bryng not our trespass*) to remembrance
O blissed I̅H̅U̅ of thy hygh goodnesse
graunte or we deye shrift hosill and repentance.

(6) Though thou be myghty and art eke mcable [? *mercyable*]
to alle folkis that mekely theym repente
we wrecchis contrious [? *contrarious*] and culpable
to alle outragis redy to assent :
but of hool herte and will in our entent
of olde and newe and vecious governance
of youthe and age and of tyme myspent
graunte or we deye shrifte hosill and repentance.

(7) Of our confession receive the sacrifice
by our tonge offerid unto the
that we may feyn in alle our best guyse
meekly with davyd have on us merce :
save alle our soles that they not cankered be
with iron olde ruste of disesperance
whiche of hool herte knelynge on our kne
graunte or we deye shrifte hosill and repentance.

This is the end of the scroll on the south side of the chapel. It then continues round on the west side; but this part is in worse condition than the rest, and only one verse is partially legible; and even this one is very imperfect. The words decipherable in it are (doubtfully) :—

＊ ＊ ＊ ＊ ＊ ＊
heryng this voyse after we shall ＊ ＊
＊ ＊ that place in God ye ＊
and vices al from thens doremewe
thyn holy gost close in that tyme view
parte not lyhtly make such chevesaunce
to encrease in I H S and vices to eschewe
and or we dye shrifte hosell and repentaunce.

The inscription on the north side has been much mutilated, large portions having been cut away to let in the heads of iron bolts, which have been inserted in modern days for coarse repairs. The remains of the verses run thus :—

Save us thyn servants ＊ ＊ in thyn mercy
for lak of whiche let us not be confoundid
[As iron bolt let in ＊ hope stante fynally
here : inscription cut.] ＊ the I H U and groundid :
for our [? *trespase*] I H U thou wert woundid
naked on the roode by mortall gret penaunce
by whiche the power of Satan was confoundid
graunte or we deye shrifte hosell and repentaunce.

With wepyng eyen and contrite chier
[¶ *Hear*] us I H U and our compleyn conceyve
us most unworthy to lok the to [Iron bolt let in here] [¶ *nere*]
whiche in ourself no vertu aperceve :
but of thyn mercy by grace us receive
by synful leving brought unto owtrance
praye we wyth good hope whiche may us not deceyve
graunte or we we deye shrifte hosell and repentance.

Cryenge to the   *   *   *   *   *
whiche with thyn blood wer * and made
and on cherthursday† gaf us to   *
thyn blissed body I H U in forme of bred
to us most synful graunte or we be ded
*   *   *   *   *
that wyth sharpe thorn wer * outreged
or we passe hens shrifte hosell and repentaunce.

And piti our request in especiall
graunte us I H U while we be her alyve
evyr to have emprynted in our memoriall
he rememberaunce of thyn wounds lyve :
[Iron bolt let in here.]   with the speer that did thyn herte ryve
[¶ *the Crown*] of thorn which was no final penaunce
langage and tonge us onely to shrive
the holy uncion shrifte hosell and repentaunce

All the tokens of thyn passion
we praye the I H U grave hem in our memorie
duely marked myd centre of our reson
on calverie thyn tryumphal   *   [Iron bolt]   [¶ *victorie*]
man to restore to thyn eternall   *   [¶ *home*]
by mediacon of thy meke deliverauns
out of the exile vysyt and transitone
when we hens passe shrifte hosell and repentaunce

Of mercy requyreng now in tyme
of our myende the myd poynt most þfound
this woord I H U our fyne witt to enlumyne
in lenghte and bredt lyk a large wounde :
alle idill thoughtes avoyde and confounde
thyn   *   *   *   cast at chaunce
the roop and peler to which thou wer bounde
graunte or we deye shrifte hosell and repentaunce.

Of this prayer mekely we make an end
under thyn mercy full supportacion
precious I H U graunte wherer we wende
to have memorie upon thyne passion :
testymonyall of our redemcion
*   *   *   *   *
*   *   *   *   *
graunte or we deye shrifte hosell and repentaunce.

---

† Char Thursday, or Shear Thursday, was the old English name for Maundy Thursday

This concludes the poem. There are some further verses on the cornice on the east side, but they are of a different character. Some of them are much defaced, and in great part illegible. What remains appears to be as follows :†—

Oh man sette up thine eye an see
what mortall peyne I suffred for your trespace
with pitous voys I crye and seye to the
behold my wounds behold myn blody face :
behold the rebukes that doth me so manace
behold myn enemes that don me so despice
*   *   *   retayn now to grace
was [*myn blood ?*] offered in sacrifice.

Behold my love and geve me now ageyn
behold I died your ramsion for to paye
se how my herte open [*? bleed*] and pleyn
your gostly enimyes only to affraye :
a harder batayle no man myght assaye
of alle the tryumphys the grettest [*? high*]
*   *   ye men no leger [*dette I paye*]
I gav my blood for you in sacrifice.

Turne now agyn your synnys ye forsake
behold and se if ought be left behynde
how·I to mercy am redy you to take
gyve me your hart and bêth no more unkynde :
your love and mỹ togedir doth hee bynde
and lete him never parte   *   *   wyce
when ye wer lost [*? I did you fynde*]
my blod I guevid for you in sacrifice.

Enprynte theese thyng in your inward thought
and grave hem dep in your remembrannce
thynke on theym well and forgete theym nought
al this I suffred to don you allegeaunce :
and with my seyntes to geve you sufficiaunce
in the hevenly courte for you I did devyse
a place eternall [*? of reste and pleasounce*]
for which my blood I offered gavid in sacrifice.

---

† It is curious to compare with these verses, the authorship of which is uncertain, the stanzas (27 in number) at the end of John Hardyng's "Chronicle," called "A lamentable complaynt of oure Saviour and Kyng eternall to sinfull man, his brother naturall." The poem commences as follows :

"Brother abyde ! I the desire and praye
Abyde, abyde, and here thy brother speke ;
Behold my body in this blody waye
Bruysid and betyn with whippes that wold not breke."

John Hardyng was living in the year 1465.

The first five lines of the next verse are quite gone.

    *   *   *   *   *

have on your weye and beth of right glad chier
*   make day [? *forward*] on your pylgrymage
*   now thyn tyme ye shal abide here

    *   *   *   *   *

cometh on my frend myn *   * most [*dear ?*]
for which I offered myn blood in sacrifice.

This last verse, which is greatly defaced, completes the inscription on the scroll border. On the centre ridge girder of the roof, which, like all the rest, had been highly coloured, there were on both sides a series of small labels, each bearing a sentence in abbreviated Latin, and forming a litany. Many of these, which are yet legible, run as follows, each label being here given separately :—

South Side of Centre Girder.	*North Side of Centre Girder.*
Per mysterm nce	Propicius esto
Incanacois tuĕ lib.	Parce nobis dne.
Per nativitatĕ tua lib.	Ab omni malo
Per scam circmsisiōm	Libera nos dne.
Per baptism *	Ab insidiis diaboli lib.
Per temptionem lib *	Ab omni imundicia
Per crucĕ et passionĕ	Mentis et Corpis lib.
Per glor resurcionĕ	Ab imundis cogitaciōbs
Per ascensionem	Improvisa * lib.
Per ğam ɪti spus	
Succure nobis dne.	
In die judicis lib.	

On the lower west girder there is a scroll like the upper ones, on the commencement of which is painted a hooded figure, with the hands joined in prayer. The six inscriptions on this scroll are, with the exception of a few words, almost effaced. In the first verse, the 4th, 5th, and 6th lines remain thus :—

to sle the dragon with hys hedes sevene
dauntyng the power of this * * levene
out of his thraldom to make you God free.

The second verse commences,—

O alle ye daughters of Jerusalem.

But the rest of the verses are too much defaced to make sense of.

In the Clopton or Kentwell chancel aisle, there is placed (by permission) an altar tomb of white marble, in memory of Vice-Admiral Sir Hyde Parker, Bart., who was lost with all hands in H.M.'s ship *Cato*, about 1782; and for his son Sir Harry Parker, Bart., who died

1812. Also above it a mural monument of coloured marbles, made at Malta, erected by the officers and crew of H.M.'s steam frigate *Firebrand*, to the memory of Captain Hyde Parker, R.N., who was killed in storming a Russian battery at Sulina, on the Danube, 1854, aged 29. The inscription runs as follows :—

"In memory of Captain Hyde Parker, of H.M.'s steam frigate *Firebrand* (eldest son of Vice-Admiral Hyde Parker, C.B.), who fell gloriously while leading on his men to the storm of a Russian fortification at the Sulina mouth of the Danube, July 8th, 1854, aged 29 years. The British burial-ground of Pera, of Constantinople, holds all of him that could die ; but so long as a great intellect, a high and spotless character, and devotion to his country, even to the death, can command love and respect, so long will his name live in the foremost ranks of those who died too early for all save their own fame.

"This monument is erected by the officers, seamen, and marines of H.M.S. *Firebrand*, the last sad tribute of their honour and affection."

THE CHANCEL.

In the chancel is a beautiful and very costly tomb of alabaster and coloured marbles (said to have been made in Italy) to Sir William Cordell, Knight, Speaker of the House of Commons, and a Privy Councillor in the reign of Philip and Mary, and Master of the Rolls under Queen Elizabeth. He was granted Melford Hall and manor after the dissolution of the Abbey of Bury. He founded and richly endowed the Hospital of the Holy Trinity in Melford, and died 1580. This fine tomb has six columns, supporting a canopy, on the front of which is his shield of arms in the centre, with a shield of arms at each corner, with many quarterings, and underneath is the recumbent figure of the knight, in armour. At his feet is a cockatrice, which was his crest, which is also represented in all the panels of the canopy ; and in recesses at the back and sides are four female figures of the cardinal virtues. The Latin inscriptions on the monument run thus in two panels :—

> 1st. Hic Gulielmus habet requiem, Cordellus, avito
> Stemmate vir clarus, clarior ingenio.
> Hic studiis primos consumpsit fortiter annos,
> Mox et causarum strenuus actor erat.
> Tanta illi doctrina inerat, facundia, tanta,
> Ut Parlamenti publica lingua foret.
> Postea factus eques Reginae arcana Mariae,
> Consilia, et patriae grande subibat opus.
> Factus est et custos Rotulorum ; urgente senectâ
> In Christo moriens, cepit ad astra viam.
> Pauperibus largus, victum, vestemque ministrans
> Insuper Hospitii condidit ille domum.

This is quaintly rendered in English by Fuller in these verses :—

> Here William Cordal doth in rest remain,
> Great by his birth, but greater by his brain;
> Plying his studies hard his youth throughout,
> Of causes he became a pleader stout.
> His learning deep such eloquence did vent,
> He was chose speaker of the Parliament.
> Afterwards, knight, Queen Mary did him make,
> And counsellor, state work to undertake,
> And Master of the Rolls.   Well worn with age,
> Dying in Christ, heaven was his utmost stage.
> Diet and clothes to poor he gave at large,
> And a fair Almshouse founded on his charge.

2ndly.
> Hunc senait Princeps, senait Respublica tota
>   Esse virum meritis et pietate gravem.
> Vir pius et justus quem non a tramite rectâ
>   Sive odium poterat flectere sive metus.
> Qui quod pollicitus fuerat servavit et idem.
>   Qui vitare malos novit, amare bonos.
> Primus amicitiæ cultor, convictor amœnus;
>   Candidus et vitæ factus ad omne decus
> Nec dubium est qui sic vixit vitamq' reliquit
>   Quin nunc cælicolos spiritus inter aget.

There are many more of the Cordell family buried in the vault in the chancel, but, strangely enough, none have any monumental records. In the chancel are also mural tablets for Sir William Parker, the 7th baronet, died 1830; and for Sir Hyde Parker, the 8th baronet, who died 1856. Also for Admiral Sir Hyde Parker, Knight, and for his sons, Admiral Hyde Parker, C.B., died 1854; Lieut.-General John Boteler Parker, C.B., died 1851, and Lieut. Harry Parker, of the Coldstream Guards, killed while carrying the colours of the regiment at the battle of Talavera, 1809.

———

Among other mural tablets in the church there are monuments to John Moore, of Kentwell, 1753.

Rev. Jas. Johnson, Rector of Melford, 1740-1.   (His son became Bishop of Worcester.)

Elizabeth Parker, of Kentwell, widow, 1833.

Frances Almack, wife of Richard Almack, Esq., 1840; and Jane, wife of the Rev. Henry Buckberry Faulkner, of Westgate House, Melford, 1832.

Mrs. Harriet Oliver, a great benefactress to this parish, had only a hatchment, and no other memorial.

Besides the Martyn and Clopton pavimental slabs there are stones in the floors of the aisles, with inscriptions to the following persons:—

T

South Aisle.

Rev. John Leroo, Rector of Melford, who died 13th January, 1819, aged 65 ; and to his two wives, Mary, who died 21st December, 1793; and Ann, who died 17th October, 1805. This slab was originally in the choir, and the inscription goes on to say, "Their remains are deposited beneath, and two yards to the right of this stone, facing the Altar." (This and some of the other slabs have been removed from their original positions.)

The Rev. Nathaniel Bisbie, D.D., Rector of Melford, who was deprived 1689, for refusing to take the oath of allegiance to King William III. The inscription is very illegible, and a blank piece of stone has been let into it. He is thereon described as "Qui dubiis rebus sibi constans," &c. He died 1695, aged 61. His wife was the daughter of William and Elizabeth Hurton, of Melford.

William Hurton, who died 1723.

John, son of William Hurton and Elizabeth his wife, died 10th July, 1702, aged 1 year and 5 months.

Elizabeth, daughter of the same, died 21st February, 1702, aged 8 months.

John Drew, 1684, inscribed "Spe certi Resurectionis futuræ per Christum ad gloriam mortales reliquæ Johannis Drew nuper de Melford in Com: Suffolk generosum vitam hanc melior. . . . . Kalendar Aprilis Christiana MDCLXXXIIII. Ætas suæ LII. Vixit post funera virtus."

Adjoining this westward, is another slab to a Drew, who died in 1700. This is much worn and defaced, and part of the inscription is illegible :—

"Mors. . . . . Hic jacet. . . . . . . Edwardus Drew nuper de Melford in comitatu Suff. . . . . Novembris anno ætat. suæ LIIIII. . . . . per quam expectat Resurectionem felicem MDCC."

Charles John Drew, Esq., who was murdered at his own door in Hall Street, Melford, in 1740, by his only son, is also buried here. The son was hanged at Bury.

Another slab records the wife of a Drew.

"Spe resurgendi hic jacet Brigitta Sumersett, quondam uxor John Drew nuper de Melford in comitatu Suffolciæ generosi mortem obiit Sexto die Decembris, Æræ Christianæ 1723, anno ætatis suæ. . . ."

Giles Stewart died 19th November, 1764, aged 52, and Anne his wife, daughter and heiress of John Hamond, of this place, who died 13th August, 1779. Also four sons, who died infants.

The Rev. Charles Edward Stewart, who died 7th October, 1819, aged 68. "A wit, a scholar, and a gentleman." Also his wife, Anne Alethea, daughter of Richard Wallin, of the island of Jamaica. She died 19th June, 1790, aged 38 and a half years. Also Elizabeth Lucy, their daughter, who died 19th July, 1800, aged 12 years.

John Hayward died 1st December, 1812, aged 70, and Elizabeth his wife died 16th March, 1825, aged 80.

Mary Beales, wife of William Beales, surgeon, died 15th May, 1807, aged 63, and Mary their daughter, widow of the Rev. Philip Wynter, died 5th Nov., 1807, aged 37; and Anne Beales, also their daughter, died 13th May, 1849, aged 74.

William Beales, M.D., Fellow of Caius College, Cambridge, and Chief Magistrate of Bury, who died 8th Dec., 1820, aged 44.

William Beales, senior, of Cambridge, died 27th April, 1728, aged 83.

Anne, daughter of Giles Stewart, and wife of Thomas Glubbe, of Boxford, born 20th Jan., 1742, died 11th Oct., 1784, aged 43.

At the west end of the *North Aisle* are, Robert Spark, died 10th February, ... aged 62, and Mary his widow (who married George Bolton, Esq.), died 18th August, 1714, aged 74.

John Crisell, formerly of Cavendish, B.A., of Saint John's, Cambridge, died 3rd Sept., 1723, aged 41. In memory of whom this stone was placed by John Moore, of Kentwell Hall, Esq., 13th August, 1749.

Joseph Howlett, Gent., died 8th July, 1781, aged 60.

A curious hatchment which was in this church has been removed to the Lady Chapel, with others. It was of 1635, to Viscount Savage, with many quarterings.

As described in the accounts of Church Furniture, there were in this church several altars, independently of the High Altar. Besides the credence with a holy-water stoup under it, in the Kentwell Chapel, indicative of an altar, and which, as usual, was on the south side thereof, there still exist several credences, which show the sites of altars: viz., on the northern side of the north pier of the chancel in the Clopton Aisle, there is a credence.

To the west of the present north aisle screen, in the north wall (near where the tablet of the Magi now is) there is a credence.

On the south wall of the church, nearly opposite, there is a credence.

Near the oldest Martyn tomb there is a holy-water stoup.

By the north door of the Clopton Chapel, near the recumbent effigy of Sir William Clopton, there is a holy-water stoup.

There is also in the north wall by the Clopton Aisle, a very curious and perfect piece of sculpture in alabaster, which bears traces of gilding and colour, representing the offerings of the Magi. This is the "tabyll of alabaster," mentioned in the churchwardens' accounts of the 2nd of Edward VI., in the long list of "gere takyn down by the Kyngs commandyment": thus, "Item, sold to Mr Clopton the

Alt^r of alebast^r in our Lady's Chapell, vi^s· viii^d· Memoran^d left unto Mast^r Clopton ii stonys at the ends of the Alt^r in Mast^r Cloptons yelde, and the *tabyll of allebaster* in the seyde yelde, and a lytell tabyll in Sent Anny's Chappell, and all the gere th'in, to dres up the Chappel and dyscharge the churchewardens, and *to do yt at hys plesur.*" This sculpture was found beneath the floor, where probably Master Clopton had placed it, in hope that his faith might once again finally, after its changes and reverses, become the established religion of the land, and that this sacred altar-piece might then reappear, *after many days,* when the Puritan rage for cleansing the church had again abated. In this curious ancient basso-relievo of the offering of the Wise Men, the three kings exactly answer to the description given of them by the Venerable Bede. *Melchior*, King of Arabia, having presented the apple of gold, which the infant Jesus holds in his hand, is in the act of offering with his left hand the thirty gilt pence in something like an urn, while with his right hand he is taking off his crown. *Balthazar*, King of Saba, is following with a box of myrrh, and *Gaspar*, King of Egypt, who is young, and has no beard, is the last, and has a jar of frankincense. The pillow of the Virgin is supported by a female, and at the foot of the couch Joseph is sitting in a chair.

This curious relic is in fine preservation, but requires a better setting than it now has, to show it to advantage.

As has been already noticed, there still exist several credences in the church, which denote where altars formerly stood: the following altars are enumerated in the various accounts; viz. the High Altar; Jesus Altar (in the Martyn Chapel); John Hill's Altar; St. Anne's Altar; St. James's Altar; St. Edmund's Altar; Our Lady's Altar (in the Lady Chapel).

As to the images of saints formerly in this church, the roll is a long one, and though some of their niches remain, yet where many of them stood, can now be only matter of conjecture. There were, Our Lady; Our Lady and her Blessed Son; Our Lady of Pity; St. Saviour; Jesus; The Trinity; St. Anne; St. Leonard; St. John the Baptist; St. John the Evangelist; St. Peter; St. Anthony; St. James; St. Catherine; St. Margaret; St. Mary Magdalene; St. Edmund; St. Osyth; St. George; St. Thomas; St. Christopher; St. Andrew; St. Loy (variously called St. Eligius, St. Eloy, and St. Loye, a. 659). All of these had coloured hangings and other ornaments belonging to them; besides which are enumerated sundry cloths for "divers other saints," besides the above 23 named. The niches for the four Evangelists remain in the chancel, and those for the 12 Apostles in the Kentwell Chapel.

There were four if not five priests of chantries here; viz., a chantry founded by William Clopton, of the then yearly value of £6. 6s. 8d. Another by John Hill, yearly value £7. 5s. The master of the

College of Sudbury for the time being had the sole nomination of the priest of this chantry. Another by Jeffery Foot, £6. 13s. 4d. Our Lady's Priest, £4. Mr. Martyn's Priest. Mr. Richard Martyn, by his will, dated 13th June, 1500, bequeathed 8¼ marcs (£5. 13s. 4d.), to be levied yearly for ever on sundry lands, for the salary of a good and well-disposed priest to pray for his and his relations' souls, every holyday, at the altar of the south aisle of Melford Church, and every week-day at St. James's Chapel (on Chapel Green). This was again confirmed by the will of Roger Martyn in 1535, who directed a brass to be placed in the wall of the same south aisle, recording the endowment. This brass is gone, but the place where it had been affixed to the wall is yet plainly visible.

In the churchyard are two tombstones of great antiquity, but bearing no record; besides many others, which, though not so ancient, are yet of interest as connecting-links with old personal histories belonging to Melford. On the outside of the church are also the matrices in the stones, from which several brasses have disappeared.

THE LADY CHAPEL.

Although the present Lady Chapel appears to have been, as to date, the last completed addition to the church, it is certain that the older church had also a coeval Lady Chapel attached to it. In the will of John Waryn, a fuller of Melford, dated 1448, there is a bequest of forty shillings for the reparation and amending of the Lady Chapel. In the will of Richard Moryell (or Meryell) a sum of two shillings and eightpence is left for the mending of the Lady Chapel, *at his interment.* So he was probably buried in the old chapel. The date of this will is 1456. In 1472 Thomas Germayn left to the repairs of the chapel of the Blessed Mary, in the churchyard of Melford, twelve pence. All these bequests clearly refer to the former Lady Chapel.

Old John Clopton, John Hill, and Richard Loveday appear, by the inscription outside the chapel, to have shared in the erection of the new edifice, though John Clopton was the principal person concerned therein. Its rebuilding, as shown in the inscription, was not completed till 1496. As already recorded in the history of the church, John Clopton, by a codicil to his will, dated 1497, left 100 marks (£66. 13s. 4d.) for the garnishing of the Lady Chapel, and the cloister (as he calls it) around it, and which, he goes on to say, he had newly made in Melford churchyard; and we therefore mainly owe to him this beautiful specimen of the architecture of its particular period. This fine chapel has, at various times since the Reformation, suffered every sort of desecration; it was long used as a parish schoolroom, and subsequently, not only as a store-place where past rectors kept their garden-frames and utensils, but even as a coal-cellar and fuel-store, in which yet living persons can recollect hunting rabbits which had got in from neighbouring preserves through the broken doors, in hard winter weather; and many of the windows were blocked up to save reglazing.

Notwithstanding such abominable misusages (which have been now abated) this chapel yet remains very perfect. Its fine carved stonework, and the (now empty) canopied niches for saints, are still fresh, and but little damaged. The plan of the building is curious, consisting of a small choir and chancel combined, round which runs on all four sides a broad aisle, or, as John Clopton, the builder, calls it, "a cloister." This is open to the centre space on the north and south, and is partly closed on the west by a carved stone screen. Among its ornaments are the cinquefoil badges of the Darcy family, and round the cornice is a running scroll of the same pattern as that in the Clopton Chantry, but without inscription. There are also some old monumental slabs in the pavement. It is to be hoped that the restoration of this fine Lady Chapel (of which the cost would not be very great) may be some day effected, when it would again become a perfect architectural gem.

The following entry relates to the conversion of this building into a school for the village.

1670.

Conversion of the Lady Chappel into a Publick Schoole for Melford.

Sir Robert Cordell, Baronet, gave to ye chapel at ye east end of ye church, about to be fitted into a schoole, because it was much ruinated, and under great decays, 3 trees, containing six loads of timber, and a certain wainscotted pew within ye chappell (whereof the master's seats were made) for and towards the finisheinge & repairinge of ye same.

M' Roger Clopton, Clerk, heir of Kentwell (with the consent and approbation of Sir Thomas Darcy, the present proprietor), gave towards ye same 2 trees containing three loads of timber—which timber was imploy'd for ye makeinge of the tables, seats, and benches, and other necessarys towards ye school, and ye resydue thereof was sold.

Subscriptions given to ye repaire of ye same.		£.	s.	d.	Disbursements were	£.	s.	d.
						46	0	4
Total		18	15	0				
Sale of timber		9	6	0				
Other sums		5	2	6				
		33	3	6				
Given by Dr. Bisbie out of his goodwill and free benevolens		12	16	10				
		46	0	4				

Several persons were beneficial hereunto with their carts & teams —particularly John Drew—Rob⁺ Sparke at ye Parke—Will. Caston— Thos. Windle—Robert Hammond of Rowhedge, &c.

This History of the Church cannot be concluded without noticing the state into which, in this century, it had finally fallen.

In the churchwardens' book is a memo., entered under date of 1828, by Mr. Almack, who was churchwarden for many years. Among other things he mentions as follows, as to the then state of the church.

"The roof of the middle aisle was found to be in a state of great decay. It was repaired, releaded, the clerestory walls screwed in, and several hundred pounds expended in necessary repairs.

"The walls of the church had been whitewashed in the upper part, and coloured with yellow ochre below. The whitewash was nearly an inch thick in places. Traces of the 'superstitious pictures,' defaced in pursuance of the injunctions of Edward VI., were visible when the flakes of white were chipped off. The outer doors were painted pea-green. Almost all the pillars of the church were surrounded with pegs for hats, and on the walls were many rows of pegs.

"The windows at the west end of the church were partly blocked up with brick—the south-west one about two-thirds, and the north-west one about a fourth. The windows in the Martin Chapel were also partly blocked up. The great east window was partly blocked up with brick in the centre. At this time Mr. Almack collected from other parts of the church, the old painted glass, now in the east window, and with much toil and care arranged them therein as they now are. The windows of the Lady Chapel were all, except one, filled up with lath and plaster. (Even in late times a rector of Melford, like some of his predecessors, used this Lady Chapel to store his coal and fuel, garden produce and frames and utensils!) The paths of the church-yard were muddy and ungravelled.* The two parts of the old choir-screens, still existing, were much broken, and were whitewashed. The font stood in the north-west corner of the church, painted a stone colour; it had a broken pinnacle cover. The large pews in the church were all of irregular height. The church gates were of wood, decayed. Two of the bells were broken.

"At this time the gallery at the west end of the church was erected.

---

* As has been truly remarked by many writers, in no country is "God's acre" so ugly and ill kept as in England. The old entries as to the churchyard generally only refer to the mending of its pales and gates, except one in 1682, which states as follows: "This year ye churchyard was planted al round with ash trees, but some were cut up by travaillers for sticks, some destroyed by ye poore, few prospered or were permitted to grow." One other notice has been already alluded to, that on the occasion of a visitation, the briars around the church were cut away. In 1665 the Rector says that he fed his horse in the churchyard, and the feed was worth £2. 10s.

"There was an accumulation of much earth, up to the quatrefoil string-course, varying round the church from two to three feet in depth."

Many of these abuses were remedied at that time, and the church made somewhat more decent; yet its state was very unsatisfactory, when, in 1868, it was determined to make a restoration of the interior. It was still disfigured with pews of every size, and of every variety of lining, old green, blue, and red baize, dirty and shabby. The aisles were laid with common clay tiles, covered with dirty matting. The hideous gallery erected in 1828, was still at the west end, with a trumpery worn-out old organ in it; two of the old choir-screens remained, but much mutilated, partially repaired with deal, and painted brown. The fine old font was under the gallery, and was covered with yellow paint; and, in short, the whole appearance of the church was still very lamentable. £400 was borrowed on the security of the church rates, and a large sum raised by subscription of the parishioners generally, towards defraying the expenses.* The cost of restorations of the Clopton Chapel being further defrayed by Captain Bence, that of the Martyn Chapel by Mr. Westropp, and that of the choir by the Rev. Charles Martyn, the patron of the living, and Sir William Parker, jointly. The restoration of the chancel was deferred for a time. A new organ was purchased at a cost of over £500, and a new stone tower arch was built to correspond with the architecture of the church, in lieu of the existing plain, round-headed brick arch of the previous century. The total cost amounted to £3,282. On the Rev. C. Martyn coming to the living, he, as has been already stated, altered, repaired, and restored the vestry, and the priest's chamber adjoining, both of which were in a deplorable state, and made many other good and substantial improvements.

Much remains to be done by the inhabitants of Melford. The restorations of the tower, and of the interior of the Lady Chapel, and the renovation of the stonework of the many windows, are still required. Yet that which has been already accomplished leads to the hope that a new and brighter era has dawned for Melford Church; and that the care of the present and future generations will somewhat atone for the cold and wanton neglect of their forefathers, and may help to restore to the grand old edifice some of the long lost beauties which had been lavished upon it by the old builders and benefactors.

---

* Independently of this, some minor portions of the restoration were undertaken by individuals, and the church porch was tiled by the persons whose initials are on the tiles.

CHAPTER VI.

THE MANOR OF THE RECTORY OF LONG MELFORD.

AS in a measure belonging to the history of this church, the details of the Rectory and its appurtenant manor must be considered in conjunction therewith. As has been already mentioned, the old church of the eleventh century had a coeval endowment from Earl Alfric; but, as has also been explained in the relation of how that grant was afterwards affected by the partition of the church property with the Hospital of St. Saviour at Bury, the possessions of the Church of Melford became diminished; and though some addition was afterwards made thereto, yet the portion appropriated to St. Saviour's never reverted again to it, but at the Reformation fell into secular hands.

From the Chartulary of the Abbots of Bury of their manor of Melford, in A.D. 1287, we can balance the property of Melford Rectory at that time as against its original grant. By the following schedule of tenants and their holdings and rents of the manor of Melford Rectory, it appears that the quantity of land then left pertaining to the Church of Melford was 112 acres, besides a further quantity of about 60 acres, part of which was probably of the gift of Abbot Sampson, and perhaps also included a third of the lands of the before-mentioned benefactress, Juliana de Bonard, to be taken as against the original grant of 261½ acres from Earl Alfric in the eleventh century. It is, however, difficult to trace and reconcile the various quantities of rectory land at different subsequent periods, and in the year 1684 we find the glebe land estimated at 131a. 3r., churchyard included; and it was finally settled in 1839, under the Tithe Apportionment Act, at 129a. 2r. 18p., at which it now remains.

In the survey made in the 14th of Edward I., A.D. 1287, John de Norwold being Abbot of Bury, among the free tenants of Melford, not in demesne, the manor of the Rectory, with all its holdings at that time, is set forth. The entries (translated) run thus:—

"The parson of Meleford holds a manor in the town of Melford, with 100 acres of land, 8½ acres of meadow, 8 acres of pasture, and half an acre of wood, of the holding, from which the aforesaid church is endowed, and he has free right of bull and boar, and he claims the right of assize of bread and ale (regulating the prices of bakers and ale-

U

sellers) of his homagers; and these rights are of the gift and charity of Sampson, formerly Abbot of St. Edmund's.

"Also the said parson holds in the said town of Melford 52 acres of arable land, which his villeins hold of him, with their houses; and 1 rood of mowing meadow, 6 acres of pasture, and half an acre of wood. He has also 7 cottars who hold an acre and a half of land, with their houses, paying 2 shillings a year.

"Johannes, son of Hugo, holds of the said parson a messuage, with 4 acres and 3 roods of land, for 3 shillings and sixpence a year.

"Johannes, the merchant, holds of the said John III acres and III roods of land for 21^d a year.

"Robertus Coyl and Andrew his brother, hold half an acre and a rood of the said parson for 3^d a year.

"Galfridus de Falsham holds of the said parson II acres and a half of land for 5^d a year.

"The said G. holds of Galfridus Alain II acres of land for 2^d a year.

"Johannes, the merchant, holds of the said parson v acres of arable land for 30^d a year by himself and his tenants, and he renders three suits to the Manor Court of the parson.

"Richardus Cole holds of the said John of the same feoff half an acre of land for 2$\frac{1}{4}^d$ a year.

"Adam Vel holds of the said parson XXII acres of land for 9^d a year for himself and his tenants, and he renders three suits a year to the Manor Court of the parson.

"Galfridus Veel holds of the said Adam I acre and III roods of land for 8^d a year.

"Sevicha del Hel holds from the said parson I acre of land for 12^d a year.

"Johannes atte Wattere holds of the said parson I acre and a half of land for 6^d a year.

"Willelmus, son of Hugo, holds of the said parson XII acres of land for 47^d a year for himself and his tenants of the said feoff; and he renders three suits a year to the Manor Court.

"Johannes de Agum holds of the said William I acre and I rood of meadow, and half a rood of pasture for 5^d a year.

"Lucia, sister of William, holds of the said William I acre of meadow for 2$\frac{1}{4}^d$ a year.

"Willelmus Joce holds of the said parson a messuage with an acre and a half of land for 18^d and 3 suits to the General Court yearly.

"Richardus Cole holds of the said parson two acres and a half of land for 11^d, and 3 suits to the Court of the parson yearly.

"Johannes le Huyrer holds of the said parson an acre of land for 12^d, and 3 suits to the Court of the Manor.

" Stephanus de Cranende holds of the said parson one acre and a half of arable land, and one rood and a half of meadow and pasture for 9ᵈ a year.

" Thomas Wyot holds of John de Lausel [Lawshall] one acre of land for 2ᵈ a year.

" Richardus Folk holds of the said parson a messuage with one acre of land for 3¼ᵈ a year, and 3 suits to the Court.

" Willelmus Corpyng holds of the said parson one acre for 4ᵈ a year.

" Henricus, son of Robert the Reaper, holds of Willelmus Palmere a messuage and three acres of arable land for 5¼ᵈ a year.

" Rogerus Harold holds from the said parson two acres of land for 7ᵈ a year.

" Isabella de Ally holds of the said parson a messuage and three acres and a half of land for 12ᵈ

" Walterus le Poer holds of the said parson a messuage with an acre and a half of land for 1¼ᵈ a year.

" The same Walter holds from Juliana Galant an acre of land for 5ᵈ a year.

" Richardus Cole holds of the said parson two acres of land for 9ᵈ and 3 suits a year to the Manor Court.

" Willelmus Paumer holds of the said parson a messuage and two acres of land for 7ᵈ and 3 suits a year to the Court.

" Thomas Wyot holds of the said parson a messuage with three roods of land for 1ᵈ a year.

" Robertus Alwyn holds of the said parson three acres of land for 13ᵈ a year.

" Thomas Wyot holds of the said Robertus an acre and a rood of land for 5ᵈ a year.

" Richardus, the Salt-fish Merchant, holds of the said parson seven acres and a half of land for 22ᵈ a year."

[This latter merchandise was a trade of itself, and an important one; for the population generally lived on salt fish for more than half the year.]

From the foregoing detail, which may also be compared with the Chartulary of Melford Hall, it would appear that the average rental of the arable land of the Rectory or Church land was, in A.D. 1287, at the rate of fourpence halfpenny per acre. Sir John Cullum, in his valuable and learned History of Hawsted, Suffolk, gives the average rental of land there at about the same period, as being fourpence per acre, which very nearly tallies, allowing for the superior quality of the Melford land to that of Hawsted. But it must be borne in mind that a nominal money rent at that time furnishes no criterion of actual value. Till about fifty years prior to the above date, scarcely any coin was in general circulation. Rents were paid mostly in kind, combined with personal services ; and money was, as a rule, only to be found in the coffers of the Barons or other great people ; and though we may consider the purchasing property of a coin in the 13th century, compared with the present time, as being about thirty times its nominal value, yet this affords no definite clue to the relative commercial worth.

As only part of the Rectory land was at that time let, it is difficult to form a correct idea of the value of the whole of the Church property, including its manorial rights, tithes, services, &c. But in what was called "The Domesday Book of the 49th of Edward III.," 1375-6, folio 22, the Rectory or Church property of Melford was then stated to be of the annual value of thirty marcs, or £20 a year.

According to "Cox," it is entered in the King's Books as of the value of £23. 6s. 8d., or thirty-five marcs a year.

Now comparing this with the estimated value of the Rectory before the apportionment of two-thirds of it to St. Saviour's Hospital, of which we have fortunately one record, the increase of value in 200 years is shown.

Jocelin de Brakelond, in his Chronicle of the Abbey of St. Edmund from 1173 to 1202, enumerates the churches belonging to the Abbey, with their respective values in the time of Abbot Hugh, somewhat before the year 1180. He divides them into two classes, one of which he terms the Churches of the Manors and Soccages of the Abbot, comprising 35 churches, of which Melford was one ; the second class he calls the Churches of the Manor of the Convent, numbering 31 churches. Of all these 66 churches and livings, Melford is valued the highest by far, being estimated at that time at £40 a year. So that when, very few years after the above date of 1180, two-thirds of Melford Church had been assigned to St. Saviour's Hospital, the value of Melford Rectory was reduced to £13. 6s. 8d. But in 1375 we find this value increased to £20 a year. In 1534, William Newton, then rector, valued the living, with glebe and manor, at £31. 14s. 6d.

In 1647 this had increased to £183. 3s. 11d. a year.[*] On the restoration of King Charles II. in 1660, after the living had been held by the six Puritan ministers, who, with one exception, left no accounts, the value was still about £183 ; but in the following year, with the return of law and order and increased prosperity and larger

---

[*] Mr. Seth Wood, the first Puritan minister here, gives a detail as to how this amount was made up : viz. Rent of Cranmoor glebe, £42 ; glebe farm near the church, £30 ; churchyard and rent of college house, £3 ; small piece of glebe near Stanstead, 8s. ; glebe grove, 2s. 6d. ; rents of the Rectory manor, £4. 6s. ; and the remainder of the sum of £183 was made up of £103 as the value of the tithes, fees, &c. Twenty years later these rents had only been raised by £3, but the tithes had largely increased ; and in 1673 the tithes to the rector were worth £164. 9s. 6d.

agricultural production, raising the value of tithes whether taken in kind or by composition, it rose to £224. 7s. 11d. The income thenceforward continued to increase, and thus in 1665 we find it £234. 7s. 8d.; in 1670, £260. 19s. 7d.; in 1675, £265. 13s. 9d.; in 1680, £281. 3s. 4d.; in 1685, £290. 13s. 6d.: and so it has gradually risen steadily down to our own time; when, on the Commutation of Tithes, the award of the Commissioners, dated the 13th of June, 1839, based on the averages of grain for seven years, from 1828 to 1835, allotted to the Rector of Melford, in lieu of tithes in kind, a commuted sum of £839. 19s. 3d., which, in addition to the rent of 129a. 2r. 18p. of glebe land and the Rectory, is now the value of the living; to which there is also attached a small manor, with rights over 170 acres, the tenures being fine certain. Dr. Bisbie, in his notes, states that he held the Court Rolls of this manor dating from the year 1412 to 1642, but the Court Rolls from the former date, for nearly 220 years, now no longer exist. It seems somewhat strange what can have become of them, for as Dr. Bisbie held them, it is certain that they had survived the pillage of the old rectory by the Puritan mob in 1642; besides which, the oldest roll now existing of the Rectory manor commences in 1630 and ends in 1641. It is 15 feet in length. Among the early entries in the former ancient, but now lost rolls, of this manor, were the following: viz., in 1418 (1st Henry V.) the surrender of a messuage in Cranmore called "Algors," by John Bonerd to William Bonerd, at a rent of 7 shillings a year, and the labour of one man for a day in autumn. These names are curious, for probably they were descendants of the family of the Bonards, who had possessed land in and around Cranmoor in the year 1199. In 1429, William Gerold, of Glemsford, was presented by the Rectory Manor Court, and fined 20 pence for cutting down an ash tree by Glemsford Mill; and for improperly diverting the course of the stream at Glemsford Mill, this same person was ordered to amend the same under a penalty of £10. In the reign of Henry VII. a grant was made of the site of an ancient mill called Glemsford Mill, to be held of the manor of Glemsford by copy of Court Roll. There is a Glemsford water-mill recorded in Domesday Book. In 1471, Robert Chrysell, of Stanstead, was amerced 20 pence for illegally taking fish valued at 3s. 4d. from the fishery of the manor of the Rectory. In 1507, Margaret att Hill was amerced 6 pence for trespassing with beasts and horses on Stoneyland, near Cranmere; upon which she made a claim before the Manor Court of a right of Boar and Bull, which does not appear to have been denied.

From early days until about the year 1750, the Rectory or Glebe house or Rectory Manor-house, as it was variously called, stood where the parsonage farm near Cranmoor now is. In the agreement made in the King's Court at Westminster in 1199 (already recorded in full), this was called the " Capital Messuage of Cranmere," and seemingly was not part of Earl Alfric's grant; but, subject to some reservations of rights, had been given with the adjoining land to the Church of Melford by Juliana, wife of Richard de Bonard, who died prior to 1199. From a terrier exhibited and delivered at Bury St. Edmunds, A.D. 1613, signed by Francis Clopton and Christopher Tenant, churchwardens of Melford that year, the parsonage house is thus described :—

" The scite of the Rectory containeth an acre, wherein are built one Manour house, containinge twelve severall rooms, smal and great, with an outhouse and the office of the Dairy with five rooms, built in the side of ye yarde : one garden containeing one rood : one orchard planted containeing one rood : al which are inclosed with a moate : one close or ponde yarde, with a sluce, and a swann's tofte, and two fish pondes, and one smal crofte enclosed, containeing halfe an acre : one Dove-coate with a smal flighte of Doves, and one Pound belongeing to the Manour."

The Francis Clopton who made this return was buried at Tostock, the 11th March, 1638.

The old Rectory Manor-house has been pulled down and replaced by a lath-and-plaster double cottage; but at the back, on the west side, there yet remains a portion of the wall of the old house from the ground to the roof, which was part of the main chimney-stack. It is built of stone rubble, with bands of tile, some thin and some of the thickness of Roman tiles, and the corners are formed of dressed stone quoins. It is noticeable that among the flint rubble-work, some pieces of wrought stone have been used, which were evidently once part of the headings of small round arched windows, as though the materials of an even yet older house had been used in the construction of this old wall.

From the low-lying position of this old Rectory, surrounded by water and swamp, it was probably a rather unhealthy site. In 1604, the then rector lost there four of his children from the plague, which at the same time was very fatal in other parts of the parish; and shortly afterwards two more of this family died there. Subsequently, the same rector, the Rev. William Gilbert, removed from this house, and came to live in Melford town until his death in 1618; and he let the old parsonage at Cranmoor with 64¼ acres of land around it, to John Carver of Melford, husbandman, on a three years' lease from 1615, at a tithe-free rent of £38 a year, to be paid half-yearly at Mr. Gilbert's dwelling-house in Melford ; and the Rector reserved to himself half the pigeons or young doves which should at any time be in the dovecote, and also the fishing, fowling, swan-marks, and land swans, and the use of the Rectory manor pound and a barn.

At a subsequent period in the same century, it appears that

another rector, Dr. Bisbie, also let the old parsonage-house to a tenant.

The inconvenient, lonely, and perhaps unhealthy situation of this old house, and its distance from the church, probably led eventually to the erection of another house on the site of the present Rectory, part of which older house is incorporated with this one. In 1775 the new house is described, not as the Rectory, but as a house lately erected, abutting on Melford churchyard towards the north, containing 10 several rooms, with a small yard and garden. In 1784, Robert Butts (son of the Bishop of Ely), the then rector, added to this house two parlours. In 1791 it appears to have been still further added to by Mr. Leroo, the Rector, and it is then described as "the Rectory or parsonage house, lath and plaister walls, and covered with tiles, standing upon one rood of ground, and containing 16 rooms, with offices, court-yard, and garden; part of the building having lately been erected and the rest very much improved by the Rector, Mr. Leroo, and is now his dwelling-place."

The old Rectory at Cranmoor then commences to be described as "a cottage, formerly the parsonage house."

About the year 1832-3 the Rev. Edward Cobbold built on to the present Rectory, and made it externally much as it now remains.

In olden times there stood near the churchyard another house, which was not used as rectory, but was termed the Parish Priest's house, and it was also sometimes called the College. This house was described as standing on the north side of the churchyard, and was bequeathed by the will of Robert Harset, clothmaker of Melford, dated 1484, who, after his wife's life-interest therein, desired that it should belong to the priests of Melford; and especially that the new parlour and chamber over it should be occupied by the priest of Jesus's Altar. The name of "College" may have arisen from the fact that Harset allowed the west end of the house to be used as a schoolroom, "wher the childern lerne"; and he expressly desired that the said portion should continue to be so used. This house, which Harset valued at twenty marcs (£13. 6s. 8d.), contained eight rooms, a stable, and a little house adjoining, with a yard before and behind. A priest (not the Rector) dwelt and had a chamber there, with a lock and key. One rector, however, Parson Malet, is recorded to have lived in this house in the reign of Queen Mary (1553—1558). Some of the chantry priests, such as Sir Richard Dodington and Sir John Gayton, are mentioned as occupants; and as late as 1679, the Rev. Samuel Middleditch, who was Dr. Bisbie's curate, lived in the lower story of this house, and held the garden, paying a rent of £1 a year.

This house is represented in old maps of 1580, 1613, 1619, and 1677, and was more fully described as standing near the churchyard stile, and as being bounded on the south by the churchyard, on the west by the manor-house of Monks, on the north by the yard of the said house of Monks, and on the east by the barn of the said manor-house. (This manor-house and the parish priest's house have both been long pulled down).

About the year 1567, the owner of Kentwell, Francis Clopton, claimed the priest's house and took possession of it; but on what ground he founded his claim does not appear; and the proceeding was the more strange, as his ancestor, old John Clopton, was the supervisor of Harset's will, and, from the expressions contained therein, the Clopton family evidently enjoyed the testator's implicit confidence. Mr. Clopton's arbitrary proceeding led to some litigation, and for many years this house was in dispute and going to decay. The following letter was written on the subject by Sir William Cordell, then Master of the Rolls, dated 1567, to Mr. Simon Cawston, a yeoman, who farmed some of the tithes, and was tithe-gatherer to *Mr. Humphrey*, at that time the parson of Melford. This letter clearly expresses Sir William Cordell's opinion, as a lawyer, of the rights of the case, and from its context also shows that, subject to the right of a room in the house for the use of an officiating priest, the remaining part of the house was let by the Rector to his tithe-gatherer or farmer, who again sublet it to a tenant. Thus, in 1608, one Robert Playle hired the garden, the kitchen, with two rooms over, and the great chamber over the hall, for twenty shillings a year.

The letter runs thus :—

" To my loveing neighbour, Simon Cawston, at Melford.

" Neighbour Cawston,

"I understand by your letter that my Cosin* Clopton hath given warning unto Ward, your tenant, of the Parish Priests house in the Churchyarde to pay no more rent unto you. I marvel he will show so much folly therein to challenge that wch his father and his ancestors never had, but hath continued with the parson. Keep you the possession of it, as you may doe by the order of the law: and if he have any right unto it, let him demand it against the parson and you, and if he doe recover it lett him enjoy it: But I think it will be too hard for him to recover it, and you shall have my help soe far as I may lawfully doe, and therefore let me be advertized as you shal have occasion. Thus, with my hearty commendations to you and your wife, fare you well.

" From the Rolls this 7th of November, 1567.

" Your loveing neighbour and friend,

" WILL^M CORDELL."

* Distant cousin by marriage, Sir Wm. Cordell having married Mary Clopton.

The Cloptons, however, continued to hold and to let the house until 1613, when they abandoned their claim; but the house had fallen into a ruinous state, and no one would repair it, though it appears that in return for its use by the parish priest, and also as a vestry for the transaction of parish business, it had formerly been repaired by the churchwardens on behalf of the parishioners; however, prior to the year 1660, they denied their right, and refused to repair it. This again led to litigation between the then rector, Dr. Bisbie, and the parish, which resulted, in 1665, in his obtaining full possession of it, when he dealt with it as shown in the following memorandum, written by him in 1669 :—

Memorandum, dated the 4th May, 1669.

THE CHURCH HOUSE.

"The house called ye Church house, anciently employed for ye service of the Church, contained in length 76 foot, and in breadth 41 foot and an half, besides a little yard at the west end thereof—and it abbutted West on ye foresayd yard—North on ye Churchyard—East and South on ye yard now Charles Ward's, (late Haxall's) and is held by Copy on ye manor of ye Rectory, and pays rent per annum xviii pence, and ye foresayd yard per annum r^4

"Anno 1660, when Nathaniel Bisbie, D.D., Rector of the Church of Melford, came first into ye liveinge, he found the foresayd house in very great decay, especially as to the East part thereof; neither would the Churchwardens, or others of the inhabitants of Melford, pay its customary rent or do such suit and service at ye Lord's Courts, as was usuall to be done for ye same—though notice was duly given to them openly in ye Church upon a Sunday after Evening Service, and moreover by Josias Lee, ye bailiff, afterwards at their own houses.

"Wherefore the said house was put into proclamation and soe continued for two or three years: in which space of time it was presented (for being much in decay) at ye episcopal visitation anno 1661, into ye Bishops Court at Norwich: but found noe redress: wherefore, in 1662, Doctor Bisbie cited John Knopp and Thomas Halstead, Churchwardens, into ye Court at Bury, to shew reasons why they, (as formerly their predecessors had done) should not repaire it; upon which the chief inhabitants of ye towne being called together after Evening Service, into ye Chancell, concluded that it should forthwith be done, and accordingly ordered ye Churchwardens by a writinge under their hands to certify ye same into ye Court, and thereupon the Court was satisfyd.

"Nevertheless the house sunck more and more under its ruins, and for two years more nothing was done. Whereupon at an

Ecclesiastim Visitation for ye Church of Melford, the then visitors were desired to take cognizance of it—but upon weighing, adjudged, that it did not belong to them, nor their Court to enforce its repaire.

"This being understood, address was made to Sir Robert Cordell and Sir Thomas Darcy (both inhabitants of the towne of Melforde and Justices of the Peace) to intreat their interest, and power to interpose, that if possible, an utter devastation might be prevented :—Whereupon rates by them were offerred to be made, for its sudden repaire, but by ye rest of ye inhabitants opposed. Afterwards free subscriptions by them, ye parson and some others tendered, but without success. Wherefore the parson (as Lord thereof) took advantage of the forfeiture and caused the house to be seized for him, and to his use, Anno 1665.

"The seizure being made, the parson pulled down all ye East end of it unto ye great chimney, containeinge in length 52 feet. The tyles of ye same being generally blown off, the walls broken down, the floor and joyces all rotted, insomuch that it could not in anywise endure ye hardship of another winter: and of its ruins raised the sum of £19. 7. 6.

"The parson being thus imbursed with the foresayd £19. 7. 6. repaired ye other end of ye forementioned house, and settled it upon ye parish Clerk, 'durante beneplacito' (as will appear by ye Court Rolls belonging to ye Rectory) intending ye same for him and his successors in that office, towards the encreas of their maintenance; and with ye remainder made up the vestry, which was then useless, for ye like offices of ye towne as ye foresayd house was designed for ; where-upon he disbursed on the whole £20. 19. 9. Soe that the parson instead of enriching himself by what hath been done, is out of purs thereby the sum of £1. 12. 3, and willingly gives ye same to ye uses above sayd—and furthermore protests that if by any art or means he could have prevaild upon ye inhabitants of the town to have repaird ye sayd house, he would never have seized upon it, or pulled it downe.—In witness whereof he hath put to his hand the day and year above written.

" NATHANIEL BISBIE."

Another memorandum goes on to state that " Sir Robert Cordell of Melford Hall, Baronet, did after ye wastinge of the foresayd house, for himself and ye conveniencys of his family, build an house, called a coache house, upon part of the ground whereon ye sayd Church house lately stood, on ye East end thereof, affixinge ye same unto ye sayd house; wᵗ sayd Coache house he at present useth for the bestowinge his coach and horses duringe his or his family being at church upon Sundays and Holydays ; and as for all other days and times, ye parish Clerk enjoys the same for such uses as he thinks good."

Sir Robert's act appears to have been an arbitrary one, for there is a note added to this entry in Dr. Bisbie's writing, "Quo jure?"

This furnishes rather a quaint illustration of the fashion of that day; the fine ladies and gentlemen from the Hall declining to walk even up the Green to church, but requiring, every Sunday and Holyday, their ponderous coach and horses to draw them the few hundred yards which intervened between the Hall and the Church, and then having a shelter on the spot for their grand equipage during service-time, before reconveying the smart gentry their three minutes' drive home in state, before the eyes of the admiring rustics. Yet these great people, on a quarrel with the Rector, refused for several years to give him any Easter offering, which was then customary from all classes; and we find them afterwards, repeatedly, from 1676 to 1681, presenting to the Rector, at Easter, the munificent gift of *two pence*, which was the smallest sum that any poor person in the village contributed.

The duty of collecting these Easter offerings appears at that time to have devolved on the curate, when there was one. Sometimes the gift was in kind, in lieu of money; thus in 1684 the parson received one pair of silk gloves, which he valued at 6s., and another pair of gloves worth 5s. There is also mention of an *Apricock* tree, worth 1s. And there is a notice of an offering to the Rector by Lady Darcy, on the occasion of her being churched, of gloves worth 18s. 4d.

Two of Dr. Bisbie's curates are named; viz. the Rev. John Firmin, who became rector of Stanstead; and the Rev. William Steuckley.

In the long list of 47 rectors of Melford, already enumerated, there is a hiatus from 1643 to 1660, during which time six Puritan ministers were in possession of the living. Suffolk, as one of the associated counties during the Rebellion, was decidedly Parliamentarian, anti-Royalist, and Puritan in its sentiments and sympathies, and these ministers appear to have been well and cordially received, and to have been liked by the inhabitants of Melford, as shown by the testimony of one of them who was five years in possession, and by the character given by Dr. Bisbie of the last one; and another of them continued till his death, and his son after him, settled in the parish after the Restoration, and resided in Westgate Lane, and acquired some property there. A few particulars concerning them exist thus in the quaint expressions of that day, which also refer to the plunder of the Rectory by the Puritan mob, a further account of which will be found in the chapter relating to Melford Hall.

"On or about A.D. 1643, the Rev.ᵈ Doctor Warcyn, D.D., Rector of Melford, after holding the living for 25 yeares, was most unjustly (by the then prevailing powers) sequestered from his benefice and parsonage of Melford, he being one of the first, upon the rebellion breakinge oute, that was plundered by ye rabble rout of ye countree [in 1643], insoemuch that not onely the writeings and other the evidences of his owne time, but those alsoe that did belong to Mr Gilbert, Doctor Jones, and other his præddecessors, were supposed and confidently said to be lost and destroyed, through ye rudenes and fury of the then enraged misguided multitude.

"The Reverend Doctor being as aforesaid, for his Loyalty sequestered, the Revenue of ye sayd parsonage of Melford was granted by the Committee of Parliament, for that and such other like purposes then sittinge, unto Mr Seth Wood, late minister of Lenton in Lincolnshire, by order bearinge date the 30th daye of October, Anno D^ni 1643."

In 1648 Mr. Seth Wood resigned, and returned to Lincolnshire, being succeeded at Melford by Mr. Samuel Boardman, his brother-in-law, of the same faction, to whom he wrote the following letter relative to such portion of tithe as he conceived to be due to him on quitting the sequestrated benefice, his stay in which appears to have been all along uncertain, as he says that he was under an engagement to return to Lenton.

"1648.   Dr Sir,

"That I may doe you that succede me noe wrong, nor injure my neighbours of Melford, from whom I have received all civil respects, you may hereby take notice, that I shall leave wholly to your use the great tithes of Corn & Hay, craveinge onely some allowance as you shall think meet in your discretion, for such hay as became due before my departure and your entrance: which yet I would not gather, because I would not render intricate your account with the neighbours. I have received onely for my labours sinc the last harvest (though I stayed till the poynt of this present harvest)—some tithes &c., of some persons (as per schedule), of other of whom either through straights of times, or their refusal to pay me till they saw who should succeed, I could not get them :—I desire you therefore let Thos: Lee the Sexton gather them in your name for me. What you please to allow me for the Hay, or what shal come to your hands of these Tithes, or the arrears of Lord's Rent, if you keep a Court, I pray you give it into the hands of Mr Hobert, and hee will conveigh it to me in Linconshire.

"This is all S^r, more then my most fervent wishes y^t Melford may proove an happy province to you, and that you may bee a full blessing in the Gospell to them. Soe prayeth y^r poor predecessor and fellow-servant to our best Lord.

"Seth: Wood."

During this sequestration of the living until the Restoration, the following Puritan ministers, whom the Churchmen called intruders, were deputed by the Rebel Parliament to take clerical charge of Melford, and to receive the profits and tithes of the Rectory :—

1. Mr. Seth Wood, who was appointed in 1643, but resigned Melford and returned to his former cure in Lincolnshire in 1648.
2. Mr. Samuel Bordman, brother-in-law of the first minister, appointed in 1648. He died in 1653. His son continued to live at Melford for many years after the Restoration.
3. Mr. Ralph Brideoak, appointed probably in 1653.
4. Mr. Seth Wood. (Query: was he a son of the first minister ?) ·
5. Mr. Peter Sainthill.
6. Mr. Claudius Salmasius Gilbert. Dr. Bisbie describes him as "the honestest, peaceablest, most learned, and best principled of y* packe ; who, if he had not wanted a good title, might have deserved as good a liveinge."

Two of the above-named Puritan divines had been ministers in other parts of Suffolk before their appointment to Melford ; for in the "Humble Petition of the Ministers of the Counties of Suffolke and Essex concerninge Church Government, presented to the Right Honourable the House of Peers, on Fryday, May 29, 1646," two of the signatures among the Suffolk ministers are those of "Mr. Samuel Bordman" and "Mr. Peter Sainthill." Mr. Bordman's son Samuel continued, after the Restoration, to reside in Westgate-lane, Melford, and acquired property here ; and there is an entry in the Court Rolls of the Rectory Manor, dated the 15th September, 1662, to the effect that he was amerced, for setting and continuing his pale upon the lord's waste, the sum of sixpence, and had warning given him to remove the same before Christmas following, under pain of an amercement of 3s. 4d. In 1663 this waste was granted to him at a quit-rent of 6d. a year. He also owned the Black Lion Inn, and he lived to the year 1670.

These ministers' tenure being very uncertain, and in the disturbed state of the land it being difficult to enforce legal rights, they seem to have gladly accepted any composition which they could secure, in lieu of tithes and other profits ; and thus, at the Restoration, the income of the Rectory had certainly not improved, and the church had also been allowed to decay, for the ministers would not repair their part of the chancel, and Sir Robert Cordell, taking advantage of the reign of confusion, and the patronage being taken out of his hands, also refused to repair his part, endeavouring to make them believe that they ought to repair the whole.

With the Restoration law and order returned, and Dr. Warcyn was reinstated in the Rectory and benefice, from which he had been sequestered nearly seventeen years, at the close of his very advanced life. Whether Dr. Nathaniel Bisbie, who succeeded him shortly after, acted as his curate, does not appear plainly. He was then a young man of 26, and in orders, an M.A. of Christchurch, Oxford, and afterwards D.D.; and in the following year, Dr. Wareyn, who was worn out with age, let to him all the profits, tithes, rents, &c., of the living, which had become due during the preceding year, for the sum of £120. Old Dr. Wareyn being then of the great age of 96 years, and, as he himself said, " superannuated and unfit for the further service of the Church," voluntarily resigned the living into the hands of the patron, Sir Robert Cordell, of Melford Hall; and his urgent request that Dr. Bisbie might succeed him in the living, was complied with. The old doctor died very soon after his retirement, and was buried at Borley, in Essex, the 9th July, 1661.

Dr. Bisbie was instituted 12th November, 1660, by Dr. William Juxon, Archbishop of Canterbury (Dr. Anthony Sparrow being then Archdeacon of Sudbury), and he was inducted on the 14th November, by the Rev. Francis Craven, vicar of Acton. During the thirty years that he held this living he greatly improved its value, and zealously asserted the Church's privileges, and recovered many of its lost rights, though this involved him in repeated litigation. Many of the present inhabitants of Melford can remember how sore and vexed a subject was the gathering of tithes, whether in kind or by composition, before the Act for their commutation; and how fruitful a source of contention it was between the parishioners and the Rector, and what ill blood it often caused. It was the same in Dr. Bisbie's day; and though the matter of detail of tithes is now no longer of consequence to us, yet from the care bestowed by him on this subject, laboriously as he has recorded it all, much clear knowledge is gained of Melford in his day; and, being obliged to push his researches into the past, he becomes to a considerable extent the historian of this parish.

Commencing with the time when he began to farm the tithes, &c. from Dr. Wareyn, his grievances began; thus, quoting his own words and quaint diction :—

" Beinge a stranger to ye place and altogether unexperienced in sæcular concerns, and not capacitated to claime or demand the respective dues till ye yeare was elapsed, I was forced to take accordinge to ye former composition made by ye intruders [he always calls the six ministers thus] : and indeed the Church had been soe pilfred, and the revenues thirof soe embezled, through the late times of sequestration, some payeinge noe tithes, some little instead of much, few or none above halfe their dues, that upon account I found myself, had not ye resignation devolved ye liveinge upon me, a looser rather than a gainer by ye bargaine.

" In 1661, the Revenues of ye liveinge were this year £183 : 0 : 11 : Among other offrings I received of my Patron and his Lady, out of their goodwill and respect, for a sermon preached by me upon ye 30th daye of January, beinge ye daye of ye martyrdome of Kinge Charles ye first, there being noe law known at that time for ye constraininge and enforceinge ye same, in *gold worth* : £2 : 6 : 0.

"Many other of ye inhabitants of Melford ought to have payd tithe to me, who did not doe so :—For beinge accustomed in the late times of confusion to pay none, or but little, and takeinge advantage of myne unacquaintance with them and their estates, they woulde not discover to me what my dues were, nor where they were to be taken, nor how :—Soe that for this yeare alsoe, I was imposed upon by some, and defrauded by others.   The Clown resolveing, if possible, to be too hard for the Schollar !

"The custome of Melford for great Tithe to the Rector, was based upon a valuation sette upon ye yearly rents of ye landes in the Parish, according to an Act of Parliament for the Revenue of ye Poll money, made Anno 166$\frac{2}{4}$, by Robert Sparke, Thomas Halstead, & John Knopp, inhabitants of the said Parish.

"The customs of the Small Tithes were then as followeth: viz.

"Those whose houses stand in the Hall Streete of Melford pay for the herbage of every cow they doe keepe, yearly, one Penny.

"They that dwell oute of ye sayd streete, and elsewhere within the parish, pay yearly for every cow they doe keepe, Four Pence.

"The Parson is to have the seventh calfe throughoute ye parish, if soe many happen to fall: and if not, then he is to take four Pence for every calfe under the number of seven : and if there chance to bee eleven Calves or more, then he is to have one Calfe in kinde, and Four Pence apiece for the other.

"If there bee four Lambes or less, the Parson is to be allowed Three Half-pence apiece for every one of ye said lambes : but if there bee five lambes, then the lambe is to be valued by the owner, or else by ye parson, and ye parson to take ye lambe or else one halfe of ye money for which ye lambe was valued.

"And soe of Swine, he is to have the seventh Pigge.

"Of Geese the seventh Goose.

"Of Wool, either the tenth Pound, or the tenth Shillinge.

"Of Hops ye tenth Pound.

"Of Apples, Pears, &c., tithe also.

"These tithes had been leased to Mr. Hobart of Melford, but the memory of these things through the length and confusion of ye time wearinge off, and noe enquiry beinge made concerninge them, the full knowledge of them came to be lodged in M⟨r⟩ Hobarts breast onely, whose self interest was at that time soe great, and whose conscience afterwards soe large, that he would have swallowed most of them, those especially which lay on ye east side of ye waye leadinge from Sudbury to Bury, prætendinge they belonged to him by Vertue of a lease from ye Hospitall, and that they were within his precint;

had not I, by a diligent and chargable enquiry into forrayn records and writeings, encouraged thereunto by several broken papers of Doctor Wareyn's, received from his executors, resolutely put a stop unto ye same, and possessed myself, as opportunity favoured me, with many of ye tithes : and thus have I waded through ye enquiry whether there be any such tithes as are, and are called, partible tithes. But beinge perfectly tired with ye long and wearisome pursuite of these matters, I must for the present dismiss the enquiry, and give a small respit and divertisement to myself."

The details of inquiry into tithes after this are extremely minute and very voluminous, though they are now but of little interest, excepting in a few details. It appears that in 1581, 1582, 1583, the parsons gathered the tithes of Lineage and Spelthorn woods in kind, taking from Lineage one year, 9 loads, and in the year 1671, from Spelthorn, 16 loads, worth 8s. a load.

In 1672–3 a quarrel arose between the Rector and Sir Robert Cordell, of Melford Hall, the patron of the living, on the double subject of tithes and the right of sitting in the chancel (as so called, but really in the choir) of the church ; Sir Robert claiming to be free from all tithes, great or small, on the old demesne lands of Melford Hall. It was evident that he was in error as to these tithes, but he was obstinate in the matter, and a suit was commenced against him. A similar case had been tried in 1608–10 by Mr. William Gilbert, who was rector from 1599 to 1618, against Sir William Waldegrave and others, trustees of William Clopton, their ward, as to demesne tithes, &c., which came to the Kentwell estate, on the partition of the Abbey lands. This suit was finally adjusted in 1614. Dr. Bisbie, desiring to get a copy of the old bill and the answer thereto, communicated with a lawyer in London thereon. The following reply from him is curious as showing the state of the public records at that time :—

"London, Dec' 3ʳᵈ 1674.

" WORTHY DOCTOR,

"I have searched Sir John Marsham's Book, and find the suite as I do verilie believe. I searched from 1606 to 1612, which is two yeares before and two yeares after, but finde noe other than this wch is in these words followinge, viz': ' Evelin then Clerk, Termino Michaelis, 8° Jacobi 1610, Will Gilbert de Com: Suff: Clericus, quær: con: Will Waldegrave, Will et Rob' Playle def: Billa filat 17 Octob: Respons : 4 Dec' p. Waldegrave: Repb: 13 Feb.—John Derbyshire, Clerk in Sir John Marsham's office.' Michaelmas term than began a fortnight sooner than now it doth.

"I yesterday went to the Tower,* and spent all the forenoon in

* _Memo._—All the Rolls to the last year of King Charles I. had been removed to the Tower.

searcheinge the Records which lye in the White Tower. But suche confusion in keepinge of Records did I never see : throwne all abowt, trampled and trod on ; soe that though the Bill and Answer may be there, yet it is ten to one to find them. But I told Mr Rylie, who telleth me that if I will paye a souldier, wch he can hire for 12 pence a daye, to remoove the bundles, his sonne shall look over them.

"I have advised with an ancient Clerk in the Six Clerks Office, who is of opinion that if upon searche the Bill and Answer cannot be founde, yet foreasmuch as the suite is founde entered in the Six Clerks Booke, and the originalle depositions in the Examiners Office ; and the office haveing been burnt downe since, wch was Anno 1620, that upon mooveing the Court, they will be allowed to be used as evidence.

"Y^{rs} to Cõmand,

"JOHN TABOR."

"For Dr. Bisbie, Rector of Melford.

The Six Clerks Office referred to in the above letter was a very ancient office of the Court of Chancery. Originally they forfeited their places if they *married ;* but they were permitted to do so by the 24th and 25th of Henry VIII., 1533.

Sir Robert Cordell was at last, in 1676, forced to give in, but in his perverse obstinacy he refused to sign, and never did sign, the agreement, which was at length made for him by his son, who became afterwards Sir John Cordell, whereby it was decided that the lands in dispute, which included Melford Hall and grounds, part of the park, woods, and meadows, amounting to 630 acres, should pay as *Demœne lands, a small tithe* only, of £10 a year, and that the owner of Melford Hall should supply to the Rector of Melford every year, from his deer park, *a plate of fat venison in the summer season, and a plate of fat venison in the winter season.* As the Rector, in his accounts, values this venison at the then amount of 16s. 4d. for each plate, it must have been a considerable quantity. From the accounts of 1647–8 it would appear that the park had paid tithes from £2. 5s. to £3, and also some tithe venison.

These conditions were duly fulfilled up to 1690, when, after Dr. Bisbie had been deprived of the living for refusing the oath of allegiance to William III., Lady Cordell, the widow of Sir John (son of Sir Robert), made an endeavour to set aside the agreement which had been entered into with Sir Robert Cordell as to these tithes. Dr. Bisbie, however, having been appealed to, refused to keep silence in a matter affecting the welfare of the church, though he had no longer a personal interest in the living ; and he then gave a full account of how the matter had stood seventeen years before, and he added thereto further details. Among others he says that the park, meadows, woods, &c., in all above 600 acres, were, according to the Poll Bill of anno 166½

Y

rated at the yearly value of £256. He also asserts, though questionably, that the abbots of Bury, before the dissolution of the Monastery, always paid some tithe of the demesne lands which they held in hand, to the several rectors of Melford; and among others he cites here, for the first time, Bulneymoores and Le Churche Tye, and he quotes an entry from the Rectory Manor books of Dr. Egidius Dent, Rector of Melford 1474, in these words :—

"Item Jurati dicunt quod Rector Ecclesiæ de Melford et Successores sui, debent habere pasturam in le Bulnymere cum duabus Bestiis ibidem pasturandis a festo Inventionis Sanctæ Crucis usque finem Sancti Petri ad Vincula, cum Bestiis Domini Abbatis de Bury, manerii sui de Melford Hall absque contradictione alicujus, sicut prædecessores sui ex antiquo tempore habuerunt: et similiter debet habere pasturam quolibet decimo die de la Churche Tye pro bestiis et bidentibus depascendis per totum annum."

By the Court Rolls of the 23rd of Henry VII., this is not called le Churche Tye, but Viridarium de Melford Tye.

So it appeared that the parson of that day (1474) laid a claim, but which was not acknowledged by the Abbot, to have in lieu of tithe, in the one case, a joint feeding for two beasts with the beasts of the Abbot on Bulneymoor, from one before-mentioned feast day to another; viz. from 1st May to 1st August; and in the other case to have an entire and separate feeding both for beasts and sheep, every tenth day throughout the year, over le Churche Tye, presumably Melford Green. And they further endeavoured to show that trespassers on that tenth day were as punishable by the parson in his court, as they were on the other nine days by the Abbot in his court; and a case was quoted that seven persons were in 1501 cited to the Rectory Court for trespassing over "*le Churche Greene* de Melford" with pigs and sheep, and they were each fined a small sum. But it is not stated whether the fines were ever paid, or whether le Churche Greene meant the *Churchyard* or Melford Green.

Whatever may have led to these claims, it does not appear that they were maintained. In the three grants of the fair and market on the Green, no notice is taken of any rectorial right, nor is there any such mentioned in any of the abbots' voluminous terriers. The abbots certainly acknowledged no such rights, and in the lease granted by John Reeve de Melford, the last of the abbots, 26th of Henry VIII., of Melford Hall, for thirty years to Dame Pennington, widow, there is particularly leased to her the entire "feedings of the Green of Melford," without any reservation of the tenth day to the Rector. And after the dissolution of the Abbey, the Green was, with other parts of the estate, and with the fair, &c., granted absolutely by the Crown to Sir William Cordell. And in all Dr. Bisbie's minute tithe accounts there is no other mention of the Green, or of any profit derived from it, nor did he ever exercise any right over it. And there is nowhere else any mention whatever of this claim, which never seems to have been substantiated.

Sir Robert Cordell's quarrel with the Rector also embraced the subject of the right of seating in the chancel (or choir) of the church, —about which a considerable wrangle ensued before the vexed matter could be settled; and as therewith was also brought into dispute the question of repairs of the chancel between the Rector and the owner of Melford Hall, who was also the patron of the living, it may be of some interest to record the squabble as handed down by Dr. Bisbie, in his own words :—

"This year alsoe 167$\frac{3}{4}$ Sir Robert Cordell: Bart.: denyed me a seat in y⁰ Chancell of y⁰ Churche of Melford, for myselfe and my family to sit in: sayeinge that I ought to repair the whol Chancell, but to have no use of it: though it was sufficientlie prooved to him that Doctor Wareyn, my immediate prædecessor, and likewise Mᵗ Gilbert his prædecessor, both seated themselves and their familys on the south side of ye sayd Chancell, claimeing to themselves a right not onely to sit, but to bury there. And that the Quire seat was pulled down about the yeare 1662, when Mᵗ Thomas Hobart was Churchewarden, and the great seat wherein the sayd Sir Robᵗ Cordell doth now sit was then erected in the place thereof by the sayd Mᵗ Hobart at the appoyntment and by the direction of the sayd Sir Robᵗ Cordell.—Nay though I offerred to resign to him and to his use the sayd south side of y⁰ Chancell, resserving for myself and my successors to bury our dead therein, provided that the sayd Sir Robᵗ Cordell would cause a seat to be erected for me, and for my family in the Churche, to which he then payd Churchwardens Rates, and appropriate the same to me and my successors, yet that was alsoe refused and rejected by him.—Whereupon I forbore to repaire the Chancell, and would not end my suite about Tithes till that alsoe was accorded.

"Thus my claime is,

"1ˢᵗ That ye parsons of Melford had seated themselves and their families at the Weste end of the South side of ye Chancell, and the owners of Melford Hall, immemorially on the Northe side of ye sayd Chancell.

"2ⁿᵈ That ye present great seat at the South side wherein Sir Robᵗ Cordell and ye *males* of his family do sit was erected by Mᵗ Thomas Hobart, his Steward, then Churchwarden, about 1662.

"3ʳᵈ Till that seat was erected, Sir Robᵗ Cordell with the *males* of his family, sat constantly with his Lady, and the rest of the *females* of his family, on the North side of ye Chancell."

In 1676 the Rector abandoned the mooted right of sitting in the chancel. An agreement was finally entered into as follows; viz., that the owners of Melford Hall were to continue to occupy the seats in the chancel exclusively, and that a seat should be erected in the *body of the church*, westward over against the said great seat for the use of the parson and his family, which was accordingly done at the expense of the parish; Mr. Hobart and Mr. George Street being churchwardens.

This new seat remained as the Rectory pew from that time until the restoration of the church, 1867, when the owner of Melford Hall voluntarily relinquished his right to the chancel or choir seating, in order, and on condition that this part of the chancel might be stalled, and *used for the seating of a surpliced choir, and the officiating clergy only*, during the services of the church.

On the debated point of the repairs of the chancel, Sir Robert Cordell argued against the parson, that Dr. Bisbie had, at his own cost of £30 and upwards, repaired the whole of it in 1661. To which the Rector replied, that on coming into the living immediately after the troubled times of sequestration, he had indeed done so in ignorance of the joint custom of repair; but that before that time the north side had been always repaired by the owners of Melford Hall, the patrons of the living; and that the intruding Puritan ministers, in whose times the dilapidations happened, refused to repair the south side of the chancel when desired to do so by Sir Robert Cordell, unless he at the same time would repair the north side. And the parson further contended, that whereas the owners of Melford Hall have, as he admits, a right of one-fourth of the chancel on the north side to bury in, and another fourth part of the same on the south side also to bury in, being the place where the monument and vault belonging to the family is built, and they also sitting in the chancel, it was but reasonable that one half of the chancel should be maintained by the family.

Whereupon it was agreed, that the south side of the chancel should entirely and wholly be repaired and maintained by the parson and his successors, and the north side thereof by Sir Robert Cordell and his successors. And accordingly the leads thereof were mended, September, 1679, by the appointment and order of *John Cordell, Esq.*, his son. It is evident from this, as well as from a following passage, that though Sir Robert Cordell finally allowed these agreements to be entered into for him, and they were afterwards fully kept, yet his pride would not allow of his carrying them out in person, as the partially defeated party, and so his eldest son's name is used in the matters; and at a town meeting called to make a rate to and for the repair of the church in 167⅚, John Hobart and George Boston being then churchwardens, it was by the township consented to and agreed, that in regard that *John Cordell, Esq.*, had one half of the chancel to repair at his own proper costs and charges, the lands in his own occupation, viz. the Homestall, Park, and Broadmeadow, should no more be rated to the church, but remain as of former times, rate-free; and accordingly the said lands were excused in the rate then made, as also again in 1679-1680, and long subsequently.

After Dr. Bisbie's time there is but little of importance to relate as regards the Rectory. During the eighteenth century, the rectors here, as elsewhere, probably plodded on, as regarded their office, in the dull, lifeless, careless routine mode which was the distinguishing evil mark of that era in most country parishes; and particularly in counties which, like Suffolk, had not even Jacobite tendencies to rouse them from their lethargy. The old Doctor himself was a stanch adherent to the House of Stuart, and sacrificed all prospects in life for the maintenance of his principles; for (as he expresses it), "on his refusal to forego his faith and sworn allegiance to King James II., and to transfer the same to the Prince of Orange," he was, in 1689, ejected from the benefice of Melford, which he had held for thirty years, and he was succeeded by Dr. Felton, a Fellow of Cambridge, who favoured the new succession. Dr. Bisbie was the author of several published sermons, copies of which are now rare. They bear an impress of pedantic scholarship, and are the outspoken expressions of a stanch Royalist high churchman of that day. Among them the following are noticeable; viz., *Prosecution no Persecution*, preached at the assizes at Bury St. Edmund's, 22nd March, 1681, and dedicated to " my ever honoured patron, Sir John Cordell, of Long Melford, Baronet, one of his Majesties Deputy Lieutenants for the County of Suffolk; and to the vertuous and truly religious Lady, Dame Elizabeth, his wife;" another, named *The Modern Pharisees;* two sermons on *Anarchy and Sedition*, preached 1682-3, at Bury assizes, and published by request of Thomas Waldegrave, Esq., who was High Sheriff of Suffolk at both these assizes, the judges named being, at the first one, Mr. Justice Windham, and at the second, Lord Chief Baron Montague and Mr. Serjeant Holloway; and a sermon called the *Bishop Visiting*, preached at Bury before the Bishop of Norwich, the 3rd May, 1686, and dedicated to him.

Although it appears that Dr. Bisbie was not wholly free from that obsequiousness and servility which the clergy of his day displayed towards people of rank, yet he seems on occasions to have asserted his position and rights, and those of the church, against the titled owners of the two great Halls, in a far bolder and more spirited manner than was usual at that time. Although this book purports only to treat of men and manners in so far as they pertain to Melford, yet the following little detail of positive facts, as relating to this immediate neighbourhood, may serve as an illustration of the position of the clergy in society towards the close of the seventeenth century.

This sketch is taken from a personal MS. diary, written by a clergyman and a scholar, who was domestic chaplain to a family of rank in a great house only a few miles from Melford, in Dr. Bisbie's time. The worthy chaplain, in his journal, tells us with perfect simplicity and good faith, and as ordinary matter of course, that he associated generally with the upper servants, in whose society he appears to have been far more comfortable than in the parlour. When the family were alone, he commonly dined with them, sometimes at 12 and sometimes at 2 o'clock; but when company was entertained he seldom dined with the higher circle, and if honoured with an invitation to table, he was expected to retire before the close of dinner, when he adjourned to the steward's room, where he made his little jokes and paid compliments to Mrs. Betty, my lady's woman. In the family circle he was not allowed to enter into the general conversation, but was expected to be useful and subservient, and to toady his patron and patroness, and to fetch and carry for any of their noble visitors, from whom he occasionally received a present of a guinea for his services, which he accepted with profuse expressions of gratitude; and when the great house was full of guests, he had to give up his bedroom; and his Reverence tells us that he then shared a bed with either the butler or the steward!

Before his death, in 1695, Dr. Bisbie compiled a narrative of some of the vexatious disputes which had occurred between him and the Cordell family, and he closed his account thereof as follows :—

"Thus ended all ye controversys between Melford Hall and yͤ parson, and may never more any arise soe long as there is an owner at the Hall, and a parson in Melford."

And though his expressed hope has not been completely fulfilled, and that since his time many disputes have arisen, some often but trivial, some faulty on one side, some on both; and though in the frailty of human nature, with its infirmities of temper, it can scarcely be possible that the intercourse of neighbours should always run uninterruptedly smoothly, yet we may so far echo the long since recorded sentiment of the old parson, by the hope that the improved state of society in the present day has corrected the former evil tone of arrogance and exclusiveness, and by thus engendering a more genial relation between all classes, has tended to promote the better feeling of general goodwill and neighbourly kindliness.

CHAPTER VII.

KENTWELL.

IN the time of Edward the Confessor, Kentwell belonged to Seward, and was held by his undertenant Algar; but in 1086, this manor, together with six others (of which one was the lesser of the two Lavenham manors), formed part of the possessions of Frodo, the brother of Abbot Baldwin, of St. Edmund's. Translated from the abbreviated Latin of the Domesday Book of 1086, the following is the record entered therein :—

" *Suffolk.—The Hundred of Babergh.—XII.—FRODO.* [*Possessions, among others, of Frodo.*]

" In the time of King Edward the Confessor, Algar held *Kane-wella* under Seward, a freeman of Meldon, as a manor containing two carucates of land with Soke. There were thereon at that time 7 villeins, and afterwards, and now 4 villeins. There was then, and subsequently, 1 bordar; there are now 3. There were always 2 ploughs belonging to the demesne. There were then and afterwards 2 ploughs belonging to the Homagers of the manor; there now remains 1. There are 8 acres of mowing meadow. There has always been one horse at the Manor house. There were then 5 working oxen; there are now 8. At that time there were 30 swine; there are now 40. Then 80 sheep, now there are 50. At that time and subsequently, this manor was valued at 40 shillings; it is now worth £4."

Frodo, the owner of Kentwell at the Domesday survey in 1086, is known to have left at least two sons, named Alan and Gilbert, who both attested an important deed of grant of Abbot Albold between the years 1115 and 1119. Of their families we have no record, but it appears that about the period of from 1145 to 1148 a person named Galeus held this manor; for in the Bull of Pope Eugenius III., endowing the Abbey of Bury with certain tithes, it was decreed that the manor of Melford should pay a sum of 20 shillings a year, and the land of Galeus in Melford was to pay 10 shillings a year. And as at that time there was no other property in Melford which could have been assessed in such proportion to the Melford manor, except the then existing manor of Kentwell, it seems tolerably certain that Galeus was the owner of Kentwell. As to whether he was a descendant of Frodo through either Alan or Gilbert, his sons, there is no clear evidence; nor as to who were his immediate successors; though a Thomas de Mendham, living in 1188, is recorded to have been a descendant of Frodo; but whether he also owned Kentwell does not fully appear. There was a family of " De Kentwell " in the 13th century; and in one of the Chartularies of the Abbey of Bury, among a number of leases and conveyances connected with Melford, the name of *Sir Gilbert de Kentewell* appears as an attesting witness to a deed executed between Abbot Hugh Northwold and Lokereus, son of Absolon, of Melford, between the years 1218 and 1228.

A curious deed exists which was made between John Camerarius, of Shimpling, Suffolk, and *Richard de Kentwell*, clerk, and which was dated at Shimpling *in the churchyard, on Sunday next before Pentecost*, 1294. The selection of such a place for the execution of a document may seem strange; but the reason for this was, that, as sometimes the custom at that period, in order to make the conveyance as solemn and public as possible, the legal deed was read to the congregation in the churchyard, after divine service, that all present might know the contents, and be witnesses thereto if future occasion required.

The name of another person in some way connected with Kentwell appears repeatedly in the 14th century; for *John de Luton* attested Melford deeds of the Abbot of Bury in the several years 1816, 1817, 1823, and 1830.

It is said that a " Sir Edmond de Cornwall was of Kentwell in the county of Suffolk, whose son John died without issue." This Sir Edmond was the grandson of Richard de Cornwall, living in 1280, and who was the natural son of Richard, Earl of Cornwall and Poitou, King of the Romans, who was the second son of King John of England by his third wife, Isabel of Angoulême. The statement as to his ownership is however somewhat shadowy, and seems difficult to reconcile with the fact that in 1251 the manor of Kentwell was in the King's hands, and was granted by King Henry III. to Sir William de Valence, who is recorded in the Abbot's Chartulary of Melford of 1287, as holding therein a manor comprising 360 acres of arable land, 4 acres of mowing meadow, 5 acres of pasture, 17 acres of wood, a windmill, and a warren; besides 52 acres which his villeins held from him. Four persons are specially named as holding between them 50 acres of the lord's land; three of whom were again allowed to sublet it. The four tenants are thus described :—

" Stephen de Sidulvemere holds of the said Sir William xx acres of land for his under-tenants at 20 pence a year. [Sidolves Mere was near Ballingdon.]

" John, son of Capell, holds of the said Sir William x acres of land for his under-tenants at 10 pence a year.

"William Maupas holds for himself and his parceners a messuage and x acres of land for 10 pence a year.

"Matilda Wodefoyle holds of the same Sir William x acres of land for 10 pence."

The name of this latter tenant, *Matilda Wodefoyle*, is noticeable at the above date; for Wodefoyle, now called Woodfowles, was a reputed manor of Kentwell, from which this person, in the common custom of the period, no doubt received her appellation.

It would appear that the Kentwell Manor (with perhaps some of its adjuncts) was granted by King Henry III. to Sir William de Valence between the years 1252 and 1272; and though in the Melford Chartulary the Abbot of Bury, as lord paramount of Melford, includes De Valence in the roll of his free tenants, exacting from him a small yearly rent in free soccage in lieu of all services, the account goes on to state that this particular manor was held by the said noble "in chief from the king."

This Sir William de Valence married Joane, daughter of William de Montchensy by his wife Dionysia (daughter and heiress of Nicholas de Anesty), through whom the earldom of Pembroke descended, after the failure of the title in the family of Mareschall, and whose son, Aymer de Valence, was the last Earl of Pembroke of this latter line, being murdered in France on the (23rd?) 27th June, 1323; when, dying without issue, his niece carried the manor of Kentwell to her husband, the Earl of Athol.*

William de Valence was killed in battle in France in 1296, and his body was brought to England and buried in St. Edmund's Chapel, in Westminster Abbey. On his fine tomb his arms are repeated as a pattern in diamond-shaped panels, enamelled in gold and colours on copper. These are alternately Gules, three lions passant regardant, Or; and barry Argent and Azure, an orle of martlets, Gules. These arms are again repeated on the cushion beneath the head of the recumbent figure. The shield he holds only shows the second coat of arms, and on the azure bars is a delicate running pattern in gold, and on the argent bars a similar tracery pattern, rather broader; and the outlines of the martlets are picked out in gold.

Through the above-mentioned marriage of de Valence's niece and co-heir, Kentwell passed to David Strabolgie, Earl of Athol, who, in 1333, conveyed it to Sir Robert Gower and his heirs, and in 1388 the

---

* In Gage's History of the Thingoe Hundred, the family connections are differently given. He says that Dionysia was the only child of William de Mountchensi; that she married Hugh de Vere and died without issue, when her fee descended to Aymer de Valence, son and heir of Joane, cousin of William Mountchensi; and that, after the death of Aymer, it came to the Earl of Athol in right of his wife, Joane Comyn, sister of Aymer. The particulars in the text are taken from the Suffolk Archæological Society's Report, Wright's History of Essex, and Camden's "Britannia."

King confirmed to the said knight in fee the Manor of Kentwell, in the county of Suffolk. Gower's daughter Joan married one William Neve, of Wyting, and she and her husband had a pardon granted to them in 1366 for having entered on the Kentwell property, on the death of her sister, without process in the King's Court; and they were restored after the seizure by the king, on payment of 100 shillings. In 1368 this manor is said to have belonged to John Gower, the poet, and in 1373 to Sir John Cobham, and soon after passed to the family of Mylde, and the Cloptons obtained it by an intermarriage with that family.

The Cloptons had been long settled in Suffolk before they acquired this property. They are named in the Suffolk Domesday Book as feudatories of the Honor of Clare; and the name of Thurstan de Clopton appears as a witness to a grant of land at Hawkedon to the Abbot of St. Edmund's in the year 1154; and his son, Robert de Clopton, gave to St. Edmund's Abbey four acres that Thurstan de Clopton had held " in villa de Clopton," which was a hamlet of Wickhambrook.

The Manor of Kentwell was brought to the Clopton family by the marriage of Sir Thomas Clopton, Knight, with Katherine, daughter and heiress of William Mylde, Esq., of Clare, in the county of Suffolk. The will of this Sir Thomas Clopton, who died 1383, is dated 8th March, 1382, and was proved the 12th October, 1383. He was buried in Chipley Priory. At that time, and for nearly two hundred years after, the manorial residence was not called Kentwell, but "Lutons." In the wills and documents of successive Cloptons, till the year 1563, constant mention is made of the Hall or Place of Lutons, as the dwelling-house of the family; but in that year reference is made to the *new mansion-house of Kentwell Hall*. From many expressions and references, as well as from a careful comparison with them, of the existing features of the ground, there is, if not a certainty, at least a strong presumption, that Lutons Manor-house stood in or about the wood now called the "Pond Plantation" of Kentwell. Old Mr. Martyn, in his account of Melford church, prior to the Reformation, speaks of " Lutons House, near to the Ponds in the Park, where there was a little chapel of Saint Anne." The will of Sir William Clopton, who died 153$, mentions particularly the vestments and decorations in this private domestic chapel. As to the "Ponds in the Park," mentioned by Mr. Martyn, there still remain in the wood which now derives its name from them, as the Pond Plantation, the large rectangular artificial fishponds, one of which is at a much lower level than the others, together with a series of several smaller stews, such as in past times were generally attached to these old manor-houses. Near them stand some magnificent venerable old oaks of immense age, which were once probably very near the house of Lutons; and the calm quiet beauty of these ancient fishponds, now hidden in the depth of the wood which has grown up around them, with their unruffled stillness, on a summer's day, only broken by the occasional passage of waterfowl, or by the flapping of great fish upon the surface, forms a most picturesque and charming sylvan scene. Outside the wood the existence of similar splendid old oak-trees on land which is now arable, leads to the conclusion that the park in olden days extended up to, and partly around this wood, so that Lutons (if on this site) was surrounded by the park. No traditional details seem to exist as to the style of the old manor-house, and there are no remains of it; for probably, from its early date, and the scarcity of natural enduring building material in these parts, it was a timber-framed house; and on its being pulled down, its materials, if sound, would have been used up again, or if decayed, converted into fuel, leaving no traces behind it, saving those peculiarities of site and aspect and configuration of ground which here point so strongly to its presumed position.

The tenures of the several manors pertaining to this estate were repeatedly described in the various inquisitions on the wills of successive Cloptons.

In early ones Lutons is stated to be held of the Abbot of St. Edmund in free soccage for 16 pence a year in lieu of all services; and after the dissolution of the Abbey it is described as held on the same terms "from the Crown and from the Hundred of Babergh, which Hundred was formerly parcel of the ancient possessions of *the Abbot of St. Edmund's.*"

A portion, called the Messuage of Blakes, is described in similar terms to the above, before and after the dissolution of the Abbey, as held at 6 pence a year.

The Manor of Woodhouse and Woodfowles was held of the Earl of Sussex, and of his Manor of Shimpling, for 2 shillings a year.*

The Manor of Kentwell was held originally of the King in chief, and of the Castle of Norwich, by a fourth part of a knight's service; and afterwards by a further payment of 65 shillings a year to the governor of the castle. But about the time of the Rebellion, it is noted thus:—
" It seemeth there hath been a license or pardon of Alienation sued out ignorantly or unawares, as if the same had been holden in chief only; and processes have thereupon issued out of the Treasurers Remembrauncers Office in the Exchequer, which were discharged, some of them in the year 1645.

---

* As to a part of this manor there exists a notice that in the 15th of Edward IV., 1476, one Walter Jermayn held Woodhouse for 13s. 4d. a year, and he requested to be allowed the sum of 10s. 3d. for a thousand of wood which in that year had been made in the grove called Woodhouse, and which had been wrongly included in his hire. The parson of Stanstead on this occasion took a hundred of wood for his tithe.

In 1287 there is a mention of one Matilda de Woodfoyle, as already recorded.

"To this manor belongeth a Court from three weeks to three weeks, and many rents of Assize of Free Tenants—and of two or three customary or Copyhold Tenants—their Fines arbitrable."

The Manor of Monks, in Melford, which was originally included in the one-third of the Melford Church property alienated by Abbot Sampson to the hospital of St. Saviour, Bury, was granted by King Henry VIII., 23rd December, 1545, after the dissolution of the Abbey, to Sir William Clopton, the then owner of Kentwell, to be held of the Crown in chief by the fortieth part of a knight's service, and an annual payment of 32s. 4½d. at Michaelmas. This patent was renewed, enlarged, and confirmed by King James I.

In the patent the contents of this manor are thus described (in Latin):—

A pightle called Le Barneyard, containing by estimation 1 acre.

A close of arable land next Le Barneyard, with the site of the Manor-house, 6¼ acres.

A building called Le Tiled Barne.

Four enclosures of meadow and pasture called Bargate field, Crow medow, Middlefield, and Prestly field, and containing together 58 acres.

A parcel of land and marsh called Le Cangle, containing ¼ acre.

A pasture on Kentwell Down, near the park, containing 4½ acres and 27 perches.

Five parcels of land and pasture between the mansion-house and the cross called *Clopton's Cross*.

Two groves of wood between the mansion-house and the road leading to Bury.

Also all tithes of hay, grass, and grain, and all other tithes of the above lands; and also all other tithes of lands from the tenement called Bochers, on the east side of the said road to the end of Melford Park.

A further account states thus:—"To this manor belongs a Court from three weeks to three weeks, and many rents of Assize of free tenants and of divers customary or copyhold tenants, whose fines are arbitrable; but only one tenement lately [*i.e.* circa 1640], in tenure of William Miller, deceased, which is claimed to be certain, upon every alienation and descent."

On Monks Manor there formerly stood a manor-house, concerning which no descriptive records remain, except that it continued to be named in the abuttals of the Priest's house or College, as Monks Manor-house, with barn, buildings, and yards. Its site was therefore somewhere near the north-east end of the church, probably where part of the broken ground in Kentwell Park, near the churchyard, indicates the position of former buildings; and a house, which presumably was this Manor-house, is shown as standing on that spot near the College or Priest's house, in the Melford Manor maps of 1613 and 1615, and also on an old map of 1677. The date of its erection and of its destruction are equally uncertain, though perhaps from some context it may be surmised that it was pulled down towards the close of the 17th century. It is mentioned in one document as still existing in 1674.

Sir Thomas Clopton, who through his wife acquired the Manor of Kentwell, probably occupied the old house of Lutons, as he made his will *at Melford* the 8th of March, 1382, whereby, among other bequests, he left " to Master John, the chaplain of the parish of Melford, half a marc " (6s. 8d.). This John was perhaps a chantry priest, he certainly. was not the rector, for Thomas de Grynesby was rector at that date.

Sir Thomas's widow (she was his second wife), who was the heiress Catherine Mylde, remarried Sir William Tendring, whose father was also Sir William Tendring, of Stoke, who married Margaret (daughter of Sir William Kerdeston, of Claxton, Norfolk). Sir William Tendring the elder is said to have died in 1375, and his wife in 1394, and they were both buried in the old Priory Church at Sudbury. Sir William de Kerdeston was the son of the second baron of that name, but a doubt hung over his legitimacy, and he was never summoned to Parliament as a baron.

Lady Tendring, Sir Thomas Clopton's relict, made her will the 24th February, 1403, leaving the following bequests :—

To the High Altar of Melford a marc (13s. 4d.).
To Thomas, her husband's chaplain, half a marc (6s. 8d.).
To Margaret, her maid, a marc (13s. 4d.).
To her two gentlemen chamberlains, to each 40 pence.
To John, her husband's cook, 40 pence.
To Thomas, the baker, 40 pence.

This lady also left, among many bequests to her daughter Alice Tendring, who became a great heiress, and the ancestress of the Howards, all her head-gear, except two fillets of pearls of lesser value, and all her keverchefs; also a furred cloak and other furs, a long chest, and her napery, &c. She further left to Sir John Howard, the husband of her daughter Alice, a piece of silver gilt, called a Flatpoc, with a cover for the same. She bequeathed to Sir William Clopton, her son by her first marriage, a piece of silver, or covered cup, with six silver shells ; a bed of white worsted stained with figures of men and women, and another bed and mattress; a Paris napkin, with a long towell of the same workmanship; a green vestment for a chaplain ; a missal ; and *a book called a Byble* (in manuscript) ; a piece of silver called a stondynggepec (query, standing piece) with a cover with the head of a leopard ; and a chest called the great cofre. Finally she left to every beggar coming to her burial, two pence.

After Sir Thomas Clopton's death, his son *Sir William* continued to reside at Lutons, which in his will he mentions as his dwelling-

house; he died in 1446, and his effigy is on the recessed mural tomb
in the north aisle of the choir of the church. After him there succeeded his son by his second wife, *John Clopton,* who married Alice
Darcy, and who is so intimately connected with the history of Melford,
as the great benefactor and restorer of this church. His career has
been already briefly noted in connection with the church. His lot
was cast in troubled times, and being an intriguer of a strong political
bias, he narrowly escaped with his life, when on the 22nd of February,
1461, his fellow-prisoners in the Tower, John de Vere, the 12th Earl
of Oxford, his son Aubrey de Vere, John Montgomery, and Sir
Thomas Tuddenham, were all beheaded on Tower Hill for their attachment to the Lancastrian party. The Earl and his son were buried in
Austin Friars, London. Old John Clopton, however, managed to make
his peace, and he lived to the ripe age of 75, and was buried in Melford church, in the Easter tomb. His will, which is dated 4th November, 1494, three years prior to his death, is very curious as illustrative
of the manners and customs of that day. It is a document of considerable length. Among other dispositions he mentions the mortuary to be paid in kind at his burial. These mortuary fees claimed
by the priests sometimes led to great scandals. The clergy asserted
themselves to be entitled to the best suit of clothes which had belonged
to the deceased; and there were instances in which by the grave-side
the officiating priest tore off a mourner's doublet, declaring that it
had belonged to the dead man. The custom led to such infinite
abuses, that an Act was passed in the 21st year of Henry VIII., which
regulated mortuary fees, and also controlled the exorbitant probate
duties of the bishops' courts. John Clopton in his will says as
follows :—

"Also I wull that the parson have my best hors at hys eleccion
for hys mortuary, according to the lawdabill custome of the towne.

"And forasmuch as I knowe well that prayers is a singuler
remedie for the delyveraunce of soules in purcatory, therfore I wull
that ther be disposyd for me and Dame Margarete Leynham [daughter
of Dame Annes Fray, of whose will John Clopton was executor] within
a monith next after my discease, fifty marcs [£33. 6s. 8d.] for two
thousande masses and diriges under this forme followynge."

He commences the apportionment thereof with Shene, the Charter-
house of London, and the House of Sion, to which latter he leaves an
especial legacy for masses for his soul; adding thus,—" consydering
that I am a Broder of the place."

Persons of rank were often, in this sort of lay form, brethren of
the principal religious orders, and they were thus supposed to parti-
cipate in the benefits of the prayers of the monks while living, and
after death they were to be especially prayed for by these communities.
As the affiliated lay brethren generally bequeathed legacies or made

gifts to their adopted house, perhaps the monks' prayers might be given on a sort of principle that "qui pro alio orat pro se laborat." Sion was a Carthusian house, one of the strictest orders in England. There were two establishments; one of monks of Sion, and one of nuns.

He then continues the distribution of the masses, and the four-pences apiece for them, among the Friars of Sudbury, Clare, Babwell (beyond the Banna leuca of St. Edmund's), the Grey Friars of Col-chester, the White Friars of Maldon, the Blackfriars of Chelmsford, the Black Friars of Thetford, and the Austyns (Augustines) there; the Priory of Colne; every monk in Bury besides the abbot, the prior, the sexton, the cellarer, and the hospitaller; the nuns of Thetford, the nuns of Hoddington; and the priests of the churches of Melford, Lavenham, St. Gregory, St. Peter, and Allhallow in Sudbury, Glems-ford, Cavendish, Boxted, Hartest, Shimpling, Lawshall, Hawsted, Alpheton, Stansted, Acton, the Waldingfields, both the less and the more, Chilton, Liston, Foxearth, and Clare; together with divers private priests, who were all to receive certain sums for masses for his soul. The bequests to the following anchorites and anchoresses for the same object are deserving of special notice:—

"Also, I wull that the Anker of Busshopesgate, and each of the Ancors of Norwiche have 6ˢ 8ᵈ.

"Also I wull that the Anker of Bury have 20 shillings for two Trentallis." [A trental was 30 masses, one on each consecutive day for 30 days after the burial; or sometimes all together on the 30th day, so often referred to in old wills to be observed as the month day.]

"Also I wull that Dame Johan Lampett, Auncores [Anchoress] of Carewe, have 3ˢ 4ᵈ to praye for me, and for the saide soules."

The mention of these persons is of double interest, not only on account of the names of different then still existing Anchorholds, as they were called, and their recluses, but also because such reclusoria are seldom mentioned so late as the date of this will, 1494. From the 14th to the middle of the 15th century, there are many histories of anchorites and anchorholds. These varied greatly in their freedom of external communication, and in their sizes, and were commonly cells either attached to the church or in the churchyard, and were inhabited by male recluses, generally singly, but sometimes in pairs, or by soli-tary female recluses or anchoresses. Although not strictly pertaining to this history, a few observations may be permitted in explanation of this subject; particularly as one notice which is on record of these ancient anchorholds relates closely to this neighbourhood. On the 28th of January, 1433, the Mayor of Sudbury petitioned the Bishop of Norwich to admit Richard Appleby, of Sudbury, to the order of Hermits, the mayor, with the assent of the inhabitants and church-reeves, having granted to him to live with John Levington, a hermit, in his solitary place and hermitage, which had been made at the cost of the parish in the churchyard of St. Gregory's church, to dwell together as long as they should live, or whichever should live and dwell the longest. In 1443 Thomas Scrope, who was a recluse at Norwich, resigned and left his anchorhold (a rare occurrence) and became suffragan to the Bishop of Norwich, and died near the great age of 100 years old; he was buried at Lowestoft.

Bishop Poore's ancient book, entitled the "Ancren Riewle," is full of paternal advice for anchorite recluses, and particularly for anchoresses. He alludes to the gossiping habits that had crept in on the part of lax anchorites and anchoresses, with those who brought them their food and necessaries, which were generally conveyed through a small trap or window, open to the churchyard; and he quotes what had almost grown thereon into a proverbial saying, "From mill and from market, from smithy and from anchor-house, men bring tidings." And yet, in the earlier days, the act of adoption of the life of an anchorite recluse or of an anchoress was as grave and sad an event as could well be imagined,—a self-consignment to a living tomb. The ceremony, if it may be alluded to in a few brief words, ran thus:—Solemn service was read over the "includendus"; the recluse took the vow at the altar of the church, put on the vestment, and, mass ended, a taper which had been burning on the altar was given to the recluse and a procession was formed. First came the choir, then the "includendus," then the bishop or priest, followed by the people, singing a solemn litany, proceeding to the cell. The priest consecrated the cell and its altar, then led in the "includendus," carrying his lighted taper, and blessed him. Then the tone of the service changes, and he is now called the "inclusus." He (or she) in solemn silence throughout, is then built up into the cell, or otherwise the cell is securely closed, and the choir and congregation slowly retire, chanting appropriate psalms, leaving the "inclusus" to his solitary life, never more to mingle in the business of the world, or to step over the threshold of that living tomb! Who can tell what broken hearts, what burning passions, have been shrouded under that recluse's robe, or what wild cry of human agony has been stifled under that solemn silence, while he or she was being built up in the cell. When the last strain of that processional chant had died away, and the recluse's taper had burnt out on the little altar, was that the end of the tragedy, or only the end of the first act?

Any how, old John Clopton, who in his long chequered life had well known the opinion held of the sanctity of these anchorites and anchoresses, before the monastic rule had become lax and debased, placed much faith in their intercession for his soul, and left them money, which would be expended by them in sustenance, for they were dependent for support on charity alone.

Many other quaint matters are contained in John Clopton's will; such as a bequest to "praye for Longe's soule of Laushull that was slayne with thunder;" and the residue of his personal estate, after a multitude of bequests, he directs "shall be divided into four parts, whereof two parts shall go to sad preestes and vertuous, to sing a trental for me, and to find vertuous scolers to scole; the third part, to buy frise and lynone clothe for gownes, shirtes, and smokkes; and for pesonne, berryng, and coles, for to help the pouer peple hereabowte in Lenton seasonne;—and the fourth parte shall goo to the mending of high waies betwix this towne and Bury, and to supply to the friers of Sudbury, and to the friers of Clare, eche howse a barell of herryng in Lentone and 40 stockfisshes, and for the novis of the saide howsis, eche hous a cade [1000] of sperlyng."

Although John Clopton's will reads as if he had been a most orthodox Roman Catholic, it yet contains one little entry which leaves a doubt whether his predecessors, if not he himself, had been inclined to the precursory Reformation of Wycliffe; for in his will he left, "to my especialle gode Maister Willyam Pykenham *my Bible in Englisshe.*"

William Pykenham was the Rector of Hadleigh, in Suffolk, who built the beautiful Gate-house near the Rectory of that town in 1495.[*]

As John Clopton died in 1497, this Bible in the Vulgate must have been one of very early date, the possession of which by a layman would almost be accounted heresy.

Probably this was a Lollard copy, one of Wickliffe's translation, of which many were circulated between 1877 and 1414, and perhaps was the identical one which had belonged to his grandmother, the wife of Sir Thomas Clopton, who may have been inclined to Lollardism at heart, if not openly, for by her will she bequeathed to her son *a Bible.* Perhaps this heretical taint had affected other members of the family, for Sir Thomas Erpingham, who married her cousin Joan Clopton, was forced, for his sin in favouring the heresies of Wickliffe, to build the west gate of Norwich Cathedral, which continues to bear his name, and still remains with the word "Pena" many times sculptured thereon, and in a canopied niche in the pediment is his effigy in armour, kneeling, and begging for pardon. He fought in the battle of Agincourt, and died 1428, and was buried in the choir of Norwich Cathedral.[†] Yet it is remarkable that John Clopton, who, as far as we can judge from his own words, was a bigoted Romanist, with full faith in friars, monks, and religious orders, the corruption of which Wickliffe denounced so bitterly, should have cherished this early copy of the

---

[*] William Pykenham was made Archdeacon of Suffolk in 1471.

[†] In a document of the Corporation of Norwich, of 1409, Sir Thomas Erpingham is called "Steward of the King's household."

Bible in English which had been anathematized, and should, as a precious though dangerous gift, bequeath it to his dear friend William Pykenham.

Old John Clopton was succeeded in Lutons Manor-house by his son, *Sir William Clopton, Knight,* born 1450, and who made his will the 14th October, 1530, by which he bequeathed to his eldest son John " all the hanginges within the haule, parlure, and greate chamber, with the beddinge, quysschyns, tables, formes, and stoles within them ; and the stuffe of my chapell, as auter clothes, boke, chalesse and vestementes, being and servyng on or for the workyndayes, within the saide chappell." From this, and from the bequest of his father to Melford Church of certain cloths and vestments, which he says he had *at home,* they appear to allude to their private chapel of St. Anne, in or near the house at Lutons. He continues : " And whereas I have diverse peses of broderid workes of silke, and gold, to fornesch and serve for the hole suete of westyments as well for a coope vestyment, diacone and sub-diacone, I will that my executours do bye cremysyn welwett or clothe of golde, yf my goodes will extende unto it, for to accomplissch this same suete of vestmentes in forme before writen, which suete of vestymentes, every parcell thero, I gyve and bequeth to Melford Chirch, so that this same coope, vestimentes and every parcell therof schall be at the commandement of hym that God schall provide to be my heyre male and *dwell at my place at Lewtons,* and such tyme as schall fortune to be any marige at my saide place, and immediatly after to be delyvered unto the Chirch Wardens ayen." He leaves, after the death of his wife (the third wife, Thomasine Knevit, who survived him), to his son John the cross of gold, " which I where dayly abowtte my necke," as an heirloom to his heirs male, with this very curious proviso, " upon the condicion that they and every of them dow lenne the same crosse unto women of honeste, being with child, the tyme of ther laboure ; and immediatly to be surely delivered up ayen." He leaves to his wife for her life his *Manor and Place of Lewtons, where he dwells,* and entails it afterwards ; and among many bequests he leaves 40 shillings, and the tenement and ground called the Saffron Pane, to *John Cordell, his servant, and his wife Emme.* Sir William Clopton died 1537, aged 80, and was buried in Melford Church, as he directs, near his two first wives. The stone slab for him, which has lost the brass, and has only one shield left for his first wife, Joane Marrow, has been moved from its original place in the chancel floor, in front of John Clopton's tomb, into the north aisle. The next occupier of Lutons was Sir William's son *John,* by his first wife, Joane Marrow. He made his will a few days before his death, on the 5th October, 1541, whereby he bequeathed to his wife Elizabeth (Roydon), who survived him, " the hangynges, beddynge, testores, and all oder the appurtenaunces withyn the grett chamber, and as muche brede corne, and ale corne, as shall fynd hyr howse oone hole yere after my decesse." He also left to his godson, John Cordell, a merlyg,* or wevell.

To his son William, who succeeded him, he leaves "the hangynges, bede, and testour, with all the appurtenaunces, belongyng to *my chamber callyd my Lorde ys chamber:* also I geve hem the hangynges of my hall and my parler." This will was proved on the 5th November, 1541, John Clopton having died the 21st October in that year. Among the witnesses was Sir John Gayton, priest, of Melford.

His wife Elizabeth remarried a Mr. Robert Withersby; she survived her son William Clopton, the heir of Lutons and Kentwell, who died at the age of 53, and who was buried at Melford 19th August, 1562. He was the grantee from the Crown, in 1545–6, of the manor of Monks, of the dissolved abbey of St. Edmund's, and was the builder of *Kentwell Hall,* but in what particular years does not appear; probably, however, the house was not completed till but a short time before his death. His mother, in her will, dated 1st December, 1563, fifteen months after his death (her will was proved 26th April, 1564), mentions for the first time the *new Mansion-house of Kentwell Hall* as the family dwelling-place. She left to one of her grandsons the furniture of her house in Sudbury, comprising " one joyned bedsteade, three steyned courteynes of redde saye, a testorne of silke wroughte with lyons of golde uppon the same, seven peces of steyned hanginges, a feather bedde, a boulster, one pellowe, two pellow beres, three paire of sheates, a cusshein, a chaire, a joyned stole, a rounde table, two shorte table clothes, sixe napkins, one shorte towell, one brasse potte, one paire of pothokes, a chamber potte, and one candlesticke."

To two other grandsons she leaves her *two harnesses, called corslettes.*

After this time Kentwell Hall became the dwelling-place of the elder branch of the family, and probably the old house at Lutons was pulled down when the new hall was built.

Many other Clopton wills contain quaint entries, of which only a few can be here mentioned. It is noticeable that all older wills generally deal only with personalty, or what was termed movable goods; the explanation of which is said to be that till the 32nd year of Henry VIII. a man could not dispose of his lands, which are therefore seldom referred to in the old wills. The law was in that year modified by the Statute of Uses.

Edward Clopton, in 1504, leaves to Sir William Waldegrave, Knight, "the crosse of golde which I was wont to were on my cape" (cap).

Dorothy Clopton, in 1508, gives " to my Cosyn Kateryn Froxmer

* Merlyg: query, Mertlage, a devotional church calendar. A John Cordell appears to have died in 1564: if the same, was he the father of Sir Wm. Cordell?

my bedes of corall, gawdyed with x bedes of golde, and a derke tawney velvet frontlet, and a gette of mynkes, *the which she gave me hir selfe.*

"Unto my fader [she was daughter of Sir Wm. Clopton and Joane Marrow] a serpentyne bede, and a broche of golde with an ymage in it, and a tablet of silver and gilte, beseching hym of his daiely blissyng.

"I geve to my broder Robert, my gret bedes, of whit yvery, and 20 nobles, which myn *unkill Marowe* gave me.

"Item : I geve to my broder Fraunceys my pomandyr of sylver.

"Item : I geve to my broder Poley, my golofer with a saffir.

"Item : I geve to litell John Poley my ryng with the visage.

"Item : I geve to my suster Gattes, my best bonet of blak velvet, garnyshed with crymson velwet, and a frontlet of orange colour, and a blak goune furred with blak, and my best kyrtill of worsted.

"Item : "I geve to litell John Gattes a payre of agglettes of sylver.

"Item : I woll the parson of Long Melforde have a payre of bedys of gette gaudeyd with jesperes, and a purse of blak velwet, not fully fynyshed, lying in a coffer of myne."

She also left to various persons five gowns and nine head-dresses of rich materials.

She bequeathed altogether eight sets of beads, of jet, coral, ivory, and jasper, and variously gauded with silver, silver gilt, gold, and amber. Such sets of beads, which were at this period commonly passed by will, consisted usually of from 30 to 70 beads in number, every tenth one being a larger and more valuable bead than the rest, called a Gaude, for a Paternoster. The set left to Katherine Froxmer, of coral with ten golden gaudes, must have been unusually large, for it would have had 100 or 110 beads. These strings of beads, or rosaries, were worn in various ways, both for ornament and for devotional purposes, and were very often pendent from the girdle.

Mistress Dorothy Clopton, who died single, made Mr. William Skerne, parson of Melford, her executor.

John Clopton, whose will of 1524 was proved 1528, bequeathed "to the foure prisons in London, Newgate, Ludgate, and the two Compters, 2ˢ 8ᵈ to eche prison in bred, to be delyvred to the poure prisoners." There was also to be said for his soul in the church of St. Margaret, Lothbury, a trigintall of masses.

Francis Clopton, in 1559, leaves to the reparation of Melford Church 40 shillings; and to his wife Bridget all interest and profit of the *lease which he holds of Melford Hall Park* for an unexpired term of years; and also to her the millhouse, yards, and hop-yard at Bridge Street, which he had purchased from the churchwardens and feoffees of the parish of Alpheton, subject to an outgoing of four pence a year for scouring (cleaning) Alpheton Church.

Thomas Clopton, of Kentwell Hall, in 1598, left to his wife Mary

Waldegrave "the use and occupacion of all my *waineskott and glasse* in and about my mancion, to be and remaine as they nowe are, and by noe meanes to be removed or altered; and also the occupyinge of the hanginges of tapestry whiche serve for my grete chamber of my saide house, for forty yeres, yff the saide Mary shall so longe live." He then entailed the same; but his son was the last male Clopton who owned Kentwell.

George Clopton, of Sudbury, who was buried at St. Gregory's, left, in 1565, to his son Thomas his house in the North Street, Sudbury, which he lately bought of John Bregenes; a legacy to his eldest son Francis, directing that he be set to school to write, read, and cast accounts, and be bound prentice in London to some good occupier.

William Clopton, of Groton, 1615, gives "unto my sonne William, all my bookes and armor, excepte such armor as my wife shal be compelled and constrayned to use and shewe forthe at the trayninges and musteringes of souldiers, duringe her life."

Priscilla Clopton, widow, of Boxted, 1632, gives everything to her daughter Bridget Clopton, except her stammell pettycote, which she gives to Bridget Horman, her niece.

This lady makes her mark to her will, not being able to write.

Francis Clopton, of Haughley, in 1689, leaves to the minister that shall preach his funeral sermon 13s. 4d.

The elder branch of the Cloptons became extinct as to male heirs with the children of Sir William Clopton, who, though twice married, died in 1618 at the age of 27; and his two sons by his second wife Elizabeth, daughter of Sir Giles Allington, of Horseheath, and widow of Sir Henry Pallavicini, of Babraham, died as infants in 1618 and 1619. Sir William's first wife had been Anne, daughter of Sir Thomas Barnardiston, of Clare Priory, "a gentlewoman of exact beauty and comeliness and of exemplary piety," who died at the early age of 20; and their daughter Anne became the heiress of Kentwell. She was carefully brought up by her grandmother, Lady Barnardiston, at Clare Priory, and while yet a child various negotiations appear to have been entered into for her marriage, both with the eldest son of Sir Thomas Coventry, the Lord Keeper of the Great Seal, and with James Fiennes, son of Lord Say and Sele; and finally with Sir Simonds d'Ewes, of Stowlangtoft, and M.P. for Sudbury, who married the heiress of what was then described as "that stately house of Kentwell in the town of Melford, with an estate of about £500 per annum lying round about it," in the year 1626, when she was not yet 15 years old, and he was about 24. Some years afterwards they had several children, but a fatality seemed to attend them. Their first son, named Clopton, "a goodly sweet child born," died soon after his birth, "through the cursed ignorance or neglect of such as were employed" about the lady during her confinement. Two other sons, twin-born, survived but a few hours their premature birth, which was occasioned "by some hurt to Lady d'Ewes by travelling in her coach in Bury streets during the festival;" and her fourth son, also named Clopton, died before it was two years old of the rickets, which were produced "by their pitching upon a proud, fretting, ill-conditioned woman for a nurse," and aggravated by the unskilful treatment of "Doctor Despotine, an Italian physician at Bury."*

Lady d'Ewes, the last of the Cloptons who possessed Kentwell Hall, died at Stowlangtoft Hall of small-pox, in 1641, at the age of 29, after an illness of ten days.

Sir Simonds d'Ewes was a learned man and a distinguished antiquary, but Dr. Bisbie describes him as "a great Bigot and Beautefeau in the Rebellion," whatever the expression may mean. He remarried, and died 1650, when the Kentwell estate descended to his daughter Sissilia, the only surviving child of his first marriage. She married Thomas Darcy, of St. Osyth, who came to reside at Kentwell Hall, and was created a baronet in 1660, at which period he made considerable repairs in the interior of the house (Lady Darcy was buried at Melford, 1st June, 1661). In 1676-7 he sold Kentwell and its manors, when the particulars of the parts sold with the Hall at that date were stated as follows:—

1676–7.

The Manors of Kentwell and Monks, Melford, with the lands thereunto belonging, were sold in the above year by Sir Thomas Darcy, Bart., to Thomas Robinson, Esq. The particulars whereof were as follows:—

In the Landlord's own hands.

Acres.		Value of Rental.
		£. s. d.
150	Park, orchards, gardens, and yards, about 150 acres, at 15s. per acre . . .	112 10 0
50	Park lay and Maypole field, about 50 acres, at 13s. 4d. per acre . . .	32 0 0
21	Crow Meadow, part arable, and tithe-free, 21 acres, at 20s. per acre . . .	21 0 0
37	Upper Monks and small crofts, most tithe-free, about 37 acres, at 14s. per acre .	25 0 0
2	The hop-ground, stocked and planted, near 2 acres, at £3. 5s. per acre . . .	6 10 0
	The tithe of hay, corn, &c., of 800 acres of land belonging to Monks Manor . .	31 0 0
	Free and copyhold rents of both manors .	14 0 0
260		£242 0 0

* Jasper Despotin, "Doctor of Physicke," of Bury St. Edmund's, by his will, dated in 1648, directs ten rings of gold to be made, of the value of 20s. sterling apiece, with a death's head upon some of them, and to be disposed of among his friends.

Let to Tenants.

Acres.		Value of Rental.
		£. s. d.
210	Zeph. Lungley, for Monks Manor, mostly tithe-free, about 210 acres, at 10s. an acre	100 0 0
260	Robert Golding, for the Kell farm, about 260 acres, at 6s. per acre . . .	82 0 0
80	Ditto for another tenement, and lands, 80 acres, at 6s. per acre	25 0 0
65	John Pask, about 65 acres, at 6s. per acre .	20 0 0
55	William Smith of Stanstead, about 55 acres, at 6s. per acre	16 0 0
12	Edward Smith, of Stanstead, about 12 acres, at 7s. 6d. per acre	4 10 0
682 —		
41 ⎫ Wood.	Robert Golding, for underwood of about 41 acres, at 6s. 8d. per acre . . .	13 13 4
10 ⎬	Ditto for underwood, 10 acres, tithe-free, at 8s. 6d. per acre.	4 9 2
25 ⎭	Edward Johnson, for underwood, 25 acres, at 7s. 6d. per acre	9 7 6
76 —	Widow Huggins, for a tenement and yard .	1 10 0
1018 Total A.	Total . . .	**£518 10 0**

Kentwell Hall is described as a " very faire brick house with 12 wainscot roomes, the park stored with above 150 deere, a double dovehouse, fish ponds, and other conveniencys, besides timber on the grounds and woods considerable. It is an excellent good aire, within 3 miles of Sudbury, 3 miles of Lavenham, 5 miles of Clare, all three market townes; about 9 miles from St. Edmunds Bury, about 14 miles from Colchester, and about 18 miles from Ipswich."

It is not stated what sum was realized by this part of the property and the Hall. The purchaser, Mr. Thomas Robinson, Protho-notary of the Court of Common Pleas, was subsequently knighted, and was created a baronet by Charles the Second in 1681-2, and on the 2nd of August, 1683, he lost his life by jumping out of his chamber window in the Temple, to avoid the fury of a fire which had broken out near his chambers. His son, Sir Lumley Robinson, survived him but a short time, for he died 2nd June (query 6th June), 1684; and Sir Thomas, the third baronet, sold Kentwell. Thus the estate again changed hands, and was owned for a time by the families of Moore and Logan. During some of these changes many of the old documents and papers relating to Kentwell became scattered, and it is to be regretted that reference cannot now be made to them, for they would doubtless contain matters of interest, and furnish further history of this fine old place, of which there is now but comparatively little available documentary record.

Since its erection more than three centuries have rolled over it, and far from detracting from its beauty, time has only served to add thereto, by imparting to it its present lovely mellow tones and shades of colour, and rendering more venerable the old trees around it.

Of the two old halls of Melford, built at nearly the same period, Kentwell is in many ways the more beautiful at the present time, as its exterior has been less altered and modernized by so-called improvements than Melford Hall. It therefore retains far more of its original style and character, and no one can now look at it without admiration as a very fine and excellent specimen of the best class of the sixteenth century manor-house.

Its general peculiarities are well preserved; most of its mullioned windows exist in their original proportions, though cement has in some places been substituted for their stonework. Its moat remains complete and perfect, access being gained to the house at two points by bridges over it; and the old timber and bricknogged brewhouse and offices, the bases of which are washed by the moat, are as picturesque objects as well can be; and the beauty of the whole is further enhanced by the approach through the handsome lime avenue, which was planted by Mr. Thomas Robinson in the year 1678, all the trees in which appear to have been pollarded.

The general plan of the mansion is much the same as that of the sister house,—what was commonly called the E shape; the main hall being in the centre, and one of the two wings being devoted to offices. It contains, among other curiosities, some painted glass coats of arms of great antiquarian interest.

They appear to have been put up by the former possessors at different periods, and most of the arms belong to the family of Clopton and their connections by marriage; but the glass varies much in date. Among these coats of arms are,

Clopton impaling Trussell; for Sir William Clopton, the great nephew of the first owner of Kentwell, and Frances Trussell, his wife.

Howard impaling Tilney.

Denston impaling Clopton; for John Denston, of Denston Hall, Suffolk, and Catherine, daughter of Sir William and sister of John Clopton.

Clopton impaling Waldegrave; for Thomas Clopton, who died 1597, and Mary Waldegrave, of Smallbridge, Bures, who died 1599.

De Vere impaling Howard; for the 12th Earl of Oxford and Elizabeth Howard; they married 1428, and he and their son Aubrey de Vere, Sir William Tyrell, Sir John Montgomery, and Sir Thomas Tuddenham, were all beheaded on Tower Hill, 22nd February,

1461, when John Clopton, their fellow-prisoner, alone escaped their fate.

Tendring impaling Mylde; for Sir William Tendring, Knight, of Stoke-by-Nayland, and Catherine Mylde, widow of Sir Thomas Clopton, the heiress who brought to the Cloptons the Kentwell estate.

Clopton impaling Mylde; for Sir Thomas Clopton and the above-named Catherine Mylde.

Bouchier impaling Plantagenet; for Henry Bouchier, Earl of Essex, 1461, and Isabella, daughter of Richard, Duke of Cambridge, who was beheaded at Southampton, 1415.

Clopton impaling Franceys; for William Clopton, who died 1446, and his second wife, Margery Franceys, who died 1423. (His first wife was Margery Drury.)

Erpingham impaling Clopton; for Sir Thomas Erpingham, Knight of the Garter, and his second wife, Joan Clopton. He was at one time in great danger, as a suspected Lollard: he died in 1428, and was buried in Norwich Cathedral, of which he built the beautiful west gate as a penance for his heresy.

Clopton impaling Darcy; for John Clopton and Alice Darcy. He died 1497, and is buried in the Easter tomb in Melford Church.

Clopton impaling Barnardiston.—There was more than one inter-marriage of these families: this glass was probably for Sir William Clopton, who died 1618, and his first wife, Ann, daughter of Sir Thomas Barnardiston, of Clare. She died 1615.

Harleston impaling Clopton; for John Harleston and Alice Clopton, who was born about 1410.

Howard impaling Molines; for Sir John Howard and his first wife, Catherine, daughter of Richard Lord Molines. Sir John Howard was created Duke of Norfolk, and was the

"Jocky of Norfolk be not too bold,
For Dickon thy master is bought and sold,"

who was slain at the battle of Bosworth, 1485, and buried at Thetford. His wife Catherine was buried in Stoke-by-Nayland church, where there is a fine portrait of her in brass.

Howard impaling Tendring; for Sir John Howard, grandfather of the above, and Alice, daughter of Sir William Tendring and Catherine Mylde. In 1416 Sir Walter Clopton and William Clopton were trustees for Sir John Howard and his wife.

Arms of England and France quarterly.

A shield of the arms of *Clopton*, quartering 19 other coats of arms. There is a similar painted shield on the wall of the Clopton Chapel in Melford Church.

2 B

Besides the arms above mentioned, there are several other shields and various quarterings of arms.

About midway between the moat in front of the house and the north end of the avenue, on each side of the road, there are signs of extensive foundations of buildings which have been at some time removed. They are more plainly visible in hot summer weather, from the colour of the grass over them. The present stables being of a modern date, it has been conjectured that the original stable buildings in two blocks, with the entrance-road between them, were on the site of these old foundations. Such an arrangement was not uncommon in former days; and in a rude map of 1677, a wall and gateway is shown across the entrance-road, considerably in advance of the moat in front of the house. If it was so, these buildings must have spoiled the aspect of the Hall from without, as well as injuring the view from within; and perhaps some such reason may have led to their removal.

In 1826 a fire occurred, from which Kentwell appears to have narrowly escaped destruction. The dining-room was burnt, and the fire extended through the house to the garden side, and from thence can be traced the portions of the external wall which it became necessary to rebuild.

No stranger who, on a sunshiny summer's day, walks down the beautiful long avenue of lime-trees, planted nearly two hundred years ago, and now forming a natural arch of foliage overhead, and, emerging from its shade, comes into the full view of the gloriously-hued stately pile of building facing him, can for a moment wonder that among the many picturesque beauties of Melford, its inhabitants are justly proud of Kentwell Hall.

CHAPTER VIII.

MELFORD CHARITIES.

MELFORD is fairly rich in charities. Many are derived from ancient inhabitants, whose lines had fallen in this pleasant place, and some also from persons who had only known it as their first early home; their fortunes having led them to dwell elsewhere, yet whose thoughts to the end still fondly clung to the dear old birth-place. These, mindful of the divine precept of almsgiving, when their turns drew nigh to start on that last long journey, on which they could not carry their worldly substance, bequeathed some portions thereof for deeds of future charity and mercy to their poorer neighbours of Melford, as well as for the maintenance and repair of that grand old church, into which they in their early days had been solemnly admitted.

Probably, in point of date, the first charitable bequest which still exists, was given by the will of *Robert Colet* in the 15th century. When it is remembered that then, and indeed for centuries after, the best roads of this country were mere green tracks, rough and rutty in summer, and in winter almost impassable with deep mire, it appears but little strange that a person living at that time should consider that he was doing a real charity to his neighbours and their descendants in leaving a provision in trust for the improvement of the wretched roads over which they had to travel. So Robert Colet left his lands at Rodbridge, called "Nelys," for the repair of the highways of Melford for ever.

In various repetitions of this bequest in the Melford terriers, different dates have crept in, such as 1408, 1480. In the old transcript copy of the will of Colet, in the Melford Black Book, the date appears as 1414. Whether this also was not an error seems doubtful, for this land was apparently that which had belonged to Roger Nell, and continued to be called by his name, as Nelys or Nell's; and if so, the following conveyance of it by Nell's widow to Robert Colet for £20, did not pass till the year 1458, and Colet's bequest must therefore have been subsequent to that date.

The conveyance from Isabella Nell (now in the parish chest) is beautifully written on parchment, with a seal attached in good preservation, of Richard Martyn (R. M.), with his cloth-mark. The substance of it runs thus, translated from the Latin:—" We, Isabella, formerly wife of Roger Nell, of Melford, Richard Martyn, and John Waryn at the brook, of the same town, have conveyed to Robert Colet, John Clopton, gentleman, William Colman, chaplain, and John Amyot the elder, of Melford, the lands and tenements in Melford which had belonged to the said Roger [Nell] and which formerly were of the dimission and feoffment of Laurence Martyn, John Dowe, and Simon Amyot, of Melford; to have and to hold to the said Robert Colet, &c., their heirs and assigns, of the feoff in chief of the lord, by the services due on these conditions following; viz., that the said Robert Colet shall pay or cause to be paid to the said Isabella, her heirs, executors, or attorney, £20 of lawful money of England in manner and form following; that is to say, at Easter next following the date of this deed, and at the feast of St. Michael, at each 20 shillings; and yearly during nine years immediately following, 40 shillings, in equal portions, in like manner, at the feast of Easter and Michaelmas. In witness whereof the said Isabella and all the named persons have set their seals. These being witnesses:—Roger Moriell, Robert Sparwe [Sparrowe], Roger Ponder, Walter Hervey, John Kent, and others. Given at Melford the 1st day of October, in the 36th year of the reign of King Henry the Sixth " [1458].

Of the various persons named in this deed, many are clearly to be identified. Richard Martyn died in 1463; John Waryn, who was one of several of the same name at about that period, is distinguished as John Waryn "at the brook:" he was a fuller by trade, who is described as holding land in 1442 in Smaley meadows and by the bridge there. John Clopton, of Kentwell, died in 1497; Laurence Martyn died in 1460; John Dowe, a fuller, and Simon Amyot, held lands in Melford in 1442; Roger Moriell's name is on the walls of the church; Robert Sparwe (Sparrowe) died 1468. Roger Ponder, in 1442, held land adjoining Walter Hervey, who lived near Wissendale; John Kent died in 1482. Robert Colet was, in 1442, next door neighbour, in Hall Street, to John Waryn.

COLET'S CHARITY.

Robert Colet's Will as entered in Melford Black Book.

"The last Wyll of Robert Colet whyles he lyved of Melforde within the dyocesse of Norwyche mayde the thyrde daye of May, in the yere of oure Lorde God, a thousande fure hundrythe and furton. [?] Amongest oder legacyes he gave and bequethed hys place and lande in Radbryge Strete called Nelys in these worde:—

"I wyll that Henry Chandeler have my place and lande in Rad-bryge Strete, the wyche ys called Nelys to ferme for tenne yeres wyth

syx horse and a carte paying therfor yerly xxvi˟ viii˟, and at the tenne
yeres ende I wyll he shal leive as many horse and a carte, wyth a
tumberell and a plowe, as he haith at the begynnynge and of as goode
walew as they be prysed, or els the pryse therof: the wyche
xxvi˟ viii˟ yerly over the reparacyon and rente payde, I wyll yt be
bestowed in the hyghe wayes of Melforde by the advyse of myne
execoutours and supervysor. And I wyll that the sayd Chandeler have
the trymynge of the reparacyon of the hyghe wayes befor any may.
And after the tenne yeres ende I wyll that my sayd place wyth all the
sayd stuffe be lette to ferme to the moste walew and the profytte that
grow therof besyde rente and reparacyon that yt be bestowed yerely
on the hyghewayes in Melforde: requyryng and desyryng myne
execoutours and supervysor that they put the sayd lande and place in
feoffament so that the profytte therof may goe to the hyghe wayes in
perpetuyte."

The executors: Charles Elys and John Houthe.

In this will the horse power for so small a farm seems considerable, there being six horses for forty acres of land; especially as at that
time it was customary to use oxen mainly for ploughing.

The property which Colet bequeathed, together with two cottages,
adjoins Mr. William Mill's land at Rodbridge, and is now let to him
(on a 12 year's lease from Michaelmas, 1865) for a gross rent of £62
a year, and the proceeds are paid to the Lavenham Highway Board on
behalf of Melford parish.

The old churchwardens' "Black Book" gives the full abuttals of
this land (page 129), and it is all shown on the Melford Manor maps
of 1580 and 1613. This land was originally about 40 acres, but in
later times it was reduced to about 38 acres by the sale of a small
portion to realize money to redeem the land-tax on the remainder.
There has also been an exchange of part of this land, thus: 15a. 1r. 26p.,
formerly in five pieces inconveniently scattered and dispersed among
lands belonging to Mr. William Jennings (now to Mr. William Mills,
of Rodbridge), were exchanged for other land belonging to Mr. Jennings, containing 16a. 3r. 13p., lying in one compact piece, adjoining
the remainder of the original land of Nelys.

JOHN HILL's CHARITY.

1495.

John Hyll, or Hill, a clothier of Melford, gave to the poor of
Melford for ever, his quit-rents, or, as then called, white rents, of Bower
Hall, Pentlow, and a wood there, altogether now producing the sum
of £12. 14s. 2d. a year, the wood having been converted to tillage. This

charity having been applied for a considerable period, with the consent of the parishioners, to the free education of a certain number of poor boys of Melford, is now paid for that object to the funds of the National School, where eleven poor boys are taught free of charge.

In the reign of Henry VII., Bower Hall, in Pentlow, belonged to John Hill, a clothier of Long Melford, whose name is recorded outside the church, and who by his will, dated 4th May, 1495, gave all his manor aforesaid (except the white or quit-rents and wood belonging thereto) unto Sir William Hogeson, to pray for the souls of him and his friends in the church of Melford. The white rents and woods he gave to the poor of Melford, and a chantry was founded for him in Melford church, called "Hill's Chantry." With the above white rents were dues of four capons, and one day's work in hay-season and in fowling, yearly, besides 14½d. for rents and services in Pentlow. The wood was about nine acres. Questions having arisen about this charity, it was confirmed by a grant from King Edward VI. at the suit of Sir William Cordell. The charity was well paid for many years, till at last default was made by certain persons, particularly by one John Gooday; whereupon a commission for charitable uses was obtained, 16th September, 1663, and the commissioners, upon a full hearing and inspection of records, decreed, on the 15th October following, that the owners of this manor should pay to the church-wardens of Melford all arrears, and the said quit-rents for ever; and that these parish officers should have the ownership of the wood; which order of the commissioners was confirmed by a decree of Chancery, 6th April, 1665, and a writ of execution was issued out the 12th May following.

Subjoined is part of John Hill's will.

Extracts of the Will of John Hyll (or Hill).

A.D. 1495.

" The last wyll of John Hyll whyles he lyved of Melforde within the dyocese of Norwyche, mayd the iiiith daye of May in the yere of our Lorde God, a thousande coco, ᵐ, and fyftene [1495].

" Amongest other legacyes he gave and bequethed the whyte rente and woode belongyng to the Manor of Bowre Hall in these worde followyng :—

" *Item :* the whyte rente and the woode wich belongyth to the sayd manor and ys above excerpt, I will yt be dysposed by myne excutors under thys forme; that ys to say, that certayn of my tenne-mentes wich be porest, whose namys I have in a byll expressed, the next halfe yere rent after my dyssease I gyf them, to pray for me and my freuds.

"*Item:* the fyne of the alynacion of Panels when so ever yt fall I wyll yt remayn to the reparacion of the Churche in Pentlowe foresayd.

"*Item:* I gyf and bequeth unto John Godwyn as long as he dwellyth or abydyth in the towne of Melforde in syknesse and in helth, whether he be in servyce of the towne or not in servyce, of the foresayd whyte rentes, vj⁴ viij⁴ the yere, duryng hys lyf to be payd by myne excutors once in y⁴ yere, and I wyll that no porcion of the sayd vj⁴ viij⁴ be put to the fulfylling of hys wagys, nor that he tayke never a peny the lesse in the towne for thys my gyft, for thys intent I wyll the sayd John have yt alonely to have my soule in remembraunce.

"*Item:* the resydew of the sayd whyte rent and woode I wyll yt be desposed amonge the poore pepull in Melford aforsayd by the hande of myne executors or there executors or assygnes for and in paying the kyngs taxe whan yt falleth, and whan yt falleth not, I wyll yt be dysposed dyscretly in almes dede to the porest pepull within the sayd town—and who so yt be that after the dyssease of myne executors that hayth the gatheryng and dystrybucion of the sayd whyte rent and woode, I will he have ech yere of the same for hys labour vj⁴ viij⁴ [6s. 8d.], and once in the yere to gyf accompts therof unto the heyres executors or assygnes of my forsayd executors. And for lacke of heyres or executors unto the churchwardens within the sayd town.

"Executors to thys wyll, John Barker of Acton, Gylbert Barker and John Barker at the Hert (and Robert Bery my servante ?) *This in brackets is written in another hand.*

"Wuytnese   Mr. Thos. Aleyn alias Carver."

"1541. *Memo.*—The sealed wyll remayneth in the college of Sudbury and openly seen in Melford Church before these men— Gyles Elys, Will™ Kyng, and Thos. Barker, and the wryter herof, Sir John Gayton, the v⁴ [5th] day of August, año dñi milîimo quiñgent quadragessimo primo."

In another hand as follows :—"The dedes and other wrytynge remayneth in the custodye of Sir Edward Turrell" [in other memo's called "Turrett." He was a priest].

"The accompte of John Gager gatherer of the whyte rente of Bowerhall belongyng to the use of poore peple and the kyngs taxe when yt falleth in Melford wich ys yerly iij⁴ iij⁴ v⁴ [£3. 3s. 5d.] mayd ye seconde daye of November from ye feast of the annuncyacion of our lady, yt was in ye xxx yere of our soverayne lorde ye Kynge [Henry VIII.—1540] unto the feast of Saynt Mychell in xxxiv yere of our sayd soverayne lorde ye Kynge [1543] as yt apperyth by hys byls delyvred into the honde of the churchwardens in the presens of Thomas Barker, Richard Smyth, Gyles Elys, Wyll™ Maye, John

Cordell, Wyll^m Kyng, Wyll^m Smethe, Thomas Crysall, Thomas Waltre, & other.

"And y^t ys agreed y^t who so hayth the gatheryng of ye sayd whyt rente y^t he shall gyfe hys accompte yerly herafter apon all sowles day y^t ys to say the seconde daye of November before the honest men of Melforth and churchwardens of ye same for the tyme beynge how y^t he hayth gathered and dystrybuted ye sayd whyte rente accordyng unto ye wyll of John Hyll the Donator and gyffer therof."

There is a species of terrier of this land, with its abuttals, at page 127 of the old Churchwardens' Book.

1694.

The Account of Nathaniel Bisbie, D.D., and Mr. John Knopp, touching the Pension issuing out of the King's Exchequer to the Poor of Melford; as also touching the Bower Hall Estate, in Pentlow, Essex, of the Gift of *John Hill* to the said Poor, and now settled by the full consent of the Inhabitants of Melford upon the Free School of Melford, for the Educating of Eleven Poor Boys, made the 18th Day of April, A.D. 1694.

Receipts.	£.	s.	d.
Out of the Exchequer yearly	2	18	1

Hill's Charity.

	£.	s.	d.
Quit-rents of Bower Hall Manor at Michaelmas yearly .	4	4	2¼
Four Rent Capons due from some of the said tenants yearly at Christmas	0	2	0
Bower Hall Woods yearly at Candlemas-day . . .	2	5	0
House in the said woods yearly at Lady-day . . .	1	18	0
Value of Hill's Charity A.D. 1694 . . .	8	9	2¼

6s. 8d. paid yearly to the collector of these rents.

Many of the original deeds, confirmations, and decrees relative to this charity are in the iron-bound chest in the vestry of Melford church.

Although in 1694 the parishioners in vestry decided on applying this charity to educational purposes, this resolution is liable to be rescinded in like manner at any time, as the testator made no appointment of his bequest to any such purpose, but left it to the *poor* of Melford. And therefore, although the proceeds of this charity may be paid to the National School of Melford, it cannot be treated by the Government school authorities as being an endowment belonging to the National Schools.

Skyrn's or Skene's Charity.

A.D. 1510.

Mr. William Skyrn, sometimes called Skerne, and at others Skene, who was formerly a parson of Melford, bequeathed certain lands in Melford called "Thumbs," to be applied in equal shares for the poor of Melford and for the maintenance of Melford Church. Two cottages still belonging to the parish, on the east side of Day's Lane, at the top of Cranmoor Hill, were a part of this property, and were on the site of the homestall of Thumbs. The land was in many small detached pieces, lying amid the Kentwell estate, much scattered and difficult of access, and in 1839 an arrangement was made between the parish and the owner of Kentwell Hall for an exchange of lands, whereby the parish, in lieu of seven scattered pieces of inferior land, containing about 11½ acres, acquired the two fields, now called the Back Lane Allotments, on the east of the town, which are of excellent quality, and from their position much better adapted for the purpose of charity land.

In 1862–3, when the Great Eastern Railway line from Melford to Bury was made, a small portion of this exchanged Back Lane Allotment land was required for the line; for which land the company paid to the parish the sum of £200. This money was by the direction of a vestry meeting invested in £213. 16s. consols, in the names of Sir William Parker and Captain Edward Robert Starkie Bence, as trustees for the parish, who receive and pay to the churchwardens the dividends, amounting to about £6. 5s. a year, which, with the rents of the Thumbs cottages and land, the allotments (including Day's Lane and High Cross, which came from other sources), comprising in all 13a. 1r. 2p., amount to an average gross sum of about £37. 9s. a year, the net proceeds of which are applied equally between the poor and the church; but the outgoings of rates, tithe, land-tax, &c., diminish the amount considerably.

There appears to be some confusion as to the acreage of Skenes. The entire quantity of the Thumbs land was said to be originally 16a. 3r. 24p. (on the board in the church 20a.), nine pieces of which, amounting to about 10 acres, were held by free tenure from the Rectory manor at a quit-rent of 2s. 3d. a year. This land is now, however, part of the Kentwell estate by the exchange. The ancient abuttals of the land are fully given in the Melford churchwardens' Black Book, page 130.

The following is an extract from the donor's will:—

" A.D. 1510.—The Artykyll of the last wyll of Mr William Skyrn, somtyme parson of Melford, wich dyssesyd the xxii daye of Apryll in the yere of our Lorde God a MCCCCCX concernyng the londe in Cranmere called Thommys and Marke in these wordes.—

"And wher as I have bargaynyd with Maister Mertyn for a certeyn tenement called Thommys and Merke, and other parcells, havyng as yet none estate therin, yf yt can be seen by myne executours and supervysor that they can have suernys in the londe, that my executours paye up the resydew of the mony, and the profyt therof to go to the poore pepull of Melford by the dyscrecion of my executours :—and after ther desseys, by the parson of the Churche of Melford and the churchewardens of the same by the space of $\frac{XX}{III}$ and XIX yeres [99 years], and after the yeres of $\frac{XX}{III}$ and XIX to be sold by the parson of Melford and the churchewardens of the same, and the mony therof cummyng the one halfe to the poore pepull and the other halfe unto Melford Church.

"The utentycall dede herof wyth thys seyd artykyll upon the backe therof, remaynyth in the tresure huch within the vestre of the seyde church."

The lands to the said use were put in feoffment by a deed, bearing date 12th December, in the 9th year of Henry VIII., A.D. 1518.

In the churchwardens' books the rent of this land is given as in 1679, at £10 a year, 1706 at £12.

KING EDWARD THE SIXTH'S GRANT.

King Edward the Sixth gave a pension for ever to the poor of Melford, to be paid from the Exchequer. The amount is now £2. 12s. 9d. a year.

RICHARD SMITH'S CHARITY.

1560.

Richard Smith, of Barkston, in the county of Leicester, but who was a native of Melford, gave, in 1560, a sum of £1. 10s. charged on land at Mendlesham, in Suffolk, called "Crow Croft," to be distributed annually at the Feast of St. Thomas, for the benefit of the poor of Melford. This is now given in the money distribution called the " Widow's Gift."

WILLIAM CHAPLYN'S CHARITY.

1575.

William Chaplyn, of Melford, gave in 1575, a tenement called Cook's House (now two cottages under one roof), at Cuckoo Tye, in this parish, for the relief of the poor of Melford. The proceeds of this now amount to £7. 16s., and the net amount, after payment of out-goings, is given in the "Widow's Gift."

JOHN CORDER'S CHARITY.

John Corder, by his will, devised the sum of £2 a year for ever, to be given to the poor of Melford in bread, and he charged his lands at Lawshall, called "Kings," with the payment thereof. This charity is no longer given in bread, but now forms part of the "Widow's Gift."

MOORE'S CHARITY.

26th December, 1700:

Mr. John Moore, of Kentwell Hall, bequeathed to the minister and churchwardens of Melford, for the time being, £300, to be paid within one year after his decease, upon trust to purchase an estate, and to use the rents, profits, &c., for the payment *for ever of a schoolmistress* to teach and instruct 10 *poor boys* of the said parish to *read* English, and 10 *poor girls* of the said parish to *read, and sew, and knit*, and to buy necessaries to sew and knit with, until they can be sooner put out and provided for; and ordered that such school should be under the govern-ment and direction of the governor for the time being of the hospital of Melford, called the Trinity Hospital, and of the minister and church-wardens of Melford for the time being.

This now goes in support of Crouch's School for life. This money had some years ago to be transferred and reinvested, and an expense of £19. 18s. 6d. was incurred thereon; and in order that the charity should not be reduced by this expense, the parish paid this sum in 1863, and they take from the dividends £2. 3s. 6d. a year, until they shall be recouped, which will be about 1873; until then Crouch's School only receives about £9 a year. After Mrs. Crouch's death, this money may be available to *national schools* for 10 *girls* and 10 *boys*. The £300 is now invested in £372. 19s. 1d. reduced annuities.

DR. JOHN MAYOR'S CHARITY.

John Mayor, doctor in divinity, devised by his will forty shillings a year for ever, out of his estate lying in Rayden, in Suffolk, to be dis-tributed yearly upon Christmas-eve, to twenty poor families dwelling nearest to his house in Melford, who keep their parish church constantly.

The family of Mayor were long settled in Melford. They were resident at " Prowdes " prior to 1580, and were perhaps the same family as mentioned in Foot's will in 1512.

JOHN MOORE'S CHARITY.[*]

1700 (?).

John Moore, late of Kentwell Hall, Melford, by his will bequeathed to the minister and churchwardens of Melford for the time being, the sum of £100 on trust, to purchase lands and tenements, and distribute the rents thereof annually among 20 poor old men or widows, of above the age of 60 years, who do not take alms of the parish, and who frequent the Church of England.

This £100 was at one time invested in land at Icklingham, but in 1775 this land was sold, and the proceeds, amounting to £155, were invested in the purchase of a house and premises in Melford, which were used as a parish workhouse, and of which the rent was then £6 a year. After the New Poor Law Act, the house was sold by order of the Poor Law Commissioners, and was purchased by the Rector of Melford, realizing £170. To this sum was added £76. 19s. 2d., which arose from sale of timber on Bower Hall Wood being stubbed up, and some other parish money was also added, and with the total amount the five cottages in Hall Street, near Liston Lane, were built, and the proceeds arising from their rentals, being a gross sum of £19, is thus apportioned by consent: £4. 4s. 6d. as interest on the Bower Hall and parish money, is applied to the national schools (the Pentlow charity being applied to this use); another part, after payment of outgoings, goes to the poor, and the surplus to the repair of the church.

MRS. HARRIETT OLIVER'S CHARITY.

2nd September, 1825.

Mrs. Harriett Oliver gave by her will to the overseers and church-wardens of Melford, the interest of four thousand pounds, three per cent. consols, to be applied in the purchase of coals to be distributed amongst the poor of Melford annually; on whose behalf a deed of trust was obtained, the expenses of which, with duty, have reduced the gross amount to £3,634. 3s. 3d. three per cent. consols. The said last-mentioned sum was standing in the names of trustees under the said will, by a decree in the Court of Chancery; but after the death of the Rev. Edward Cobbold, in 1861, who was one of the trustees, this fund was transferred to the Charity Commissioners by Richard Almack, Esq., the last surviving trustee.

---

[*] The Charity Commissioners' Report gives the date of this charity as 1713, and they spell Mr. Moore's name as Moor.

MISS FREWER'S CHARITY.

25th April, 1857.

Mary Frewer by her will devised as follows: "I direct my executors to purchase £100 of the same stock as that in which the late Mrs. Harriett Oliver's charity money is invested, and in the names of the same trustees for the time being, and I request that the same trustees for the time being will receive the dividends thereof, and pay the same to the officiating minister, for the time being, of Melford Church, to be by him applied in any manner he may think proper for the benefit of the Sunday or Church-school at Melford aforesaid for ever."

In pursuance of this direction, the executors paid the duty on the legacy, £9. 12s., and £87. 5s. 6d. for the purchase of £89. 19s. 6d. three per cent. consols: this stock, like the last-mentioned charity stock, was transferred to the Charity Commissioners in 1861 by the last surviving trustee, R. Almack, Esq.

OSMUND'S CHARITY LANDS.

Various bequests of money and goods had been made at different times, in olden days, by John Barker and sundry other persons (some of whose wills are here given), for the repairs of the church and highways of Melford, and for the good of their souls. Of these legacies some were left in kind, and others as remainders. About 300 years ago certain of these bequests were realized, and the sums, amounting to £80, were together invested in the purchase of land at Stoke-by-Nayland, now known as "Osmund's Charity Land." Its name of Osmund's is very ancient, for in a conveyance from Matilda, widow of John Marchaunt, it is so named, and is described as abutting on the land of the Priory of Prytewelle. This deed is of 1419, and is attested, among other persons, by Ph. Mannok (of Gifford's Hall). There is another conveyance of it in 1497, from William Whepstede, of Boxford. In the year 1575 the inhabitants of Melford agreed that the apportionment of the rent of this land, about 20 acres, should be at the rate of two-thirds for the repair of the church, and the other third equally between the poor and for the repair of the highways of Melford. The rent, which now amounts to £35, should be so apportioned, after payment of outgoings. The land is let on a twelve years' lease from Michaelmas 1872, to Mr. C. Worters.

The following document is the agreement for this division:—

"Forasmuch as the sayde tenemente callyd Osmunds with purtenances was purchasyd with the Churchys monye, the poores, and the hye wayes; but the gretest summe was of the Churches monye. Yt ys therfore agreed uppon thys XIII of August A° D^d 1575 by the best of the inhabyters of thys towneshypp of Melford that a convenyent rate and dyvysyon of the yerelye profytte and revenewes of the premysses shal be made and from hencforth observyd by the Churchewardens there alwayes for the tyme beyng, accordyng to suche severall portyons of monye—viz. of the Churchys, the poores, and the hye wayes layd owte for the sayd purchase as afooresayd wich dyvysyon and rate aperyth as in manner and forme followyng.

"Furst—The sayd Churchewardens of the yerelye profytte of the premysses to be ymployed by them to the use of the Churche of Melford and of our Lady's Chappell thereunto adjoynyng at ye Est end for so long tyme as the same are letten for iiij^{li} [£4] by yere, shall receyve and take p. añn. liij^s iiij^d [53s. 4d.], and to the use of the poore xiij^s iiij^d [13s. 4d.], and to the use of the hye wayes xiij^s iiij^d [13s. 4d.], and when the same shall be letten for fyve Powndes by yere then they shall receyve thereof to the use of the poore xvi^s viii^d and to the use of the hye wayes lykewyse xvi^s viii^d p. añn.

"So two partes of the sayd Tenemente called Osmunds ys to goe to the reparacyons of Melford Churche and the Chappell, and the thyrd parte to be equallye devyded betweene the poore and the hye wayes."

In another handwriting there follows thus :—

"And now [1677] beying letten for viij^{li} p. añn there ys to be payd to the use of the Churche and our lady's Chappell aforseyd p. añn. v^{li} vj^s viij^d and to the poore xxvi^s viii^d p. añn and to the hye wayes xxvi^s viii^d p. añn."

In another handwriting :—

"The Churche ys to paye the oute rente yf the ferm : dothe not :"

In 1775 the rent had increased to £15 a year : it now amounts to £35 a year. So this land has increased in rental value nearly ninefold in the last three centuries.

Of late years an erroneous custom has crept in of paying onethird of the rent for the highways, and so now to the Highway Board ; whereas a moiety of this third should go to the use of the poor.

Some of the following are parts of the charities which eventually were realized and invested in "Osmund's." The copy of John Barker's will is very illegible. Barrell's charity, which follows, was perhaps one of these : the land appears to have been adjacent to King's Lane, but cannot now be clearly identified.

BARRELL'S.

1508.

John Barrell's bequest for the good of his soul; and a reversionary benefit for the poor of Melford.

"The last wyll of John Barrell whyles he lyved of Melforde within the dyocese of Norwych, mayd the syxt daye of the month of September in the yere of our Lorde MCCCCO and VIII. Amongest other legacyes he wylles and bequethes hys tenement in Foteforde Strete in these wordes: viz:—

"And I wyll that my tenement in Foteforde Strete wyth the londe pastures and all other the appurtenence unto the same tenement belonging shall remayn in feoffes hands immedyately after my dyssease for $\frac{xx}{iiii}$ and nynetene yeres [99 years] unto thys use folowying. That they be letten to ferme by myne executours to the most avauntage and that wyth the mony therof cumyng out the Rents yerely payd, all reparacions thereof mayntened and sustened, shall yerely kepe my obyt in the seyd parysh churche of Melforde for the yeres abovesayd. And of the overplus I wyll that the parson of Melforde have yerely XIId for the bederoll kepyng therein my name, and for hys dylygens.*—And the resydew therof cumyng, yf any be, to be dystrybuted and gyfn to the poor pepull dwelling wythyn the sayd towne of Melforde by the dystrybucion of myne executours. And I wyll and requyre all my feoffes of and in the sayd tenement, londe, and pastures wyth appurtenance that they and everyone of them shal delyver or do to be delyvered, a suffycyent and lawful astate of me in the same premysses unto syxtene suer honest persons dwelling wythyn the sayd town of Melforde at such tyme as they and any of them shal be therto convenyently requyred by myne Executors accordyng to the performacion of thys my testament and last wyll. Morover I wyll that when it shall fortune x or XII of the sayde XVI persons to dyssease then I wyll those vj or iiij then lyvyng mayke and delyver a new estate on agayne unto other XVI persons wich at that tyme shal be thought most convenyent unto the sayd use and so to contynew as long as yt may please God to endure.—Furthermore I wyll that after the dessease of myne Executors that the profytte cummyng of the sayd premysses shal be at the dysposycion of the parson of the sayd churche of Melford wich ys or shal be, and by the Churchwardens, and so to order unto the forseyd use.—And after the tyme of $\frac{xx}{iiii}$ and nyncteen yeres [99 years] to bo solde by the feoffes and dysposed for my soull and my frends soulls within the parysh of Melford.

* So he bequeathed his property that his obit day, or anniversary of his death, should be kept in the church for ninety-nine years; and yearly a shilling to the parson, to keep his name on the bederoll, or roll of dead persons for whom Mass was to be said.

"The approved wyll and xiiii pecys of evydens belonging therto remaynes in the tresure huche within the vestre of the sayd church.

"The Executors Mayster Willm Skyrn somtyme parson of Melford and Jeffere Foot."

(This Geoffrey Foote's will follows next.—He died before 1512.)

The abuttals of this land are in the old churchwardens' book, page 130.

THE BEQUEST OF GAFFERYE FOTE (FOOTE).

A.D. 1512.

To find a priest at Melford and 40s. to the poor of Melford.

"Inprimis geven by Gafferye Fote certen londe to the fyndyng of a pīt. at Melford and xl^s to the poore peple of ye same towne within the dyosese of Norwych, Anno Dom' mv°xii, as followyth.

"I wyll that all my londe and tenements, medows, pastures, woodes, rente and fruite, with th' appurtenance wych I have, or any man to my use within the countye of Essex be put in feoffement to other persons namyd by myne executryce and supervisor to the coste of my last wyll and the profitte of the wyche londe I wyll how my wyffe shall have and enjoye duryng her lyff, and after her deth to remayne to John Fote my brother and the heiers males of hys bodye lawfullye begotten—and for lacke of yssue of the sayd John, I wyll yt shall remayne lykewyse to Willm Mayer: and for lacke of yssue of the sayd Mayer or for not performyng this my wyll to remayne unto John Danyell and his heyers: and yf the sayd Danyell dye withoute yssue or else that this my wyll be not performyd of his part or his heiers or executors, that then I wyll all the premisses to remayne to Sr Roger Martyn and his heiers performyng this my last wyll and testament, and for lacke of heires as aforesayd of ye sayd Roger to be sold and to goe to Melford; wyche wyll ys to geve yerelye unto a prest to syng in Melford x markes and a other part of the profitte of the premisses to the kepyng of my erth daye for evermore; and thereat. to be geven to Prestes, Clerkes, pore men and wemen wythyn Melford xl shillings to praye for owre sowles for evermore.

"Sole Executryce I make Jeane my wyffe, and Sir Roger Martyn, Supervysor.

"Alle the premissis ys in the occupying of John Mayer, son to foresayd William.—And further I wyll the Prest shal syng iii dayes in the weke at Sent James Chappell [on Chapel Green], the resydew at Melford Churche, wythout resonable lett.

"The Copye of thys wyll remayneth in Sir Roger Martyns handes and kepyng, and in J. Mayers.

With reference to Foot's bequest of his lands in reversion for prayers for him for ever, it may be noticed that twenty years after the date of this will, legislation on this subject had become necessary.. In 1532 it was enacted that lands could only be burdened with bequests for prayers for souls, or for priests to sing for the dead, for twenty years; after which the lands were to relapse to the heir. By long usage the custom had become so settled for persons to leave by will a sum to be expended in masses, that the priests eventually came to consider such bequests as an absolute right and perquisite. At last a case arose which induced a revolution of feeling in the matter. A Gloucestershire gentleman named Tracy had left no money to be expended in masses for him; and as by his will he had bequeathed his soul to God through the mercies of Christ, declining the mediatorial offices of saints, the priests took advantage of this as a confession of heresy, to revenge themselves on him even after death; for as soon as the contents of his will were known, they actually dug up his dead body and burnt it.

A.D. 1513.

JOHN BARKER'S CHARITY (part to Melford Church).

Extract from Barker's Will.

" The last Will of John Barker at the Feste, whyles he lyvyd in Melford within the dyocesse of Norwyche, made the XIII daye of Februarie in the yere of our Lord God MCCCCCXIII. Amongest other thyngs he gave and bequethed to Melford Churche and other goode usys his howse callyd the Feste with other tenementes and legaces in maner and forme followyng.—

" *Imprimis.* I bequethe to the Hye Aulter of Melford Churche for the Tythes and offerynges forgotten, III* IIII*. *Item.* I bequethe to Margarete my wiff my place called the Feste which I dwel in with the appurtenaunces, and the twayn ferms called 'Frikkers' and 'Cuoples,' with ther garthings; those of the sed . . . . . [query *Frikkers*] lyeth on the Southe syd of my foresed place; and the other on the Northe parte of my foresed place for terme of lyffe: and after her dissese Gylbert and Robert my sonnes: and after ther dessese without yssue, I wyll that the foresed place &c. with appurtenaunces be solde and the mony therof applyed to the use of the reparyng of Melford Churche and our Ladys Chappel.

" *Item.* The plate bequethed to my sonne for the chyldren yf they dye wythout yssue before they cum to yeres of XX*, to the use as befor sed.

" *Item.* I bequeth to the gyldyng of the Ymage of the Trinitye before my wyffe's grave XLVI* VIII*.

2 D

"*Item.* Also al the londe and pastures which I bowte of M^r Rg^{r.} Martyn and John Marby late of Melford lyinge in the Nether Bulney I give and bequeth as aforsed.

"The copye of thys wyll remayneth in Mr Rogere Martyn's hande."

There was also another bequest, failing his children's heirs, of a close of land lying in Hundon, or its price, to Melford church and the chapel of our Lady. There is also a note of a subsequent date, that "M^r Cār. Danyell of Acton marryed Margery the wyff of the fore-namyd John Barker." She was Barker's second wife. She gave to Melford church a chalice weighing 16¼ ounces.

The Feste, which was a place of some importance, stood on the west side of Hall Street, near the site of the Crown Inn; and its premises included those now Mr. John Bullingbrook's, and others, and Smaley meadows. In the Manor maps of 1613 and 1615 it is called "the Fosse;" and it is evident that this part of the property did not lapse to the church for want of heirs.

The following extracts are among the records of other charitable bequests to this parish, which, alas! have long since been lost; who shall now tell how or when? Some, perhaps, in the troublous unsettled time of the Rebellion, for one or two are traceable till after the year 1600; and some small plots have also been lost in compara-tively modern times. Although we may lament the unscrupulousness of those who in former days thus removed the old landmarks of our poorer neighbours, we may therefrom also take to heart the lesson of the imperative duty of all parishioners to watch jealously over their parish charities.

A.D. 1520.

SYMOND HALL'S [A LOST CHARITY].

Symond Hall, of Long Melford, husbandman,—Charity to Melford Church.

"The Bequest of Symond Hall of Long Melford in the countye of Suff. husbondman unto Melford Churche in manner and forme fol-lowyng, the IX daye of Marche in the yere of our lord God MV^oXX [1520].

"*Inprimis* I give unto Agnes my wyffe my tenement wyche I dwell in with all ye londes therunto belongyng as yt aperyth by the copye of the same that she hath for terme of her lyff paying the Rent and bering the reparacions during her lyff, and after her decese I wyll all the same tenemente and londe be sold by myne executors and the mony therof cummyng I wyll yt be bestowyd by myne executors and supervisur in dede of charyte within the towne and churche of Melford aforseyd.—

"*Item* I geve unto ye sayd Agnes my wyff all my copye hold londes and tenements with th' appurtenences in Melford terme of her lyff paying ye rent and beryng ye reparacions and after her decesse I wyll all ye sayd londe and tenements be sold by myne executors and supervisor and the same to be distributyd in dedes of Charite within the towne and Churche of Melford aforsayd as they shall thynke most best and convenient to the Homage of God and merytt of my sowle.— Also I wyll the sayd Agnes my wyff have my II croftes of pasture wyche were late John Barrell's for terme of her lyff paying ye rent and after her decesse I wyll yt be put in feoffement to the use of Melford Churche and speciallye to the reparement of the glasse wyndowes on the sowth syde of the Churche of Melford.—Executors Agnes my wyff—Gyles Elys—and Sir Wm Clopton supervysor. The copye of this wyll remayneth in Robert Alfounder's hande."

There is a note to the foregoing; viz., "The foresayd Agnes made a wyll of ye II parcelles of pasture, wherein she had but a state for terme of lyffe as yt apperyth in the premisses: wherfore yt ys adnithilated and for ye purporse of non effecte."

The recital of this charity continues in the various terriers of the parish after 1770, but in that of 1791 there is appended for the first time the remark that this, with Hopkyn Hayward's Charity, *had long been lost.*

The following abuttals of this land were also given :—

"Inprimis: one pece of grounde wyche lyeth by the Gawtes house, betweene the londe of Willm Elys of the southe parte, and the londe of Robert Tyler alias Alfunder, sumtyme Symond Hall's of the North. The one hede abbuttyth uppon the hye waye ledyng from Melford to Berye Sent Edmunds towards the est: the other hede abbütt upon the londe now Sr Will. Cloptons quondam the Monks, called Bargage Feld towards the West, and yt conteyneth 1 acre, 1 roode, et di."

On reference to the Melford Manor map of 1580, this land is there named "Melforde Tounc Londe," and its position, agreeing with the above description, is clearly shown, as a strip of land, now belonging to Kentwell Hall, nearly opposite to High Street farmhouse, the south fence thereof coming down to the pond on the west side of the high road, by Lilly's, the woodman.

There is also the description of another piece, which is perhaps now part of the Parish High Cross Allotment land.

"Item an other pece contcynyng 1 acre et di, and XX perchys and lyeth beyond the hye crosse on the est syde of the forseyd hye waye between ye grove now of Thomas Martyn, quondam Symonds Halles of the sowthe part and the londe of ye sayd Martyn quondam Halles of the north. The one hed abutteth upon the sayde londe towerds the Est, the other hede lykewyse towerds the West : the wych hede hath a lane ledyng from and out of the forsayd Berye hye waye to the said pasture."

The following are again lost charities :—

" The ABBUTTALLES of dyverse londes geven to dyvers usys within the towne of Melforde by the gyfte of dyverse men as followyth.—

" Inter alia : Londe callyd Hopkyn, alias Copping, Heywarde.

" *Item :* a pece of arryble grownd conteynyng 1 acre, 1 roode, and 10 perchys, lying betweene the londe of Sir William Clopton, quondam the Hospytelers, callyd Bargage feld, of the Weste parte, and the londe of Sir Wm Clopton of the Est. The one hede abbuttyth upon the londe of Robert Tyler, alias Alfunder, towards the Sowth, and the other hede abbutt upon the sayd Sir Wm Cloptons londe quondam the Hospytellers towards the Northe.—The meres of ye sayd parcell hath alwayes been mowed by the fermers therof: and the waye to the sayd pece lyeth thorew the monkes yerde by the churche yerde syde, and so into Bargage feld. The wyche John Marshall, Robert Cornysshe, and Willm Spon [Spooner] hath usyd.

" *Item :* an other pece of arryble lying in this pece together conteynyng VIII acres and di : betwene the londe of Sir Wm Clopton and the londe of Robert Tyler, alias Alfunder, of the Weste parte : and the hye waye ledyng from Melforde to Berye Sent Edmund of the Est. The one hede abbuttyth uppon the londe and grove of the sayd Sir Wm Clopton quondam the Hospytellers, towards the Northe : the other hede abbutt uppon the tenemente of John Grengras towards the Sowth.

" The sayd IX acres, III roode, and X perchys, called Hopkyn, alias Copping, Heywardes, was of the gyfte of Sir Wm Clopton of Kentwell to the Orgayne player in Melforde Churche, as by hys Wyll, and a dede annexed therunto, sealed wyth hys seale and subscrybed wyth hys hand playnly apereth, beying in the custoyde of Mr Rychard Clopton of Fordehall, gentleman ; as also by a lease remaynynge in the churche boxe, made to William Sponer therof, he beyng orgayne player ther, playnlye doth apere, wych wyth the forsayd wyll and dede, Roger Martyn of Long Melforde, Esquyre, under seales dyd sec. For the testymonye of the truth wherof the sayd Roger Martyn hath subscrybed thys wyth hys owne hande.

" Dated the laste yere of Quene Marye 155⅞.

" Teste me ipso, ROGERO MARTYN.

" *Addendum.* The one of the sayd peces, viz. the fyrst pece of Hopkyn Heywarde conteynyng 1 acre, 1 roode, and 10 perchys, lyeth on the Est syde of Bargage feld by a mere, wych mere is now broken upp, and so lyeth now into the sayd feld withoute mere or dole. The mere beying whole and untowched all Quene Maryes tyme and alwayes befor.

"Teste me ipso: ROGERO MARTYN."

Note in a different handwriting.

" Yt ys thowght that S' Frawncis Clopton had in custodye afterwarde the forseyd wyll and dede annexed, wyth Spons lease : after whom succeded Sir William Clopton hys brother : thys put owt here the effecte and substuns beying suffycyentlye recyted befor."

This lost charity land belonged in 1377 to Robert Copping, and in 1471 to Robert Hayward, then to Sir William Clopton, who gave it for the use of the organ-player of Melford Church. In 1580 part of it was still charity land; but in a rental of 1584 it is described as land *formerly* belonging to the churchwardens of Melford.

" MELFORD IN SUFF.

" Agreement for Hopkyn Heywards of Sir Will™ Clopton's gyfte. Rent 13ˢ 4ᵈ

" *Memo.* Yt ys fully agreed thys XII™ daye of August Aᵒ Dᵐⁱ 1566, betwene Frawncis Clopton of Kentwell Esquier on the one part & Thomas Smythe & John Grenegras Churchewardens of Melford abovesayd on the other part that the sayd Frawncis Clopton shall ferme and occupye the londs latelye in the tenure and occupying of the wydowe Spones tyll Mychylmas next payyng therfore de claro for the whole yere occupying therof that shal end at the sayd feast, thyrtene shyllyngs iiij ᵈ. Thys agreement was as abovesayd agreed between the sayd partyes in the presens of thes men subscrybyd—

" By me—ROGER MARTYN.
By me—SYMON CAWSTON.
By me—THOMAS DYCKE.
By me—JOHN GROSSE.
By me—THOMAS SMYTHE."

There is a further note in 1556 to the effect that Mr. Richard Clopton and Mr. Roger Martyn, as churchwardens, had possession of all the charity lands, except one piece of Hopkyn Heywards, which was then lost : and from other memoranda it appears that the remainder of this land had lapsed to Kentwell before 1600.

THE HOSPITAL OF THE HOLY TRINITY.

To the foregoing goodly roll of charities bequeathed to their poorer brethren of Melford by so many bygone worthies, one has yet to be added, exceeding them all in its munificence; the foundation and endowment of the "Hospital of the Holy and Undivided Trinity," by Sir William Cordell. Camden, in his "Britannia," says, "As you enter Long Melford from Clare, you see a beautiful hospital lately built by that excellent person Sir William Cordall, Knight, Master of the Rolls." During his lifetime he built the original hospital for the support of twelve aged brethren, a warden, and two lay sisters to attend upon them; and he maintained it until his death. By his will, dated the 1st January, 1580, he created a trust and an endowment of this charity for ever, naming among his trustees some very distinguished persons who had been his friends in life, and whom he thus describes :—

"Sir Thomas Bromley, Knight, Lord Chancellor of England.

"Sir William Cecil, Knight, Lord Burleigh, and Lord Treasurer of England.

"Anthony, Lord Viscount Montague.

"John, Bishop of London.

"Edmund, Bishop of Norwich.

"Sir Francis Walsingham, Knight, one of her Majesty's principal Secretaries.

"Sir Christopher Wray, Knight, Chief Justice of England.

"Sir Walter Mildmay, Knight, Chancellor of her Majesty's Court of Exchequer.

"Sir Thomas Gawdy, Knight, one of her Majesty's Justices of her Pleas.

"Mr. Alexander Nowell, Dean of Pauls.

"Mr. Gabriel Goodman, Dean of Westminster.

"Sir Gilbert Gerrard, Knight, her Majesty's Attorney-General.

"Edmund Plowden, Esq.

"George Carey, of Cockington, in the county of Devon, Esq.

"Thomas Andrews, of Bury, in the county of Suffolk, Esq.

"William Necton, her Majesty's Feodary of London and Middlesex, gentleman."

To these he bequeathed in special confidence and trust as follows :—

"All that my messuage or tenement which I have newly erected nighe unto the Church of Melford, commonly called the Hospitall, or Almeshouse, wherein I have divers poore folkes presentlie inhabitynge, with the garden enclosed with a pale on the south side of the saide garden."

And then continues a description of the lands and tenements and hes with which he endows the charity; and its purpose, viz., for twelve poor brethren and a warden, to be sole or unmarried, of the age of sixty, or not less than fifty-five years, for whom a daily diet is prescribed of three mess of meat among them, with some augmentation and increase thereof on Christmas-day and three days following, New Year's-day, Twelfth-day, Candlemas-day, Easter-day, and the two days following, Whitsunday and the two days following, Trinity Sunday, Midsummer-day, Michaelmas-day, and All Saints'-day; and that the brethren should be allowed five shillings a quarter each in money, and the warden ten shillings a quarter, and from the residue of the revenue, an allowance yearly of forty shillings each to two honest widows of fifty years at the least, the one to be cook and butler to the poor folk, and the other to wash their linen and clothes, and both to brew and bake and attend to them in time of sickness; and in consideration of these services to be allowed to have such remains of food as were left by the brethren; and the further overplus of the estate to be employed in repairs of the almshouse, beds, bedding, and linen, and the rest to provide for the warden and brethren once a year against holy mass, one frieze gown, and every second year against Easter, another gown of a sad colour of four or five shillings the yard, if the issue and profits will extend thereto, (as they will if frugal order be set down for the daily diet). Also, that there be yearly for ever appointed a godly, virtuous, and learned man to preach two sermons yearly, on Good Friday, on the Passion of Christ, in the parish church of Melford, which the brethren are to attend, and for which he is to have twenty shillings. And he gives to his next heirs in continuity the patronage of appointment of the warden and brethren; and in default of such appointment within eight days after notice received, then that the nomination shall rest with the parson and churchwardens of Melford for the time being; and in default of their appointing within their eight days, then the nomination shall be made by the Bishop of Norwich for the time being, who is also constituted visitor of the Hospital.*

Until an Act passed in the reign of William IV., Melford with other parishes was in the diocese of Norwich. It is now in the diocese of Ely.

Although the actual endowment of the Hospital was only made under Sir William Cordell's will of the 1st January, 1580, the charity was founded and supported by him in 1573, and the appointment of the first warden, Robert Durrant, bears date that year. The Royal Charter for the Hospital did not issue till the 29th June, 1591.

* When the Charity Commissioners visited Melford they borrowed from this Hospital the original trust-deed to show to Lord Brougham as a curiosity. After a time its return was requested, but the only answer which could ever be obtained from these Commissioners was, that the deed was mislaid and could not be found!

The following is a list of all the Wardens of the Hospital, with the dates of their appointments :—

Name.	Date.	Name.	Date.
Robert Durrant	1573	Luke Morley	1750
John Allen	1597	Thomas Cadge	1752
Gilbert Somerton . . .	1607	John Bouttell	1757
John Hills	1632	John Abell	1758
Ralph Swindell	1649	Giles Jarmin	1764
Henry Cupper	1652	Benjamin Smith	1779
[Removed 1656.]		Thomas Wright	1779
Edward Cordell	1656	Francis Beales	1782
Howell Davys	1658	William Harrington . . .	1798
John Wood [clerk] . . .	1664	William Brome	1804
Robert Burket	1671	Edward Knopp	1806
Thomas Page	1684	John Phillips	1812
William Nicholson . . .	1686	Joseph Fitch	1823
Henry Lemynge . . .	1686	John Batterham . . .	1833
Thomas Wingfield . . .	1688	William Fordham . . .	1846
Edward Parfrey	1700	William Henry Cowey . .	1857
Abraham Kerrington . .	1725	George Cater	1862
Andrew Clarke	1733	Charles Cushing Spilling .	1869

Making a total number of 35 wardens in 299 years, with an average duration of office of about 8½ years each.

Among Doctor Bisbie's records, there is an entry under date of 1624, which he appears to have copied from a record of that period, as to the then rental of the Hospital lands. It runs as follows :—

"Shimpling Hall, comprising 656a. 3r. 37p., was let for £72. 8s., besides a fee farm rent to the Earl of Essex, of £22. Also to supply to the Hospital 40 loads of wood; and 12 quarters of wheat, worth then £1. 6s. 8d. per quarter.

"Giffords, 90a. 0r. 8p., let for £23, and a fee farm rent to Wm. Cutler, of £2 a year. Also to supply to the Hospital in kind a quarter of wheat, worth then £1. 6s. 8d., and 5 quarters of barley, worth then 12s. a quarter.

"Tithe Barn (Cox Green), 24a. 3r. 33p., let for £47 a year and 12 quarters of barley, worth then 12s. a quarter."

The total income thus being about £170, besides fuel; as against £144 in value about the year 1580.

In 1686 the rentals are given as,—

Shimpling Hall, £135 and 15 quarters of wheat, and wood supply as before.

Giffords, £24 and 8 quarters of barley.

Tithe Barn, £56 and 2 quarters of malt; making a total income of about £260, besides fuel. And it is mentioned in the accounts of 1686 that after all expenditure and the purchase from income of some property in the street, there yet remained a balance in hand of £152. 11s. 7¼d.

If these figures are correct (as there appears no reason to doubt), two points are very noticeable; viz., that in 1624 the rent of Shimpling Hall was only at the rate of about 3s. 4¼d. per acre, when the Melford Hall estate land was let at an average of 8s. per acre; and on the other hand, the extraordinary rent of the Tithe Barn farm at about £2 per acre; a very exceptionable instance, of which no explanation is given.

Till 1633, the old building of the Hospital was inclosed with a pale fence, and the present outer old wall was built at this date, as shown by the accompanying letter to Lord Savage, requesting that he would grant a small additional space to be inclosed from Melford Green.

"To the Right Honble. the LORD VISCOUNT SAVAGE, Lord of the Manor of Melford, in the county of Suffolk, and Patron of the Hospital of the Holy and Blessed Trinity, of the foundation of Sir Wm. Cordell, Knt., in the same town.

"The humble Petition of us, your Lordship's Tenants, the Inhabitants there, on the behalf of the Warden and Brethren of the same Hospital, humbly sheweth unto your good Lordship, that forasmuch as the Warden and Brethren, with your Lordship's approbation, and the consent of such others to whom in that case it doth or may appertain, have determined to build a wall of brick in lieu of the pales compassing the woodyard and garden belonging to the same Hospital, and for that it appeareth that the woodyard is at the straightest to turn a cart in, and the already pale inclosing the garden place and yard stand so near adjoining to the fruit trees there growing, whereby a great part of the fruit is oftentimes stolen or lost: our humble suit therefore unto your Lordship is that your Lordship would be pleased (the premises considered) to grant and give license to them to take and inclose into the said garden and yard lying south-east from the said Hospital, about four or five foot of ground, parcel of the Green called Melford Green, the soil being your Lordship's inheritance; and the pasture of so small a quantity of ground of no moment. And they shall be bound to pray for your Lordship and your noble posterity, &c. And we shall have cause to remain thankful to your Lordship for their sakes, whereby the same shall be enlarged, they benefited, and none prejudiced.

"R. WAREYN (Rector).	"FRA. HALL.
THO. AGGAS.	JOHN OKLE.
GRE. HUBBART.	JOHN BARKER.
JO. EVERED.	JOHN HAMONDE.
ANDREW BYHLE.	THOMAS SHEPARD.
RICHARD GARLIS.	J. PET. CRESWELL.
EDWARD DREWE.	RO. MALPAS.

Thus indorsed.

" I am contented that fowre or fyve foote be taken to enlarge the garden of the Hospitall as itt is desired for the good of the Hospitall.

" This 25 of Aprill 1633

" SAVAGE."

The board in the church states the original value of the endowment of the Hospital at £144 per annum.

Some of the old terriers of Melford, which generally were uncorrected repetitions, vaguely state the income of the Hospital some time after its foundation, at *about* £300 a year; and the terrier of the year 1784 adds, " this is now of the value of upwards of £500 a year." Without entering on the details of the progressive income of the charity, which would be tedious, it suffices to note, that 80 years after the above date the income had increased to £961 a year; and the gross income is now £1,308: the net amount received for the use of the Hospital being £1,292 a year, which will continue steadily increasing in the future.

Various visitations have been made at sundry periods, and the statutes have been amended by successive Bishops of Norwich to meet the altered circumstances of time and custom, as well as to reform abuses which had crept in. An instance of gross misgovernment is recorded during the wardenship of John Hills, who was governor of the Hospital from 1632 to 1649, when the Countess of Rivers was the hereditary patroness. That strong-minded, uncompromising royalist lady was not likely to pass over in silence any misconduct of which she was cognizant, and the following letter from her to Hills, the warden, is very characteristic :—

" GOVERNO'—

" Many complaints have come to me of yo' house, both by yo' selfe and most of the Bretheren, as in tipling, wenching, and in suffring yo' said Bretheren to take their owne pleasures in goeing up and downe as they list themselves, contrary to the statuts and ordinances of the house. These are therefore, to require you that theise abuses be reformed in yo' selfe, and to inflict punishment upon such of your said bretheren as hereafter shall offend and breake any of the saide statuts or ordinances, and to informe me who they are that shall contemne the p'formance hereof.—See you faile not.

" Melford, 24 Novembris, 1641.

" E. RIVERS."

All charities such as this one are peculiarly assailable by jobbery and mismanagement, and the annals of this hospital tell similar sad tales of past years; let us hope, never again to be repeated. Doubtless, ere long, the grave question must arise whether the benefits of this charity are capable of extension. The income has increased enormously since the founder endowed it, while the number of inmates remains unaltered. Thus, the original endowment was at the rate of less than £10 per head all round; the income is now within a little of £87 a head; and is annually increasing, independently of the rising value of land; so that, fully allowing for the difference of the present mode of living, and of the altered value of money as compared with three hundred years ago, it can scarcely fail to be observed that the large sum of nearly £1,300 a year is in excess of the requirements for the support of so small a number of persons drawn from the working classes, for whom the pious founder of the charity, by the expressions of his will, clearly contemplated only a provision of simple frugal comfort in their old age.

On the election of a warden, he is obliged to go to Norwich to be sworn in before the bishop. In these days of railroads, this is of little consequence; but in olden times, when the journey had to be made on horseback, over bad roads and perhaps in the winter season, it must have been a matter of grave importance to an elderly person, who may be was obese, and perhaps not a distinguished equestrian. The brethren are sworn in at the Hospital, and in their case it appears to have been considered necessary that there should be an extra amount of hard swearing, in which they commence by blessing the Queen, and vowing that they will keep her duly informed, and disclose to her (it is not stated whether by post or telegram) if any radical republicans in Melford should propose to make Dilke or Odger president of the British republic. They then proceed to curse the Pope in the true orthodox Exeter Hall fashion, and they declare that "they do from their hearts abhor, detest, and abjure, as impious and heretical, that damnable doctrine and position, that princes excommunicated or deprived by the Pope, or any authority of the See of Rome, may be deposed or murthered by their subjects." Having thus far disburdened their consciences, the brethren next in due form renounce the old and young Pretenders, by "solemnly and sincerely declaring that they do not believe that any of the descendants of the person who pretended to be Prince of Wales during the life of the *late* King James the Second, and since his decease pretended to be and took upon himself the style and title of King of Great Britain, hath any right or title to the crown of this realm; and they accordingly renounce, refuse, and abjure any allegiance to him." And finally they do their utmost to secure the liberties of England, by acknowledging "upon the true faith of a Christian, that the succession to the Crown stands limited to the Princess Sophia, Electress and Duchess Dowager of Hanover, and the heirs of her body being Protestants"! And having recited all this, with the addition of many long words, it is to be hoped that the newly elected brother clearly understands and feels edified by what he has sworn.

A few words more are necessary to explain a point very constantly remarked upon by strangers to the place. Looking up the Green towards the fine old church, every one is led to wonder why the comparatively modern Hospital should have been placed in such a position as greatly to hide, and certainly to mar the effect of the splendid church, which is now only partially seen rising above it, but which would otherwise be, as it certainly once was, so grand and prominent an object from the village.

The reason for this breach of good taste rests partly on a fact of squirearchal pride. If the Hospital had been built further eastward on the top of the Green, it would have partly stood on a strip of soil belonging to the manor of Monks, which had then become vested in the owner of Kentwell. Possibly the founder, who had opposed his neighbour of Kentwell in the matter of the Church-house, was not on sufficiently friendly terms to ask the favour of placing his hospital thereon.* So he built on his own ground; and though the choice of site was unfortunate in point of appearance, it was rendered less so, at that time, by the nature of the original building; for it was a low modest one of only one story high, infinitely more picturesque than the present stuck-up edifice, which was the result of a job perpetrated but few years since, and which has not added architecturally to the beauty of Melford.

ANCIENT EXTINCT BEQUESTS.

Besides all the before-mentioned legacies and benefactions, many other curious ancient records exist of minor bequests by parishioners and priests of Melford. Some of these are very interesting and noticeable, not only from the remote pre-Reformation date of several of them, but also on account of the variety of purposes for which these legacies were bequeathed. They were mostly absolute gifts, to be expended for specific objects; such as the fabric of the church and Lady Chapel, and for their ornaments, vestments, furniture, and plate. In like manner, also, to St. James's Chapel (on Chapel Green). Also donations to the poor; to the highways; for the repair of the church

------

* The two great Melford proprietors of that day appear not to have been on very friendly terms. Probably the ancient knightly family of the Cloptons looked on Sir William Cordell, though a deserving self-made man, as one of the yeomen-bred upstarts whom the Reformation pushed upwards with a mushroom growth, and against whose class the old families had the additional grievance that at the dissolution of the monasteries, the bulk of the lands which their ancestors had in ancient days given to the Church was bestowed on the low-bred followers of Cromwell, the *novi homines* of the day, who were utterly despised by the old gentry.

bells (this seems to have been a favourite form of bequest); for the keeping of the testator's obit day; and towards the support of the various guilds within the parish. Among the donors are several of the persons whose names are recorded as taking prominent parts in the rebuilding of the church, and who were living at that time.

The following extracts from these old wills (some of which are in Latin) are here given in English, according to the priority of date.

As by the wills of 1448, 1456, and 1472, there are bequests for the reparation and amending of our Lady's Chapel, there was evidently attached to the *old church* a lady chapel, which was replaced by the present one, which was completed in 1481.

1443.

Roger Richards, of Melford.

(Latin will.)

For the repair of the road, from the lane called Fotysford
Street (King's Lane) . . . . . . xx^d.

1448.

John Waryn, of Melford, Senior, fuller.

To the amendyng of the reparacion of the Bellys . . III^s. IIII^d.
To the reparacion and amendyng of owre Ladyis Chapel in
the seid toune of Melford . . . . . . XL^s.
To fourty persones of men and women, fourty gounes of
Colchester russet: the prys of a yerd of brodcloth II^s:
a clos table in maner of a trestel.
For the makyng of everye goune aforn rehersed VIII^d. . VIII^d.
To the supportacyon and helpyng of Seynt Marye Gilde of
the toune of Melford. . . . . . . VI^s. VIII^d.

John Waryn, senior, lived on the west side of Hall Street in 1442, and John Waryn, junior, lived on the same side of the street, and possessed part of Broadmeadow.

1456.

Richard Meryell (or Moryell), of Melford.

To the reparacyon of the Belles of this toune . . III^s. IIII^d.
To be stowed on to the quer Copys [Choir copes] of this
Cherche . . . . v^{li}.
I bequeth to the seyd Cherche to be stowed ther as moste
plesyng to God . . . . v^{li}.

I quethe to the mendyng of owr Ladyes Chapel in seyd
    towne to my teyrment   .   .   .   .   .   .   II^s. VIII^d.

So he was buried in the older Lady Chapel.
The name of Roger Moryell is inscribed outside the walls of the church as a
benefactor.

1459.
Thomas Swyfte, of Melford.
(Latin will.)

For the repair of the Bells   .   .   .   .   .   .   xx^d.

1459.
Rose Wareyn, of Melford.
(Latin will.)
A bequest for the Bells.

To the Guild of Jesus   .   .   .   .   .   .   XIII^s. IIII^d.
To the repair of the road at Prowdys bregge   .   .   .   XIII^s. IIII^d.

Query : Was she the wife of Richard Wareyn, who, in 1442, lived near Chapel Green,
Prowdsbridge being in the present Rotten Row, Melford.

1401.
Henry Turnour alias Dyer, of Melford.
(Latin will.)

For the repair of the Bell broken in ringing   .   .   .   III^s. IIII^d.

1464.
Roger Carter, of Melford.
(Latin will.)

I leave to the Chapel of the Blessed James, in Melford, in
    the street called Horstree [a mis-spelling for Hall
    Street]   .   .   .   .   VI^s. VIII^d.

1468.
Robert Sparrow, of Melford.
(Latin will.)

I leave to the Sacristan of this church for the time being,
    for ringing the bells, making my grave, and for the
    religious offices belonging to my burial   .   .   .   II^s.

The name of Robert Sparrowe is on the north side of the church, with that of Marion his wife, as benefactors thereto. He is noticed in Chapter III., in the account of the Church.

1472.

Thomas Germayn, of Melford.

(Latin will.)

For the repair of the Chapel of the Blessed Mary in the churchyard of the said place . . . . . . XII^{d.}

1477.

John Gente, of Melford.

This will relates to some property on Melford Green, and to personalty.

1477.

Nicholas Groome, of Hallestrete, Melford.

To the reparacyon of ye belles . . . . . . VI^{s.} VIII^{d.}
But I woll that myne exeoutours delyver yt not, on to ye tyme they onderstond the need.

1479. ·

Margaret Heede, wife of Thomas Hede, of Melford, fuller.

(Latin will.)

For the maintenance of the Mass of Jesus in the said church . . . . XII^{d.}

1479.

Richard Brightewe, of Melford.

To the Chapell of Seynt Jamys . . . . . III^{s.} IIII^{d.}

1480.

Rosa Germon, of Melford.

(Latin will.)

Leaves to the support and benefit of the Guild of Jesus in Melford, *one cow and sundry utensils.*

The following will contains some curious items :—

1481.

Roger Howe, of Melford.

Leaves to the Guild of Jesus 2 keen, that ys to saye by the gwelt-ments of myn two dowghters that ben passed.

To the cherche werk of Melford xxvi˟ viii˟ yff my goodys in alle thynges accordynly wyll extende so largely, or ellys I bequethe to the seyd werk xx˟

To myn wyffe alle myn hyvys with beyn, that is to seyn II qwyke and VI idell hyvys.

I woll that myn wyffe and myn sone wone stylle in myn hows to Mychellmas on the wyttemete of the keene and to have wete and maete lymmytyd by the dycrecyon of myn executours.

Gyles Dente the parson of Melford myn executour.

The meaning of the above appears to be as follows :—

First.—To the Guild of Jesus two cows, independently of what was already bestowed in portions on his two daughters.

Secondly.—It is evident that the rebuilding of the church, or some portion thereof, was yet in hand.

Thirdly.—The bequest to his wife of two working hives and six idle hives of bees is very curious.

Fourthly.—His wife and son were to be provided until Michaelmas, in his house, with the milk, butter, and cheese from his cows, and to have wheat and meat at the discretion of the executors. (He was twice married: his wives' names were Alison and Elizabeth.)

The name of Roger Howe, or Hoo, as there spelt, was on the painted glass of the 10th window, south side of the church, with his two wives.

1482.

John Kente, of Melford.

To the reparacyon of the hyghe weye betweene the gilde
alle, and memberys crosse .   .   .   .   .   .   xxx˟

Query: Where was this Guildhall, and where was the Member's Cross? Some of this family held land at Rodbridge, adjoining the Moryells' lands.

1482.

Richard Plandon, of Melford.

I wyll that xxvi˟ viii˟ that myn wyffe bequethe me of her owne proper goodys that yt shal go to an . . . . . . of copyr and owtgylte in Melford Cherche, and yiff yt coste more I wolle yt shall be made good of myn owne propyr goodys.

1484.

Robert Harset, of Melford, Clothmaker.

In the name of the fadyr and son and holy Gost, Amen. The last daye of february in the yeer of owr lord God, an: MCCCCLXXXIIII^to I Robert Harset of Melford Clothmaker in the diocesse of Norwyche, of an hooll mynde and wyth a vyfed remembraunce make myn wyll and testamente under this manner of forme.—

Fyrste and formest I bequeth and commend my sowle to Almygthy God my creatur and maker, and to the blyssyd mayd and modyr our lady Seynt Mary, and to alle the celestyal courte of hevyn, and my body to be buryed wythynne the Cherche of Melford on ye south syde afor the aulter of Jesus by the sufferaunce and lycens of alle the paryshe. Itt's my wyll to have a ston of marbyll to ly on myne grave. Item: I bequeth yat fyrst and formest my detts that I owe be truly tent and payd.—Item: I bequeth to the executours of Master Gylys Dente* xx^a for tythis and offeryngs forgette.—Item: I bequeth to the reparacyon of the bellys III^a IIII^a—Item: I bequeth on C^ll for the sustentacyon and mayntynnans for to help the yeerly salere to the preeste of Jesus for to pray for me and for my wyffe and for alle my kinred and good dowers in the Cherche of Melford. The wyche C^a ys owyng to me by trew dett and covnante by the grace of God to be payd at Ester next comyng, to me or myn executours by Thomas Elof, mercer of Sudbury.—Item: ytts full my wyll that also meche lond of profytabyll and good lyveled be bowte be the good consell and good mastershepp of my master John Clopton, wyth ye consent of myn executours as that forseyd C^a may extende unto. When the lyvelod ys bowte, itts my wyll that yt shall be subdewed and gevyn to the helpe and sustentacyon of the forseyd masse of Jesus. Item: I requere myn executorys and beseche my master Clopton that this forseyd lyvelod be purved foras sone as it may uergently after my decease: and what tyme this forseyd lyvelod is bowte itts my very wyll that Master Rychard Dodyngton now beyng Jesus preeste have this foreseyd lyvelod: and more that I trust my wyfe wyll do more therto and she may spare yt terme of his lyffe bothe in sykeness and in helthe, thow ytt be so that he be benyfysyd so that he contynewe Jesus preeste. *Item:* itts my wyll that he be not lemet to non owre to say masse, but at his lyberte in dewe tyme. *Item:* itts my wyll after the decess of myn executours that the eldest and rygth eyer lawfully begotyn of the

* It appears questionable whether, in transcribing this will, an error has not been made in its date, and whether it should not be 1485. Giles Dent, the Rector, did not make the last codicil to his will of April, 1484, till ✝ July of 1484, and his successor, Thomas Aleyn, was instituted in September of that year; so that Giles Dent was living at the date given of Harset's will, viz. in February, 1484, though Harset therein leaves a bequest to Dent's executors.

stok of Master John Clopton shal be patron and gever of this foreseyd supervyse as long as yt endureth. *Item :* itts my wyll that myn obet shal be kepte be the space of x yeer, and evyry yeer vi˙ viii˙ to bere the charges therof.—*Item :* I bequeth on to the parson of Melford or ys debete iiii˙ to remembyre my sowle an hooll yeer in his bedroll. —*Item :* I bequeth to Annes Harset my wyff xx", and she for to be delyveryd v" yeerly for her sustentacyon and levyng be my executorys unto the hooll summe be payd. *Item :* I bequeth to my forseyd wyffe my mancyon that stondys in the Cherche yeerd on the North esyde wyth alle ye comodytes therof duryng her lyffe, except ther the chyldren lerne, in at the West ende of my place, at that I wyll shal goo stylle on to that same use as longe as yt ye howse endureth. And after the decess of myn wyffe I graunte and wyll that yf my master Clopton in specyall, or any other man or woman wyll buy this forseyd howse, I will that the pryce therof shal be xx marks to thys entent, that yt may long unto the preestes that long or shall long unto the Cherche of Melford, and on specyal I will that Jesus preeste have the newe parlour and chambour theron for his esment. *Item :* itts my wyll that x" of this forseyd xx marke be dysposed unto the reparacyon of our ladyes chapell, and the v markes that remaynyth I bequeth fyve noblys to John Harset my broder. I bequeth to Roberte Harset the sonne of the foreseyd John Harset on shorte blewe gowne wyth a dowbelet, a sherte, and a cappe, a peyer of hoses and peyer of shone ; and these forseyd shal be delyvered unto the forseyd John and Roberte after the dyscrecyon of my executorys when they thynke most nede.—*Item :* I bequeth onto my forseyd wyffe alle my howsolds that I have, and after her decess that she dyspose them charytable after her own wyll for the wele of her sowle and myn both.—In aspecyall it is my wyll that myn wyffe shal leve in the handys of myn executours or in the handys of Jesus preeste my grete foldying tabyll and a grete potte of brasse, a basen and an ewer of latyn : a chafour of latyn for colys : iiii platers and iiii pewter dysshes, ii sawsers and a spette : an awndyryn, a bordcloth and ii towells, a jake and a salet and a pole : thes forseyd bequests to be occupyed yff it be so that the preestes be dysposed to goo to comons with june themselffe.—*Item :* itts my wyll that yff Jesus preeste wyll goo to comons with june his chambyr he shal ocupye the forseyd stuffe.—*Item :* I bequeth v marke the wiche John Whale, schomaker, is bownd bye oblygacyon to pay on to me or to myn executours, every yeer a marke unto the tyme that the forseyd fyve marke be payde, I wyll that the gaderes [gatherers] wiche gadyr for the masse of Jesus shal have vi˙ viii˙ of this forseyd of this fyve marke for this entente, to make upp x marke a yeer yff it be so that Master Rychard Dodyngton contynew Jesus preeste.—*Item :* I bequeth unto *Thomas Dyer, child unto ye forseyd Master Rychard Dodynton* vi˙ viii˙ a yeer unto the forseyd fyve marke be payde off, yff it be so that he be dysposed to be a

preeste, or ells not.*—*Item :* I bequeth unto Master Rychard Dodyngton
a lytyll faldyng tabyll.—*Item :* I bequeth unto Mawte Crysale my aunte
fyve marke in mone, such tyme as Thomas Eloff shal pay for the last
bargayn that he made with me for IIII clothes.—*Item :* I bequeth unto
the forseyd Mawte my best blew gowne and also suche parte of stuffe of
howsold as my wyffe is dysposed to depart wythall.—*Item :* itts my
wyll yff any casualte falle that my goodys will not performe this my
forseyd wyll that everye bequeste be lessened after the dyscrecyon of
myn executours to the most plesure of God and helthe to my sowle :
whom I ordeyn and make Thomas Eloff, Master Rychard Dodyngton,
and my wyffe Annes Harset. *Item :* itts my very wyll that thes forseyd
myn executours shal have the consell and mastershep in executyng of
this my forseyd wyll of my good master John Clopton, and in specyall
in bying of the forseyd londe : wiche Master Clopton I make supervysor
of this my forseyd wyll.

These recordes : Master Roger Smyth : Syr John Talbott : John
Boonys : John Mason, and Robert Revers.

(Proved at Melford, 15th March, A.D. 1484.)

In the old painted glass of the 13th window on the south side of the church was
an inscription praying for the souls of Harset, of Agnes his wife, and of John and Robert.
As long ago as 1688 this inscription was much mutilated. It has since been lost. It
would seem that the house mentioned in this will was that afterwards known as the
Priest's house, or the College, concerning which Dr. Bisbie, the Rector, had a long
litigation.

1487.

John Berde, of Melford.

To the bying of a Canape to hang over the blyssyd Sacrament in the seyd parysshe cherche of Melford   .   .   xˢ

1487.

John Farnan, of Melford.

To the masse of Jesus kepte in the seyd parysshe cherche of
Melford, II acres of londe lyinge in Fotysforde [King's Lane] for evermore, provydyd alway that yff y' happe the seyd masse to be loste and
not kepte, then I wyll the profyte of the seyd londe be done in wex
brennyng in the honor of that most holy name of Jesus in the seyd

* This bequest sounds curious. How came the celibate priest in 1484 to have this
son ? and it seems strange that this issue should be mentioned in this will, together with
the condition annexed. Sir Richard Dodington, priest, is recorded as having given a
Hymnal noted to Melford Church.

cherche.—Also I bequeth to the peyntyng of the Roodlofte in the seyd cherche, xˡⁱ· in good and lawful mony.—*Item:* I bequeth to the reparacyon of the bellys beyng in the stepyll of the seyd cherche vɪ·ˢ vɪɪɪ·ᵈ—*Item:* I bequeth to the reparacyon of the cawsway from the gate of the seyd cherche alle the lengthe of the grene xxˢ·—*Item:* to Alys myn wyffe as long as she ys a wedowe my tenement lying in Hallestrete agenst Newe Crosse.

Is this the same person as named in the old painted glass of the 15th window on the south side of the church, therein called Firmin, Alice being also named ?

1500.

Richard Martyn, of Melford.

13th June.

My body to be buried in the South Ile in Melford Church, by my wife, which I did make for me, my wife, and my children to lye inne. I bequeth xLˡⁱ to the reparacon of the said ile. Item: to the high Awter xxˢ· Item: to our Lady Chapell in Melford Church yarde xLˢ· Item: to the 4 ordre of ffriers, that is to say Clare, Babwell, Sudbury and the White ffriers in Cammbrigge, eche of thym xxˢ· Also, I bequeth to Saint Jamys Chapell in Melford xxˢ· Also I will that every prest dwelling in Melford, being at my obite, both at Dirige and Masse have eche of them xɪɪ·ᵈ: and every grete clerke dwelling within the said towne ɪɪɪ·ᵈ, and every child ɪ·ᵈ, and every other prest comyng to my sayd obite to have ɪɪɪɪ·ᵈ And in like wise I will that every prest and clerke have at my xxxᵗ day. Also I will that at my said xxxᵗ day a good Diner be ordeyned for all my neighbours dwellyng within the said towne, bothe for riche and poore yf it please them to come therto. Also I will that every poor man that will come at the said xxxᵗ day and take almes, that eche of them have a peny. [Then follow further bequests for 20 year days, masses, and trentalls for his soul.) Item: I bequeth to the reparacion of high wayes within vɪ myle of Melford xxˡⁱ. Item, I will a prest be had and ordeigned for ever to pray for my soule [&c.] and to keep his service every holyday in Melford Church, and he to sing at the Auter in the South Ile aforsaid, and every week day at Saint Jamys Chapell: and to say aftre the Gospell allway De profundis. Item I bequeth to the Mariage of poore Maydenes in Melford xx marc [£18. 6s. 8d.]. Item; I bequeth to the Maister of the Colledge of Sudbury xLˢ· prayeing him to helpe my body to the erthe and to praye for my soule [&c. &c. &c.]

(Will proved 11th September, 1500.)

1516.

Laurence Martyn, of Melford (and London).

13th November.

My body to be buried in the Churche yarde of Melford Church on the southe side by the wyndowe of the 7 sacraments. I give to the high Awter of Melford Church xx⁵ Also I will it be spent at my vii day xx⁵. Item: I will there be spent at my xxx⁴ day to preests, clerkes, and pour people xL⁵, but not in festinge the riche people. Also I give the profites of the lands called Higgells and Reyners, lying in Monkysylly in fawte of my heires male to the commontie dwelling in Melford to the dischardinge of Taxys, Kyds, and Subsidies forever. [He also gives a residue in certain other lands for the reparation of Melford Church for ever.] And all the residue of my goods, my will perfourmed I bequeth unto Elizabeth [Cheke] my wyfe soo that she doo ley a gravestone upon my grave, and doo my name graved theron and kepe iiii yere my yere day in Melford Church, [&c.].

(Proved 16th December, 1518.)

Executors—his wife Elizabeth and Sir James Hewer, his priest.

1525.

John Howes, of Long Melforthe.

To be buryed in the Churche porche of Melforthe.
To the reparacyon of the Churche porche . . . iii⁵ iiii⁴

A slab which had been inlaid with a brass, which was then gone from it, was removed from the church porch in 1866 and placed within the church.

1525.

Clemente Thressher, of Long Melford.

To bye some jowell for Jhesus aulter wythyn the same Chirche of Melford by the advise of my executours to be occupyed and usyd there to the honor and wirship of the holie name of Jhesu . . . . xxvi⁵ viii⁴

In the pre-Reformation list of church goods this person is described as "Mother Thresser, otherwise called Clementi Thresso, widow," and as having bequeathed to the altar of Jesus an altar-cloth of satin, purchased in 1526, for 31s. 8d.

1534.

John Fyske, of Melford.

To be buryed wythn the Chercheyerd off Melford, nyghe on to the yle of Jhesus ther.

1535.

William Norman, of Melford.

I wyll have III^{li} of wax to be striken in VII tapers without any hart candle, and to be sett aboute my herse the daye of my buryinge.

To Saint James Chappell an aulter cloath.

To Peter my master's servant a twybill, a hand sawe, a hatchet, a stryer, and a playne.

To Roger Coker's sonne a Coate of Dodde.

Judging from the bequests, this man was probably a carpenter or builder.

1535.

Margaret Owers, of Melford.

Bequests of dress.

1535.

Roger Martyn, of Melford (Bencher of Lincoln's Inn).

20th of April.

My Body to be buryed in the South Ile in Melford Churche, which my father caused to be made, before the image of our blessed lady of pyttie, betwixt my tombe and the place where my last wyfe [*Alice Forde*] lyeth buryed [&c.]. Item : I bequeth to the high Aulter xx^s At my burying day I wille every prest dwelling within the said towne of Melford, and doing his dutie the said daie have vi^d; and every grete clerke within the seyd towne, and doing their dutie IIII^d; and every childe that can sing in the quere dwelling in the seyd towne to have II^d; and every other childe a peny: and every other prest that cometh to my seyd burying daie IIII^d· [Then follow bequests for the keeping of his 30th day, for Placebo's, Dirige's, Requiems, &c., for his soul; mentioning the name of Nicholas Pate as a great clerk of Melford Church.] Item : I bequeth to the maryage of true poor maydens within the towne of Melford, tenne pounds : to every oon of them the daye of their sayd maryage fyve shillings. I will yf any godsone of myne help to bere me to church he to have for his labour xII^d· Item : because common dooles be prohibit and put awaye be Act of Parlyament, therefor I have wrytten my mynde herafter, how, and in what forme I will have usyd at my burying daye to poor people within the towne of Melford: and in like wise at my xxx^{ti} daye for the comfort of my soule.—I will the preest [endowed by his father] have every yere more for his salarie xx^s to sing yerely every weke daye in the weke in saynte Jamys Chapell in Melford: and every holydaie at Melford Churche, helping furthward the service of God.—I will have an obytt kept every yere in Melford Church for my fathers soule and myn for evermore to endure, and yerely to be gevyn and distributed xlvi^s viii^d in forme folowing: that is to seye, to. prests, clerks, and childern within the quire, and ringing of the greate bell Tenne shillings: and Thirtie shillings in peces of beef and good loves made of wheate to be delyvered the next daye before any seyd yerely obytt daye to the poor creatours, householders in Melford as ys nede to give Almes to, to pray for my fathers soule and myn: and vi^s viii^d to twenty coppyle meane persones, man and wyfe, to offer their devosion yerely at the offering of the masse, and every copill to receyve at the sayd offering iiii^d [A bequest of a reversion as follows]: Two partes therof to the poor creatours in Melford in brede and flesshe every yere against Christmas: and in Lenton, herring red and white. And the third parte, to the comfort of Melford Church, saynte Jamys Chappell in Melford, and high wayes.—Item, I bequeth to my lorde of Bury [Abbot John Reeve de Melford] of the money he owith me, whiche ys fourtye pounds, Tenne pounds therof, so he paye the rest to myne executours, trusting he will remember my soule, and be good Lorde to myn heyre.—Item: I bequeth and give my greate sylver Sensors lying in my chest in my counter to Melford Church, to serve the worship of Jesus for evermore, and my soule to be remembred therfore in the suffragis of the parissheners. Item: I bequeth to Mr. Awdely, now my lorde Chauncellor for a poor remembraunce, a greate salte of sylver percell gilt, lying in my counter in the chest I sytt on. Item: I bequeth to Sir Thomas Jermyn, knight, for a poor remembraunce, my kerving great knyves with gilt halftis. Item: I bequeth to my lady Milborne [her husband, a native of Melford, was Lord Mayor of London 1521] for a poor remembraunce a Ringe of golde with a stone, and two olde Nobles. Item: I *bequeth to the heremytt now lying and being at Saynt Jamys Chapell in Melford* an Aungell noble of gold, for to bye hym therewyth a cote, and so to have every yere tene yeares immedyatly after my deth [&c. &c.].

(Will proved at London, 14th October, 1542.)

This is a very long will, and contains many bequests besides those here enumerated.

1538.

James Hewer [Mr. Martyn's priest], of Melford.

To everie of the twoo parisshe Clarkes III⁴

To everie of my maistors pore folkes which he useth to give almes onto at Saint James Chappell. . . . . . .

To the reparacyons of Saint Jamys Chappell III⁵· III⁴

To Roger Martyn my bibill bounden in twoo partis and my cowcher lieinge in my maister's chappell,—and my fflat coffer with a springe lockke.

To Sir John Skurre, Jhesus preest, my booke which he hath in kepinge, oon payer of Bedis of jasper of ten bedes, with II silver bedes at everie ende and a litill silver ringe.

1543.

Sir William Bretyner, preest of Melforde.*

I geve to the reparacions of Melforde Chirche by the discrecion of myne executors XIII⁵· IIII⁴, soe that the parishnors and chirchwardens be contented that I shal have my buriall within the same Chirche; ells not.

I will that there shal be distributed and geven at everie of the daies of my buriall, and thirtie daie, by myne executors or there assignes amongst preestes, clarkes, and poer peple of the same towne of Melforde XL⁵ of lawful mony of Englande; and speciallie amongst the poer, aged and needie persons as bene bedrede, lame and blynde, by the discretion of myne executors. And amongst them and other straunge peple being poer comynge and beinge at my seyd buriall, I will that my sayde Executors shal geve and distribute XXVI⁵· VIII⁴, and more yf neede require, desyeringe and requiringe the same poer peple to praie for my soule and all Xpian soules : and after the distribution of the same allmes I will that monicion and warninge be geven unto all the same poer peple that they shal not resorte nor com unto my seyd thirtie daye for any doale, consideringe yt ys prohibit by the lawe. But all such as shal be appoynted to have and receve the same shal have and receyve the same at there owne howses. My obit to be kept for 10 yeres. And to spende everye yere yerelie at my sayde obytt among preestes, clarks, and poer peple of the same towne, rynginge of belles, and lytinge of candells XVI⁵· VIII⁴· *Item :* I geve unto my good Ladye Dame Thomasyne Clopton, a pledge that I have of hers, of dyvers coynes of golde of the valew of IIII⁽ᵗ⁾

To Mary Clopton my goddowghter XL⁵ of lawfull mony, and a sufferante of golde.

---

* He was not a rector, but probably one of the chantry priests.

1544.

John Cawndysh [Cavendish] of Long Melford, Preest.

My body to be buryed within the Chirch of the sayde towne of Long Melforde.—*Item :* I will ther be bestowed at my buriall daye to foure preests II* and to Sir Robarte Reader VI* and unto three clarkes II* a pece, and unto three chyldren III* : and I will there be XII poer men abowte my herse and eche of them to have II* a piece. Also to the light and the grave makinge, and the soule knell, and the rynginge of all the bells I will there be bestowed IIII*

Item : I will there be geven the same daie to poer folkes at there howsen within the towne of Melford XX* And also I will there be bestowed the same daye in meate and drinke amongst honest neighbours that shal please to be at my buriall where my executours will appoynt them XXVI* VIII*—*Item :* I will there be bestowed at my seventh daye XX*—*Item :* I will there be bestowed at my XXX*ᵗᵉ daye to prests, clarks, also to the poer peple of Melforde at there howsen, and unto other honest peple in meate and drinke, lyke manner as I have before apoynted them at my buriall daie.—I wyll and bequethe unto the two women that shal wynde me VIII*, and unto IIII men that shal bere me to the church and laye me in the grave, eche of them IIII*

Item : I will there be kept a yearely obytt for me and my frendes in Melford Church as long as my executors shal have in there handes of my goodys, and thereoppon yearelie to be bestowed to prestes, clarks, and speciallie to the poer peple, and the comforte and releve of prisoners XXVI* VIII*

[He left a reversion of property to nephews and nieces] to provide a taper of one pounde waxe to burne afore the sepulchre at Ester tyme the space of VIII yeare next after my decesse.]

My best carpett coshyn as yt will laste to remayne to Melforde Church under this condicion that yt be used in the parson's seate for hym or his parishe preeste uppon the holy daies : so that yt be thus used, or ells to be at the wyl of my executors or supervisor.

John Cavendish was not a rector, nor was the person whose will here follows, Thomas Hoore. Both were probably chantry priests.

1545.

Sir Thomas Hoore, preest, of Melford.

I will that myn executors or there assignes shal provide and bye as moche good whyte and wheaten breade as shal amounte unto the

2 G

somme of tenne shillings yf they convenientlie maie have yt; which
breade I will that my saide executors, or there assignes shal distribute
and gyve the daie of my buriall amonges poer peple of the same toune
at there dyscretions: and for lacke of breade to gyve as moche mony.
Item: I will that my saide executors shal dystribute and geve the sayde
daie of my buriall amonges prestes, clarkes, candells, and ringinge of
belles, as it shal seme onto them conveniente and mete after the rate
of my poer degre by there dyscretions.

I bequeth to Richard Martyne, Esquier, my byble and my booke
called "the Castell of helth."

To Mr. Roger Martyne, his sonne, my litle booke called "the
Castell of helth."

This book, the "Castle of Health," was one of the many grave and learned works by
Sir Thomas Elyot, and was written in 1541. Elyot, who was knighted by Henry VIII,
died in 1546.

1549.

Robert Moore, fuller, of Melford.

I gyve onto the poore ffolks boxe to thuse of the same poore ffolks
within the sayde toune II^d

1550.

John Cawger, the Elder, yeoman, of Melford.

Bequest of certain furniture.

This person and the following one were churchwardens of Melford together, in 1549.
John Cawger's, otherwise Gager's, father, Robert, left five pounds to the church, which
John paid about 1544.

1558.

Simon Colman, clothier, of Melford.

A payement of XL.^s yearlie to the Cherchewardens of Melford to
be paide within the Churche of Melforth at the place called Jhesus
Aulter on the southe syde of the Churche at the feste of All Saintes,
betwene the howres of tenne and foure of the daie for ever. And the
saide mony so receyved by the saide Cherchewardens to geve and
distribute unto the porest peple of Melforth at the feste aforesaide or

within twentie daies after the saide feste of All Saintes, and the saide Cherchewardens do make yearely thereof accompte onto the parsonne of the same toune of Melforthe and onto vi or viii of the cheife of the parrish upon Sainte Stephans daie nexte insuinge the saide feste of All Saintes, and the saide Cherchewardens yerely tak for there paines xii^{d.} of the same mony.

1559.

Gyles Shawe, of Melford.

Bequest of quern and other utensils.

CHAPTER IX.

MELFORD HALL AND MANOR.

INSEPARABLE in its rise and progress as is the history of the Church from that of Melford generally, scarcely less so is that of Melford Hall and its appurtenant manor, and especially during the period from the Conquest to the Reformation, for its owners, the successive abbots of St. Edmund's, were the lords paramount, and Melford, with most of its inhabitants, was under their sway.

In Chapter I. the particulars have been already recorded of the gift of Melford and its manor to the Abbey by Earl Alfric, in the time of Edward the Confessor. In the "Nigr. Regist. de Vestiario" of St. Edmund's, fol. 124, 125, and in the Register of Walter Pinchbeck, p. 178, there is a schedule of the Abbey lands, the heading of which, (translated from the Latin) runs thus :—"These are the manors which St. Edmund [the Abbey] had in his demesne, and these are the lands of his men [vassals and feudatories], which they also held at the time when, by order of King William, a survey of all England was made on sworn oath as to every one's lands, that each person, on interrogatory, should relate the truth as to his own land and property, and also as regarded others who dwelt in his neighbourhood. These the saint [Abbey] and his men also held at the time when the said king was alive."

In the schedule is then described :—

"*In Melford :* 12 carrucates of land : 17 villeins : 30 bordars, and 2 socmen holding 80 acres."

The Domesday Book of 1086 more fully details the Abbey possessions in Melford, as has been already described, and these particulars may be yet further amplified; and they are also confirmed by the survey of the 14th of Edward I., A.D. 1287, compiled from the report of Salomon of Rochester, Thomas de Sudington, Richard de Boiland, and Walter de Hopton, the king's justiciaries itinerant. This was set forth in the White Register of the Abbey, folios 119 and 247 (also in the Register Pinchbeck, folio 234, and in Abbot John de Norwold's Melford Chartulary), in which the description commenced with a recital of an ancient survey. This older record (translated from the monkish Latin) runs as follows :—

"The Abbot of St. Edmund, as Lord of Melford, holds a manor in this vill from the king in chief, by a free grant in perpetuity, as well as by the right of his lordship of St. Edmund. And there are in the same eight hundred acres of arable land, twenty-four acres of mowing meadow, fifty-three acres of separable pasture, and three hundred and sixty acres of wood. And he has rights over this manor of Furca and Tumberell; also of Bussellus, Lagen, and other measures; and to hold in frankpledge and to implead all trespassers; and he has rights of Barony; and he has also the right of use of his vassals' working cattle; and he has Infangthef and free warren over his lordship, and . he has two water-mills, and free right of Boar and Bull.

"The advowson and gift of the Church of Melford also belongs to the Abbot; and this church is endowed with two hundred and thirty-six acres of land, ten and a half acres of meadow, eleven acres of pasture, and four acres of woodland, from the gift of Alfric, son of Widgar [or Withgar], formerly the lord of the said barony.

"The said Abbot also possesses in this vill [township], in the said lordship, six hundred acres of arable land, which his villeins hold of him with their messuages; he also has four acres of land, which his cottars hold of him."

From the above it appears that the Abbot's rights over his manor of Melford were virtually unlimited, even embracing the power of life and death; for he had the right of "Furca," or gallows, on which he could hang felons. He had also "Tumberell," or the right of pillory, on which he could punish misdemeanants, and also scolds and unquiet women among his vassals. And he further had "Infangthef," or the right to pass judgment for any theft committed, or on any thief taken, within his manor. He appears also to have had the privilege of assize of food and drink; for he claimed "Bussellus," or the right to control all measures in his manor, his own bushel to be the standard for all; and "Lagen," or the measure for liquid, in like manner. As regards his two water-mills, he had almost a monopoly of milling; for no person except a freeman could have his corn ground at any other mill than the lord's. Besides the right of use of his vassals' working cattle, the privilege of Boar and Bull above mentioned was an oppressive and vexatious one, for the lord could depasture these animals at will on the meadows or lands of any person within his manor. The Abbot also claimed numerous personal services from his manorial tenants, including the ploughing of his demesne lands, the reaping his corn, and his haymaking: and his bordarii had to rear fowls for his supply.

The following curious rent-roll of this manor in the year 1287 gives the rents and suits and services of tenants of lands. The statutory oath of fealty from a freeman to his lord, ran thus: holding his hand on the Scriptures, he said, "Hear you, my lord, that I shall be to you both faithful and true, and shall owe my faith to you for the land that I hold, and lawfully shall do such customs and services as my duty is to you, at the times assigned.   So help me God and all his saints."

The villein's oath to his lord in like manner, ran as follows: " Hear you, my lord, that I from this day forth unto you shall be true and faithful, and shall owe you fealty for the land which I hold of you in villeinage: and that no evil or damage will I see concerning you, but I will defend and warn you to my power: so help me God and all his saints."

Some of the names in the following rent-roll deserve special notice. Translated from the Latin text, it runs thus :—

The REGISTER of ABBOT JOHN DE NORWOLD, " de itinere Salamonis de Roff: et sociorum suorum," made in the 14th and the beginning of the 15th year of the reign of King Edward I., son of King Henry III., A.D. 1287. As in the 247th page of the Register Pinchbeck, and in folios 174 and 234, and in the Abbey Register.

The Chartulary of Abbot John de Norwold.

A.D. 1287.

Roger de Boleneye holds from the Abbot xxIIII acres of arable land, III acres of meadow, v acres of pasture, at 12 shillings a year of the above-named feoff, for himself and his tenants [*the last five words are almost obliterated in the original Latin text*].

Robert de Boleneye, his brother, holds from the above Roger 1 acre . . . . . . [*rest obliterated*].

The lands still called the Bulney's and Bulney-moors probably derived their names from this family.

John Peytenyn holds of the said Roger 1 acre of meadow for 2 pence a year [*almost obliterated*].

Walter Bercarius holds of the said Roger II acres of land for 8 pence a year.

Robert Bridebec holds of the Abbot a messuage, xxx acres of land, III acres of meadow, and IIII acres of pasture for 8 shillings a year, and 3 suits to the Manor Court annually.

Peter Porterose holds of the said Roger I acre of land for 8 pence a year; also II cottars hold of the said Roger half an acre of land with their cottages for 12 pence a year.

William de Melforde holds of the said Abbot LXIII acres of land, III roods of meadow, and VII acres of pasture for 21 shillings a year, by himself and his tenants.

His daughter Joan married Alexander de Walsham, Lord of the Manor of Brockley.

Richard Dune holds of the said William VII acres of land for 20 pence a year.

Hervey Kenege holds of the said William III acres of land for 12 pence a year.

Alan Boydon holds of the said Abbot XLI acres of land and I acre of meadow for 6 shillings and 4 pence a year, and 2 suits to the Manor Court.

Robert Yue holds of the said Abbot XIV acres of land and I acre of meadow for 5 shillings and 4 pence a year.

Adam Wyth holds of the same Abbot XVIII acres of land, and VI acres of meadow, and I acre of pasture for 10 shillings and 4 pence a year.

Robert de Wolpet [Woolpit] holds in the said town from the said Abbot I acre and a half of land for 6 pence a year.

Gilbert le Son holds of the Abbot II acres of land for 2 shillings a year.

Henry, son of Robert the reaper, holds of the said Robert [de Wolpet] I acre and a half of land for sixpence halfpenny a year.

John Peytenyn holds of the Abbot XXX acres of land, IIII acres of meadow, and III acres of pasture for 7s. 9d. a year, and one pound of cumin.

Also the same John holds of Sir Gerard de Wacheaham XXX acres of arable land, which the said Sir Gerard holds of Sir Peter de Chalesworth [Chelsworth], and Sir Peter again holds of the Earl of Gloucester, and the Earl holds of the King. And the said John pays to Sir Gerard for the said holding, for himself and his tenants, a fourth part of a pound of peppercorns.

In 1279, Sir Gerard de Wacheaham is mentioned as lord of Stanstead. The earl named here was Gilbert de Clare, surnamed "the Red," 3rd Earl of Gloucester and 7th Earl of Hertford.

John the merchant holds of the above-named John V acres of land of the feoff of the Abbot for 2s. 2d. a year.

Robert de Wolpet holds of the same John VII acres of land and II acres of pasture, which are part of the before-mentioned XXX acres of land belonging to the aforesaid feoff of Clare; and he pays for his part 38d. a year.

William Pede holds of the said John II acres and a half of land, of the *feoff of the said Earl*, and pays for his land 14 pence a year.

Marc the carpenter holds of the said John I acre of land for 16 pence a year.

Walter Dypel holds of the said John I acre for 5 pence halfpenny a year.

Clarus le Chalmiere [? the thatcher] holds of the said John 1 acre and a half of land for 16 pence a year.

Robert Deine holds of the said John I acre and III roods of land for 4 pence.

Alex de Sundesham holds of Petronilla Peytenyn II acres of land for 9d. a year, and the said Petronilla holds of the Lord Abbot of St. Edmund.

Geoffry, son of Thomas, holds of the said Abbot XXI acres of arable land and III acres of meadow and pasture for half a marc of money [6s. 8d.] a year, and 3 suits to the Manor Court.

Ralph Pottok holds of the said Geoffry II acres and I rood of land at 8d. a year.

Walter Dypil holds of the said Geoffry I acre and a half of land for 6d. a year ; and Gilbert Sad holds of the said Geoffry IIII acres of land for 18d. a year.

William Pede holds from the said Geoffry III acres of land for 11d. a year.

Isabell Caldwell holds I acre of land and half an acre of pasture for 20d. a year.

Robert de Berton holds of the said Geoffry V acres of arable land for 10d. a year.

* . . * . . * . . * [*part effaced by injury to the parchment*] V acres of land from Robert de Berton for 11d. a year.

* . . * . . * . . * [*part effaced*] said feoff a messuage and II acres of land for 82d. a year, and 3 suits to the Manor Court.

* . . * . . * . . * [*part effaced, but from what follows in the next entry one of the effaced names was Martin*] IIII acres and a half of land for 24d. a year.

Hugh, son of Arnold, holds of the said Martin III acres of land for 6d. a year.

Alan, son of Jordan, holds of the said Martin II acres and III roods of land for 8d. a year.

William Elys holds from the said Martin II acres of land for 4d. a year.

The name of Elys continued in Melford for several centuries.

Galfridus Deniel holds of the said Martin IV acres and a half of land for 14d. a year.

Also the said Martin has 5 free tenants who hold in all I rood of land of the said feoff, with their houses, for 2s. 4d. a year.

Henry, son of Robert the reaper, holds of the said Abbot I acre . of land for 1d. a year.

Dominus John de Beauchamp * holds in chief from the said Abbot, of the same feoff, without intermediary, a messuage and CXX acres of

---

* This was a member of the old knightly family of De Bellocampo, of whom many members were buried in the old priory church of Sudbury. The arms of the family in the time of Henry III. were, Gules, a fess between six billets Or.—" Antiquarian Repertory," p. 97.

arable land, IV acres of meadow, and II acres of pasture for 8s. a year, and 3 suits annually to the Manor Court.

Robert Grapynel holds of the said Sir John, of the aforesaid feoff, X acres of land for 4s. a year.

Also the said Sir John has in free tenure from the said feoff, III roods of land, which his free tenants hold of him for 3s. 6d. a year.

Robert le Neuman holds from the said Robert Grapynel I acre and ⅓ of land for 1d. a year.

John de Cramaville holds from the said Abbot CXX acres of arable land, X acres of mowing meadow, XX acres of separable pasture, and two water-mills, of this feoff, for 30s. a year, for himself and his tenants, and 3 suits to the Court of the Manor.*

The same John holds VI acres of arable land and II acres of meadow, which his villeins hold from him, with their houses, and he has also two cottars, who hold one acre and a rood of land for 16d. a year, and one cottar for 9d. a year.

William, son of Hugo, holds of the said John V acres of land and III acres of meadow for 22d. a year.

John de Lausel [*Lawshall*] holds of the said John XII acres of land and II acres of meadow for 6d. a year.

Geoffry de Belenye [*Bulney*] holds of the same John I rood of land for 1½d. a year.

Alan de Rokewode holds in chief of the said Abbot XXX acres of land and X acres of meadow, and XVIII acres of pasture for 12d. a year, and 3 suits to the general court of the Abbot. The said Alan has eight free tenants, who hold I acre and a half of land for 8s. a year.

Alan de Rookwood was thirty years old at this date. He was made Vice-Dean of Sudbury.—(See Cullum's " Hawstead.") He married Elizabeth de Clerbecks, a member of a family very early settled at Acton, in Suffolk.

William Fussho holds of the said Alan II acres and a half of land for 13d. a year.

Robert le Neuman holds VIII acres of land among his tenants at 2d. a year.

Julian Galint and his son Ralph hold of the Abbot in chief VII acres of arable land for 24d. a year.

William de Busso holds of the said Julian I acre of meadow for 1d. a year.

Walter Whithune holds of the Abbot a messuage and IV acres of land for 20½d. a year, and the same Walter has V tenants under the same feoff, who hold free, in all, IV acres of land for 16½d. a year.

* This was the land on Cranfield farm, which for 400 years after continued to be described as " alias Cramavilles," and the mills were probably on the site of what was Hun mills, afterwards the paper-mill. The two mills are in another place described as being under one roof.

William Gamen holds a messuage, IV acres of land, and II acres and a half of pasture for 10s. a year.

Thomas, the cordwainer, holds V acres of land and a messuage of the said Abbot for 34d. a year, and 3 suits to the Manor Court.

Gilbert le Son holds of the said Thomas I messuage and II acres and a half of land for 12d. a year, and the same Thomas has 3 cottars who hold in all 1 rood of land at 17d. a year.

Adam Raysun holds of the Abbot I messuage and VII acres of land for 2s. a year.

Isabella Gruddi holds of the Abbot IV acres of land for 14½d. a year. The said Isabel has 8 cottages which 8 free cottars hold for 3s. 11¼d. a year.

Richard Dune holds of the said Abbot a messuage for 4s. 4d. a year and III suits to the Manor Court.

Walter Bercarus holds of the said Richard 1 acre and a half of land for 4d. a year.

Gerneys Congeley holds II acres of land of the said Richard for 6d. a year.

Roger Positus holds of the said Richard II acres and III roods of meadow for 8d. a year.

Walter Dipil holds of the said Richard I acre and a half of land for 6d. a year.

William the merchant holds of the said Richard III roods of land for ½d. a year.

Ralph Puttok holds of the said Richard II acres of land for 6d. a year.

John the miller holds of the said feoff a messuage from Peter Porterose, and he again from Richard Dune, for 8½d. a year.

Robert Dune holds of the said Richard V acres of land for 19½d. a year.

Gerneys holds of the Abbot a messuage and I acre of land for 8d. a year.

Gilbert Wade holds of the Abbot I rood of land for 1d.

Robert de Sell holds of the said Abbot a messuage, XV acres of land, and I acre of meadow, for 7s. 6d. a year, and 3 suits to the Manor Court.

Robert, son of Walter, holds of the above Robert IV acres of land and I acre of meadow for 16d. a year.

Walter Muriel holds of the said Robert I acre of land for 6d. a year.

Gilbert Hervey holds of the said Robert III roods of land for 1d. a year.

Juliana Galant holds of the said Robert a messuage for 1d. a year.

John the cowherd holds half an acre of land for 2d. a year.

Thomas, son of Positus, holds II acres of land for 5d. a year.

Petronilla Peytenyn holds II acres of meadow for 1d. a year.

Gilbert de Pantria holds of the said Abbot a messuage and xv acres of land, and iii roods of meadow, for half a marc [6s. 8d.] a year. His cottars for 6d. a year.

This was on the present High Street farm, where the land is still called "Pantria."

Robert, son of Walter, holds of the said Abbot a messuage, with lxvii acres of land, ii acres of meadow, ii acres of pasture, and i acre of wood, for 3s. 8d., and 3 suits to the Manor Court.

The same Robert holds also viii acres of land and i acre of pasture of the feoff of the said Abbot, and pays to Sir William de Valence 29d.

Richard Lytel holds of the said Abbot a messuage and ii acres and a half of land for 3½d. a year.

Robert, son of Walter, holds iii acres of land from John Hamelyn for 2d. a year.

William de Busso holds iii acres of land from the said Robert for one clove a year.

Geoffry, son of Alan, holds of the said Abbot xv acres of land, iii acres of meadow, ii acres of pasture, and v acres of wood; doing for this to the Court of the Hundred of Babbergg [Babergh] half a suit [or service] a year.

Also Geoffry holds of the said Abbot xv acres of land at 4d. a year.

Ralph de Elmeswell holds of the said Geoffry ii acres and a half of wood for 1d. a year.

William de Pyro holds of the said Geoffry a messuage and v acres of land for 6d. a year.

William, the son of the blacksmith, holds of the said Geoffry a messuage and i acre of land for 12d. a year.

Juliana Galant holds of the said Geoffry xi acres and a half of land for 4d. a year.

John the merchant holds of John de Lausel iii acres and iii roods of land for 12d.; and the latter John holds from Sir Gerard de Wachesham, and the said Sir Gerard holds from Sir Peter de Chalesworth, and the said Sir Peter holds from the Earl of Gloucestre, and he from the King.

Richard le Parker [park-keeper] holds of the said Abbot xxxiiii acres of land, ii acres of meadow, and i acre of pasture for 15s. and 3 suits a year to the Manor Court.

John Peytenyn holds from the said Richard i acre of pasture for 13d. a year.

Richard de Eya holds from the said Richard ii acres and iii roods of arable land and iii roods of pasture for 18d. a year.

William Sweyn holds of the said J. [?] a messuage and iiii acres of land for 4s. 1½d. a year.

2 H 2

John Peytenyn holds of the said William II acres of land for 13d. a year.

Robert de Wulpet [Woolpit] holds from the said William IIII acres of land for 12d. a year.

William del Husso holds of Sir John de Beauchamp a messuage, with X acres of arable land, for 3s. a year.

Ralph de Elmeswell holds from the said Abbot a messuage, with XVI acres of land, for 4s., payable to the Hospital of St. Saviour of St. Edmund.

So this land, though alienated by Abbot Sampson's grant to St. Saviour's, was still feudatory to the Abbot.

Petronilla Peytenyn holds of the said Ralph VIII acres of arable land for 2s. 0½d. a year.

Sir William de Valence holds of the said Ralph VII acres of arable land for 8d. a year.

Geoffry and Richard, brothers of Sir William, hold of the said Ralph III acres and a half of land for 3½d. a year, and half a service to the Hundred of Babbergg, and 3 suits to the Manor Court of the Abbot of St. Edmund.

John, son of Alan, holds of the said Abbot LX acres of land, IIII acres of meadow, and III acres of pasture for 6s. 9d. a year, and 3 suits to the Manor Court.

Kabell, son of William, holds of the said John III acres of land for 12d.

Petronilla Peytenyn holds in the township of Melford of the feoff of the Earl of Gloucestre, XLVI acres of land and I rood of pasture, and pays yearly a quarter of a pound of pepper to Sir Giles de Wachesham. And Sir Giles holds from Sir Peter de Chalesworth; and Sir Peter from the Earl of Gloucestre; and the said Earl holds in chief from the King.

Besides the land which Sir William de Valence held as a sub-tenant of the Abbot, as already mentioned, he also held the manor of Kentwell, which is included in the rent-roll of the Abbot's free tenants. This manor had been granted to De Valence between 1252 and 1272, as more fully explained in Chapter VII. With Kentwell the manor of Lutons was held of the Abbot in free socage for 16d. a year in lieu of all services; and the manor of Blakes in like manner for 6d. a year.

The roll of De Valence's manor runs thus:—

Sir William de Valence holds a manor in Melford of CCCLX acres of land, IV acres of meadow, V acres of pasture, XVII acres of wood, and one windmill; and he holds a warren in chief from the king by one knight's service. The said Sir William holds in this town LII acres of land, which his villeins hold of him.

Stephen de Sidulvemere holds of the said Sir William xx acres of land for his under tenants at 20 pence a year.

The place whence this Stephen took his name was also spelt Sidolves Mere: it was near Ballingdon, and there was there a chapel of the Brothers of St. Thomas the Martyr.

John, son of Capell, holds of the said Sir William x acres of land for his under tenants at 10 pence a year.

Matilda Wodefoyle holds of the same Sir William x acres of land for 10 pence.

William Maupas holds for himself and his parceners a messuage and x acres of land for 10 pence a year.

From all these curious and elaborately detailed accounts it will be noticed how greatly rentals varied, and into what small portions the holdings came to be divided by the process of repeated sublettings, at a considerable profit. Some of the very small rents named were doubtless only manorial rents combined with services. Thus some of the land bears only a rent of one-third of a penny per acre; some a halfpenny. A farm of 126 acres, at three farthings per acre; and in the case of a messuage, with two water-mills and 140 acres of excellent land, at the present Cranfield, the rental for the whole lot was only £1. 10s. However, where real rents can be arrived at with any degree of certainty, it appears that some exceptionable arable land was let as high as 1s. 2d. per acre; but the average may be struck at about 5d. per acre for arable land here. Pasture, however, was dearer, and mowing meadows let for considerably more. As a comparison, it may be noted that arable land at Hengrave, of a poorer quality than the soil here, was worth, in the year 1264, 4d. per acre rent; meadows 1s. per acre; but it must be borne in mind throughout, that personal and other services were exacted besides the money rent, from the tenants. About the time of this chartulary (1287) land was commencing to rise in value; and by the following survey, which Abbot John de Tymworth caused to be made of his Melford lands in 1386, it will be noticed that a much higher value was estimated than that of 100 years before. The rent of arable land then rose to an average of 7d. per acre; pasture to 1s. 5d.; while the mowing meadows, which it is true in this case were accommodation lands of a fancy value, were priced at the then very high rental of 3s. 9d. per acre. A hundred years subsequently we find the crop of hay from an acre estimated at the value of 5s.

Woodland was then, in comparison, of far higher value than at present; for it not only furnished the chief supply of fuel and building material, but it was also an important feeding-ground for stock, with its beech-mast and nuts and acorns. In the Domesday book Melford is described as possessing woodland, giving enough mast and acorns for depasturing sixty hogs; which would have been about eight acres to a hog. One point in these surveys must attract attention; it is the very small proportion which the grass-land bore to the arable. In Domesday Book, 1086, the grass-land mentioned in Melford, which was probably only the *mowing meadow* land, is recorded as 50 acres. In 1287, mowing meadows are measured separately from pastures. On the Melford manor and De Valence's manor together, there were at that date about 92 acres of mowing meadow and 134 acres of pasture; Saint Saviour's had 8 acres of mowing meadow and 3½ acres of pasture; and the Rectory manor had 3¾ acres of meadow and 14 acres of pasture; making the total of the grass-land in Melford 255½ acres. It is at the present day 1,083 acres; and yet, owing to its natural situation in the valley, there was more grass-land here in the olden time than was usually the case; for, comparing with other localities at the same period, the proportion of mowing meadow here would have been only about 78 acres. In those days, and indeed for long after, the cultivation of grain was the main object of agriculture, for, except in great houses, meat was seldom a general article of food; bread and salt-fish being the principal diet of the lower classes; and the great number of fast days observable before the Reformation must have tended still further to lessen the consumption of animal food, while it increased that of vegetable production. There was, however, in addition to the grass-land, a portion of feeding-ground which should be taken into account; for the borders of the arable lands were then wide, with large hedges and bushes, and these headlands probably grew a considerable quantity of rough cattle-food. It was not till the commencement of the 16th century that pasture became really valuable, and that restrictions were made against breaking it up; for we then find that if a tenant broke up and sowed with corn any pasture, the landlord was to have one half of the crop grown thereon; and in 1628 there is a covenant in a lease, that from pasture broken up without permission the tenant was to forfeit the entire crop.

SURVEY of the MANOR of MELFORD, according to ABBOT JOHN TYMWORTH's CHARTULARY of A.D. 1386.

Extent: Manerii predicti prout sequitur.

Translated from the Latin text.

This record was made on an inquisition in a Court of the Manor by Walter Kench, Roger Stalon, Richard Nel, Walter Nel, Robert Chiep, Walter Chiep, Richard Stalon, Henry Proudfot, Henry Goche, Thomas Heyward, Robin Bryon, and William le Shephirde, who declare on their oaths that the contents and values are as follows, on a measurement in perches of 16½ feet.

Arable Land.

	Per Acre.
In the field called Le Melnefelde, which contains cxxx acres of land, and which is worth £4. 17s. 6d. a year, being at the rate of	9 pence.
In the same field cxxx acres, worth £2. 3s. 4d., being at the rate of	4 pence.
In Estonfelde c acres, worth £3. 15s. a year, being at the rate of	9 pence.
In the same field clxiii acres, worth £2. 14s. 4d., being at the rate of	4 pence.
In Addernefelde cxxvi acres and iii roods, worth £5. 5s. 7½d., being at the rate of	10 pence.
In the same field lx acres, worth £1, being at the rate of .	4 pence.
In Vynyonnestoft xi acres and a half, worth 9s. 7d., being at the rate of	10 pence.
In the field called Chisewyk xxv acres, worth £1. 0s. 10d., being at the rate of	10 pence.
In Le Bulneye xiii acres, worth 10s. 10d., being at the rate of	10 pence.

Total Dcxxxix [639] acres and 1 rood, at £21. 17s. 0¼d., being at the rate of 7 pence per acre.

It is difficult to understand the above computation, for the total acreage named would amount to 759 acres, which, at the sum given of £21. 17s., would make the acreage value 7 pence; whereas the 639 acres at that rental would be at the rate of 8 pence per acre. Perhaps it was a clerical error of the scribe.

Mowing Meadows.

	Per Acre.	
	s.	d.
In the field called Brademedewe xxv acres, worth £5 a year, being at the rate of	4	0
In le Neuemedewe iv acres and 1 rood, worth 12s. 9d., being at the rate of	3	0
In le Holmes i acre, worth 3s., being at the rate of . .	3	0
In le Pond i acre and a half, worth 5s., being at the rate of .	3	4
In le Parkmedewe ii acres and a half, worth 7s. 6d., being at the rate of	3	0
In le Smalemedewe ii acres, worth 5s., being at the rate of .	2	6
In le Pondmedewe iii acres, worth 12s., being at the rate of .	4	0

Total xxxix [39] acres and 1 rood, worth £7. 5s. 3d. a year, being at the average rate of 3s. 9d. per acre.

Pasture Land.

	Per Acre. s.	d.
In the piece called Reydone IX acres, for £1 . . .	2	2
In the piece called Smalemedewe VIII acres, 16s. . . .	2	0
In Okslades X acres, for 13s. 4d	1	4
In Bulneymoor XVI acres, £1. 4s.	1	6
In [Conlesu] called Eldebery V acres, 6s. 8d.	1	4
In Parkcrofte IV acres, 2s.	0	6
In le Parkmede we called Conlesu IV acres, 8s. . . .	2	0
In the Small Park in le Launes V acres, 2s. 6d. . . .	0	6
In le Russelynesleye IV acres, 2s.	0	6
In le Calfpightel called Eldebery V acres, 6s. 8d. . .	1	4

Also a part round Addernefeld for 1s. 6d.

„ part formerly divided near le Wylves, 3d.

„ fruit of the garden, with herbage and its curtilage, £1. 6s. 8d.

Total rental, £6. 9s. 7d. ; about per acre . .	1	5

Woods.

In the Great Wood [Elmsethe] CCLX acres by estimation, in which can be made yearly 600 fagots,
at 8d. . . . .

For the agistment [stock-feeding on mast and acorns]
in the same, worth yearly £2 . . . .

In the wood called Lenynge LXXXX acres, a sixth part of which is yearly XV acres, worth £2. 12s. 6d. .	8	6 per acre
In le Speltne by estimation LXXX acres, and the wood worth £2. 7s. 10d. a year	8	6 an acre
In le Small Park LX acres, and the wood is worth £1. 10s. a year	3	0 an acre
Cutting of thorns in various places is worth . .	0	12 a year
For Aunag [? depasturing] of pigs worth . . .	6	8 a year
About 490 Acres. Total £9	6	0 a year

As this total of £9. 6s. is the sum of the figures named above, it
follows that in the first item of the Great Wood, the 600 fagots
were valued at 8d. per 50 fagots.

Melford Manor.

Customary Receipts by the Abbot by payment in money, or by
value of services.

A.D. 1886.

	£.	s.	d.
In money, for manor fines and dues	13	12	1
Court fees this year, deducting the expense of the steward .	9	5	1
Profit of the Hall water-mill, deducting expenses . .	8	13	6

	£.	s.	d.
Mader [used for dyeing in the cloth trade] sold this year	0	2	0
Apples and pears sold this year	0	3	0
Value of apples and pears had this year out of Melford Hall garden	1	0	0
Rent of the Sudbury farm, with various parcels of land; viz., by computation XI acres at le Clatydon; III acres in Humberchar; and various others in the Sudbury farm	3	1	1
Rent of the farm of Oldhalle this year; viz., a messuage and XXIV acres of land in divers pieces; XIV acres of land in divers pieces; V acres of the demise of Edmund Mundekyn; XI acres of the demise of Henry Whytynge; and VI acres le Oldehalleweye .	5	2	10
Rent of divers parcels of pasture, by computation; viz., II acres and a half in Brademedewehille; III acres and a half at Heydech; I rood and a half in Bulneye; II acres and a half at Melnemerchs, and Halles-treteweye; II acres and a half at le Greneweye and Roymers; III acres at Lackfordestrete; half an acre in le Melnedam; half a rood in le Pightel; II acres in the roadway under the Small Park; I acre in the way by Coppedebush; III acres at Brodemoor; III acres and a half at le Chapmannesmoor; IV acres at Mikelleye; I acre of the ditch or stream round Addernefeld and Vynyonnescroft; and III roods in the roadway between Chesewyk and Vynyon-nescroft .	4	5	9
Cropping and lopping of trees sold this year	0	15	8
Value of the [compulsory] service of the smith for the iron-work of the manor ploughs this year .	0	10	0
For XI capons, at 2½d. a capon [dues from tenants] .	0	2	3¼
For XXIV hens, at 1½d. a hen [ditto] .	0	3	0
For CCCCLXVIII young pigeons this year, from six manor pigeon-cotes, at four pigeons for 1d. .	0	11	5
For the value of CIII and a half cartings performed for the lord by his tenants, with their own animals	0	18	7½

[There next appears a word the meaning of which is not very plain. The entry runs thus]:

CLXXXII Gavilhirthes, at 8d. each	6	8	0

Query: Was this word intended for the same as Govelherd?

LIX cacases of pigs [or porkers] at 4d. each .	0	19	8

2 I

Value of the rendered services of Villeins.

	£	s.	d.
XXIV threshings and winnowings of corn for the lord, valued at	0	6	0
LXXXXVI cartings of dung for the lord, valued at 1d. each .	0	8	0
Mowing XLVII and a half acres of meadow for the lord, valued at 4d. an acre	0	15	10
XIX cartings with oxen for the lord, valued at . . .	0	3	2
Winter labour by villeins, of 6,219¼ works, valued at 3 works for 1d.	10	7	2¼
Autumn labour by villeins of 1,205 works, valued at 3 works for 1d.	2	0	1¼
Also 1,339 further works at the same price . . .	2	3	5

Total, £72. 8s. 9d.

Total of the whole Rental of the Abbot's Manor of Melford, this year 1386, £117. 6s. 7¼d.

And there remained to the Abbot a stock of four cart gelding horses, 16 entire cart-horses, 20 oxen for work, 33 cows, and 216 sheep, of which the stock-taking value is only set down at the low sum of £11. 10s., though, according to the general prices of that date, their selling value would have been over £20.

The common husbandry custom in this neighbourhood, at the above period appears to have been to keep about the same number of working oxen as of horses for agriculture, or generally nearly so.

It appears from the Chronicle of Jocelin de Brakelond that in the year ending Michaelmas, 1181, the whole of the rentals of the Abbot of Bury from all his many manors amounted to £326. 12s. 4d.: this was exclusive of the revenue of the monks of Bury, who had their separate portion and income of the Abbey lands.

Going back a little in point of date, after having thus shown the rental which land in this part commanded in these early days, it may be interesting to note a few of the various prices of produce,— labour and stock, as compared therewith. At the commencement of the 13th century the average price of a hen was about a halfpenny; sheep, 5¼d. each; hogs, 1s. each; oxen, 5s. 6d.; cows, 4s. 6d.; mares, 3s. each. In 1202 wheat ranged generally from 2s. to 3s. 6d. a quarter. In a very great dearth in 1126, amounting almost to a famine, wheat rose to over 6s. a quarter, as recorded by Henry of Huntington. The villein tenants of a manor were not allowed to grind their corn at any other mill than the lord's mill; but the freemen could have their corn ground where they chose; as in the case of Haberdon Mill, quoted by Jocelin de Brakelond. In 1225 it was enacted that millers were only to have a halfpenny a quarter for ordinary wheat-grinding; and for gleaning-corn a toll of the meal was to be deducted in lieu of money payment. Labour was at about three farthings a day wages, together with some victuals, but neither wheaten bread nor beer. Towards the close of the century, in 1287, the average price of wheat in this neighbourhood appears to have been about 4s. a quarter; but in the following year, 1288, a season of extreme heat, the price of wheat fell to 3s. 4d. a quarter. The average produce of the good corn lands was about 10 bushels an acre.

The bailiff of a manor had his meals at the lord's table, below the salt. The plough-driver slept in the same building as his working oxen. It was said of him, that to be a good servant, he ought to be lively and full of singing, cheering with his tunes the labouring cattle; he should feed them, be fond of them, and sleep with them every night; scratch, curry, and wipe them.

The following prices of daily labour in this part of Suffolk (without meat or drink except in harvest) in 1387-1389, are extracted from Ruggle's "History of the Poor," and from Sir John Cullum's "History of Hawstead;" but various other authorities on these points, as in the matter of the price of corn in those times, differ somewhat in their details.

	d.
Wages of haymakers and weeders by the day	1
Wages for mowing meadows by the acre or day	5

The Abbot only estimated the price of mowing at this date, in his farm accounts, at 4d. per acre.

A reaper per day	4
A reaper, per acre	7
Threshing wheat, per quarter	4
A man filling a dung-cart, per day	3½

Sixty years later some of the prices of labour had risen; for instance—

The labourer, haymaker, &c. now received	2½
The mower	6
The reaper, by the day	5

In 1514 the wages of the mower and of the reaper by the day appear not to have increased; while the wages of a labourer were now 3½d. per day; and the price per quarter for threshing wheat was as much as 1s. 1d.

In 1317 a labourer's diet consisted of two regular meals a day; viz., what was called dinner at 9 a.m., and supper at 5 p.m. In harvest time he received in addition to his wages, two salt herrings a day, some skim-milk and cheese, and a loaf of bread, made at the rate of fifteen loaves from a bushel of wheat. When the crop was harvested, his wages were paid partly in money and partly in kind by a share from the crop, which would have to last him till the next harvest. Prior to, and even subsequently to that date, the general state of the lower orders was very miserable. Of the labouring classes some were serfs or bondmen, entirely the property of their masters. In some old deeds there are stated particulars of the transfers by sale or gift of some of this description of serfs; and not only of the individuals themselves, but of their chattels, and of all their *families and progeny, whether born or to be born.* Others were villeins, who were attached to the manor or estate on which they resided, and were irremovable from it. Among these latter there were various distinctions, but the condition of all was very degraded. Some in return for their services were only entitled to a bare maintenance from their lord, while others could also cultivate plots of ground for their own profit. Some again had the occupation of cottages, while others habitually lived and slept with the oxen. Besides being poorly fed and ill-housed, restrictions were placed upon their clothing; for it was legally enacted that carters, ploughmen, oxherds, shepherds, swineherds, and other servants in agriculture, were not to be allowed to wear any manner of cloth, but only blanket stuff and russet wool. In some cases it would appear that a few articles of clothing were supplied by the lord to his labourers, for there is an entry in the accounts of the Prior of Burchester in 1425, of two yards of russet for the shepherd, price 2s. 2d., and thirty pairs of winter gloves for the men, 4s. Notwithstanding the miserable condition of the lower orders, they were forced to bear part of the national taxation; and one of the clauses in Magna Charta for their relief, prohibited that villeins should be "amerced beyond safety to their wainage;" the meaning of this protection being that the villein should not by excessive fine or taxation be deprived of his rude cart or wain, wherewith he rendered his service to his lord, in carrying out manure to the lord's land, harvesting, and the like; for otherwise the wretched creature had to carry it all on his back.

For some time subsequent to the Norman Conquest the condition of these classes was at its worst. Population had decreased throughout the kingdom, while the taxation had been greatly increased. In the Domesday Book, in the account of Melford, we find that the number of irremovable villeins had been maintained as in the time of Edward the Confessor, while the freer bordarii or husbandmen of a better class had diminished from 35 to 10. Where there had been eight ploughs there were only six left; and while there had been enough homagers or tenants to maintain twenty ploughs, the number of ploughs had dwindled down to thirteen; and though the proportion of principal taxpayers who bore the burden of the public imposts had thus diminished, yet the gelt or government tax on the township of Melford had been raised from £20 to £30 a year.

After the "Black Death" Plague of 134$\frac{8}{9}$ (which raged throughout the diocese of Norwich and in other parts) the population had been so much reduced, that the price of labour increased enormously. There had long been a custom of commuting some of the serf-labour, never very profitable, for money payments; but when the supply of working men became inadequate to meet the demand, and that they could therefore almost dictate the price of wages, endeavours were made by several enactments to regulate them arbitrarily; and in addition, an attempt was made to revive in full all the worst oppressive parts of the old serf-labour. The discontent engendered by these injustices led in a great measure to the rebellion of Wat Tyler in 1381.

In 1389 the worst part of the old system of villeinage had almost become extinct; but what the poor people had gained in freedom of person was counterbalanced not only by grinding taxation but also by enforced pauperism. For whereas the villein irremovable had formerly been entitled to maintenance for himself and family from his master, who was bound to support him not only while able to labour, but also in sickness and old age, and when unfit for work; now that he had become his own master, when either want of employment, sickness, or the helplessness of old age came upon him, he was totally unprovided for. But men will not starve when they can either beg or steal; so mendicants, thieves, and vagrants began to swarm throughout the land, and the destitute poor now first appeared as a distinct class of the community. The traffic over the highways of the country had been difficult enough before from natural causes; the rural highways being almost impassable except on foot, and the larger roads between the market-towns, besides being rough rutty green-ways, varied in the low places by deep sloughs of mud, were now rendered yet more difficult for traffic by their insecurity, being infested by vagrants, robbers, sturdy mendicants, and other loose characters, so that it became necessary that an Act should be passed directing that every highway leading from one market-town to another should be cleared, for the space of 200 feet on each side, of every ditch, tree, or bush in which a man could lurk to do hurt; and if a park was near a highway, it was ordered to be removed to the same distance, or to be carefully defended by a wall or otherwise, so that it should not serve as a harbour from which malefactors might issue forth to attack the traveller. The state of the country roads did not however improve till long after this ordinance.

Without entering further upon the manners and customs of the Middle Ages, it may just be noticed in illustration of these early days, that in the reign of Edward III., 1327 to 1377, the neighbouring town of Colchester contained 359 houses, some built of mud, and the better kind of timber, having wood lattice windows unglazed, but perhaps in a few of the best houses filled in with horn; and yet there were at that time only about nine towns in England of greater importance. The number of the inhabitants was about 3,000, so that the houses must have been much overcrowded. The entire property of the town, including the furniture and clothing of the inhabitants, was only valued at £518. Twenty-nine trades were carried on in it. The tools of a carpenter at Colchester were a broad axe, value 5 pence; another axe, 3 pence; an adze, 2 pence; a square, 1 penny; making the total value of his implements only one shilling. The tools and stock of a blacksmith of the highest order were priced at 12 shillings. The whole stock in trade and household goods of a considerable tanner there were estimated at £9. 17s. 10d.; a mercer's stock at £3, and his whole household property at £2. 9s. The trades of brewer, baker, and miller were carried on by women as well as by men.

Returning, after this glance at the state of our forefathers in olden times, to the immediate history of Melford Manor, notice must be taken of the early, and, in those days, most important grants to Melford, of weekly markets and an annual fair; the marts and channels for all the general merchandise of those days.

The first of these charters was granted by King John. The patent existed in the Tally Court of Westminster up to a comparatively recent date; but there does not appear to be a copy of it among the existing Abbey records of Melford, although they contain the subsequent grants to the same effect.

This one was, however, confirmed and extended by a charter of King Henry III., dated July, 1235. The following is the Latin text, to which is appended a rough translation :—

Melford Fair and Market.

1234.

CARTA de Anno Regni Regis Henrici Tertii, Decimo Nono.

Pro Abbate Sancti Edmundi.

Rex Archiepiscopis &c. salutem. Sciatis nos concessisse et hac carta nostra confirmasse pro nobis et heredibus nostris, dilecto nobis Xþo Henrico Abbati Sancti Edmundi, quod ipse et successores sui Abbates ejusdem loci habeant in perpetuum unum Mercatum singulis septimanis per diem Jovis apud manerium suum de Meleford—et quod habeant in perpetuum unam Feriam ibidem singulis annis duraturam per tres dies, videlicet in Vigilia et in die et in crastino Sanctæ Trinitatis—Nisi prædictum Mercatum et prædicta Feria sint ad nocumentum vicinorum mercatorum et vicinarum Feriarum—Quare volumus et firmiter præcipimus pro nobis et heredibus nostris quod prædictus Abbas et successores sui Abbates ejusdem loci habeant et teneant in perpetuum prædictum Mercatum et prædictam Feriam bene et in pace cum omnibus libertatibus et liberis consuetudinibus ad . . . . . . Mercatum et Feriam pertinentibus. Nisi prædictum Mercatum et prædicta Feria sint ad nocumentum vicinorum Mercatorum et vicinarum Feriarum, sicut prædictum est.

His testibus

Venerabilibus ~~Presbiteribus~~ *Patribus*

R. Dumelm : ⎫
J. Bath : ⎬ Episcopis
W. Carl : ⎭

T. Mar. Com. Pembróke
H. de Burgo Com. Kent
Radulpho filio Nicholi
Godefrido de Crancumb
Johanne filio Philippi
Galfrido Dispenser
Galfrido de Cauz
Henrico de Capella
et aliis.

Datum per manum Venerabilis Patris R. Cycester Cancellarii nostri apud Westmonasterium viij die Julii, et mandatum est Vicecomiti Suffolcii quod prædictum Mercatum et prædictam Feriam per Ballam suam clamari faciétur et ibidem teneri sicut prædictum est ut supra.

(Translation.)

Melford Fair and Market.

The Charter of the 6th month of the 19th year of the reign of King Henry III.

123⁴⁄₅.

For the Abbot of St. Edmund.

The king to all Archbishops, Bishops, &c. &c., greeting.

Know ye that we have granted, and by this our charter have confirmed, for ourselves and our heirs, to our beloved in Christ, Henry, Abbot of St. Edmund, that he, and the abbots who succeed him, shall have in perpetuity at their manor of Melford, a weekly market on Thursday. And that they shall also have in perpetuity at the same place a yearly fair, to last three days; viz., on the vigil, day, and morrow of the Holy Trinity; unless the said market and fair should be to the hindrance of neighbouring markets and fairs. Therefore we will, and we do for ourselves and our heirs firmly grant to the said

Abbot and his successors, that they may well and peaceably have and hold for ever the said market and fair with all liberties and customary rights belonging to the same; unless the said market and fair should be to the hindrance of neighbouring markets and fairs, as aforesaid.

These being witnesses hereto.

The Venerable ~~Priests~~ *Fathers*

RICHARD DURHAM ⎫

JOHN BATH   ⎬ Bishops

WILLIAM CARLISLE ⎭

GILBERT MARSHAL, Earl of Pembroke

HUBERT DE BURGH, Earl of Kent

RALPH, son of Nicholas

GODFREY DE CRANCUMB

JOHN, son of Philip

GEOFFRY DISPENSER

GEOFFRY DE CAUZ

HENRY DE CAPEL

and others.

Given by the hand of the venerable Father Richard Chichester, our Chancellor, at Westminster, the 8th day of July. And the High Sheriff of Suffolk is commanded to make proclamation by his bailiff of the holding of the said market and fair in the said place, as is aforesaid.

As will be seen in the Latin text of this charter, the name of the first attesting witness is there given as T. Mar., Com. Pembroke. It is so in the attested copy of 1767, from which this was transcribed; but it would appear that this initial letter of the Earl of Pembroke's Christian name was a clerical error, and should have been G; for *Richard* Marshal, the third earl, was killed in Ireland in 1234, and was succeeded by his brother *Gilbert*, the fourth earl, who was killed by the fall of his horse at a tournament in 1241, and who was therefore the person who attested this deed, unless perhaps Earl Richard had done so before he proceeded to Ireland. Anyhow the initial T was an error, as it must have been either R. or G.

Two points in this charter are worthy of special remark; viz. that the days of the annual fair were the eve of Trinity, Trinity Sunday, and Monday. At that period it was by no means unusual for fairs and markets to be held on a Sunday; and in 1317 a presentment was made at Colchester, that the Abbot of St. Osyth's market on Sundays was injurious to the trade of the town of Colchester.—In the 15th century, however, it appears that a general revulsion of feeling had commenced on this subject; for in 1449 a petition was presented to King Henry VI. against the " holdinge of Feyres and Marketts on

Sundayes;" wherein it was represented that they caused great profanation of Sundays and the principal holy-days, such as Whitsunday, Trinity, &c., and praying an amendment of the special grants of olden times, which included these days.—The king granted this petition.—And secondly, it is a matter of curiosity to read the great historical names of the attesting witnesses to the charter of the fair and market of this village. Moreover, there is a peculiar coincidence in the fact of its bearing the signature of Sir Godfrey de Crancumb, together with that of the great Hubert de Burgh, the justiciary, with a notable event in whose life, this knight (who is sometimes called Crawcombe), two years later, bore so prominent a part. When the noble minister was forced, by the intrigues of his enemies, encouraged by the ingratitude towards him of one of the falsest and meanest of our kings, to flee from London, he received a royal safe-conduct, relying on which he started to join his wife at St. Edmund's Bury; but he had scarcely begun his journey, when the King, notwithstanding his plighted faith, sent Sir Godfrey de Crancumb, with 300 armed men, to seize him. They surprised him in bed at Brentwood; he contrived to escape, almost naked, into the parish church, and took refuge at the altar, with a crucifix in one hand and the Host in the other, hoping that the sanctity of the spot would insure him respect. But his furious enemies, headed by Sir Godfrey de Crancumb, regardless of the sacrilege, burst into the church, and having dragged the earl forth, placed him on horseback, nearly naked as he was, tying his feet under the girths, and so conveyed him to the Tower of London.

This violation of sanctuary raised such an outcry, that the king was reluctantly forced to order Sir Godfrey and those who had seized the earl, to reconvey him in safety to the church from whence he had been taken.

Hubert de Burgh was buried in 1243 in the Black Friars, London.

This charter of Melford fair and market is only briefly referred to in a few words, in the posthumous edition of Archdeacon Battely's (Latin) History of the Antiquities of Bury St. Edmund, published in 1745.* He gives no copy of the text of the charter.

Another copy of this charter of 123¼ is noted thus:—"True copy of the Record in the Tower of London, examined by Henry Rooke, chief clerk of the Records of the Tower of London, and attested the 30th July, 1767, by me, S. CLARKE."

The next charter, of a hundred years later, is yet more comprehensive, and includes, besides the ratification of the grant of the market and the fair, the duration of which latter is extended, the

* Dr. John Battely, Archdeacon of Canterbury, was brother of Nicholas Battely, rector of Nowton, also a learned author. They were sons of Nicholas Battely, of Bury, apothecary, who was buried at St. James's, Bury, in 1680.

renewed liberty also of free warren in Melford, among numerous other places. Like the former charter, it is of so much interest that it is here given in its original text (freed from abbreviations), as well as the translation thereof:—

CARTA DE LIBERA WARENNA in omnibus Dominicis Sancti Edmundi habenda, et de Mercato de Melforde per diem Jovis singulis septimanis habendo : et de una Feria ibidem singulis Annis per IX dies duratura ; ut prius in Registro Richardi, Abbatis, folio 88, folio S. E., sequitur in hæc verba.

A.D. 1330.

Edwardus Dei gratia Rex Angliæ, Dominus Hiberniæ, Dux Aquitaniæ, Archiepiscopis, Episcopis, Abbatibus, Prioribus, Comitibus, Baronibus, Justiciariis, Vicecomitibus, Præpositis, Magistris, et omnibus Ballivis, et fidelibus suis salutem—Sciatis quod cum per cartas progenitorum nostrorum quondam Regum Angliæ dudum concessio fuisset tunc Abbati et Conventui de Sancto Edmundo quod ipsi et successores sui in perpetuum haberent liberam Warennam infra Burgum de Sancto Edmundo et extra in omnibus locis suis, ac dilecti nobis in Xp̄o nunc Abbas et Conventus loci prædicti et predecessores sui virtute dictorum verborum generalium · habuerint a tempore confectionis cartarum prædictarum liberam Warennam in omnibus Dominicis terris suis in Comitatibus, Norfolciæ, Suffolciæ, Essexiæ, Hertfordiæ, Lincolniæ, et Northamptoni :—et nobis supplicaverint ut pro ipsorum securitate in futuris velimus eis loca prædicta specificare, Nos volentes præfatis Abbati et Conventui gratiam in hac precatione [?] facere specialem concessimus et hac carta nostra confirmavimus præfatis Abbati et Conventui quod ipsi et successores sui in perpetuum haberent liberam Warennam in omnibus dominicis terris suis de Sancto Edmundo, Cheventone, Magna Saxham, Parva Saxham, Hargrave, Magna Hornynggeserth, Parva Hornynggeserth, Lacford, Fornham omnium Sanctorum, Fornham Sanctæ Genoveve, Fornham Sancti Martini, Nowton, Whepstede, Westle, Risby, Downham, Mildenhale, Parva Bartone, Hæringewelle, Ikelyngham, Elvedene, Hoptone, Hildercle, Rykynghale, Wattlefeld, Conæeweston, Stantone, Elmesette, Honæeweston, Langham, Troston, Ingham, Culeforde, Westowe, Bradefelde Monachorum, Bradefelde, Semcler, Hægesete, Clopton, Welpit, Whinstone, Rugham, Pakenham, Magna Bertone, Rosshebrok, MELLEFORDE, Cokefeld, Boxford, Grotæne, Sæmere, Chelæsworth, Lelleseye, Oldhawe, Brokford, Palgrave, Rædgrave, Wertham, Cotton, Bekles, Wirlyngeworth, et Saham Monachorum in dicto comitatu Suffolciæ.

Chebenhale, Rungeton, Tylneye, Tyveteshale, Thorp Abbis, Sothereye, Estbradenham, Aylesham, Brook, Castre, et Wikylburgh, in dicto Comitatu Norfolciæ.—Herlawe, Wrabenase, et Tedenhowe, in

dicto Comitatu Essexiæ.—Werketon in dicto Comitatu Northamptoni.
—Stapelford in dicto Comitatu Hertfordiæ.—Et Waynfleet in dicto
Comitatu Lincolniæ : cum tamen terræ illæ non sint infra metas forestæ
nostræ.—Ita quod nullus intret terras illas ad fugandum in eis, veluti ad
aliquid capiendum quod ad Warennam pertineat, sine licentia et voluntate ipsius Abbatis et Conventus veluti successorum suorum, super foriffaturam nostram decem librarum.—Concessimus etiam de gratia nostra
speciali et hac carta nostra confirmavimus iisdem Abbati et Conventui
quod ipsi et successores sui in perpetuum *haberent unum Mercatum,
singulis septimanis per diem Jovis apud manerium suum de Meleforde,
in dicto Comitatu Suffolciæ, et unam Feriam ibidem singulis annis per
novem dies duraturam ; viz., in Vigili et in die Pentecoste et per septem
dies proximos sequentes,* nisi Mercatum illud et Feria illa sint ad
nocumentum vicinorum mercatorum et vicinarum feriarum. Quare
volumus et firmiter præcipimus pro nobis et hæredibus nostris, quod
prædictus Abbas et Conventus et successores sui in perpetuum habeant
liberam Warennam in omnibus dominicis terris suis prædictis :
cum tamen terræ illæ non sint infra metas forestæ nostræ. Ita quod
nullus intret terras illas ad fugandum in eis, veluti ad aliquid capiendum
quod ad Warennam pertineat sine licentia et voluntate ipsius Abbatis
et Conventus veluti successorum suorum super foriffaturam nostram
decem librarum et quod habeant prædictum Mercatum et Feriam apud
manerium suum prædictum cum omnibus libertatibus et liberis consuetudinibus ad hujusmodi mercatum et feriam pertinentibus ; nisi
mercatum illud et feria illa sint ad nocumentum vicinorum mercatorum
et vicinarum feriarum, sicut prædictum est.

His testibus :—
    Venerabilibus Patribus,—
            H. Lincoln, Episcopo-Cancellario nostro,
            B. Episcopo Sarum,
            Johanne de Eltham, Comite Cornewallæ, fratre
                nostro carissimo,
            Rogero de Mortuo,
            Marc, Comite Marchiæ,
            Willo de Monteacuto,
            Olivero de Ingham,
            Hugone de Turplytone, Senescallo Hospitii
                nostri,
                    et aliis.

Datum per manum nostram apud Notyngham, tertio decimo die
            Septembris, Anno regni nostri quarto.

    The following is the translation of the Charter of Free Warren in all
demesnes of the Abbey of St. Edmund's, and of a weekly market on

Thursdays at Melford, and of an annual fair of nine days' duration at Melford, from the Vigil of Pentecost. Given by King Edward III. at Nottingham, 13th September, 1330, to Abbot Richard Draughton; and confirming the former charters of King John and of King Henry III. as entered in the Register of Abbot Richard, folio 83, in these words following :—

Edward, by the grace of God, King of England, Lord of Ireland, Duke of Aquitaine, to the Archbishops, Bishops, Abbots, Priors, Earls, Barons, Justiciaries, Sheriffs, Governors, Magistrates, Bailiffs, and to all faithful subjects greeting. Know ye, that whereas a grant by charter was formerly made by our ancestors, kings of England, to the then Abbot and Convent of St. Edmund, that they and their successors should have for ever a free warren over their burgh of St. Edmund and over all other places appertaining to them; and whereas our beloved in Christ the Abbot and Convent of the aforesaid place and their predecessors, by virtue of the said terms, have had from the time of the said grants a general free warren in all their demesne lands in the counties of Norfolk, Suffolk, Essex, Hertford, Lincoln, and Northampton; and as they have prayed us that for their future security we should specify these places: now we, willing to show special favour to the Abbot and Convent in this matter of their petition, do grant and by this our charter confirm to the Abbot and his successors for ever, that they shall have free warren in all their demesne lands of St. Edmunds, Chevington, Great Saxham, Little Saxham, Hargrave, Great Horringer and Little Horringer, Lackford, Fornham all Saints, and St. Genevieve, and St. Martin, Nowton, Whepstead, Westley, Risby, Downham, Mildenhall, Little Barton, Herringswell, Icklingham, Elvedon, Hopton, Hindercley, Rickinghall, Watfield, Coneyweston, Stanton, Elmsett, Honeyweston [or Hoveweston?], Langham, Troston, Ingham, Culford, Westowe, the Bradfields, Hesset, Clopton, Woolpit, Winston, Rougham, Pakenham, Great Barton, Rushbrook, MELFORD, Cookfield, Boxford, Groton, Semer, Chelsworth, Lindsey, Oldhawe [? Aldham], Boxford, Palgrave, Redgrave, Wortham, Cotton, Beccles, Worlingsworth, and Monk Soham, in the said county of Suffolk.

Chebenhall, Runcton, Tilney, Tivetshall, Thorpe Abbotts, Southery, East Braddenham, Aylsham, Brooke, Castle Acre, Wikylburgh (?), in the said county of Norfolk.

Harlowe, Wrabness, and Tedenhowe (?), in the said county of Essex.

Warkton, in the said county of Northampton.

Stapleford, in the said county of Hertford.

And Waynfleet, in the said county of Lincoln.

Unless the said lands should be within the bounds of our royal forests. And further that no one shall enter these lands, either flying from justice into them, or to seize in them anything belonging to the warren, without leave and consent of the Abbot and Convent or their successors, under pain of forfeiting ten pounds. We also by our special bounty grant, and by this our charter confirm to the said Abbot and Convent, that they and their successors shall have in perpetuity *a weekly market on Thursday at their manor of Melford*, in the said county of Suffolk, and also *a fair there yearly of nine days' duration; viz. on the Vigil and on the day of Whit-Sunday, and for seven days next following*, unless the said market and fair are a hindrance to neighbouring markets and fairs. Wherefore we will and do fully grant to the said Abbot and Convent and their successors a free warren for ever in all the aforesaid demesne lands, provided they are not within the bounds of our royal forests, and that no one may enter these lands either flying-from-justice, or to seize anything in them belonging to the warren, without consent and permission of the Abbot and Convent, or their successors, under a penalty of a forfeiture of ten pounds; and that they shall hold the said market and fair in their manor aforesaid, with all free rights and privileges belonging to such market and fair, provided that they are not to the hindrance of neighbouring markets and fairs as aforesaid.

These being witnesses hereto —

· The Venerable Fathers,—

  H. LINCOLN, Bishop, our Chancellor,

  B. SALISBURY, Bishop,

  JOHN DE ELTHAM, Earl of Cornwall, our dear brother,

  ROGER DE MORTM° (MORTIMER),

  MARK, Earl of March,

  WILLIAM DE MONTACUTE,

  OLIVER DE INGHAM,

  HUGH DE TURPLYTON, Steward of our Hospital,

    and others.

Given under our hand at Nottingham, the 13th day of September, in the fourth year of reign.

The witnesses to this charter, like the former one, were very great people. John of Eltham, the second son of Edward II., who was created Earl of Cornwall in 1328, must have been but a youth at the date of this attestation. Some writers, as Stothard in his "Monumental Effigies," say that he died at Berwick-on-Tweed in 1334, aged 19. This, however, is an error, for by a document dated 20th June, 1336, he was clearly alive at that date; and though his death is involved in some obscurity, he appears to have died very suddenly, and it is suspected, by a violent death, at Perth, in the month of September or October, 1336. Sir Bernard Burke follows this date. There is a very fine monumental effigy of him on the south side of the choir in Westminster Abbey, in which, however, the face, though young-looking, would convey the idea of a somewhat older man, from being represented as wearing a moustache.

It is evident that the Roger de Mortm° was Roger Mortimer, the Queen-mother Isabella's favourite, who was with the court at Nottingham at the date of this charter, and to whom undue precedence is given in the attestation, as his signature follows that of the king's brother, and precedes those of the great barons; and his name was affixed hereto only a few weeks before his seizure and subsequent execution: and thus this deed of the 13th September, 1330, has, like the former one of 1234, the coincidence of two names of persons who closely affected each other's fates being appended to it as joint witnesses. In this case, on the 19th of October, 1330, the plot concerted between the King and Lord Montacute, whose name is also attached to this charter as a witness, was put into execution, and shortly before midnight Montacute and his associates seized Mortimer in Nottingham Castle (from whence this charter was dated), and he was hanged on the 29th November following at the common gallows, then called "Elmes," near Smithfield, where his body hung two days and nights naked before it was interred in the Grey Friars. His grandson, Roger, married Philippa, daughter of Lord Montacute.

The William Lord Montacute who signed the charter was the third baron of his name, and became afterwards Earl of Salisbury. He was a Knight of the Bath, and when he attested this deed, he had just returned from an embassy to Rome. This distinguished warrior, who was crowned by Edward III. *King of the Isle of Man*, died in 1343, of hurts received in a tilting at Windsor.

The next witness, Oliver de Ingham, was created a baron in 1328, and was one of the twelve guardians of King Edward III. He died without male heirs in 1344.

In this latter grant of the fair the time for holding it was altered from Trinity to Whitsuntide, and the abbots were allowed to extend its duration to a period of nine days, which included both Whit-Sunday and Trinity Sunday; but this long continuance of the fair being in after-times found inconvenient, fell into desuetude. When the market was first abolished does not appear, but probably in the 17th century, and before 1676. There yet remains on Melford Green the base of the old Market Cross, and as it is shown on the Manor map as still standing in 1615, having been repaired at the close of the previous century, it is natural to presume that the Puritan mob, who sacked Melford Hall and injured the church during the Rebellion, in their general hatred of the holy symbol, then demolished the cross. An old writer, who must have been somewhat of a satirist, remarks that the origin of these market crosses being placed on such sites, was to remind those who resorted to market, of the virtues of truth and justice.

In connection with the early history of Melford Manor, there is in some records a mention of an event which is somewhat irreconcilable in its dates and terms; for it is stated that it appears from the Hundred Rolls of the third year of King Edward I., 127$\frac{4}{}$, that John Walraven, escheator to the king, destroyed the cattle and damaged the Park at Melford, while the manor was in the king's hands, after the decease of Edmund, Abbot of St. Edmund's. These names and events not being applicable to the Abbey in reference to the date, it must be surmised that the account in the Hundred Rolls of the time named does not apply to that year, but is merely an after-record of an event . which had occurred some few years previously, and in the previous reign: for Abbot Edward, or sometimes called Edmund de Walpole, died on the 2nd January, 1256, and Abbot Simon de Sutine succeeded him 19th February, 1257, and was Abbot of Bury till 1279. It is to be noticed that there was therefore an interval of a year during which the Abbey was in the king's hands, between the death of Abbot Walpole and the appointment of his successor. Probably, therefore, the event alluded to occurred between 1256 and 1257, in the interval of the abeyance of the Abbacy, and in the reign of Henry III.; and considering the constant indigence and unscrupulous rapacity of this king, who earned the name of the "sturdiest beggar in Christendom," it is probable that he seized the opportunity given him by a short lapse in the succession to the Abbey of St. Edmund, to plunder all he could from its manors while in his power; and this very period was one in which he was more than ever impecunious.

Certain expressions of an old writer, relative to St. Edmund's Abbey about that time, tend somewhat to confirm this conjecture; thus: "Quomodo, Rex vacante sede nummos extorserit." Probably the king's officers, besides money, also seized cattle, or anything they could lay their hands on, belonging to the country houses of the Abbey (as at Melford Hall) while the Abbacy was thus in abeyance.

The following charters, conveyances, and agreements exist in the various Melford chartularies of the several abbots, relative to this manor and estate. The originals are all in abbreviated Monkish Latin, on parchment; and though their headings are here retained, a précis of their general substance is given in English, and they are here placed in the order of their dates. They are in all respects very curious and interesting documents, bringing to light Melford lands and people in far back times; and some of the attesting witnesses to them were distinguished personages. In explanation of the fact of so many such witnesses signing deeds of comparatively little importance, it should be borne in mind that documents of this nature were very commonly executed at Courts of the Hundred or other public meetings. And ancient deeds were often dated on a Sunday, being executed in churches or churchyards, for the greater publicity and notoriety.

ABBOT ANSELM.

CARTA ANSELMI ABBATIS de terris ibm concessis Roberto fili Walteri, cum servicio de terra Nicholi: fili Durand* pro servicio VIII milit̃: inter cartas Abbatis, &c.

A.D. 1119—1148.

Anselm, Dei gratia Abbot of St. Edmund, to the faithful in Christ of *France and England*, greeting. Know all men, &c., that I have given and granted to Robert, son of Walter, certain lands in Melford of the feoff of St. Edmund, and the service of the land of Nicholas, son of Durand, holden by tenure from St. Edmund in fee and heritage, by eight knight's service. This I had before given and granted by the counsel and assent of Talbot, the Prior, and the whole chapter of the convent. And these are witnesses on the part of the Abbot:—

WELNARDUS, Clerk.	WELNARD DE WRIDEWELL.
WILLIAM, Magister.	WILLIAM, son of Anselm.
PETER, Clerk.	REMALD, the Camerarius.
†GILBERT BLUNDUS.	JOHN DE LANAL.
RICHARD, son of Walter.	ALBERT DE MARSICA.
GODEBOLD DE KIRKEBI.	SEWARD, the Hostiarius.

And on the part of Nicholas, these:—

THOMAS, the Chaplain.	ROGER DE BILL.
ADAM, Clerk.	GUDO, son of Daniel.
ROBERT, son of Hugo.	RUNGOTUS LUND.
HUMFREY DE MUNDAVILLE.	ROBERT, nephew of Ralph.
ALAN, son of Odo.	ALURED DE NORTH.
JOHN, his son.	ROBERT, son of Alan.
GEOFFREY, son of Humfrey.	WALTER, his brother.

ABBOT ORDINGUS.

QUIETA CLAMA COMITIS ALBERICI de x libris quas de manerio Melforde solebat annuatim percipere. Inserit in Registro Johannis North-woldi folio q. e. inter cartas Abbatis a.1. prout sequitur in hæc verba.

A.D. 1148—1156.

Earl Alberic of his free will and pleasure hath given to the Abbey

---

* The family of Durand are mentioned as proprietors of land in Suffolk in the Domesday Book, as is also a person of the name of Blundus.

+ Gilbert de Blund, about the year 1100, founded the Priory of the Virgin Mary at Ixworth; it was held by Canons Regular of St. Augustine.

of St. Edmund and to Abbot Ordingus, and to the Convent of Stapleford, ten pounds of his receipts of the manor of Melford, binding thereto his heirs and successors.

Witnesses hereto :

ROBERT, son of William.

RALPH DE HOSDENE.

GEOFFRY ARSIT.

It is recorded of Alberic, Earl of Clare, who became possessed of part of the lands of Earl Alfric, the son of Withgar, that he claimed from Abbot Hugh (the successor of Ordingus) an annual payment of 5 shillings, alleging that this was an ancient fee due to him, as hereditary standard-bearer of the forces of the Abbey. But his rights both to the fee and to the appointment were disproved, for Earl Roger de Bigot, Alberic's relation, carried the standard of St. Edmund at the battle of Fornham against the Flemings.—" Chronicles of Jocelin de Brakelond."

ABBOT SAMSON DE BOTINGTON.

CARTA SAMSONIS ABBATIS de XXII Acris terræ et III et dim: Acris pasturæ concess: Galanto Blund pro annuo reddend: VII* et operum yemabilium estim: Inter Cartas Abbatis A. 2. prout sequitur in hæc verba.

A.D. 1180—1211.

Samson, Abbot of St. Edmund's, grants to Galant Blund and his heirs, on payment of 40 shillings, 22 acres of land, and 1 rood of land in Bulney, and 1 acre of pasture, and $2\frac{1}{2}$ acres near Lenetoft, and 4 acres of land of Richard de Brikebec, for a rent of 7s. a year, by four equal payments ; i.e., 21d. at the feast of St. Michael; 21d. at the feast of St. Andrew; 21d. at Easter; and 21d. at the Nativity of St. John the Baptist; and in each year they are to reap for the abbots on land at Melford half an acre of wheat and half an acre of oats, and to plough twice in winter and twice in spring on the arable land with their ploughs.

Witnesses hereto :

MANRIO } Chaplains.
HEBERT }

STEPHEN MAGRO.

(A) ROGER DE WALSYNGHAM.

GILBERT DE WALSYNGHAM.

(B) RALPH DE NEKETON.

WILLIAM DE ELMSWELL.

(C) . . . . . . Pincerna.

THOMAS ALBY.

ADAM TALBOT.

RICHARD FORESTAR.

ROBERT, son of Thomas.

(D) REGINALD DE BROCLEY.

WILLIAM RUSSEL.

YNO DE PRESTON.

WILLIAM, son of Holdedene.

THOMAS GERNON.

And others.

2 L

In this lease a bonus of nearly six years' rent appears to have been paid to the Abbot by Galant Blund, for the grant to him and his heirs. The rent was not quite 3 pence an acre, besides services.

(A) The two Walsynghams who attested the deed appear also as witnesses to another grant relating to Barrow, whereby Thomas de Barewe, in the Abbacy of Sampson, gave to the Church of St. Edmund a villein named Seward, son of Aluric, with all his chattels and progeny.

(B) There were many members of the family of De Neketon settled at Risby. Ralph de Neketon's land there passed to Sir Robert Hovel, Knight.

(C) *Pincerna's* proper surname is illegible in the Melford Chartulary, but in the Register of the Sacrist of the Abbey of St. Edmund's, Bury, his name is given as "Seward," *Pincerna* (*Pincerna* being the abbey wine butler or cupbearer).

(D) Reginald de Brocley, in the year 1197, held of Abbot Samson a knight's fee in Brockley, which had belonged to his father Peter. Reginald's daughter Lucy married John de Cramaville, of Melford, whose name appears as an attesting witness to several Melford deeds; and she had a son, John de Cramaville. She remarried John Algar.

ABBOT HUGH, OF NORTHWOLD.

CARTA LOKEREI fili ABSOLON de Homagio et Servicio Alexi Absolon, Walteri Palmere, et Walteri Peynton cum annuo reddi xviii*. Inter cartas Abbatis, A. 12. prout sequitur in hæc verba.

A.D. 1218—1228.

The said Lokereus, son of Absolon of Melford, sold in perpetuity to Hugh (of Northwold, Abbot of St. Edmund's, afterwards translated to the bishopric of Ely) and his successors, the homages and services of Alexis, son of Absolon, and of Walter Palmer, and of Walter the miller, in the town of Melford; viz. from Alexis 10 pence a year, payable at the four registered terms of the Court of Melford, for 5 acres of land; of Walter Palmer, 6 pence a year, payable as above, for 1 acre of pasture; and of Walter the miller, 2 pence a year similarly, for 4½ acres of arable land; and for all these the Abbot paid to Lokereus the sum of 12 shillings in money.

Witnesses hereto :

(E) Sir GILBERT DE KENTEWELL.
(F) JOHN DE CRAMAVILLE.
ROBERT, son of Thomas Brian, the Forester.
ROGER, son of William.
ADAM DE BRIKEBEC.
GEOFFREY SEMER.

WILLIAM, son of Galant.
HUGH, son of Adam.
YNONE DE PRESTON.
WALTER NEWMAN.
MANRIC, son of Philip.
HUGH, his son.
ADAM, the Clerk.

(E) In this deed alone occurs the name of Sir Gilbert de Kentewell.
(F) The family of De Cramaville, besides having estates in Brockley and Hawstead,

had considerable possessions in Melford, and held what of late years was the paper-mill, and which was then two water-mills under one roof; and they had land and a house at Cranfield, which is a corruption of their name, which sometimes occurs as "De Cranville." Some of the family were buried in the old Priory of Sudbury. In 1231, Peter, son of Alan de Brockley, released to John de Cramaville and Lucy his wife, half the advowson of the church of Brockley.

CARTA ejusdem LOKERICI de v acris terræ cum pertinentibus jacent: in Tenakercroft: inter cartas Abbatis A. 13. prout sequitur in hæc verba.

A.D. 1213—1228.

The said Lokereus surrendered to Abbot Hugh 5 acres of land, with appurtenances, which he had held in the field called Tenakercroft, for which the Abbot paid him 6 marcs (£4) by the hand of Geoffry de Semer, to whom the Abbot then sold the land. And further, it was agreed that there should be refunded to Lokereus and his heirs for ever, 6 pence a year, which he had to pay, in lieu of his due services, to the Court of Melford; for which 6 pence the said Geoffry, or his heirs who might hold this land, were to be responsible. For the perpetual security of which thing, Lokereus affixed hereto his seal.

Witnesses hereto :

ROBERT DE BOSTON.
JOHN DE CRAMAVILLE.
ROGER, son of William.
BRIAN, the Forester.
ROBERT, son of Thomas (Brian).
THOMAS, his son.

ADAM GARDINER.
ADAM DE BRIKEBEC.
WALTER LE PALM.
(a) WALTER LE NEWMAN.
(b) MANRIC, son of Philip.
ROBERT, the Clerk of the Abbey.

(a) Walter le Neweman is elsewhere called Walter de Melford. He was the son of William le Neweman, and held lands of the Abbot, now in Melford Place, between the years 1234 and 1248, which had been bequeathed to him by his father after the death of his aunt Amfreda.

(b) This Philip may have been the person who owned considerable property in Melford, and who is recorded to have been *hung for theft* about the years 1170 to 1180.

ABBOT HENRY.

QUIETA CLAMA ROBERTI, Fabri de Melford, de omnibus terris, redditibus, et de tenemento cum officio fabrili, et pratibus suis. Inter cartas Abbatis A. 8. prout sequitur in hæc verba.

A.D. 1234—1248.

Robert the blacksmith, of Melford, granted and conveyed to Henry, Abbot of St. Edmund, all lands and incomings, and the house, with the forge and smithy, which he possessed in the town of Melford, and the land pertaining thereto.

Witnesses :

(G) ROBERT DE SHARDELAWE.
HENRY DE NEKETON.
(H) ROBERT DE NEKETON.
THOMAS DE WHEPSTEAD.
ROBERT DE REDE.
GEOFFRY DE MELFORD.

BRIAN, the Forester.
ADAM, the Gardener.
THOMAS, son of Robert.
HUGO, son of Manric.
And others.

(G) The family of Shardelowe held much land in Suffolk, and had a manor in Little Barton. In temp. Henry VI. their arms were, Argent a chevron gules, between three cross croslets fitchée azure.

(H) Robert de Nekton's name is attached to a deed of Sir Robert Hovel, of Risby, in 1259. One Geoffry de Nekton was a Friar Minor of Babwell, of St. Edmund, and was suspended in 1263, with eight other monks, for contumacy, and with a threat of excommunication, under a brief of Pope Urban IV., of 1262, the Friars Minor having intruded themselves within the Banna leuca of the Abbey and refusing to quit their possession, which had been surreptitiously acquired.

ABBOT EDWARD DE WALPOLE.

CARTA HENRICI DE TITTYSHALE de uno messuagio et IV acris terræ, reddent: aule de Melford annuatim XIX^{d.} inter cartas Abbatis A. 6. prout sequitur in hæc verba.

A.D. 1248—1256.

Henry de Tisteshall (*sic* in the deed) conveys to John Brodeghe, of Thorp, in consideration of his homage and service, and 9½ marcs of money (£6. 6s. 8d.), which he has paid, 4 acres of arable land and a messuage on the said land in Melford, lying between the lands of Gylote, son of William Torleser, and lands of Adam Gru, and abutting on the road called *Hallestrete*,* to hold to him and his assigns, &c., paying to the said Henry yearly VIII^{d.}, and to the manor of Melford yearly XIX^{d.}, at four terms; viz. 4¾d. each, at St. Michael, St. Andrew, Easter, and the Nativity of St. John the Baptist.

Witnesses hereto :

WILLIAM DE HECHAM
(Hitcham).
JOHN ELGAR (? Algar).
GEOFFRY DE MELFORD.
WILLIAM, his son.
THOMAS, son of Robert.
ALAN PEYTEVIN.

ROBERT BRIDEBEC.
ROBERT LOKER.
HERVEY DE PLAYFORD.
RICHARD DE LA MORE.
THOMAS SCOTCLITO.
ALEXANDER DE REDGRAVE.

* So that Hall Street, Melford, has certainly borne its same name for more than six centuries, and probably from long before the above date.

CARTA WILLELMI DE LAVENHAM de una acra prati jacente super Regia Via quæ ducit de Meleforde versus Gippewicum. Inter cartas Abbatis A. A. prout sequitur in hæc verba.

A.D. 1248—1256.

William de Lavenham and Amicia his wife grant and convey to Edward de Walpole, Abbot of Bury, one acre of meadow in Melford, lying lengthways along the king's highway leading from Melford to (Gippewic) Ipswich (*i. e.* Bull Lane), one end abutting on a meadow belonging to the Abbot, and the other on a meadow of Edward, at the stall.

Witnesses hereto:

(1) Sir HENRY DE BELLOCAMPO, Knight.
GEOFFRY DE MELFORD.
WILLIAM DE FEYRIO.
HUGH, son of Manric, of Melford.
THOMAS GALAUNT.

GEOFFRY DE PELHAM.
(2) HERVEY DE PLAYFORD.
RICHARD DE MORE.
WILLIAM DE GUNTUN.
ALEXANDER DE WALPOOLE.
COLIN DE PELHAM.
And others.

(1) In 1253, Sir Henry Bellocampo, or Beauchamp, held the manor of Rede Hall, with two carucates of land there.
(2) Hervey de Playford also attested about this same date a deed of Walter de Risby, who sold to the Sacrist of St. Edmund's his villein, Walter FitzAylward, *with all his progeny.*

QUIETA CLAMA RICHARDI ONNE de una acra pasturæ jacente in le Lackfordstrete. Inter cartas Abbatis A. 10. prout sequitur in hæc verba.

A.D. 1248—1256.

Richard, son of Robert Onne, of Melford, granted and conveyed to Edward de Walpole, Abbot of St. Edmund's, an acre of pasture in Melford, lying in Lackford Street, among the Abbot's lands; one end abutting on the pasture of Robert Loker, towards the east, and the other end on the pasture of Matilda de la Tye. For which the Abbot gave him 8s. sterling.

Witnesses hereto:

ROBERT DE HECHAM (Hitcham).
GEOFFRY DE PELHAM.
GEOFFRY DE MELFORD.
WILLIAM, his son.

THOMAS GALANT.
ROBERT DE BRIKEBEC.
RICHARD DE BULNEYE.
And others.

QUIETA CLAMA : ADAMÆ LE FORESTER de Serjantiâ qua habuit ad boscos Abbatis Custodiend : Inter cartas Abbatis A. 11. prout sequitur in hæc verba.

A.D. 1248–1256.

Adam the forester to all who may see or hear of this writing, greeting. —Know that I have given and granted for myself, my heirs, and assigns, without reservation, to Edward [de Walpole] Abbot of St. Edmund, and to his successors the abbots thereof, all those my heritable rights to the Sergeanty * of the woods of the said abbots, with all appurtenant to the same in Melford ; not only as to the demesne woods, but also as to other rights, with all liberties pertaining to the same. And I have also given and granted for me and my heirs to the said Abbot and his successors all quiet possession of all right and claim in all fisheries around the *Small Park* in Melford, and in the water of the Stour river near the said Park. Also all homage and service and all pertaining thereto, that Thomas Galaunt renders to me for the holding which he has of me in Melford.

Witnesses hereto :

Sir THOMAS BYGOT, Knight, Steward of the Liberty of St. Edmund.
Sir WILLIAM DE HETCHAM.
Sir GEOFFEY DE PELHAM.
RALPH DE ANHUS.
RICHARD DE GEDDYNG.
HERVY DE PLECKFORD.
WILLIAM DE WALPOLE (of Brockley Hall).

ROBERT DE BRIDEBEC.
ROBERT DE ST. EDMUND'S.
ROBERT, son of Walter.
HUGH BARIL.
ADAM LE SALLE.
EDWARD DE DYS.
HUGO, son of Monte.

QUIETA CLAMA : THOM : GALAUNT de Custod : boscorum. Inter cartas Abbatis A. 16. prout sequitur in hæc verba.

A.D. 1248–1256.

Know all men, that when Adam le forester and Thomas Galaunt resigned to Edward (or Edmund), Abbot of Saint Edmund, and his successors, that heritable right which the said Adam le forester held of the Sergeanty of the woods of the Abbot in Melford, with all belonging

---

* Battely says that these sergeanties of the Abbey were to a certain extent military feoffs, rendering military services. Wives could claim dowers from the lands held in sergeanty.

to the same, the said Abbot for himself and his successors granted all of these to Thomas Galaunt and his heirs for ever; always reserving to the Abbot the rights over all the green paths, chaseways, and road-ways, which the said Abbot used to have customarily in the time of Adam le forester; and also reserving all payments and customary services for the holding which the said Adam used to have of the Abbot in Melford.

Witnesses hereto:

Sir Thomas Bigot.
Sir William de Echam (Hitcham).
Sir Geoffry de Pelham.
Ralph de Aish.
(k) Nicolas de Geddyng.
William de Walepol.

Robert de Bridebec.
Robert de St. Edmund.
Robert, son of Walter.
Adam de Selle.
Edmund de Hays.
And others.

(k) Nicolas de Geddyng, in 1259, witnessed a lease of Sir Walter FitzBernard at Risby. He bought of Ralph de Saxham a manor at Saxham, afterwards called Geddynga. His son Adam was living in 1300, according to Abbot Northwold's book of fees.

Quieta Clama: Thom: Galaunt de 1 acro pasturæ. Inter cartas Abbatis A. i. a. prout sequitur in hæc verba.

A.D. 1248-1256.

Thomas Galaunt of Melford conveyed to Edward (de Walpole) Abbot of St. Edmund's, and his successors, one acre of pasture in Melford, which had been bequeathed to him by Matilda, formerly wife of William de la Tye, and which lies by the *Abbot's Pond towards the south.*

Witnesses hereto:

Sir Thomas Bigot, Steward of the Liberty of St. Edmund.
Sir William de Hecham.
Geoffry de Pelham.
Ralph de Anhus.
Richard de Geddyng.
Robert de Bridebec.

Robert de St. Edmund's.
Robert, son of Walter.
Hugh Babil.
Adam de Selle.
Ralph de Hays.
Hugh, son of Manric.
And others.

This land, from the description, was a part of the Bull Meadow, opposite the south side of the ponds.

QUIETA CLAMA : THOM : GALAUNT de Custode Boscorum Abbatis.   Inter
cartas Abbatis A. 18. prout sequitur in hæc verba.

A.D. 1248–1256.

Thomas Galaunt, of Melford, conveyed to Edward (de Walpole),
Abbot of St. Edmund, the custody and charge of the woods belonging
to the said Abbot, with all that pertains to the Sergeanty of the woods
of the said Abbey, &c.   Together with all rights pertaining to the
said holding which Adam le forester had given to him.
Witnesses hereto :
     The same names as in the preceding document.

INDENTURA inter ABBATEM et THOMAM GALAUNT de excambio Prati et
     Pasturæ.   Inter cartas Abbatis A. 19. prout sequitur in hæc
     verba.

A.D. 1255–6.

Agreement between Edward (de Walpole), Abbot of St. Edmund's,
and Thomas Galaunt, in the fortieth year of the reign of King
Henry (III.), son of King John, by which the said Thomas conveyed
to the said Abbot, &c., 1 acre of meadow in Melford, lying between
the land of Edward del Style and the land of Richard Onne, and
abutting upon the end of the Vintners' premises in that town.   And
also 1 acre of pasture lying by the road towards Acton, between the
pasture of the said Abbot which he had of the grant of the said Thomas,
and the pasture of Geoffry de Melford.   These 2 acres being in
exchange for 2 acres of pasture lying in the upper end of " le Wynes-
meres," between the land of Walter de Bridebec and the land of Thomas
de Hal ; Thomas Galaunt paying annually 8d., which he used to pay
on the acre of pasture by the roadway near Acton, and at the same
periods.   And the said Thomas and his heirs shall be for ever free
of the payment of 4d. a year, which they used to make to the Abbot on
the acre of meadow abutting upon the end of the Vintners' premises.
Witnesses :
     The same as to the last deed.
Part of the above land was in the present Bull Meadows.

CONVENTIO inter ABBATEM et THOMAM GALAUNT de excambio diversarum
     terrarum.   Inter cartas Abbatis A. i. c. prout sequitur in hæc
     verba.

A.D. 1255–6.

Agreement made between Edward (de Walpole), Abbot of St.
Edmund, and Thomas Galaunt, in the fortieth year of the reign of

King Henry (III.), son of King John, by which the said Thomas Galaunt conveys to the said Abbot six acres and half a rood of land, in "Lynnige," which were formerly called "la Legh," in exchange for six acres and half a rood of land lying in the field called "Northo," along the land of Walter de Bridebec, and abutting on "le Wynes-meirs," the said Thomas and his heirs who shall hold this land, doing to the abbots the same customary services for this land in Northo as they formerly did for the land of "la Legh in Lenynge," and at the same periods, &c.

Witnesses hereto :

Sir THOMAS BIGOT, Knight.*
Sir ROBERT DE BORHAM, Knight.†
GEOFFRY DE PELHAM.
THOMAS, son of Sir Thomas Bigot.
GEOFFRY DE MELFORD.
WILLIAM, his son.
ROBERT DE BRIDEBEC.
EDWARD DE HAYS.
HUGH, son of Manric.
ROBERT of St. Edmund's.
ADAM DE SELLE.
WILLIAM DE WALEPOL.

ABBOT SIMON DE SUTINE (sometimes called LUTENE).

CARTA JULIANÆ GALAUNT de homagio Willi Lavenham cum Annuo Servitio iiith et Annuo Reddi : iiii^d Inter Cartas Abbatis A. 19 : prout sequitur in hæc verba.

A.D. 1256–1279.

Juliana, formerly wife of Thomas Galaunt, of Melford, being a widow, conveyed to Simon [de Sutine], by the grace of God Abbot of St. Edmund, the homage and service of William of Lavenham, for which he used to pay her annually 3 shillings, for a certain tenement which he held of her in Melford ; with all rights thereunto belonging. The said Juliana also grants and resigns to the said Abbot an annual payment of 4 pence, which the Abbot used to pay her on land which

* His arms were, temp. Henry III., Or, a cross Gules, 5 escallops Argent ("Antiquarian Repertory," p. 90). In Westminster Abbey it is simply Or, a cross Gules.
† Sir Robert de Borham was of the parish of that name in Chelmsford hundred. He died in 1265. He is described as possessing a messuage called Old Hall, with 140 acres of arable land, 14 acres of meadow, 10 acres of pasture, 4 acres of wood, a water-mill, and 23 shillings of rent in Boreham. His father held a knight's fee of the Honour of the Earl of Boulogne.

had been exchanged with him; which land lay in the park of the Abbot called "Elmesete."

For which grants and conveyances the Abbot paid to her 40 shillings in money.

Witnesses hereto:

> Sir WALTER, son of Humfrey, Knight.
> Sir ROBERT DE PRESTONE, Knight.
> (L) Sir ROBERT CARBUNEL, Knight.
> (M) Sir JOHN DE HODEBOVILE, Knight.
> (MM) Sir HUGO TALEMASCHE, Knight.
> Sir RALPH DE ALNETE, Knight.
> LAURENCE DE OFFINGTON.
> NICHOLAS DE BECLES.
> RICHARD DE BOTOLNESDALE, Clerk, Chaplain.
> GERARD DE WACHESHAM.
> WALTER DE BERNHAM.
> JOHN DE CRAMAVILE.
> ROBERT DE BRIDEBEC.
> ROBERT DE MELFORD.
> GEOFFRY, son of Alan de Melford.
> JOHN PEYTENIN.

(L) Sir Robert, son of Sir Geoffry Carbonel, held a knight's fee at Great Waldingfield, and had a grant of free warren in Newton in 1266-7. The family of Carbonel came over with the Conqueror.

(M) The De Hodebovile family are mentioned in the Abbot's chartulary as holding land in Melford about the year 1050. This Sir John was living in 1299. Margaret de Hodebovile, an heiress of this family, married Peter de Barnardiston (an ancestor of the present family), who was M.P. for Suffolk in 1300 and 1313. In 1331 she held lands at Acton which had belonged to Walter, son and heir of John de Hodebovile. He attests some of these Melford deeds, together with Sir John de Hodebovile.

(MM) Query: Is this the person who married the daughter of Berta de Wanci, of Bury St. Edmund's?

CONVENTIO INTER ABBATEM ET DOMINUM WILLELMUM DE SANCTO CLARO, de Molendino, stagno, et Breta reparandi. Inter Cartas Abbatis A. 20, prout patet in hæc verba.

A.D. 1256—1279.

This is the agreement made between the venerable father Simon [de Sutine], D. G. Abbot of St. Edmund, and Sir William de St. Clare, knight. Whereas the said Sir William has repaired his mill belonging to his manor of Lyston, the said Abbot for himself and his successors, covenants and grants to Sir William, his heirs and assigns, the Mill Pond, with the dams thereto, belonging to the said mill, as the ancestors of the said Sir William used to hold them; and also that the said Sir William and his heirs shall have the use of the bridge towards Wyffendale Mill, in so far as any one holding Wyffendale Mill can conveniently and reasonably allow; about which bridge there was formerly some contention between the said Abbot and the said Sir William, as to its perpetual maintenance and repairs, because the said abbots owned the watercourse leading from the said mill of Lyston into the Stour [*Stura*] leading to Wyffendale Mill; and if it should happen that the said Sir William or his heirs, holding the said mill of Lyston, should fail to maintain the said bridge and watercourse, then it shall be lawful for the Sheriff of Essex for the time being to distrain upon the goods of the said Sir William or his heirs, and to hold the same until the defects of the bridge and watercourse be fully made good to the satisfaction of the Abbot or his successors.

Witnesses :

> Sir JOHN DE HODEBOVILLE, Knight.
> Sir HUGH TALEMACHE, Knight.
> Sir ROBERT CARBONEL, Knight.
> Sir WALTER, son of Humfry, Knight.
> JOHN DE CRAMAVILE.
> JOHN DE LYSTON.
> WILLIAM DE GUNTON.
> ROBERT DE BRIDEBEU.
> HENRY DE DEYNHALL [Dynes Hall, near Halsted].
> THOMAS DE LYSTON Clerk.
> SEMAN DE FOXHERD [Foxearth].
> HUGH DE LA RYNERE.
> And others.

From the above it appears that, at the time named, the mill-pool of Lyston Mill, and the watercourse thence into the Stour, belonged to the Abbot, and that there was then a bridge leading from Essex into Suffolk. The family of Sancto Claro, or St. Clere, came over with the Conqueror. In 1255 there was an indictment at Chelmsford against William de Sancto Claro and Ralph de Heyron for having knights' fees and not being knighted. Only such persons as had £20 a year and upwards were to be knighted, and those who, being summoned, neglected to take the honour of knighthood, were subject to a fine. The statute was repealed in the time of Charles I. This William was Sheriff of Essex in the early part of King Edward I.'s reign, when he had a park at Danbury, where there is still a manor called St. Clere's and Heyron's. The arms of Sancto Claro were. Azure, a sun in his glory, proper.

CARTA ROGERI DE TUSSEINE de homag: et servitio 1ᵈ· pro omnibus serviciis Domini Henrici de Bellocampo et hæredum suorum de tenemento quondam Willi Manduc. Inter Cartas Abbatis A. 9, prout sequitur in hæc verba.

A.D. 1260.

I, Roger, son of William de Tusseins de Topefend [?] grant and convey to Abbot Simon, of St. Edmund's, all the homage and service, viz. 1d., which Sir Henry de Bellocampo [Belchamp] and his heirs render customarily to me for a tenement in Melford, which had belonged to John, son of William Manduc, the grantor's relation. In witness whereof the grantor has set his seal, in London, at the feast of St. Michael, in the 44th year of the reign of King Henry, son of King John [Henry III.].

Witnesses :

ROBERT DE VALEINES.
PETER DE BORGATE.
THOMAS DE LAVENHAM.
ROBERT DE PRESTON.
GODFREY DE LAVENHAM.
JOHN, son of Gilbert, of the same place.

ROBERT DE MANEWODE.
ROBERT DE MELFORD.
WILLIAM DE BELCHAMP.
RICHARD DE MERNEILUS.
JOHN LE PEYTENIN.

CARTA JOHANNIS ANDREW de v acras terræ juxta Elmissete. Inter Cartas Abbatis A. 28, prout sequitur in hæc verba.

A.D. 1256—1279.

I, John, son of Hugo Andrew, of Alfeton, have freely given, granted, &c. to God, to the Blessed Edmund and to Simon, Lord Abbot of St. Edmund, and his successors, five acres of my land in Melford, lying between the lands which formerly belonged to Thomas Galaunt and the land of Godfrey Herberd, one end abutting on the park of the aforesaid Abbot called Elmesete, and the other end on land of John de Muriens, &c. The Abbot to pay for service to the heirs of Thomas Galaunt annually 4 pence at Michaelmas. For which grant the Abbot has given me six marcs of money [80s.].

Witnesses :

ROBERT, son of Ralph of St. Edmund.
GEOFFREY DE MELFORD.
WILLIAM, his son.
WILLIAM DE SCHYMPLINGFORD.
ROBERT, son of Walter.
WILLIAM DE WOLPET.
NICHOLAS DE BOLENEYE [Bulnoy].
ROBERT DE BRIDEBEO.
HUGO, son of Manric.
RICHARD DE FALESHAM [Felsham].
GODFREY KOC.
And others.

The park called Elmsett, or Elmsethe, is now the old Park Farm, and a portion of the Dunton's Farm.

CARTA WALTERI fili Rogeri de Melford de Jure et Clam: quæ potuit habere in homagio redd: et omnibus aliis pertinentibus terræ Roberti de Melford A. 9. in hæc verba.

A.D. 1256—1279.

Walter de Melford, son of Roger de Melford, gives to Abbot Simon de Sutine his property, and all rights pertaining thereto in Melford.

Witnesses :

> JOHN DE CRAMAVILE, de Melford.
> ROBERT DE BRIDEBEC, of the same.
> GEOFFRY FITZALAN, of the same.
> PETER PORTEROSE, of the same.
> WILLIAM DE GUNTON.
> RICHARD DE FALESHAM [Felsham].

ABBOT JOHN DE NORWOLD.

CARTA WILLELMI BRIDEBEC de Melford, reddend: xvi^{d.} Inter Cartas Abbatis A.E. prout sequitur in hæc verba.

A.D. 1279—1301.

William, son and heir of Robert de Bridebec, gave to Abbot John de Norwold, of St. Edmund's, 8 pence of annual payment, which Peter Porterose paid to the said William for 3 acres of land, which he held of him in Melford in the field called *Bulneye;* and 2 pence a year for half an acre of meadow, which William the merchant, of Melford, rented of him in the field near *Bulney;* and 6 pence a year rental from Richard Prykel, miller, for a messuage in Melford, near to Fotteforde. For all which grant the said Abbot paid to the said William one marc in money [13s. 4d.].

Witnesses hereto :

> JOHN DE CRAMAVILLE.
> GEOFFRY FITZALAN.
> WILLIAM, son of Thomas.
> ALAN BOYDIN.
> SIMON, the Clerk.
>   And others.

Robert de Bridebec and Peter Porterose are both named as tenants in the Abbot's rental of 1387, as is also William the merchant.

QUIETA CLAMA: WILLELMI BRIDEBEC de Melford de Homag: Rogeri de la Tye cum annuo reddend: XII⁴ et de homag: et servitio Simoni Geryngi cum annuo redd: IX⁴ atque de homag: et servitio Walteri Bercher cum annuo redd: XVII⁴ Inter Cartas Abbatis A. 3. prout sequitur in hæc verba.

A.D. 1279—1301.

William, son of Roger de Bridebec, of Melford, granted to Abbot John de Norwold, of St. Edmund, the customary homage, service, and payment which his father had held from Roger de la Tye at 12d. a year, for three acres of land in Melford, which was sold to him. He also granted Simon Geryng's service of 9 pence for a messuage near the North Tye in Melford; also Walter le Bercher's service of 17 pence for 4 acres of land in *Bulney.*

Witnesses hereto:

HENRY DE BREGHUM, } Chaplains.
ROGER DE THENINGTON, }
Sir RALPH DE ALNET, Knight.
Sir LAURENCE DE OFFINGTON, Knight.
(N) Sir ROBERT DE NORWOLD, Knight.
Sir JOHN DE HODEBOVILLE, Knight.
(O) Sir HUGH TALEMACHE, Knight.
JOHN DE CRAMAVILLE.
ROBERT GILBERT.
SIMON THURGO.

(N) Sir Robert de Norwold owned the advowson of the church of Brockley from 1282 to after 1300, which had been granted to him by John de Cramaville, and he held a knight's fee in Brockley. He settled, in 1303, the manor of Brockley on Alexander and Joan de Walsham. She was daughter of William de Melford.

(O) The knightly family of Talemache, or Talmach, had much property in several parishes, and free warren in Hawsted, Brockley, and Somerton. Their arms in the time of Henry III. and Edward I. were, Argent, fretté sable.

CARTA DE ANNO REDDENDO XIII⁴ IV⁴ solvend: molendino de tenura Alexandri l'oer prius in Nigro Registro Vestiarii, folio e. 1. prout sequitur in hæc verba.

A.D. 1279—1301.

The Abbot John de Norwold grants to Gilbert, son of Gilbert de Elmswell, freedom for himself and his posterity; and conveys to him all the lands and tenements [a mill] formerly belonging to

Alexander Poer,* on a payment to the Abbot of 40 shillings, and also an annual payment of one marc [13s. 4d.] at the four customary periods of the year. Always reserved to the Abbot and his successors the suit and service to the Court of the Manor of Melford, and the common aid due to the Abbot. And the said Gilbert and his heirs are to cultivate with their ploughs for one day in each year certain lands of the Abbot, for his support; and also they are to help with their carts, one day in each year to carry the hay harvest of the estate; and likewise in autumn they are to help with their carts for one day annually, to carry in the Abbot's corn harvest for his support. In confirmation of which grant the said Abbot affixed his own seal and the seal of the Convent.

Witnesses hereto:

WILLIAM DE MILDENHAL,
ROBERT DE SAHAM,
   (the Abbot's Chaplains).
(P) RALPH DE ALNETO.
GEOFFRY, son of Alan de Melford.
ROBERT DE BITEBROC.

WILLIAM, son of Hugo.
JOHN DE CRAMAVILLE.
ALAN BODYN.
ROGER RE BULNEYE.
JOHN PEYTEWIN.
ROBERT DE SELLE.
ROBERT LE NEWMAN.

(P) In 1286, the family of De Alneto are mentioned as among the principal tenants of lands in Little Saxham, where Gilbert de Alneto held at that time a messuage and a considerable amount of land.

CARTA JOHANNIS MESSAGER de Melford de qdam porčone cujdā pasturæ prope molendinum de Wyffedale, concessa Abbati ad faciendum qādā fossatum ad recipiendum cursum aquæ fluentem de predicto molendino. Inter Cartas Abbatis A. 21 prout sequitur in hec verba.

A.D. 1279—1301.

I, John, called Messager, of Melford, do grant and convey to John de Norwolde, D. G. Abbot of St. Edmund, and his successors, for 4 shillings paid to me the said John Messager, that portion of pasture which I have in Melford, near the Abbot's mill of Wyffedale in the said parish, containing in width 20 feet, as marked out by certain boundaries and measurements, to make a watercourse to receive and hold the water flowing from his said mill of Wyffedale for the purpose of enlarging and widening the old watercourse flowing from this mill, in order to improve the working of this mill by the quicker flow and

* The family held land from the Rectory manor in 1287.

delivery of the water—to have and to hold the said land for a water-course with all easements, &c.

Witnesses:

GEOFFEY, son of Alan.	ADAM DE WYDES.
JOHN PEYTEWYN.	ALAN BOYDIN.
ROGER DE BOLNEY.	RALPH DE GONTON.
GEOFFEY, son of Thomas.	And others.

QUIETA CLAMA RICHARDI HOCKELEE DE LAXFELDE, de homagio Edmundi fili Adamæ de Chevyngton, Mariæ uxoris suæ, heredum et Assignatorum suorum p. quodã teñto, reddent: per annum unum Clavum Gariofili: inter Cartas Abbatis A. 22 prout sequitur in hæc verba.

A.D. 1279—1301.

I, Richard, called Hockelee, of Laxfield, have given, granted, and conveyed, &c., to the venerable father in God, John [de Norwold], Abbot of St. Edmund, and his successors, the homage of Edmund, son of Adam de Chevington, and Mary his wife, and their heirs and assigns, and all their service and annual payments of one clove, which they paid me yearly, for the tenement and pasture with which they are enfeoffed in Melford, and the said Edmund and Mary, their heirs and assigns, acknowledge to hold the said tenement in chief from the Abbot and his successors, and I, the said Richard, resign all rights, rents, and services, &c., which I had in the said tenement, &c.

Witnesses:

GEOFFEY, son of Alan de Melford.	RALPH DE GUNTON.
	ROBERT CRAPINEL.
JOHN PEYTEKIN.	ALAN BOYDIN.
WILLIAM, son of Hugo.	HENRY PEYTENIN.
ROGER DE BULNEY.	ADAM DE WYTHES.
GEOFFRY, son of Thomas.	And others.
(ᵖ) WILLIAM DE MELFORD.	

(ᵖ) Johanna, his daughter, married Alexander de Walsham, lord of the manor of Brookley, in 1303. Their son Alexander levied a fine on his lands in Melford and Alpheton, to enure himself in fee, in 1333.

CARTA ALANI BOYDIN de homagio Walteri Pryk de Aketon et hered: suorum cum Annuo redd iijᵈ Inter Cartas Abbatis A 23 prout sequitur in hæc verba.

A.D. 1279—1301.

I, Alan Boydin, of Melford, have given, granted, and conveyed to John [de Norwold], D.G. Abbot of St. Edmund, and his successors, the homage of Walter Prik, of Acton, &c., with his annual payment of 3d., which he used to pay me yearly, at the feast of St. Michael and at Easter, in equal portions,—for a piece of arable land which he held from me in Melford, called Godynescroft; for which grant, with all thereto pertaining, &c., the said Abbot has paid to me 2s. in money, &c.

Witnesses :

GEOFFRY, son of Alan.

JOHN PEYTENIN.

ROGER DE BULNEY.

GEOFFRY, son of Thomas.

ADAM DE WYTHES.

ROBERT YNE, of Melford.

ALAN DE ROOWODE.

ROBERT ATTE WARDE.

SIMON THURGOR.

ROBERT DE WOLPET, of Acton.

PETER DE BELLO CAMPO [Belchamp[.

THOMAS DE DAKEPUS.

RALPH DE MELFORD.

SIMON LE MARESCAL.

And many others, &c.

Alan Boydin, or Boydon, held fifteen acres of the Abbot in 1387. And the first seven of these witnesses were also the Abbot's tenants at that date.

QUIETA CLAMA ALANI PEYNTON de quodam Molendino cum omnibus terris, tenementis, et pertinent : quæ fuerunt Walteri le Peynton in Meleforde, vel alibi.—Inter Cartas Abbatis A 2 e. prout sequitur in hæc verba.

A.D. 1279—1301.

I, Alan le Peynton, have conveyed to John [de Norwold], Dei gratia Abbot of St. Edmund, and his successors, all claim or possession which I have or may have in a mill with its appurtenances in Melford, and of all lands and tenements which did belong to Walter le Peynton, priest, in the said town, or elsewhere. For which, with all rights thereunto belonging, the said Abbot has paid me four marks in money [58s. 4d.].

Witnesses :

Sir RICHARD DE WEYLAND.

LAURENCE DE OFFINGTON.

ADAM, parson of the Church of Schymplyng.

ADAM, parson of the Church of St. James of Ikelyngham.

THOMAS DE DAJEPUS, steward of the Manor of Melford.

PETER DE BELLOCAMPO.

ROBERT DE MARTLESHAM.

ROGER, his brother.

GEOFFRY, son of Alan de Melford.

ROGER DE BULNETE, of the same place.

Alan le Peynton was a miller. This was probably a mill at the Paper-mill, as the Hall mill and the Wissendale mill had long belonged to the Abbot. The Walter le

Peynton, priest, mentioned in the deed, was Alan the miller's brother. The next following deed refers to the same persons, and the mill in question was evidently a water-mill.

.The name of Thomas de Dajepus, steward of the manor of Melford, is spelt De Dakepus in the next deed.

Icklingham, of which place Adam the parson attests this deed, comprises two parishes, —St. James's and All Saints'.

QUIETA CLAMA ALANI FILI WALTERI PEYNTON de jure suo et clama quæ potuit habere in tenementis quæ fuerunt Walteri Peynton fratris sui—Inter Cartas Abbatis A. 29. Prout sequitur in hæc verba.

A.D. 1288.

I, Alan de Melford, miller, son of Walter the miller, of Melford, have conveyed, &c., to John de Northwolde, D.G. Abbot of St. Edmund, and his successors, all claim or possession which I have, or may have, through the gift and feoffment of Walter de Melford, my brother, in all tenements which had belonged to him, whether messuages, buildings, lands, meadows, pastures, marshes, herbage, water-mill, and moats; with ingress, egress, and every kind of right, liberty, easement, and appurtenances, presently belonging, falling or accruing to the said tenements.—For which, with all rights, &c., the said Lord Abbot John has given me four marcs sterling [53s. 4d.], &c.

Witnesses:

(q) Sir RICHARD DE WEYLAND, then chief steward of the said Lord Abbot.

THOMAS DE DAKEPUS, then steward of the Court of the said Lord Abbot of Melford.

MORGAN DE ILKETESHALE, then mareschal of the said Lord Abbot.

WILLIAM DE MELFORD.

HENRY LE VENUR [the huntsman], of Lavenham.

ADAM, rector of the Church of Lackford.

THOMES DE GRUESTED.

JOHN CLITO. And others.

Given at the feast of St. Matthew the Apostle and Evangelist [21st September], Anno Domini MCCLXXXVIII, and in the 16th year of the reign of King Edward, son of King Henry.

(q) Was the Sir Richard de Weyland, the witness to this deed, a son or brother of Sir Thomas de Weyland, Chief Justice of the Common Pleas, who was convicted of felony, and an episode in whose curious history is thus related. He escaped from custody, disguised himself, and was admitted a novice among the Friars Minors of Babwell, of St. Edmundsbury, in 1289. His retreat was discovered, but as he was in a sanctuary, forty days were allowed him, according to law, after which the introduction of provisions into the convent was prohibited. The friars soon left it through want: Weyland followed them, and was taken to the Tower. The triple option was given to him,—to stand his trial, or to be imprisoned for life, or to abjure the realm. He chose the latter, and having walked barefoot and bareheaded, with a crucifix in his hand, to the seaside, was immediately transported. Some years after, drawing near his death, he expressed a desire that his heart, at least, might after his decease be conveyed to England. This was conceded, and it was interred within the walls of the old priory of Sudbury.

His arms were Argent, a cross Gules and 5 escalopes Or, a label Azure.

QUIETA CLAMA ALANI PEYTENYN de annuo redd. x⁴. Inter Cartas Abbatis—A. 26—prout sequitur in hæc verba.

A.D. 1279—1301.

I, John, son of Alan Peytenyn, of Melford, have conveyed, &c., to John de Norwold, Lord Abbot of St. Edmund, and his successors, all rights as to the payment of 10d. a year, which used to be rendered to me by Robert Onne and Oncia, formerly the wife of Hervey Kenech, and Juliana, for the tenements they held of me in the town of Melford, &c., for which, with all rights thereunto belonging, the said Abbot gave me half a marc of money [6s. 8d.], &c.

Witnesses :

>JOHN DE CRAMAVILE.
>GEOFFRY, son of Alan.
>WILLIAM, son of Hugo.
>ROGER DE BULNEY.
>GEOFFRY LE HEYEWARD.
>RALPH DE ELMESWELL.
>JOHN the Merchant, of Melford.
>STEPHEN DE CRANEMERE [Cranmoor].
>And others, &c.

All the persons named in this deed, and the witnesses, except Hervey Kenech. Geoffry le Heyeward, and Stephen de Cranemere, were the Abbot's tenants in 1287.

QUIETA CLAMA ROBERTI WOLPET de homagio et servicio Manrici de Cranemere. Inter Cartas Abbatis A. 21. prout sequitur in hæc verba.

A.D. 1291.

I, Robert de Wolpet, son and heir of William de Wolpet, have granted and conveyed to that holy man, John de Northewold, Lord Abbot of St. Edmund's Monastery, and his successors, the homage and service of Manric, son of Stephen of Cranemere, of Melford, and Constance his wife, for a messuage house, land, and meadow adjoining, in Melford, which the said Manric and Constance his wife bought of me, next to the messuage and lands of Geoffry le Hundreder.

Witnesses :

GEOFFRY, son of Alan.
JOHN PEYTENIN.
WILLIAM, son of Hugo.
ROGER DE BULNEY.
GEOFFRY, son of Thomas.
HENRY PEYTENIN.
ADAM DE WYTHES.
ALEXANDER the Miller.

GILBERT DE PANETRUS
[*called elsewhere "de Pantria."*]
ALAN BOYDYN.
JOHN, son of John the merchant.
ROBERT JUB.
And others.

Delivered on Friday next after the feast of St. Benedict the Abbot [21st March], in the 19th year of the reign of King Edward [I.], son of King Henry.

All the parties to, and witnesses of, this deed were the Abbot's tenants in 1287. The Hundreder was the bailiff or chief officer over ten tythings.

CARTA ROBERTI GALAUNT de homagio et servitio Alani Fabri cum annuo redď : ij⁵ vend. Johanni de Boston.—Inter Cartas Abbatis A. e. prout sequitur in hæc verba.

About A.D. 1295.

I, Robert Galaunt, of Melford, have granted and conveyed to John de Boston, of Eleigh Combust, and Cristina his wife, for 20s. of money paid to me, the homage and service of Alan the blacksmith, of Melford, of 2s. a year for a tenement which he held of me in the town of Melford, payable—at Michaelmas 6d., at the feast of St. Andrew the Apostle 6d., at Easter 6d., and at the feast of St. John the Baptist 6d., &c.

Witnesses :

Sir GILBERT CASTELL, Knight.
(R) Sir JOHN DE PEYTON, Knight.
ADAM DE SHIMPLINGFORDE.
ROBERT GRAPINEL.
JOHN DE LAVENHAM.

WARIN the Warner [warrener, of Lavenham].
JOHN LE TAYLUR [the tailor].
GILBERT HERVEY.
RALPH DE DUNTON.
And others.

(R) Sir John de Peyton, Knight, was knight of the shire for Suffolk, 1301. He died 1318, and was buried at Stoke-by-Nayland. His daughter Egidia was a nun at Malling, in Kent.

Robert Galaunt, Robert Grapinel, and Gilbert Hervey were tenants of the Abbot in 1287.

CARTA ROBERTI GALAUNT de IX Acris terræ cõm.: ptin: vend: Johanni de Boston. Inter Cartas Abbatis A. l. prout sequitur in hæc verba.

About A.D. 1295.

I, Robert Galaunt, of Melford, have granted and conveyed to John de Boston, of Eleigh Combust, and Cristina his wife, and John their son, for 9 marcs of money [£6] which they have paid to me, 9 acres of arable land, of which 6 acres are in the field called "Rinlond" lying between the woods of the Abbot called *Elmsete Park*, and the land of Ralph de Dunton—one head abutting on the said park, and another on the land of the said Ralph; and one acre lies between the land formerly of William de Melford and the land of William Witynge, one head abutting on the park of Elmsett and the other on the pasture of Sir William de Selle; and another acre lies between the lands of William de Melford and William de Wytynge, abutting on the same, in the field called "le Lee," in Melford, paying to the lord of the feoff in chief one penny, at two terms of the year; viz. at Easter ½d., and at Michaelmas ½d., &c.

Witnesses:

Sir GILBERT CASTELL,
Sir JOHN DE PEYTON, } Knights.
(8) Sir PETER DE DENARDESTON, }
WARIN LE WARNER [warrener], of Lavenham.
JOHN DE LAVENHAM.
HUGO, of the same.
ROBERT GRAFINEL.
JOHN LE TAYLUR.
NICHOLAS BAREL.
GILBERT HUEY.
RALPH DE DUNTON.

(8) Two years after the date of this deed, one of the attesting witnesses, Sir Peter de Denardeston. gave evidence as a witness in the matter of Benedict, the heir of the knightly house of Blakeham, of Lackford, on his making proof of his age, in 1297, as being then over twenty-one years old. Sir Peter de Denardeston, Knight, aged 40 years, dwelling a league from Chelsworth, deposed that the year that Benedict was born, he, Sir Peter, went to Cambridge for his studies and heard civil law there for four years.

His arms were, Azure, two bars Argent, the chief Gules, a leopard passant Or.!

CARTA ROBERTI GALAUNT de X. acris terræ arabilis venditis Johanni de Boston. Inter Cartas Abbatis A. ll. prout sequitur in hæc verba.

About A.D. 1295.

I, Robert Galant, of Melford, have granted and conveyed, &c., to

John de Boston, of Eleigh Combust, and Cristina his wife, and the heirs of the said John, all my rights and possession, &c., in 10 acres of arable land of a field called "Little Croft," between the lands of Thomas Leche and the lands formerly of William Whityng, one head abutting on the road leading from the park of the Abbot called *Elmesete* towards the queech called "Roseporouch," and the other on the land of Robert of Melford, and upon the pasture of William de Melle, Chaplain; for which rights and grants the said John and Cristina have paid me 5 marcs of money [£3. 6s. 8d.], &c.

Witnesses :

> ROBERT DE ST. QUINTIN, of Sudbury.
> WILLIAM the Parson.
> WALTER DE BELCHAMP.
> ROBERT DE BERTON.
> RALPH DE DUNTON.
> GILBERT HERVEY.
> WILLIAM DE MELLE, chaplain.
> JOHN, son of John Robyn.
> ROGER, son of Hamon le holer.
> ALAN DE AQUA, of Lavenham.
> THOMAS, son of Walter de Belchamp.

Given at Sudbury, Wednesday next after the close of Easter, in the 23rd year of the reign of King Edward I.

The land mentioned here as formerly William Whityng's still retained in 1580 the name of "Whitynga." It was part of the fields on Dunton's farm, now called Hither Price field and New Close field.

CARTA ROBERTI GALAUNT de una pecia pasturæ vocata le Greneweye vendita Johanni de Boston.—Inter Cartas Abbatis A. C 3. prout sequitur in hæc verba.

About A.D. 1295.

I, Robert, son of William Galaunt, of Melford, have granted and conveyed to John de Boston, of Eleigh Combust, Cristina his wife, and the heirs and assigns of the said John, a piece of pasture called "le Greneweye," in Melford, divided by metes and bounds, between the lands of the Abbot and the bank of the stream flowing from the bridge called "le Stenenbregge," through *the Little Park*, one head abutting on "le Palmersbrok," and the other on the land called "Morynescrofte;" and also a piece of pasture called "le Brodemoor," in the said town, lying next the Greneweye and the said stream bank, one head abutting on the meadow of Kathcrine Alston, and land formerly of Robert Drake, for which grant and lands the said John and Cristina paid me £20.

Witnesses :

Sir John de Peyton, Knight.
Sir Hugo Talemache, Knight.
John de Hodeboville.
Robert de Geddyng.
(Magister) Alan de Roke-
   wode.
John de Lavenham.

Warin le Warenn.
Robert Grapenel.
Ralph de Donton.
Geoffry le Heyeward.
John Peytenin.
And others.

Given at Melford, the day of the Conversion of St. Paul [25th January], in the 23rd year of the reign of King Edward [I.].

The stream here named was evidently the Melford river, and Brodemoor probably was the present Broad Meadow.

Carta Roberti Galaunt de iij Acris et dĩ prati, vend: Johanni de Bosto. Inter Cartas Abbatis A. C 2. prout sequitur in hæc verba.

About A.D. 1295.

I, Robert Galaunt, of Melford, have given and conveyed to John de Boston, of Illegh [Eleigh] Combust, and to Cristina his wife, and John their son, in consideration of 8 marcs of money [£5. 6s. 8d.], which they have paid to me, three acres and a half of mowing meadow in one piece, in the field called "Humbelchar," and lying between the *Vineyard* and meadow of Florence de Bentham, one head abutting on the said land, and the other on the land of William de Melford, all in Melford; holding in chief of the feoff and paying thereto yearly a half-penny; viz., at Michaelmas a farthing, and at Easter a farthing,—and all usual customary services and attendance on the Manor Court when demanded, &c.

Witnesses :

Sir Gilbert Castell,
Sir John de Peyton,   } Knights.
Sir Peter de Denardeston,
Geoffry, son of Alan, of Melford.
Robert Grapinel.
Walter le Warn [? Warenner].
John Lavenham.
Hugo Lebere.
Gilbert Hervey.
Ralph de Dunton.
   And others.

The Humbelchar Meadows were those now in Wash Farm, lying between the bottom of Spelthorn Wood and the stream adjoining the Queech. Judging by the soil, the *vineyard* was probably in Lower Barnfield, Wash Farm.

Sir Gilbert Castell's name is spelt in 1300 as Castellana.

QUIETA CLAMA ROBERTI GALAUNT de omnibus messuagiis, terris, et aliis pertinent : quæ quondam fuerunt Thomæ Galaunt facta Johanni de Boston.—Inter Cartas Abbatis A. 28 prout sequitur in hæc verba.

About A.D. 1295.

I, Robert, son of William Galaunt, of Melford, have granted and conveyed, &c., to John de Boston, of Eleigh Combust, and Cristiana his wife, and the heirs, &c. of the said John, all right, possession, or claim which I have in Melford, whether in houses, messuages, gardens, ponds, vineyards, lands, tenements, pastures, feoffs rendering homages, fisheries, and all other belongings, which formerly belonged to Thomas Galaunt, my uncle, &c.

Witnesses :

(T) Sir WILLIAM DE GREY,
Sir PETER DE DENARDESTON,
Sir HUGO DE TALEMACHE,
Sir JOHN DE PEYTON,
} Knights.

(U) ROBERT DE ST. QUINTIN DE SUDBURY.
HUGO GANGE.
ROBERT DE BERTON.
GEOFFREY DE NETTLESTEDE.
GEOFFREY, son of Alan de Melford.
ALAN DE ROKEWODE.
GEOFFREY LE HEYEWARDE.
And others.

Given at Sudbury, the day after the feast of the Invention of the Holy Cross [3rd May], in the 23rd year of the reign of King Edward [I.], son of King Henry [III.].

(T) Sir William de Grey was of Cavendish. He was buried in the old priory church, Sudbury. His arms were, Azure, a fess between two chevrons Or, a label Gules.

(U) The family of St. Quintin are mentioned in after deeds.

CARTA ROBERTI GELHAM de annuo redd: VI^d Vend: Johanni de Boston, inter Cartas Abbatis A. e. g. prout sequitur in hæc verba.

About A.D. 1295.

We, Robert de Gelham and Johanna my wife, have granted and conveyed, &c., to John de Boston, of Eleigh Combust, and Cristina his wife, and their heirs, 6d. of annual payment, which Nicholas Gent, of Melford, customarily paid to me for his messuage and croft belonging thereto, in Melford; which messuage abuts on Burbegestrete, and on the land of Richard Bercarius, and lies between the land of the said Richard and of Sir Ralph de Selle; paying to us and to our heirs one grain of pepper yearly at Christmas, &c.

Witnesses:

   RALPH DE DUNTONE.
   JOHN DE SHIMPLINGFORDE.
   ROBERT GRAPINEL.
 (v) GILBERT DE PANETERIA.
   ROGER DE BOLNEYE.
    And others, &c.

(v) The family of De Panetria held lands of the Abbot, now part of High Street farm, Melford, which lands still retain their name. John Charles Pantry, yeoman, of Melford, is mentioned in 1505. The Burbegestrete mentioned in the deed was most probably the present Bridge Street, for Sir Ralph de Selle's land was near there.

CARTA ALANI BOYDIN de homagio et servitio Roberti de Sancto Quintino de Sudbury; Gilberti ad Agnum de eade; Willi, parsonæ de eade; Johannis Prentys; Theobaldi, follor; Galfridi [Fik] parsonæ; Manricii Stonhous; Prioris Sancti Bartholomei de eade; et Gilberti de Grangia de Waldyngfelde. Inter Cartas Abbatis A. 29. prout sequitur in hæc verba.

A.D. 1299.

Be it known to all faithful Christian people who shall see or hear of this present writing, that I, Alan Boydyn, of Melford, have conveyed, granted, &c., to the Venerable Father John [de Norwold], Lord Abbot of St. Edmund's, and to his church of St. Edmund, and to his successors, the homages and services, without any reserve, of Robert de St. Quintin, of Sudbury; of Gilbert at the Lamb, of the same place; of William the parson, of the same place; of John Prentys, of the same place; of Theobald the fuller, of the same place; of Geoffry Fik, the parson; of the prior of St. Bartholomew, of the same place; of Manric of Stonhus, of the same place; and of Gilbert of the Grange, of Great Waldingfield,—for all lands and tenements which the said persons hold of me, under the feoff of the said Abbot in Melford; and that neither I nor my heirs will at any future time make any claim to hold or to sell any of the said homages or services, whether in reliefs of the custody of wards, or escheats, or of manorial or demesne services. In witness

2 o

whereof I have placed my seal to this present writing.   These being
witnesses :

Sir JOHN DE HODEBOVILLE, Knight.	(w) Sir JOHN DE PEYTON, Knight.
	ROBERT DE GEDDYNGE.
JOHN DE HODEBOVILLE.	JOHN DE BOSTON.
(x) THOMAS GIFFARD.	JOHN PEYTENIN.
GEOFFRY, son of Alan.	And others.

Given at Melford, Wednesday next after the Feast of the Decollation
    of the blessed John Baptist [29th August], in the 27th year of the
    reign of King Edward, son of King Henry.

The family of St. Quintyn, mentioned in the preceding deed, were of French
extraction, and early connected with Sudbury.   Robert's father, Henry St. Quintyn,
and his brother Philip were both buried in the old Priory Church in Sudbury.   From
an inquisition made in 1275, it appeared that Robert and John de St. Quintyn exported
wool, contrary to the king's inhibition, trading through the port of Ipswich.   They are
described, with others in the same list, as " Merchants of Amiens, in France."   Robert
de St. Quintyn's wife's name is mentioned in 1301 as " Segeyna."

(w) Sir John de Peyton, in 1279, held the lordship of Ramsholt, in the Wilford
hundred of Suffolk.
(x) Thomas Giffard was of Brockley, and in and before the year 1313 held lands
there, of which there was a recital in a charter of 1326.   He married Amy, widow of
Thomas de Walpole.   In 1275, a member of this family, one Walter Giffard, treacherously
slew, in Gascony, Sir Adam de Creting, who held from William Giffard a considerable
amount of land in Barrow.   Sir Adam's son was made a prisoner at the same time.   The
motive for the murder does not appear.

CARTA ALANI BOYDYN de Annuo redd ij* quos solebant reddere Theo-
    baldus ffolour et Willelmus persona de Sudbury.   Inter Cartas
    Abbatis A. 30. prout sequitur in hæc verba.

A.D. 1279–1301.   Probably Anno 1299.

I, Alan Boydyn, of Melford, have granted, conveyed, &c., to the
Venerable Father John [de Norwold], D. G. Lord Abbot of St.
Edmund, 2s. of yearly payment in Melford ; of which sum Theobald
the fuller, of Sudbury, paid me yearly 12d. for three acres of land in
Melford, lying between the lands of Adam de Wythes and Hugo le
Paumer, one head abutting on the land of Richard Scateron and the
other head on the land of Gilbert at the Lamb, of Sudbury ; and
William the parson, of Sudbury, paid me annually another 12d. for
four acres of land lying between the lands of Richard Scateron and the

lands of the Priory of St. Bartholomew, both heads abutting on the land of Hugo le Paumer, of Melford.

Witnesses:

> ROBERT DE MELFORD.
> JOHN DE CRAMAVILLE, de Melford.
> GEOFFRY, son of Alan, of the same.
> GEOFFRY, son of Thomas, of the same.
> JOHN PEYTENIN, of the same.
> ADAM DE WYTHES, of the same.
> (Y) WILLIAM DE MELFORD, of the same.
> WILLIAM, son of Manric, of the same.
> ADAM the Clerk.
> And others.

(Y) William de Melford's daughter Joan, or Joanna, married Alexander de Walsham, lord of the manor of Brockley, who was living in 1303, and who owned the advowson of Brockley Church, which had belonged to John de Cramaville. William de Melford's surname is elsewhere given as "De Newman." Land on Rodbridge farm still, in 1580, bore the name of one of the parties mentioned in the deed; viz. "Scaterons."

CARTA ROBERTI GALAUNT de v Acris et dī Terræ vend: Johanni de Boston. Inter Cartas Abbatis A. Or. prout sequitur in hæc verba.

No date, but about 1300.

I, Robert Galaunt, have granted, conveyed, &c., to John de Boston, of Eleigh Combust, and Cristina his wife, for a certain sum paid to me, 5½ acres of my arable land in Melford, of which four acres lie in the field called Dunningworde, between the lands of Robert Gent and John de Burebregg, and one acre and a half lying in the field called Sedde, between the lands of William le Saltere and Nicholas le Cowherde, rendering to me annually in chief one clove at Michaelmas, for all customary services, &c.

Witnesses:

> Sir GILBERT LE CASTELLANE, } Knights.
> Sir JOHN DE PEYTON,
> ADAM DE SHIMPLINGFORD.
> JOHN DE LAVENHAM.
> ROBERT GRAPINEL.
> GEOFFRY, son of Alan.
> WARIN LE WARRENER [the warrener].
> JOHN LE TAYLUR [the tailor].
> ANDREW DE DUNMAWE [Dunmow], Clerk.
> And others.

2 O 2

CARTA RADULPHI DE DONTON de iij rodis Terræ vend: Johanni de Boston. Inter Cartas Abbatis A. 91 prout sequitur in hæc verba.

No date. About 1300.

I, Ralph de Donton [Dunton], of Melford, have conveyed, &c., to John de Boston, of Eleigh Combust, and Cristina his wife, and the heirs of the said John, all right and possession which I have in three roods of arable land in Melford, of which half an acre of land lies next the pasture of Sir William de Selle, chaplain, and the other rood of land lies in the field called Manlond, next to the land of the said John de Boston, &c.

Witnesses:

JOHN DE LAVENHAM.   ROBERT DE GELHAM.
ROBERT GRAPINEL.   HUBERT DE MONCHAUSY.
NICHOLAS BAREL.   And others.

Ralph de Dunton was living from 1295 to 1310. In 1309, his son Robert de Dunton, who also appears to have owned property here, sold a messuage.

Query: Did the present Dunton's farm originally take its name from this family, who owned the land, or did they derive their appellation from the land?

CARTA JOHANNÆ UXORIS WALTERI DE DITTON et Johannis fili ejusdem de iiij Acris et dī prati et pasturæ vend: Johanni de Boston—inter Cartas Abbatis, &c. &c.

A.D. 1301.

We, Johanna, formerly the wife of Walter de Ditton, of Melford, and John my son, have granted and conveyed to John de Boston, of Eleigh Combust, and Cristiana his wife, and their heirs, for 16 marcs of money [£11. 3s. 4d.] which they have paid to us, 4½ acres of meadow and pasture in Melford; viz., by Ladydowne, between the stream leading from Stenenbridge towards the house of Robert atte Pole, and the land of the Lord Abbot of St. Edmund, and the land of John de Boston, one head abutting upon Redislane and the road leading from "Balisdon" [Balsdon Hall] to Melford, and the other head on the meadow of Isabelle de Husho, which said meadow and pasture the said Johanna and John formerly bought of Master William, of Melford, and Robert Galaunt, &c.

Witnesses:

JOHN DE HODEBOVILE.   JOHN PEYTENIN.
JOHN DE LAVENHAM.   ROGER DE BULNETE.
ROBERT DE STOKES.   HUBERT DE MONTECAVISO.
THOMAS HEREWARD.   GILBERT HERVEY.
JOHN MELONN, of Acton.

Given at Melford, Friday in the feast of the Translation of St. Thomas the Martyr [7th July], in the 29th year of the reign of King Edward [I.], son of King Henry [III.].

This land was near to what are now Crabtree and Bearshill plantations, then called Ladydown Hills.

ABBOT THOMAS DE TOTTINGTON.

QUIETA CLAMA JOHANNÆ BRIDE de predicto Annuo redd: vi^d. Inter Cartas Abbatis A. l.g. prout sequitur in hæc verba.

A.D. 1808.

I, Johanna Bride, relict of the late Robert de Gelham, in my widowhood and having lawful right, have conveyed to John de Boston and Cristina his wife, all right and claim which I have in 6d. of annual payment which the said John and Cristina his wife had through our dimission to receive of Nicholas Gent, in Melford, &c.

> Witnesses :
>> ROBERT GRAPINEL.
>> JOHN DE SHIMPLINGFORD.
>> PHILIP DE MELFORD.
>> NICHOLAS BABEL.
>> HUGO, son of Andrew.
>> RALPH DE DUNTON.
>> And others.

Given at Lavenham, Tuesday next after the Feast of St. Michael the Archangel, in the 31st year of the reign of King Edward I.

CARTA ISABELLÆ DE HUSHO de ii peciis prati, vend. Johanni de Boston. Inter Cartas Abbatis, &c.

A.D. 1305.

I, Isabella de Husho, have granted and conveyed to John de Boston, of Eleigh Combust, Cristina his wife, and John their son, for a certain sum of money which they paid to me, two pieces of meadow in Melford, of which one piece lies in the fields called Humbelchar, between the lands of David of Hereford and of William Bonde, one end abutting on the meadow of Gilbert Hervey, the other on the meadow of William Brawode. The other piece of meadow lies inclosed near Stevenebridge, between the banks of the stream leading to the mill of Melford of the Lord Abbot of St. Edmund, and the way leading from Melford Hall to Lenynge [Lineage], one end abutting on the pasture of

the said John, and the other on the way and pasture beyond the fence
of the said field towards the land of Roger Warenn, &c.

   Witnesses:

JOHN DE WHELNETHAM.	RALPH DE DUNTONE.
THOMAS GIFFARD.	JOHN ROBYN, senior.
DAVID DE HEREFORD.	(z) JOHN DE MUNCHASY, Clerk.
RALPH LE HUNTE.	And others.

Given at Melford, Monday, the morrow of the feast of the Decollation
   of St. John the Baptist [29th August], in the 33rd year of the
   reign of King Edward [I.], son of King Henry.

This land is in the meadows of the Wash farm, between Spelthorn Wood and the
Queech. Steven, or Stenen-bridge, is where the present bridge stands in the meadows by
the osier-bed on the road to Lineage.

(z) Perhaps John de Munchasy's name is mis-spelt, and that he belonged to the
family of Mounchensi, who were of Edwardston, at about the above date. In the following
deed the name is again written differently.

CARTA RADULPHI DE DONTON de ij Acris terræ vend Johanni de Boston.
   Inter Cartas Abbatis A. 92.   Prout sequitur in hæc verba.

A.D. 1305.

   I, Radulphus de Dunton, have granted and conveyed, &c., to John
de Boston, of Eleigh Combust, and Cristina his wife, and their heirs,
&c., for a certain sum which they paid to me, two acres of my arable
land in Melford, in the field called Manlond, lying between the lands
of Cecilia Leche and Robert Jue, one head abutting on the land of
David de Hereford and the other on the land of William Brawode, &c.

   Witnesses:

> JOHN DE WHELNETHAM.
> THOMAS GIFFARD.
> JOHN DE LUTON.
> ROBERT GRAPINEL.
> JOHN ANDREW.
> GILBERT HERVEY.
> JOHN DE MUNCHANSY, Clerk.

Given at Melford, the day of the Decollation of John the Baptist [29th
   August], in the 33rd year of the reign of King Edward I.

This land was near the Ford Hall osier-bed.

Robert Grapinel, one of the witnesses, was a tenant of the Abbey in 1287. This
deed of 1305 is the last date at which his name appears.
Some of the Mounchensi family had possessions at Lyston, in Essex.

CARTA RADULPHI DE DONTON de q̃dam pecia terræ veñd: Johanni de Boston. Inter Cartas Abbatis A. 99. prout sequitur in hæc verba.

A.D. 1305.

I, Radulphus de Duntone, of Melford, have granted and conveyed, &c., to John de Boston, of Eleigh Combust, and Cristiana his wife, and John their son, and their heirs, &c., for a certain sum of money which they have paid to me, a piece of arable land in Melford, lying in the field called "le Walle," between the land of Chicche [Cicely or Cecilia] Leche and of John de Burbregge, and abutting on the marsh [or meadow] of the said Chicche Leche towards the east, &c. &c.

Witnesses :

JOHN DE WHELNETHAM.
JOHN DE SHRIMPLINGFORD.
ROBERT DE COKEFELD.
JOHN ANDREW.
NICHOLAS BAREL.
WILLIAM, son of Radulphus, of Shimpling.

THOMAS LE KYNG.
THOMAS LE TURNOR.
THOMAS LE MAISTER.
And others.

Given at Melford, Wednesday next after the Nativity of our Lord, in the 33rd year of the reign of King Edward [I.], son of King Henry.

CARTA RADULPHI DE DONTON de 1 rode terræ veñd: Johanni de Boston —Inter Cartas Abbatis A. 9. e. prout sequitur in hæc verba.

A.D. 1306.

I, Ralph de Dontone, of Melford, have granted and conveyed, &c., to John de Boston, of Eleigh Combust, and Cristiana his wife, and John, the son and heir of the said John de Boston, one rood of arable land in Melford, lying between the lands of the said Ralph and the *Park of the Abbots of St. Edmund's, called "Elmesete,"* and abutting each way on the land of the said John de Boston, &c.

Witnesses :

JOHN DE WHELNETHAM.
JOHN DE CRAMAVILE.
DAVID DE HERFORD [Hereford].
JOHN DE SHIMPLINGFORD.
JOHN, son of John of Lavenham.

ROBERT, son of Warin le Warrener.
GILBERT HERVY.
And others.

Given at Melford, Wednesday next before the feast of St. Gregory the Pope [12th March], in the 34th year of the reign of King Edward [I.].

This land was in the Dunton's farm.

CARTA ROBERTI DE DONTON de Annuo redd iiij^{ti} veñd : Johanni de Boston. —Inter Cartas Abbatis A. 93 prout sequitur in hæc verba.

A.D. 1309.

I, Robert, son of Radulphus de Dounton, have granted and conveyed to John de Boston, of Eleigh, and Cristiana his wife, and their heirs, for a certain sum of money which they paid me, 4d. of annual payment, receivable from Henry le Hounte for a certain messuage in Melford, lying between the messuages of Mariot Witynge and the land formerly of Robert de Selle; one head abutting on the way leading *towards the Park of the Lord Abbot of St. Edmund,* and the other head on the land of the said Robert, &c.

Witnesses :

JOHN DE CRAMAVILE.	PHILIP DE MELFORD.
DAVID DE HEREFORD.	ROBERT ATTE FRYT.
ROBERT DE COCKFIELD.	PETER LE MARESCHAL.
GILBERT HERVEY.	VINCENT DE HERTFORD.

Given at Wantñm, on the day of St. Andrew the Apostle [30th November], in the 2nd year of the reign of King Edward [II.], son of King Edward.

This messuage was on the Dunton's farm.

CARTA RADULPHI DE DONTON de qda. alia pecia terræ venñit. Johanni de Boston, inter Cartas Abbatis A. 96 prout sequitur in hæc verba.

A.D. 1310.

I, Ralph de Duntone, of Melford have granted and conveyed, &c., to John de Boston, of Illeigh Combust, and Cristiana his wife, and John their son, and their heirs, a piece of land, lying between the lands of the said John de Boston and those of Cecilia [or Cicely] Leche, one end abutting upon the road which leads from Melford Hall towards the Park [Elunsethe].

Witnesses :

DAVID DE HEREFORD.
(A) ROBERT DE ROKEWODE.
RALPH LE HUNTE.
ROBERT DE COKEFELDE.
(a) BENEDICT DE MONTECAVISO.
And others.

Given at Melford, Friday next after the feast of St. Matthew [21st September], in the 3rd year of the reign of King Edward [II.], son of King Edward.

This land was on the Dunton's farm.

(A) Robert de Rokewode, among others, temp. Edward III., made a composition for a payment of 40s. on his knight's fee to the king's eldest son.

(a) The family of Montecaviso are mentioned in the Suffolk Domesday Book.

CARTA HENRICI DE STANTON de non vendicando jus patronāt: de Melford.
Inter Cartas Abbatis, &c.

A.D. 1311.

Henry de Stanton to all faithful, &c., greeting, &c. Be it known to you, that whereas the Venerable Father Thomas [de Tottington], Lord Abbot of St. Edmund's, the real patron of the church of Melford, presented me thereto for a short remaining term, except and reserved to the Abbot and his successors the right of patronage and appointment to the church of Melford for ever, in all future vacancies, &c.; and lest my presentation to the said church by the Abbot should, for certain reasons, prejudice any of their said rights, &c., therefore I, for myself and my heirs, covenant to assure to the said Abbot, and remit to him for ever, all claim or title to the advowson of the said church, and that neither I nor my heirs will prejudice or sell any rights of the said patronage and advowson, &c.

Witnesses :
(B) Sir THOMAS DE GREY, Knight.
(C) Sir RICHARD DE LA CORNERTHE [Cornard], Knight.
Sir HUGO DE MURIENS, Knight.
(D) Sir JOHN DE GEDDYNG, Knight.
THOMAS GIFFARD.
STEPHEN DE HAWKEDON.
(E) JOHN DE WHELNETHAM.
JOHN, son of William de Cranmaville.
JOHN DE LUTON.
(F) WILLIAM BLAUNKPAYN.
And others.

Given this 5th day of December, in the 4th year of the reign of King Edward [II.], son of King Edward.

This date of the 5th December, when the deed was signed, is the very day of Henry de Stanton's institution to the living. The agreement specifies that he was only presented to it for *a short remaining term;* and he only held it for ten months, as he was succeeded on the 9th October, 1312, by Alan de Ely.

(B) *Sir Thomas de Grey* was of Cornard, and afterwards of Grey's Hall, Cavendish. He was buried at Stoke-by-Clare. His daughter Amy married John de Hengrave: he was the second son of Sir Edmund de Hengrave, who was M.P. for Suffolk 1324, and who died 1334, aged 80. Sir Edmund levied a fine, in 1314, of lands in Westley and other parishes to his son John and Amy his wife, who was endowed at the *church door* with the manor of Westley. Amy appears to have married again, for Sir Thomas Fitz-Eustace's second wife was Amy, daughter of Sir Thomas de Grey, by Alice, daughter and sole heir of Sir Richard de Cornerthe, in favour of whom a fine was levied in 1317. She became his widow in 1319; in which year she paid the king, Edward II., five marcs for free marriage; and in 1320 she executed a deed, *at Cavendish*, in favour of her father and mother, Sir Thomas de Grey and Alice his wife.

(c) *Sir Richard de la Cornerthe* (Cornard) was Sir Thomas de Grey's father-in-law, and two of the witnesses to his grand-daughter Amy's deed were Richard and Thomas de Cornerd. The arms of De la Cornerthe were, in the reign of Henry III., Azure, a fess between two chevrons Or.

(D) *Sir John de Geddyng*, of the ancient knightly Suffolk family of that name, was knight of the shire in 1273, when his arms were described as Checquy, Argent and Gules, on a fess Azure, three buckles Or.

(E) *John de Whelnetham* was born in 1276, so that he was 35 years of age at the date of this attestation. His grandmother married in second marriage Sir Walter de Bernham, Knight. The De Whelnethams' arms were, Or, a fess Azure, five roundeous Argent.

(F) *William de Blaunkpayn* was perhaps of the same family (allowing for the variations of spelling) as John de Blauncepayn, de Melford, who was presented to the living of Risby on the 13th January, 1367, by Abbot Thomas de Tottington.

ABBOT RICHARD DE DRAUGHTON.

QUIETA CLAMA CRISTINÆ uxoris Johannis de Boston de omne jure et clamâ quæ potuit habere in omnibus terris et tenementis quæ fuerunt prædicti Johannis. Inter Cartas Abbatis, &c.

A.D. 1315.

I, Cristiana, late the wife of John de Boston,* of Brende-illeye [*Brent Eleigh* or *Eleigh Combust*], deceased, have granted and conveyed to Richard [de Draughton], Lord Abbot of St. Edmund's, and his successors, all right or claim which I ever had or may have in all lands and tenements in Melford which were bought by John de Boston, late my husband, of which the Abbot claims escheat for himself and the right of his church, through the forfeiture of John, son of John de Boston, &c.

Witnesses:

Sir JOHN DE WHELNETHAM, Knight.
WYDON DE MORTNOMARE.
(c) JOHN DE SHARDELOWE.

WILLIAM BLAUNPAYN.
JOHN DE BULMER.
PETER TILLOTE.
And others.

Given at Melford, Tuesday next after the feast of the Translation of St. Edward the king [13th October], in the 8th year of the reign of King Edward [II.], son of King Edward.

For more than ten years the De Bostons had been steadily increasing their landed property here, but somehow their son then made a forfeiture, and his mother sold all her goods to the Abbot.

(a) Clement, son of William Clopton, gave to John de Shardelowe one rood of land in Cowlinge in the year 1323.

---

* John de Boston, sen., died between the years 1310 and 1315, and by the sales and forfeitures of this land, the greater part of the Dunton's farm came into the possession of the Abbot, and was attached to his Melford Hall estate.

QUIETA CLAMA CRISTINÆ uxoris Johannis de Boston de omnibus bonis et cattalis mobilibus et immobilibus quæ quondam fuerunt prædicti Johannis. Inter Cartas Abbatis, &c.

A.D. 1315.

I, Cristiana, who was the wife of John de Boston, of Brendilleye, have granted and sold to Richard [de Draughton], Lord Abbot of St. Edmund's, all my goods and chattels, movable and immovable, which I have in all my lands and tenements in Melford, which formerly belonged to John de Boston, of Brendilleye, late my husband; and the said Abbot is to dispose of all such goods and chattels as he may think fit.

To this I have affixed my seal at Melford, Saturday next before the feast of St. Luke the Evangelist [18th October], in the 8th year of the reign of King Edward [II.], son of King Edward.

It is not stated what caused the forfeiture by escheat of John de Boston, junior. Perhaps he was dead without heirs, though Cristiana does not call him her *late* son. Otherwise the escheat would have been caused by some crime or breach of duty towards the lord; as refusal to attend the Abbot's courts, or to do his appointed personal and other services.

CARTA JOHANNIS PEYTENYN de I Messuagio cum qdam peciis terræ vendit: Adame Grenelese. Inter Cartas Abbatis A. 3 A. prout sequitur in hæc verba.

A.D. 1816.

I, John Peytenyn, senior, of Melford, have granted and conveyed, &c., to Matilda, formerly the wife of Thomas Giffard, and after the decease of the said Matilda, to Adam, son of Petronilla Foot, for a certain sum of money paid to me, a messuage built in Melford, with a certain piece of arable land, the said messuage lying between the land of the said Matilda and the king's highway leading from the bridge of Glemsford towards the church of Melford, one head abutting on the tenement of John Drapar, and the other on the tenement of John Nél, and the said piece of land lying between the land of the said Matilda and that of John Nel, and abutting on the same, &c.

Witnesses:

JOHN DE LUTON.
JOHN PEYTENYN, junior.
ADAM NEEL.
JOHN MARTYN.
JOHN the Merchant.

JOHN the Miller.
REGINALD DE HELPISTON.
RICHARD DE BULNEYE.
JOHN NEEL.
And others.

Given at Melford, on Sunday next after the feast of the Apostles St. Philip and St. James [3rd May], in the 9th year of the reign of King Edward [II.], son of King Edward.

CARTA JOHANNIS PEYTENYN de qdam messuagio cum edificiis et 1 pecia terræ cum homagio et servitio 5s. 6d. vend : Adame Grenelese. Inter Cartas Abbatis A. 38. prout sequitur in hæc verba.

A.D. 1317.

I, John Peytenyn, senior, of Melford, have granted and conveyed to Matilda Gyffard and Adam, son of Petronilla Foot, for a certain sum of money paid to me, a messuage with buildings and appurtenances, and a piece of arable land containing two and a half acres, and the homage and service of 20d. arising from four acres of land which the said Matilda holds from Sir John de Hallestrete,[*] of the feoff of the Abbot of St. Edmund, and the homage and service of 10d. arising from two and a half acres of land which the said John sold to Roger Lovecok, of the same feoff, and the homage and service pertaining to a piece of land which John Martyn holds among the lands of the said Matilda of the same feoff; and the homage and service of 12d. from four acres of land which Adam Neel holds of the same feoff; and the homage and service of 2s. from six acres of land which John Neel holds of the same feoff; the situation of the said messuage and piece of land being described in the preceding grant.

Witnesses :

JOHN DE LUTONE.   ROGER LOVECOK.
WILLIAM DE ST. CLARE.   JOHN the Miller.
ADAM NEEL.   JOHN NEEL.
JOHN the Merchant.   And others.
JOHN MARTYN.

Given at Melford, on Sunday next after the Invention of the Holy Cross [15th Sept.], in the 10th year of the reign of King Edward [II.], son King Edward.

CARTA WALTERI IKELYNGHAM de parte 1 messuäg qdam Willi Coppynger rend. Adame Grenelese. Inter Cartas Abbatis A. 36. prout sequitur in hæc verba.

A.D. 1319.

We, Walter Ikelyngham and Petronilla my wife, who was the daughter of William Koppynger, of Melford, by mutual consent grant and convey to Adam, son of Petronilla Foot, of Melford, all that part of a messuage in Melford which was inherited by the said Petronilla Koppynger after the decease of the said William Koppynger, lying

* This is the only mention of this person's name. Who was he ?

between the tenements of John le Draper, one head abutting on the king's highway, the other on the garden of the said Adam, &c.

Witnesses :

THOMAS STACE.
THOMAS DE LA RENTE [Bailiff of Ipswich].
GILBERT ROBERT.
JOHN DE MELFORD [surname Grenelese].
ADAM NEEL, de Melford.
JOHN, his son.
RICHARD DEL SOLER, of the same.

Given at Gyppewic [Ipswich], on Sunday next after the feast of St. Andrew the Apostle [1st December], in the 12th year of the reign of King Edward, son of King Edward.

CARTA JOHANNIS DITTON de quam acrâ terræ, vendit : Adame Grenelese. Inter Cartas Abbatis A. 3 C. prout sequitur in hæc verba.

A.D. 1321.

I, John, son of Walter de Ditton of Melford, have granted and conveyed to Adam, son of Petronilla Foot, of Melford, for a certain sum which he paid me, one acre of arable land in Melford, lying between the lands of Matilda Giffard and of John, son of William Bercarius, one head abutting on the land of the said John, the other on the land of the said Matilda and William Brian ;—doing customary services, &c. &c.

Witnesses :

WILLIAM DE ST. CLARE.
ADAM NEEL.
JOHN the Miller.
ROGER LOVEKOO.
JOHN NEEL.
And others.

Given at Melford, Saturday next after the feast of St. Gregory the Pope [12th March], in the 14th year of the reign of King Edward [II.], son of King Edward.

CARTA WILLELMI BRYON de 1 pecia terræ vend: Adame Grenelese. Inter Cartas Abbatis A. ci. prout sequitur in hæc verba.

A.D. 1323.

I, William Bryon, of Waldingfield, have granted and conveyed to Adam Grenelese, of Melford, for a certain sum of money paid to me, a piece of arable land of two acres, in Melford, lying between the lands of Roger the blacksmith and of John, son of Alan, son of Hugo, abutting on the land of Matilda Gyffard and on the king's highway leading from the bridge of Glemsford towards Melford Hall.

Witnesses :

JHON DE LUTON.	JOHN [GRENELESE].
WILLIAM DE ST. CLARE.	ROBERT, his son.
JOHN PEYTENYN.	ROGER the Blacksmith.
ADAM NEEL.	And others.

Given at Melford, Monday next after the feast of the Translation of St. Thomas of Canterbury [7th July], in the commencement of the 16th year of the reign of King Edward [II.], son of King Edward.

CARTA JOHANNIS COLE de q̃dam peciâ Curtilagii et Gardinii vendit̃. Adame Grenelese. Inter Cartas Abbatis A. 33. prout sequitur in hæc verba.

A.D. 1327.

I, John, son of Stephen Cole, of Melford, have granted and conveyed to Adam Grenelese, of Melford, for a certain sum of money which he paid me, a piece of curtilage and garden in Melford, lying between the garden and curtilage of Walter Thoume and that of Robert Hog, senior, one head abutting on the land formerly of John Martyn, and the other on the road leading from Stansted towards Cranemere Tye ; the said Adam paying all customary services, &c.

Witnesses :·
JOHN FAYRHENED.
ADAM NEEL.
JOHN [GRENELESE].
ROBERT, his son.
ADAM SCOYL.
And others.

Given at Melford, on Sunday next before the feast of St. Dunstan the Archbishop [19th May], in the first year of the reign of King Edward III.

QUIETA CLAMA JOHANNIS DE MELFORD de q̃dam pecia terræ, data Adame Grenelese. Inter Cartas Abbatis A. 31. prout sequitur in hæc verba.

A.D. 1330.

I, John de Melford, have granted, conveyed, &c., to Adam Grenelese, my brother, all right and possession of one piece of arable land in the town of Melford, lying between the land of the said Adam and the land which Matilda Giffard and Claricia, her niece, bought of John Draparius, and abutting on the garden of the said Adam, &c.

Witnesses:
    JOHN DE LUTON.
    ROBERT GIFFARD.
    JOHN PEYTENYN.
    ADAM NEEL.
    JOHN, his son.
    And others.

Given at Melford, on Sunday next before the feast of St. Gregory the Pope [12th March], in the 3rd year of the reign of King Edward, the third after the Conquest.

INDENTA INTER ROBERTUM GIFFARD ET ADAM GRENELESE de ii cotãg. cum curtilag̃: et iij peciis terræ arabilis. Inter Cartas Abbatis A. 39. prout sequitur in hæc verba.

A.D. 1330.

This indenture between Robert Giffard and Adam Grenelese, of Melford, witnesseth, that the said Robert has conveyed, &c., to the said Adam two cottages, with their curtilages adjoining, and with three pieces of arable land, in the town of Melford, which cottages lie between the lands formerly of Matilda Giffard and the king's high road; and one of the pieces of land lies between the ground of Richard Whyp, and one head abutting on the land of the rector of the church of Melford; and another piece of land lies between the king's highway and the land of Margery atte Soler, and one head abutting on the cottage of Richard atte Soler.; and the third piece lies in the field called Bulneyefield, between the lands of the aforesaid Adam Grenelese, and one head abutting on the garden of the said Adam,—paying to me and my heirs annually, at two terms of the year, 20s., at Easter and Michaelmas, in equal portions, with usual services, &c. And if the said Adam shall die without heirs of his body, the said tenement, &c., shall revert to Robert and his heirs, &c.

Witnesses:
    JOHN DE LUTON.   JOHN ATTE HOO.
    WALTER DE GLEMESFORD.   JOHN DE WATTONE.
    JOHN PEYTENYN.   And others.
    JOHN NEEL.

Given at Melford, on Sunday next after the feast of St. Gregory the Pope [12th March], in the 3rd year of the reign of King Edward, the third after the Conquest.

DOMINUS FABER manerii prædicti cum tenuram ejusdem pāt: in Registro Richardi Abbatis: &c.

A.D. 1330.

At the General Manor Court of Melford, Tuesday next before the feast of the Purification of the Blessed Virgin Mary [2nd February], in the 18th year of Richard [de Draughton], Lord Abbot, it was presented thereto by the homagers, that Master John, "the blacksmith," held a messuage and 7½ acres of land, by the rod, and they say that he should be bound to do all the ironwork for four ploughs belonging to the lord, and that the lord should find his own wooden materials and labour for making the same, and that the said John should do this same work on the manor, at the will of the lord or of his bailiff.

CARTA ALEXI TURNOR de I ďi. acra pasturæ et gardini, et I ďi. acra terræ arabilis vendit. Adame Grenelese. Inter Cartas Abbatis A. 32. prout sequitur in hæc verba.

A.D. 1331.

We, Alexander le Turnor, of Melford, and Johanna his wife, have granted and conveyed, &c., to Adam Grenelese all right and possession of half an acre of pasture and garden, and in half an acre of arable land in Melford, lying between the land of John Cole and of Adam Scoyle, one head abutting on the land of John de Melford, and the other on the way leading to the house of John Hog. And the aforesaid half-acre of pasture and garden lies between the pasture formerly of John Fairhened and the land of the rector of the church of Melford, one head abutting on a meadow of the said rector, the other on the road leading from Stansted towards Cranemere Tye, &c.

Witnesses :

JOHN PETTENYN.
JOHN NEEL.
RICHARD HAMMOND.
ADAM SCOYL.
ADAM FETHER.
　　And others.

Given at Melford, Sunday next before the feast of St. Dionisius [9th October], in the 4th year of the reign of King Edward, the third after the Conquest.

CARTA LORÆ ATTE LOFTE de LXXIII* et iiij^{d.} dat. Adame Grenelese. Inter Cartas Abbatis A. e. prout sequitur in hæc verba.

A.D. 1332.

I, Lora atte Lofte,* have granted and given to Adam Grenelese, of Melford, and his heirs, 73s. 4d. of money annually arising from all my lands and tenements in the towns of Cockfield and Whelnetham, payable in equal portions, in each year, at Easter and Michaelmas; and if the said payments shall be wholly or partly in arrear at any time, then it shall be lawful for the said Adam or his heirs to distrain on all my said lands and tenements, till such arrears are satisfied, &c.

Witnesses :

ROBERT NEL.   ROBERT GARTYNG.
JOHN NEL.   RICHARD JUB.
PETER LE BOTELER [Butler].   And others.

Given at Cockfield, the Sunday next after the feast of Pentecost, in the 5th year of the reign of King Edward, the third after the Conquest.

CARTA LORÆ ATTE LOFTE de Cokefelde de iiij libras annui redd. dat. Adame Grenelese.—Inter Cartas Abbatis A. 39 prout sequitur in hæc verba.

A.D. 1333.

I, Lora atte Lofte, of Cockfield, have given and granted to Adam Grenelese, of Melford, and his heirs for ever, £4 of money annually, payable in equal portions at Easter and Michaelmas, from my capital messuage, and all the lands and tenements which I possess in Cockfield; and I, Lora, for myself and my heirs, covenant to pay the same to the said Adam and his heirs for ever, &c.

Witnesses :

HENRY, the Clerk of Schymplyngg.
JOHN TRISTRAM.
STEPHEN DE SIDOLVESMERE [near Ballington].
JOHN DE LAVENHAM.
JOHN HAMME.
JOHN NEL.
ROBERT NEEL.
And others.

Give at Cockfield, Monday next after the feast of Pentecost, in the 6th year of the reign of King Edward, the third after the Conquest.

* Cockfield Loft.

2 Q

ABBOT WILLIAM DE BERNHAM.*

CARTA WILLELMI ABBATIS de viii acris terræ cum unum messuagium
vocatum le Apylton, quondam Adamæ Grenelese dimiss Henrico
Peynton et Cristianæ uxori ejus et her : de corpe prædicti Henrici
legitime procreatis per annuo redd. iij⁸ viii⁴ᵈ Inter Cartas
Abbatis, &c.

A.D. 1359.

We, William [de Benham or Bernham], by divine permission
Abbot of the Monastery of St. Edmund, Bury, and the said convent,
by general consent and free will of the whole chapter, have granted
and conveyed to Henry le Peynton, of Melford, and Cristiana his wife,
eight acres of arable land, and a messuage called "le Apylton,"
which formerly belonged to Adam Grenelese, of Melford, to hold the
same to them and the heirs of their body lawfully begotten, paying
annually for the same 3s. 8d. by equal portions at Michaelmas and
Easter ; and if it should happen that the said Henry should die without
lawful heirs of his body, then the same shall revert to the Abbot
and his successors. To this deed the said Henry and Cristiana have
affixed their seal, and we have affixed the common seal of the chapter
of the convent.

Given at St. Edmund's, in our chapter-house, Monday next after the
feast of St. Luke the Evangelist [18th October], in the 32nd year
of the reign of King Edward, the third after the Conquest.

* Commonly called De Benham, but Battely and Burroughs both call him De
Bernham.

CHAPTER X.

MELFORD HALL AND MANOR—*(continued)*.

MANY different surveys of this estate were made in the times of
various subsequent abbots. One of these in the abbacy of Abbot
John Tymworth, in 1386, gives a corrected rental of Melford at that
period. It would, however, be tedious to recount all these minute
changes, and only a few are here noted as specimens of the estate
chartulary of that particular date. Though very rare, having been
originally but few in number, yet some of these chartularies of different
possessions of the Abbey of St. Edmund still exist. A few are in
public libraries, while others, like those at Melford Hall, are in private
hands. Occasionally one comes into the market; as in December,
1870, when the chartulary of Harlowe, in Essex, of the time of Abbot
Curteys, about A.D. 1431, was sold by auction in London, and was
purchased by a dealer (Jackson) for £100.

The following extracts are roughly translated from the monkish
Latin.

EXTRACTS FROM THE CORRECTED RENTAL OF MELFORD IN THE SECOND YEAR OF ABBOT JOHN DE TYMWORTH, A.D. 1386.

The Land formerly of William le Palmere.

This land is now held by John Garneys. Six acres and a tenement for 5s. 4d. a year, and to plough twice in winter and twice in
spring, in each year, with all his animals in his own ploughs, certain lands for the lord, and to reap yearly half an acre of wheat and
half an acre of oats, and three suits a year to the general court. He
also holds a tenement formerly Edmund de Harlyng's.

In 1334 to 1364, Richard de Harlyng was rector of Melford.
This land is now in Bull Lane farm, by King's Lane.

John Hunn held a messuage and 100 acres of land and meadow.

Query: Did he give the name to the old paper-mills, which were formerly called
Hunn Mills?

Land formerly of William de Lavenham.

This is now held by Sir John Sutton, Knight, 57 acres of land at 18s. a year; and to do certain ploughings, and to mow for the lord yearly two acres of wheat and two acres of oats, and three suits a year to the court.

This land was at Cuckoo Tye.

Lands formerly of Alan Boydyn.

Part is now held by John att Berye [Bury], a goldsmith, and part by the Master of the College of St. Gregory in Sudbury; and John Roghened holds two acres which were formerly held by the Prior of St. Bartholomew.

This land is near and around the old St. Bartholomew's Priory.

Lands formerly of Galfridus Messager.

Now held by John Barker, near Lolleholm.

This land was near Rodbridge, and the Barker family held there for 130 years after.

Reginald Minchyng, the tailor, holds a cottage.

John the blacksmith holds half an acre of pasture land near Smalee, in Melford.

This chartulary goes on to describe many holdings both sides of le Halle Street.

EXAMPLES of COTTAGE RENTS of MINOR BORDARII in MELFORD, under Abbot John de Tymworth. A.D. 1386.

	s.	*d.*	
Walter Pratt held a cottage and 1 acre of land for	2	2	a year.
John Bloy held a messuage and 3 roods of land for	3	0	a year.
The same held also a cottage and ¼ an acre for	2	0	a year.
Laurence Dexter held a cottage and ½ an acre for	2	0	a year.
Robert Swalowe held a cottage and ¼ an acre for	0	6	a year.
John Nerbolt held a cottage and ½ a rood for	0	6	a year.
Adam Allesner held a cottage and ½ a rood for	0	6	a year.
John Jurdan held a cottage and 30 perches for	0	9	a year.
William Pach held a cottage and 50 perches for	1	3	a year.
Richard Prentys held a cottage and 1 rood and 34 perches for	1	8	a year.

	s.	d.	
Richard Drake held a cottage and ½ a rood for . .	0	6	a year.
Roger Pekke held a cottage and ½ a rood for . .	0	6	a year.
John Lalleford held a cottage and 1 rood for . .	1	0½	a year.
Edward Bols held a cottage and 10 perches for . .	0	3	a year.
William Cook held a cottage and ½ a rood for . .	0	6½	a year.
Richard Spark held a cottage and 1 rood and 11 perches for	1	0½	a year.
Roger Dexter held a cottage and 39 perches for .	0	8½	a year.
Richard the tailor held a cottage and 1½ rood for .	1	6	a year.
Adam Bigge held a cottage and ½ an acre for . .	2	0½	a year.
Richard de Bulneye held a cottage for . . .	0	2	a year.
Henry Fabyon held a cottage and 1 rood for . .	1	0	a year.
Thomas Stagynet held a cottage and 1 rood for .	1	0½	a year.
The same held also a cottage and ½ rood for . .	0	6	a year.
The same held also a cottage and 10 perches for .	0	4	a year.
Richard Dyck held a cottage for	0	2	a year.
John Koc held a cottage for	0	2	a year.
William Cook held a cottage and 1½ rood for . .	1	4½	a year.
John Cattyshalle held a cottage and 1 rood for . .	0	11	a year.
John Gamyn held a cottage and ½ rood for . .	0	6	a year.
Richard Drake held a cottage and ½ rood for . .	0	6	a year.
Nicholas Bulneye held a cottage and ½ rood for . .	0	6	a year.
Margaret Pekke held a cottage and ½ rood for . .	0	6	a year.
John Jurdon held a cottage and 1 rood for . . .	1	0	a year.
William Dexter held a cottage and 1 rood and 15 perches for	1	4½	a year.
Richard Dexter held a cottage and 1 rood and 26 perches for	1	8	a year.
The same held also a cottage for	0	4	a year.

Henry Neel held a cottage for 1 penny and a capon yearly.

Besides the rents, these persons had to do personal services for the lord, and were entirely at his will; and, similarly to the last example quoted, bordarii had generally to raise poultry for the Abbot's supply; small plots of ground commonly rendering one chicken and five eggs.

Cottage Rents.

EXAMPLES OF RENTS of VILLEIN COTTERS of Melford Manor, who had no land attached to their cottages, in A.D. 1386.

Agnes Petyt .	5 pence a year	Johanna Carter .	1 penny a year
Edward Gent .	5 pence ,,	John Miller .	1 penny ,,
William Chiep .	2½ pence ,,	Emma Carter .	1 penny ,,
John Miller .	2 pence ,,	John at Hill .	½ penny ,,
Henry Dexter .	2 pence ,,	William Ayloff .	½ penny ,,
Robert Petyt .	1½ pence ,,	Thomas Geffery .	½ penny ,,
Roger Rous .	1½ pence ,,	John Skateronn .	½ penny ,,
Richard Skateronn	1 penny ,,	Walter Wraw .	½ penny ,,
Walter Skilcott .	1 penny ,,	Petronilla Skilcot	½ penny ,,
John Osbern .	1 penny ,,	John Garneys .	½ penny ,,
Edward Gent .	1 penny ,,	Wm. Dollyngham	½ penny ,,
John Maneves .	1 penny ,,	Robert Horner .	½ penny ,,
John Wright .	1 penny ,,	Walter Brandon .	½ penny ,,

These persons' rents appear to have been almost nominal; for they were serfs, belonging absolutely to the Abbot—body and goods.

NOMINA CUSTUMAR: DE MELFORD A.D. 1386.—Money payments in lieu of, or value of certain services.

	s.	*d.*		*s.*	*d.*
John Michel	0	6	Walter Cheep	1	6
William Peteyt	1	0	Dulcia Hervey [½ marc] .	6	8
Igelene Godemay . . .	0	3	Princia Donne	20	0
William le Proude . . .	1	6	Radulphus de la Mere . .	3	0
Robert Garland	4	0	Robert Houlot	3	0
William atte hil	1	6	Robert Stalun	2	0
William Scullot [½ marc] .	6	8	William atte hil	1	6
William, son of Osbert .	2	0	Alex. Godwyn	4	0
Edward le Chambre . .	1	0	William le Riche . . .	0	6
Richard Wodemay . . .	2	0	Roger Gernays	2	0
Galfridus Coiebat . . .	0	6	Richard Scaterun . . .	4	0
Osbert Wyan	1	6	Juliana Scaterun . . .	2	0
Reginald de Ponte . . .	5	0	Peter Scaterun	2	0
Simide Waryn	6	0	Radulphus in the Hall .	3	0
Galant Waryn	1	0	William in the Hall . .	3	4
Robert Wran	1	0	Margery Cucock . . .	1	0
Robert Proudfot. . . .	4	0	Richard Cuccok	2	0
Walter Neel [½ marc] . .	6	8	Robert atte Tye	3	4

	s.	d.		s.	d.
Sara atte Tye	4	0	Richard Benar	2	0
Richard Lytel	8	0	Walter Maur	3	0
Richard Belamy	1	6	Roger Scalim	2	0
Sara Giffard	1	0	Robert Legro	0	3
Henry le Heyeward. . .	4	0	Cecilia Leche	0	3
Robert de Bulneye . . .	2	0	Monaca Wyting	3	0
William Bussel [¼ marc] .	6	8	Ager la Ward	1	0
Roger Gooch	1	6	Radulphus de Borebrigge .	0	6
Richard Alstan	1	6	Thomas le Turnor . . .	2	0
Katherine Alstan . . .	1	0	Roger Scalim, junior . .	1	0
Hugo le Sawyer	6	8	Cristiana Scalim . . .	0	6
Peter Sancke	2	0	Roger Warrenne, of Ladi-		
Walter Jue	40	0	dene	2	0
Robert le Garryn . . .	3	4	Roger Litil	3	0
William le Warner has 2			Walter Hervey	40	0
cows, 2 young bullocks,			Thomas Bryan	5	0
6 sheep, 1 sow [¼ marc]	6	8	Adam le Sawyer, son of		
John de Borebrigg . . .	1	0	Hugo le Sawyer, pur-		
William Brawode . . .	3	0	chased from Gilbert de		
John de le hil	1	6	Pantria 5 acres of free-		
Robert Gent [¼ marc] . .	6	8	hold land	8	0

The next survey was taken in 1442, by order of Abbot William Curteys, and it contains many points of increasing interest. The names therein begin to sound more familiarly to our ears, and we are better able to identify the tenants with their holdings. Many of the families who were connected with the rebuilding of the church, and whose names remain to us in the records of the lost old painted glass, now appear in the list, and we are told where they lived, and the trades and occupations of some of them. We commence also to get a faint glimpse of the village, with its inhabitants. We find that there were two taverns in the street, with their poles for signs in front of them.* The record does not state what their signs were; perhaps they were only the general olden ones of the period, of a pole surmounted by a bunch of green, with a suspended hoop, or sometimes several hoops, covered with green twigs : these were constantly renewed when faded, and were the common signs of the taverns or alehouses of that time, in conjunction with the distinctive mark of painting *bright red*, the open wooden lattices or trellis-work in the unglazed window openings of the parlours or tap-rooms of such inns. One of these taverns was held by Roger Moryell (one of the church benefactors), and was near the old market (Chapel Green) ; and the other one, on the east side of

* Only one tavern was named in 1386. It was kept by John Onwyn.

Hall Street, was in tenure of William Martyn. There appear to have been at that time two small daily markets, probably only for minor articles of food; one held on St. James's Chapel Green, and the new market nearly opposite the Bull Inn. These markets were in addition to the more important chartered weekly market, at the cross on the great green.

There seem to have been several shops in the neighbourhood of the church, and altogether we find the following trades carried on in this village; viz., publicans, smiths, fullers, dyers, millers, masons, locksmiths, tailors, clothiers, woolmongers, and cordwainers or shoe-makers.* Doubtless there was here a barber, who, as usual at that period, was also the village leech or medical practitioner, though the name of this hairdresser and doctor is not mentioned. If the legal profession was represented by a member here, his name is not recorded; and any how, thirteen years later, this gentleman would probably have been shelved; for a petition was presented to King Henry VI. by the attorneys of the eastern counties in 1455, which represented that whereas formerly there were but six or at the most eight common attorneys in the two counties of Suffolk and Norfolk and the city of Norwich, at which time there was great peace and quiet of suits; but that now [1455] there are in these counties 80 attorneys, most of whom being needy men, do travel about to fairs and markets, and move and excite the people to undertake vexatious suits for light and frivolous causes; therefore the king is humbly prayed that he will only permit there to be in future six attorneys for the county of Norfolk, and two for the city of Norwich; and six for the county of Suffolk. The said fourteen attorneys to be elected by the chief justices for the time being. This petition was granted by the king.

In this Abbot's Chartulary of 1442 the old names of streets and roads now appear; and though in older documents Melford Hall is constantly mentioned, there now occurs the first detailed record in the Abbot's books of the description of the abuttals of the manor-house and grounds.

Extent : terr : et tent: manerii ibm̄ renōvat: et mensurāt : per perticaī : de asśis quæ continet in longitudine quincque virǵ: et dimiđ : Anno regni Henrici Sexti xx° et anno Domini Willelmi Curteys Abbatis xiiiᵃ

A.D. 1442.

The manor-house, with moats, ditches, gardens, and pastures, lieth between the road which leads to the said house on the north and

---

* The origin of the word cordwainer is said to be from the French *cordonnier*, which was originally spelt *corduanier*, because the best shoe leather was Spanish, and came from Curdua, or Cordova, as it is now called.

the bank of the Abbot's stream on the south, and abutting on the king's highway towards the west, and contains of the aforesaid measurement 14 acres and 10 perches.

The terrier then continues with descriptions and measurements of lands; many of the names remain the same, or are identifiable to this day; as Brademedowe, Stonylond, Pondmedowe, Mellefeld, Chesewyck, Bulneymoor, Bulney, Chirchewente, Shepecotewent, Longwente, Pantrieshallewente, Oxesladewente, Cleypetwente, Roughemarshewente, Palmereswente (Bull Lane farm), Highfield, Calfpyghtyl, Brakibill in the Parkmedowe, Margleswente.

Among woods :—

	A.	R.	P.
Spiltenewode	70	0	16
Lenengewode	140	2	0
Elmesetewode (now Old Park farm) . .	217	2	34
Lytle Parkwode (now in Lodge farm) . .	77	0	24

Bulneymoor pasture then contained 41½ acres, of which ten acres were allowed to be mown for hay.

Some small pastures, now thrown into the park, are described as then abutting on the large garden of the manor-house, and on the park gate.

Among the roads the following can be identified; viz. :—

Fottyforthestrete, now King's Lane.

Lackforthestrete, now Bull Lane. This road is also sometimes called "the highway to Gyppewic" (Ipswich).

Rathbregestrete, now Rodbridge.

Le Greneweye, from Cuckoo Tye to Melford Place, and including also the present Backlane.

Le Processionweye, the lane leading from the old Priory of St. Bartholomew to Stalis Tye road.

Le Clareweye, Cavendish and Clare road.

Bulneighlane, Hart Lane and Papermill Lane.

Oldewentestrete, now Hooping Lane.

Le Chircheweye, several paths and parts of roads near the church were called by this name, and particularly a way or path leading from the house called Cranevile, now Cranfield, to the Church of Melford.

Thurgoristye, now Cuckoo Tye. This was still so called after 1678.

Tallichetye, now Stalis or Stalhouse Tye. There is also mentioned a Green road (probably the present Heaven Lane by the schools) leading from Melleforde Grene to Oldewentestrete; also another way from Melleforde Grene towards the Heighstrete; besides many other field roads.

Among the lands a few appear to have been called after the families who early owned them; although more generally in old times person-derived their appellations from the lands and locality where they dwelt. Thus, Bulneys and Bulneymoors seem to have taken the name from the family of "de Bolneye" at a very early date. Cranfield is a corruption of "Cramaville," having been the property of a branch of the ancient family of that name: the site of the old manor-house is still traceable there. The Duntons was probably so called from its old possessors the "Dontones." Persons of the name of "Panetria" were early settled on part of High Street farm, where Pantries Marsh field still remains. "Monks Does," on the same farm, evidently should be "the Monks' Doles." Hunn Mills, lately the Paper-mills, perhaps took the name from John Hunn in 1386, and continued to be so called for more than 800 years.

LIST OF FREE TENANTS OF THE MANOR OF MELFORD in the 20th year of the reign of King Henry VI., and in the 14th year of the Abbacy of William Curteys, Lord Abbot of St. Edmund's.

A.D. 1442.

From this long list of names of tenants, and descriptions of the abuttals of their lands, the few following are selected as examples, and are here generalized.

Sir James Ormond, Knight, holds a messuage and 57 acres, near Tallichetye, formerly held by Sir John Sutton, Knight, and on the same payments and customary services.

Tallichetye was the present Stalis Tye. Part of the land was on the side of the road next to St. Bartholomew, and part was in the present Highlanders farm.

Thomas Gooday, the Master of the College of St. Gregory of Sudbury, held land of Melford Manor (now part of St. Bartholomew's), doing three services to the Court of Melford, and a payment of 9d. a year.

The Prior of St. Bartholomew's held similar lands with the like services, and 6d. yearly payment.

Roger Moryell held lands (adjoining or in Mr. Mills' present farm) at Rodbridge, and adjoining the lands of Nelys and the lands of Roger Ibe. He also held land in Nether Bulney and in Over Bulney. Roger Moryell also kept a tavern in le Halle Strete, on its east side, near the Oldemarket (Chapel Green), and he held a piece of the waste of the manor in front of the tavern gate, formerly held by John Sparrowe. He also held a tenement, formerly Lawrence Dyster's. He was bound to perform various services to the manor, and to mow for the Abbot 1¼ acres of wheat and 1¼ acres of oats, and to do certain ploughings annually, with his parceners.

Laurence Martyn (of the Place) held various copyholds of the manor, some of which had been granted to William Newman, and to his son Walter de Melford, between the years 1234 and 1248.

Walter Hervey held lands of the manor near Wissendale Mill. (He lived on the east side of Hall Street, near Chapel Green.)

Thomas Gooday held lands of the manor, near to the Priory of St. Bartholomew.

Roger Bulneigh held lands at Bulneys, and others adjoining Garnetts (now in Bull Lane farm and about Cuckoo Tye). He also had a messuage on the east side of Hall Street, which *he held of the feoff of the chapel of the Blessed Mary.* Several members of the family of Bulneigh held lands and tenements at various dates.

John Foot lived on the west side of le Halle Strete, towards the south end, and had some meadow land near there.

William Martyn lived on the east side of Halle Strete, near the south end. In the description of his tenure it is noted that " he held a piece of the waste of the manor by the street, in front of the gateway, into his tavern, and erected thereon a pole for a sign at the gate of his said tavern."

John Mannock held 130 acres of land at Cranfield (Cramaviles), and two water-mills under one roof, on the bank of the river dividing Suffolk from Essex, which said land formerly belonged to John de Cranvile, and previously to that to Sir Guy Bryan, knight.

John Barker held much land in various parts: some near the Bulneys, part of Chessawick, some near the Back Lane, and some about Bridge Street. He also had Forthehalle (Ford Hall) and 100 acres; and he had two shops near Melford Church, and next to the shop of Adam the mason.

Roger Ibe, of Sudbury, held land between the lands of the college of St. Gregory and the land of Sir James Ormond, Knight. He also held other lands. In 1580 there was land opposite the present Highlanders still called Ibe's Close.

Roger Cooper had land, now in Bull Lane farm, and other land and houses towards Roydon Bridge.

John Waryn, the blacksmith, held part of Chessawick, and some other land thereabout; also seven acres and a meadow adjoining, now part of Mill or Bull Field, described as " opposite the manor-house called Melford Hall, and bounded by the stream flowing from the water-mill to the bridge called Smalebregge, and also by Bulneylane, and by le Hallestrete leading towards the Church of Melford."

Smalebregge was the foot-bridge in Hart Lane, below Brook House: a dye-house stood close to the bridge; and there was another dye-house by the stream, near the corner of Mason's Allotments.

William Tye, the cordwainer, held a messuage east of Hall Street, next to the house of John Smyth, the locksmith.

Robert Colet lived on the west side of Hall Street.

Margaret atte Hill held several parcels of land in 1442. A person of the same name is mentioned as fined for trespassing on lands of the Rectory manor in 1507.

Robert Hyne, of Sudbury, held much land and a messuage called Oldehalle. This land appears to have been near Cold Hill, between Elmesete (now Old Park farm), Duntons, and Ford Hall.

Richard Smythe, the fuller, held Smalemedow (Smaley meadows), and probably also the old dye-house at Smalebregge.

John Garneys had a messuage, afterwards called "Garnett's," by King's Lane, on the present Bull Lane farm, with land adjoining, and part of "Cokhose," the present Cuckoo Tye farm. He also had part of Rye meadow, next to land described as "belonging to the Prior of Hatfield." He was to do certain ploughings for the Abbot in winter and at Quadragesima, and to reap certain crops; and court services.

Edward Gent held land by Wissendale Mill.

John Waryn, senior, the fuller, lived on the west side of the Hall Street. He belonged to St. Mary's Guild in Melford, and by his will, dated 1448, he made bequests to his guild, and to the church; and left 40 gowns of Colchester russet cloth to the poor. His son John was also a fuller by trade, and lived on the same side of the street, and had part of Broadmeadow. He also held, with Waryn the smith and Waryn the mason, land formerly belonging to the Bridebecs, who lived here in 1287.

Roger Waryn had land near Wissendale Mill, adjoining the land of the Hospitaller of the Abbey of St. Edmund.

John Waryn, the mason, had a house and some land near the church gate; described as being situated "between the road leading to the Manor-house of the Hospitaller [Monk's Manor-house] on the one hand, and on the other abutting on the churchyard of the Church of Melford."

Thomas Elys, tailor (or clothier), lived nearly opposite the present High Street farm, on land now belonging to Kentwell Hall. The site of the premises where John Lilly, the woodman, now lives, formed part thereof. Elys also had land at Bridge Street. This family owned these lands till after 1580.

John Deye, a cordwainer, lived on the west side of Hall Street, and had a shop near "le churchegate."

Lawrence Dyster held, among other lands, Nether Bulney.

John Dyster lived at Bridge Street.

Richard and William Rowe held a tenement at Rodbridge, and also one on the west side of Hall Street, which had formerly belonged to Alan, the woolmonger.

Joanna Moryell, widow of Gilbert Moryell, lived west side of Hall

Street, and held a piece of waste called Oldeflotegatespet; being a pond by Hall Street.

Thomas Neel, alias *Reve*—near Laurence Martyn's, Hall Street, and had a messuage and garden in the old market (Chapel Green).

Walter Fraunceys had lands west of the Street and near Broadmeadow.

Thomas Fletcher had a shop near the church gate of Melford, abutting on the churchway.

John Dowe, or *Dove,* tailor, among other lands, had some near the pits called "Cleypetts by the Churchtye."

Another *John Dowe,* a fuller, east of Hall Street.

John Hill, senior, lived west of Hall Street, near a lane leading to Broadmeadow.

John Berner, a smith, held, with Thomas Aldhouse, of Sudbury, among other lands, a piece of the waste of the manor in front of his gates in the new market of Melford (by the Bull Inn).

John Baleton held a piece of the waste of the manor then lately built on in Hall Street, between the pond of John Muriell, called Oldeflotegatepet, and the way (now Back Lane) leading to Lackforthe Street (Bull Lane).

Agnes Goodwen, and *John* her son, held land by Northo Strete, of the *feoff of the Chapel of the Blessed Mary,* near Churchtye.

The inhabitants of the town of Melford held a cottage (formerly belonging to Richard Pecke) called the Elmeshouse (? Almshouse), by the Churchgate Street, abutting on the churchway towards the east.

John Smyth held land now in Harefield, and *John Smyth,* the locksmith, a messuage, east of Hall Street, formerly Roger Dyster's.

Adam the mason held part of Margerys Wente Field, with other lands and a tenement and garden by the churchyard of Melford Church, and abutting on the churchway leading towards the door of the church.

Roger the fuller had a shop near the church.

Thomas Wood, of Lavenham, held a piece of land between Lineage Wood and "*the road belonging to the Earl of Oxford.*"

John Folke lived in a house in Oldmarket (Chapel Green). There appear to have been six tenements abutting on Chapel Green at that time.

Robert Hayward, alias *Sparrowe,* had a messuage east of Hall Street, and land in Nether Bulncy, and some of the present Melford Place land.

Gilbert Barker, west of Hall Street.

Roger Barker, east of Hall Street.

Henry Norfolk had a messuage abutting on Bull Lane, and land in Chesawick and Over Bulney.

Richard Cotes had part of the present Melford Hospital Tye farm.

John Ponder had 34¼ acres, now Brand's trustees.

Roger Kent had land at Rodbridge, adjoining Roger Moriell's.

John Neel, whose land is afterwards alluded to as "Nelys," had land near Rodbridge, adjoining Laurence Martyn's, Muriell's (or Moriell's), and Colys's.

Richard Waryn had a tenement and land east of Hall Street, near Chapel Green; and another one near, formerly, Alan the woolmonger's.

Thomas Waryn had land about Stallis Tye, and a right of way thereto, for his carts and ploughs, concerning which he summoned John Ballard to the Melford Manor Court for obstructing the same in the 11th of Henry IV., A.D. 1410–11, as entered in the Rolls of the said manor.

After this date, yet eight more Abbots of Bury enjoyed their Manor of Melford, and occasionally visited their old mansion of Melford Hall for recreation or repose. As to what the old Hall was like we have no existing record; and though, from certain remains and other grounds, a theory may be formed, it is too conjectural to deserve mention here. But it would appear, from a lease of the Hall granted by the last Abbot of Bury, that though a part of the house was brick, some portion was a timber-framed erection, with the usual clay wattle between, for the repair of which the tenant was bound to find all manner of clay and straw, made and laid ready. The mansion was moated round on the west, north, and east: on this latter side, as on the others, the moat ran straight; the present semicircular dry moat being a much later alteration. In the front of the house, beyond the sundial, there stood a gate-house, the foundations and paving of which still exist undisturbed, a short distance under the surface. The present park was then divided into many field inclosures, as those called Long Pasture, Horse Pasture, Nether Home Fields, &c., the site of the fences of which can be yet traced by any one who knows the history of their old positions. Many portions of ground, however, on the western side of the park were then in small inclosures, and belonged to various owners. It should be borne in mind that the present park was not at that time a deer-park, and did not probably become so till near the year 1600. The old deer-park, in which the abbots hunted, and from which many a fat buck graced their tables, was a park of a very ancient foundation.* It was called Elmset or Elmsethe, or the Great Park, and consisted chiefly of open wood, and was termed of old, "Magnus Boscus Domini," and in the Surveys of Edward I. and

* Abbot Sampson, however, never hunted; but if any guests were staying with him at any of his parks, the Abbot, with his monks, would sit in some opening of the woods to see the dogs run. The St. Edmund's breed of hounds was famous, and at Richard Cœur de Lion's request, this abbot sent to him two of the best Abbey dogs, for which King Richard gave him in return a finger-ring which had been a present from Pope Innocent III.

Henry VI. it is reckoned both as park and wood, the wood part being
in the latter survey 217a. 2r. 34p., and the whole was impaled round
and stored with deer. It occupied the site of the present Old Park
farm, and part of the Duntons farm; and those fine old oaks still
standing near the Duntons, were once in the corner of the old deer-
park, which was disparked between 1570–1580, when part of the pales
were removed (some pales remaining till 1611), and the ground was
let and was first broken up and tilled by one Robert Bentley, the tenant,
between 1600 and 1602. In 1613 it was divided into field inclosures,
but many trees still remained about it at that time. The old house or
hunting-lodge, on the site of the present Old Park farm, was moated
round. Strange to say, one quaint anecdote yet remains to us, relative
to this old park and wood of Elmsethe, carrying us back to a scene
which occurred in it no less than *seven hundred years ago!* It is no
easy matter to get at the ways and doings of men separated from us
by a lapse of seven centuries; and yet this chasm is, in a measure, bridged
over, and a dim little photograph of the past is, in this instance, presented to us, by the quaint, good-humoured journal of a monk of
St. Edmund, whose simple record reveals to us throughout his narrative
of the Abbey, the fashion of his day, much as an uncovered Pompeiian
inscription helps to unfold the history of manners and customs buried
under the wreck of ages.

Jocelin de Brakelond, the chronicler of the Monastery of St.
Edmund from 1173 to 1202, was till about 1182 the prior's chaplain.
At that date Sampson was elected abbot. His character and personal
appearance have been already described in the account of St. Saviour's
Hospital, which he founded. Jocelin then became the chaplain of the
Abbot, with whom he lived, to use his own language, day and night,
for six years. He subsequently became the almoner of the Abbey.
A contemporary monk has recorded his character in these few words:
"Master Joceline our Almoner, a man of exemplary religion, powerful
in word and deed."

In his Chronicle, Jocelin relates an anecdote as to the timber in
Elmsethe Wood, Melford, and tells the tale of diamond-cut-diamond
with evident glee.

Translated from the Latin, his narration runs thus:—

A.D. 1183–1189.

"Geoffry Riddell, Bishop of Ely, sought from the Abbot of Bury
some timber for the purpose of constructing certain great buildings at
Glemsford; which request the Abbot granted, but with bad grace, yet
not daring to offend him. Now the Abbot making some stay at
Melford, there came to him a certain clerk of the Bishop asking, on
behalf of his lord, that the promised timber might be taken at

Ælmswell, for he made a mistake in pronouncing the word, saying *Ælmswell* when he should have said *Ælmsethe*, which is the name of a certain wood of Melford. The Abbot was astonished at the request, for such timbers were not to be found at *Ælmswell.* Whereof when Richard the Forester of Melford had heard, he privately informed the Abbot that the Bishop had the previous week sent his carpenters in a surreptitious manner into the wood of *Ælmsethe* and had chosen the best timber trees in the whole wood, and had placed his marks thereon. On hearing this the Abbot directly discovered that the messenger of the Bishop of Ely had made an error in his request, and answered him that he would willingly do as the Bishop wished.

"On the morrow, upon the departure of the messenger, *immediately after the Abbot had heard mass,* he went with his carpenters into *Ælmsethe* wood, and caused to be marked with *his* mark not only all the oaks previously marked for the Bishop, but more than a hundred others, for the use of St. Edmund's [Abbey] and for the roof of the great tower, commanding that they should be felled as quickly as possible. But when the Bishop of Ely, by the answer of his messenger, understood that the aforesaid timber was to be taken at *Ælmswell,* he sent back the same messenger (*on whom he dealt many hard words*) to the Abbot, in order that he might correct the word which he had blundered as *Ælmswell,* by saying *Ælmsethe.* But before he had come again to the Abbot, all the timbers which the Bishop had desired were felled, and the Abbot's carpenters had marked them; wherefore all the Bishop could do was to take other timber, and at some other place, if he would. When I, Jocelin, saw this I laughed, and said in my heart, Thus cunning outwits itself."

By some writers the date of this transaction has been fixed as in the abbacy of Hugh (Sampson's predecessor), and in the year 1163, probably from that being the date in the margin of a previous passage of Jocelin de Brakelond's Chronicle, but which really has no reference to this anecdote; and these marginal dates are not consecutive as to the narrative. A little reflection would make it evident that the above-named year could not be correct, for Geoffry Riddell, formerly Arch-deacon of Canterbury, was not consecrated Bishop of Ely till 1174; so the event recorded must have taken place after that date, and probably, from the context of the Chronicle, and Jocelin being present, soon after Sampson's election as abbot, and between 1183 and 1189; in which latter year Geoffry Riddell died.

* The *Ælmswell* mentioned in this narrative was probably Norton Wood, Elms-well, about seven miles east of Bury. Abbot Hugh gave to Helyas, his butler (or cupbearer), 60 acres of land therein, in exchange for Helyas's land at Melford, which had before belonged to Philip, *who was hung for theft.* In attesting a deed of Abbot Anselm, Helyas signed his name as *Helyas de Meleford,* between the years 1150 and 1157.

During the rule of Abbot Sampson, many great works of restoration and rebuilding were going on in the Abbey. To these Sampson contributed largely in material from his private manors; and it appears that he provided at one time 120 *large oak-trees from his woods of Melford*, for the use of the Abbey.

After the abbots of Bury had been lords of Melford for 500 years, the great religious revolution engendered and matured by the growing abuses of the monastic rule, overwhelmed them and overthrew their house, and despoiled them of their rich inheritance; and among all their other possessions, Melford passed away from them.

When the time came that this place was to know its old masters no more, it so happened that the last of the long line of abbots was himself a native of Melford; and we may take a melancholy pride in the character of *our* Abbot, for even his bitterest enemies, seeking for cause of complaint against him, could not accuse him of any of the foul charges which were with good ground brought against most of his compeers; and they were forced to admit that his life was exceptionally free from the shocking moral taints which generally disgraced the order. John Reeves, commonly called John de Melford, became the thirty-third abbot of Bury in 1514. Shortly before the dissolution of the monasteries, the commission sent under Dr. John Ap-Rice* to inquire into the misrule of Bury Abbey, while strongly condemning the corrupt and infamous mode of life of the monks, could only speak of the Abbot thus; that he was fond of staying in his country-houses, that he had a weakness for bricks and mortar,† and that he was a stanch and zealous Roman Catholic; and except his great failing of laxity of discipline of the Abbey, they could hit but one serious blot, viz. that general rumour asserted that he was addicted to gambling with cards and dice. Their Report ran thus: "As for the Abbot, we finde nothing to sospect as touching hys livyng, but it was detected that he laye moche forth in his granges: that he delited moche in playing at dice and cardes, and therein spent moche money, and in building for his pleasure. He did not preache openly. Also that he converted divers fermes into copieholdes, whereof poor men doth complaine: also he seemeth to be addicted to the meynteyning of such superstitious ceremonies as hathe ben used heretofor."

He surrendered the Abbey and its possessions to King Henry VIII. on the 4th November, 1539; when an annuity of five hundred marks was assigned him, and he was driven from his splendid home to

---

* The chief commissioners for the suppression of the religious houses were Drs. Legh, Leyton, and Ap-Rice, ecclesiastical lawyers in holy orders.

† Abbot John de Melford built Little Horringer Hall, now long since destroyed. In the time of Charles II., the arms of the Confessor, with those of the Abbot, still remained, carved and painted, in the chief chamber of the house, which was then remaining intact.

subsist upon this scanty stipend. He is supposed to have retired at first, for a very short time, to what was called the Exchequer, at Bury, but afterwards he took up his residence in a house at the south-west corner of Crown Street, Bury (now pulled down). His arms remained in one of its windows till late in last century. We may well believe that sorrow and vexation broke his heart. The great and princely Abbot, who had administered the enormous revenues of his monastery, which it has been computed would now have been worth £250,000 annually, did not live to draw even a first half of his paltry pittance of £333. 6s..8d. a year, for he died on the 31st March, 1540, only five months after his deprivation. He was buried in the middle of the chancel of St. Mary's Church, Bury; and on the slab which covered his grave was his effigy in brass, in his pontificals, with the arms of the Abbey impaling those of his family; and bearing the following inscription, as given in Weaver's " Funeral Monuments ":—

> Buria quem Dominum ac Abbatem noverit olim
> Illius hic recubant ossa sepulta viri.
> Suffolce Melforda nomen nato Johannem
> Dixerunt Revis progenio atque patro.
> Magnanimus prudens doctus fuit atque benignus
> Integer et voti religionis amans.
> Regni qui cum Henrici Octavi viderat annum
> Ter decimum ac primum Martius atque dies
> Unum terque decem—flamine terras
> Occidit; Oh anima parce benigne Deus.

This inscription has been freely translated thus:—

" Here rest the sepultured bones of that man whom Bury formerly acknowledged as Lord and Abbot; born at Melford, in Suffolk, named John; his family and father Reeves. He was magnanimous, prudent, learned, benignant, and upright, loving the religion to which he was dedicated. Who when he had seen the thirty-first year of the reign of Henry the Eighth, on the 31st of March, sunk untimely to the grave. Spare his soul, O gracious God."

The poor persecuted Abbot was not allowed to rest quietly even in his last narrow home. His grave was desecrated and the brass torn from his slab by the Roundhead fanatics in 1643; and in 1717 the final indignity was paid to the tomb of the last mitred abbot of Bury, by his monumental slab being broken up to make room for a paltry stone to cover a person named Sutton, a purser of a ship, who was actually buried in the Abbot's grave!

Four years previously to the dissolution of the Abbey, Abbot John de Melford had granted a lease of Melford Hall to Dame Frances Pennington for thirty years; little thinking how soon the interest of his convent in this lease would have finally determined.

The original manuscript is designated "Harley number 308. fol: 71 b.," and the copy is attested by " Cha: Morton, British Museum, 21 Feby 1759."—The lease runs thus : except that some of the abbreviations are rendered in full :—

Melford Hall Manour, 1535.

This Indenture made the fourthe Daye of November in the xxvi[th] yere of the Regne of our Soverayne Lorde Kyng Henry the eight, Betwene the Reverent Father in God John Melford Abbott of the Monastery of Bury Seynt Edmunde in the Countie of Suffolk, and the Prior and the Covent of the same place on the one partie ; and Dame Frances Pennyngton wedowe on the other partie, wetnessith that the seyd Abbott Pryor and Covent with one assent and consent hath demysed, grauntted and to ferme leatyn by thes presents unto the seyd Dame Fraunces all that is their Cete of their Manour of Melford called Melford Hall, with all the Howses Buildings, gardyngs and yerdes theronto belongyng together with feadyngs of the comon called Melford Grene longyng to the seyde Manour.—And also closes whereof the on is called Parkefelde, and the other is called the Horse Pasture and two meadowes the on called Smal Medowe and the other called Parke Medowe lying in Melford aforseyd in the seyd Counte of Suffolk : Exept oute take and reservyd unto the seyd Abbott and hys successors on of the best Chaumbers within the seyd manour wyth ffree ingate and outegate into and fro the same at all tymes at hys pleasure duryng all the seyd terme of the seyd lease. To have and to holde all the seyd Cete of the seyd maner howses Buyldyngs gardyngs and yerdys and all other the premysses unto the seyd Dame Fraunces hir Heyres executours and assignes frome the feste of seynt Mighell Tharchangell last past before the date of thes presents unto thende and terme of xxx[ti] yeers frome thense nexte and immediately followyng and fully to be complete and endyd, yelding and payeng therfore yerly every yere duryng all the seyde terme unto the seyde Abbott and hys successours xi[li] iiii[s.] [£11. 4s.] of goode and lawfull mony of Englonde, att two termes in the yere, that is to say at the festes of Estern and sent Mighell tharchaungell be evyn porcons. And yf it hapen the seyd yerly ferme of elevyn pownds and foure shillynges or any parte or parcelle of the same to be behynde and onpayde after eny of the seyd festes by the space of viii dayes that then yt shal be lawfull to the seyd Abbott his successours and deputyes into all the seyd maner and other the premisses to entre and distreyne and the distresse so ther fownde to lede, bere, dryve, and carey awey and to witholde and impownde unto the seyd yerely ferme of xi[li] iiii[s.] and everie parte and parcall of the same together with thavvrage expencs and costs if eny shal fortune to be fully satysfyed and payde and yf it hapen the seyd yerly ferme or.

eny parte therof to be behynde and onpayde by the space of oon quarter of a yeere next after eny of the seyd fests in the whiche it oughte to be payde and non dystresse fownde uppon the seyd Cete of the Maner and other the premisses that then yt shal be lawfull to the seyd Abbott, Pryor, Covent and ther successours into all the Cete of the seyd maner and all other the premisses to reentre and have ayen and then clerely expell and putte owte the seyd Dame Fraunces hir heyres and executours for ever, eny thyng conteyned in thes Indenturs to the contrari notwythstondynge.—And the seyd Dame Fraunces shall fynde at hir costes and chargs the seyd Abbott or his officers comyng onys in the yeere to the Coorte and Leete of the seyd Abbott at the seyd maner to be kepte sufficient met and drynke with beddyng in ther chambre, hey and otys for ther horses by all the seyd terme for that tyme being there at the seyd Coorte and lete. And the seyd Abbott Pryor and Covent are covenantyn and graunttyn be thes presents to acquite and discharge the same Dame Fraunces hir heyres and executours of all maner owte rentes and charges goyng owte of the seyd maner by all the seyd terme, Exept the same Dame Fraunces shal paye yerly during all the seyd terme to the Baly of Babberg Hundred IIII^s, and to the Crosse Berer of the seyd Abbott for the Staffe-Acre* IIII^s And over, that the seyd Abbott, Pryor, and Covent, shal at ther costes and charges bere, kepe, and manten, all maner of reparačons, nedful and necesserey of the howses of the seyd maner, that is to sey wyndtyghte and watertyghte duryng all the seyde terme, exept the same Dame Fraunces shal at hir costes fynde all maner of cley and strawe made and layde redy for the same. And allso cary all tymbre for the seyd Maner for the reparačons of the same by all the seyd terme. And the seyd Dame Fraunces hir heyres and executours shal fell and have shredde and stowe all suche underwoode as hathe ben fellyd stowed and shredde in tymes past growynge in and uppon the seyd closes, and also shal have soficient plowbote, cartebote, hardilbote, hedgebote, and gatebote† growyng in and uppon the seyd closes and other the premisses by all the seyd terme at thassignament of the officers of the seyd Abbott—and over that the seyd Abbott, Pryor, and Covent covenanttyn and Graunttyn that the seyd Dame Fraunces hir heyres and executours shal have yeerly everie yecro duryng all the seyd terme fyve hundred woode owte of the woodes of the seyd Abbott, Pryor, and Covent, withen the seyd towne of Melford by thassignment

---

* In the "Liber de Consuetudiuibus Sancti Edmundi," folio 37, is a charter headed "Carta de Stafacria," by which Abbot Hugh gave to his clerk, Henry FitzHenry, the staffacres and tithes which Master Zacharias formerly had from the chapelries of various churches therein mentioned. These staffacres, it would seem, were certain payments or fees due to the Abbot's staff or crosier.

† Wood for making or mending gates, carts, ploughs, &c.; hedgebote being bushes or wood for repairing hedges.

of the officers of the seyd Abbott and his successours, to be felled and made and caryed at the costes and charges of the seyd Dame Fraunces, hir heirs and executours. And also Dame Fraunces hir heyrs, executours, and assignes shal have all the feadyng of the lyttyl Parke duryng all the seyd terme, so that the same Dame Fraunces ner hir assignes do non harme on to the Sprynge. And also yt is agreed betwene the seyd parties that the seyd Abbott and his successours and his deputyes shal have at all tymes free lybertye course and recourse over the seyd grownde and pastures beyng in ferme of the seyd Dame Fraunces to cary and recary woode owte of the lyttil parke by alle the seyd terme withowte ony denyall lett vexačon or trobyll of the seyd Dame Fraunces hir heyrs executours and assignes by alle the seyd terme. And furthermore the seyd Dame Fraunces covenantyth and grauntyth presentes that yf it fortune eny hurte harme or decaye to be done neoolygently by the seyd Dame Fraunces hir heyrs executours or assignes, hir servaunts or cattyl uppon eny of the howses of the seyd maner, dores, gats or walles by alle the seyd terme that then shee hir heyrs executours and assignes shal make and repare it ageyn at hir owne propre costes and charges. Allso it is condiscended grauntyd and agreed betwene the seyd parties that the seyd Dame Fraunces hir heyrs executours and assignes shal nott in no manner of wyse aleyn nor make no lease to non person or persones of the seyd Cete of the maner and other the premisses duryng alle the seyd terme withowte thassent and agreament of the seyd Abbott or his successours. Allso the seyd Dame Fraunces shal have delyvered hir at the asseallyng hereof the chaffe and strawe of all the corne growynge of XL acres of grownde of the seyd Abbott, and allso certeyn parcelles be implements of howse which the seyd Dame Fraunces shall leve, and at the prisament of indyfferentt persones by the eleccon of the seyd Abbott or hys successours re-delyver at the seyd Maner in the ende of the seyd terme or ells the pryce, whiche percellys appere particculary folowyng : Inprimis x oolers of lether, IX payer of carte trace wherof ii payer of body trace ii payer of thellbels iii carte saddyls, on plow wyth allo thynges theronto belongynge, iii shares, iii culturs, ii carte roppes, a sede skeppe, iiii comb sekks, ii Busschells, on fanne, on lader, XVI staves, ii Pycheforkes, ii payer of harrowghes, iiii longe formes, ii shorte formes, iii tabylls, ii payer of tressyls, ii Tomberelles, on leed, a schippe coffer,* and halfe a pype.—And for the more suerte of alle the covenantts, grauntts, Agreamentts and payementts in these indenturs on the partie of the seyd Dame Fraunces well and truely to be performyd observed and kepte as is abovescyd, the seyd Dame Fraunces unto the seyd Abbott and hys successours stonde bounde in the suffe of forty pownds

* The largest sort of hutches or chests were called ship-coffers.

sterlyng by hir wrytyng obligatory beryng date of these presents for
the true performaunce of the same. In wittnes wherof to the oon
partie of thes indenturs remaynyng wyth the seyd Abbott and Covent
the seyd Dame Fraunces have sette hir seale : and to the other partie
of thes indenturs remaynyng with the seyd Dame Fraunces the seyd
Abbott, Pryor, and Covent have sette ther comon seale at the seyd
monastery beforeseyd the deye and yeere above wryttyn.

BONDE.

Noṽint uniṽsi p. p̃entes me dñam Fraunciscam Pennyngton de
Melford in Com : Suff : viduam teneri et firmit : obligari Reṽend : in
Christo Patri Johĩ permissione divina Aᵬbi monasterii Sanct : Edmundi
de Bury in quadraginta libris legal : monete Anglie solvend : eidem
Aᵬbi vel successorib : suis aut suo certo attorn : ad festum Pasche
proxime futur : post datum present : sine ulteriore dilatione ad quam
quidem solucōnem bene et fidelit : faciend : obligo me hered : et execut :
meos per presentes. In cujus rei testimonium presentibus sigillum
meum apposui. Dat. quarto die mensis Novemb : anno regni Henrici
octavi Dei gratia Anglie et Franc : Regis fidei defensor et Domini
Hibernie vicesimo sexto.

The condičon of thys obligačon ys suche that yff the within
bounden Dame Fraunces Pennyngton hir heyrs execut : and assignes
observe kepe performe and fullfyll all and singler convenantts grauntts
agreamentts and paymentts as comprysed and specifyed in certen
indenturs beryng the date of thys oblygačon wythin wryttyn made
betwene the same Dame Fraunces Pennyngton on the oon partie and
the wythin namyd Reverent Father in God John Abbott of the Monastery of Bury Seynte Edmunde on the other partie whiche on the partie
and behalfe of the seyd Dame Fraunces Pennyngton yt oughte to be
well and truely observed perfourmed fullfyllyd and kepte, that then
thys presente obligacon to be voide or ells to stonde and abyde in
fulle strengthe, vertue, and effecte.

Attestation hereto.

" This copy is literal, excepting that some few abbreviations which
     might have disturbed the sense, are here wrote out at length.

" CHA : MORTON.

"BRITISH MUSEUM, February 21, 1759."

The scribe who in 1535 held the office of legal adviser to the
Monastery appears to have been little behind the lawyers of the present
day in the redundant verbosity and tedious formal repetition with
which he garnished his lease. About two months before Dame
Pennington took her lease of Melford Hall, she had hired from the
Abbey of Bury other land in Melford. For it appears that on Thursday

next after the Feast of the Exaltation of the Cross (14th September), 1535, she and Francis Johnson had let to them by the Abbot, with the consent of the Convent, three closes of land; viz., Great Monks Dole, 15 acres; Little Monks Dole, 6 acres; and New-broak-up-close, 13 acres; before held· by Robert Buck, gentleman, for 17s. a year. Almost nominal as was this rent, that of Melford Hall sounds very low, even for that time, including, as it did, the offices, gardens, the greater part of the present park, the feeding of the green, with a certain supply of wood, for an annual rent of £11. 12s., inclusive of two fees of 4s. each annually.

Dame Pennington, as a widow, married Mr. Francis Johnson, who survived her.

After the dissolution of the Abbey of Bury, the Manor of Melford appears to have been granted in the first instance to William Cordell by King Henry VIII., in the 37th year of his reign, 1546–7. There is no deed of grant of that year at Melford Hall, but the subsequent grants of Philip and Mary release the rent of £100 *originally reserved to the Crown* from this manor. The first existing grant of Melford Manor in the 16th century, is by letters patent of Queen Mary to William Cordell, her Solicitor-General, dated 26th November, 1554, confirming a former grant of the 12th of January, 1554, which was not so full and comprehensive. This patent, which is at Melford Hall, bears several autograph signatures of both King Philip and Queen Mary. Its general purport runs thus :—

GRANT from King Philip and Queen Mary to William Cordell, Esquire, Solicitor-General, of the MANOR of MELFORD HALL, with lands, tithes, fair, free warren, advowson of the church, and all rights over the said lands formerly belonging to the dissolved Abbey of Bury. Given at Westminster the 26th November, 1554.

This patent recites that a former grant under the Great Seal, had been made the 12th January, 1554; and the present one confirms to William Cordell, gentleman, Solicitor-General, on a payment of £82. 3s. 4d. to the Treasury, and in consideration of his past good, true, faithful, and acceptable services, the grant of the demesne and manor of Melford, otherwise Long Melford, with the park of Long Melford, in Suffolk, with all rights appurtenant thereto, as held by the dissolved Abbey of St. Edmund's Bury, to hold the same of the Queen and her successors, of her manor of East Greenwich, in Kent. Also the advowson and presentation of the parish church of Melford. Also the mansion-house called Melford Lodge, in Long Melford Park, with all the deer in the said park (*N.B.—This was the old deer-park and lodge, called Elmsethe, where the present Old Park farm now is*), with right of free warren. Also the capital messuage of Melford Hall (*the old hall on the same site as the present*) with two closes of land and pasture called Parkfeild, and horse pasture, and two meadows called Small Medow and Park Medow, with all buildings, gardens, belongings, &c., as lately in the occupation of Dame Fraunces Pennyngton, widow, and afterwards in the occupation of Francis Johnson (*so Dame Pennyngton was now dead, for Johnson was her second husband*). Various lands are then specified in tenure of Katherine Ellis, Francis Clopton, Thomas Campion, lands called Deymer, the Hall Mill in tenure of Christopher Hardy, Eastfields 138 acres, Oxlands, Cheswick, Bulneymoors, the fishery in the river Stour, Withindale Mill, lands held by Francis Clopton 123 acres, Little Parkwood, coppice in the same (*now Great and Little Coppice fields in Lodge Farm*), Lynage Wood, Spelthorne Wood, Proudes Farm, and all other farms, messuages, lands, &c., in Melford and Acton, and the manor and right of courts of Melford; and the right of market and fair.

This grant to Sir William Cordell also included the advowson of Rushbrook Church, Suffolk; and two-thirds of the advowson, and the next presentation, to Clipston Church, Northamptonshire; and also the advowson of Stanstead, Suffolk. It also embraced some of the lands and tithes which had been alienated from Melford Church by Abbot Sampson's grant to St. Saviour's Hospital.

The great change of ownership was thus fully completed. Melford Hall and its manor had passed away from the powerful monastery and its ruling abbots, and was now vested in secular hands. What Sir William Cordell's real religious bias was in that transitional period it is difficult to say. Queen Mary and Philip of Spain, bigots as they were, bestowed on him, or certainly confirmed to him, these church lands, and showed him favour, and confided in him throughout their reign; and again Queen Elizabeth, on the other hand, in like manner honoured him. Probably, from the training consequent on his position, he was a careful, prudent man, who, watching the then rapidly shifting changes of public opinion in this country, had learned to steer his bark wisely in the troubled waters; and though we may infer that he was a Protestant at heart, he was moderate in his religious views, while at Melford the Roman Catholic element was yet still strong among some of the leading persons of the place, such as the Martyns and some of the Cloptons; and in Queen Elizabeth's reign we find that a clergyman (or Romish priest), described as " a parson of Melford in Suffolk," but whose name does not appear among the officiating clergy of this place, and who certainly was never a rector of Melford, was included by name specially among the roll of those certified in the Exchequer Rolls to be proscribed fugitives over the seas, who were implicated in Babington's conspiracy in 1586. For with many others in the list, including Charnock and Jones, who were more actively engaged, and were afterwards executed, appears the name of

"Anthonie Wilkenson, parson of Melford, in Suffolke," as a political
refugee in foreign lands.

Soon after Sir William Cordell had acquired his manor of Melford,
he determined to build a new mansion. Probably the old Hall was
small and inconvenient, and perhaps dilapidated, and an era had just
arrived in which the taste for building fine manor-houses was a
marked feature of the age. Sir William Cordell had become a rich
man, and had then a family of children, for whom to found a great
house. His posterity never, however, inherited it, for his two sons
and two daughters all died young. He seems to have stinted nothing
in endeavouring to erect for himself a noble building on the site of the
abbot's old house. Many alterations have since been made to it, some,
alas! with very questionable taste. In the last century the stone
mullions were removed from the windows, and their openings in many
parts reduced or changed, to produce a general uniformity, destructive
of the original character of the building, one of the great beauties of
which, as in all Elizabethan houses, was its great variety of detail.
The main change in internal arrangement which has been made is in
part of the western front, for where the first floor west bedrooms now
are, was originally a long wide open gallery; the principal bedrooms
being then but few in number. The great staircase has been much
enlarged, and its original character lost, and the house has internally,
at various times, notably in 1813, been greatly modernized. In the
walls of the Cordell room are pictures of members of the two branches
of the family, evidently put in for the purpose of connecting the succeeding family of Cordell with the original possessors. They are all
inscribed, and represent:—

1. "Robert Cordell, Esquire, of London, merchant, son of William
Cordell, of Edmonton, in the county of Middlesex, whose son John
settled at Melford, and was father to Sir William Cordell." A three-
quarters length on panel, of an old man, with a ship in the corner.

2. "Sir Thomas Cordell, of London, merchant, son of the above-
mentioned Robert." A three-quarters portrait on panel of an elderly
man, with peaked beard, ruff and furred gown. In one hand he holds
richly-fringed gloves; and on a table is a skull. In a corner are the
Cordell arms and crest.

3. "Sir John Cordell, citizen and merchant, son of the above Sir
Thomas and father of Sir Robert Cordell, who redeemed the Melford
estate out of the 'Savage' family." A fine three-quarter portrait on
canvas, with a ruff and a red furred gown. He holds a letter. On a
table is a packet, and a ship under sail in a corner.

4. "Sarah, wife of Sir John, and daughter of Robert Bunckworth,
of London, merchant." This lady's dress is very elaborate, in black
and red stripes, and a splendid ruff. Round her shoulders is a chain
four times folded, pearls round her waist, and a ring sewed on to her

2 T

beautiful lace stomacher. A very fine three-quarter length portrait on canvas.

5. "Sir William Cordell, Knight, Knight of the Shire for the county of Suffolk, Speaker of the House of Commons, 4 & 5 Philip and Mary, 1557, and Master of the Rolls to the said Queen and Queen Elizabeth." He has red hair, and a red peaked beard, a rich ruff, and a black dress, slashed with red. A three-quarter length on panel.

6. "Mary, wife of the said Sir William, daughter and sole heir of Richard Clopton, Esq., third son of Sir William Clopton, by Margaret his wife, third daughter and one of the heirs of Sir Richard Bozem,* Knight." A three-quarter portrait on panel, of a dark, rather sad-looking lady, in a black dress, with a ruff and a laced cap, and holding in her hand a richly-bound book. She wears a gold ring on her thumb.

Near this room there is a curious hiding-place in the thickness of the walls and chimney, approached only through a trap panel. The cellars and basement are of great extent, and a portion of them probably formed part of the older house.

Externally, the appearance has been much altered by modernizing and changing the size of the windows, and removing some bay windows during the last century. In its original state, the house had one very peculiar feature. Between the two eastern towers, on each side of the entrance-court, high up, about level with the parapet of the roof, there was a suspended bridge, from which spectators could see the hunting and hawking, and other sports over the park, then far larger than at present. The doorways in the towers from which it was entered at each end, though now built up, are still plainly visible, and they were approached from the ground-level by the old style of winding-stairs in the towers, composed of blocks of oak round a central newel; one of which staircases complete, and others in part, still remain unaltered. When this swinging bridge was removed is not known; but it was certainly in existence in 1619. Until last century the entrance-approach to the house was very different from the present. The moat, then filled with water, continued round on the north side, but was covered over along the eastern side in front of the Hall, about 45 yards in advance of the entrance-court. There was a gateway with a bridge over the north moat. Directly opposite the front door were three separate walled-in courts: the first was entered through an open archway; the second had a gatehouse with an archway to drive through to the inner court. The gatehouse had two small turrets, corresponding in form with those of the Hall. The old stone-paved floor of this gateway still exists entire under the ground, in front of the sundial, which was moved from elsewhere to its present position. The inner

* Sir Richard Bozem died 18th August, 1525.

entrance-court, or quadrangle, was raised above the ground adjoining, and had steps up into it, where carriages then stopped, and persons went on foot from thence to the front door, along a broad centre walk, with a grass-plot on each side. The space inclosed by walls, from the corner of the house to the archway into the present stable-yard, was cultivated, and was then called the Melon-garden. The gatehouse was taken down, the north moat dried, and the present eastern semi-circular moats were dug, in order to provide earth to raise that front to the level of the inner entrance-court, with other alterations, about the year 1730. The ponds, now in two, were formerly divided into three; for there was a causeway across the larger one, since removed, on which stood a fishing-house. The earth of this bank was also probably utilized in the levelling of the eastern front. Many small buildings of various character, such as dog-houses, fowl-houses, a hop-store, in a small hop-ground near the ponds, summer-houses, and others which stood about the gardens, and some buildings in the east front, were also taken down. The bowling-house remains as it was constructed, seemingly at the same date as the Hall, except that, like the latter, its windows have been modernized. It was, no doubt, at one time hand-some in its details: the stonework at its entrance is good; and the upper story of the interior was once richly ornamented; for the panel-work, now decaying, was all painted white and much gilded. The fine bowling-green attached to it appears to be unaltered. Outside the wall, by the side of the moat next the high road, there stood a row of elm-trees, which were cut down in the present century, as endangering the old wall. The park boundary (then pales) between the lodge and Claypits pond, stood back into the park some distance. A piece was taken in late in last century, and the fence straightened to its present line of wall, and the inclosed ground was planted with trees. Somewhat about the time of the various alterations, from 1730 to 1750, many of the clumps of trees in the park were planted, and the Hare Drift road was made for access to the Lodge Farm, then newly built, and laid out for cultivation.

On the outside of the Hall there still remain the square large-headed leaden down-pipes from the roof, all adorned with Sir William Cordell's crest of the cockatrice; and in the open fireplace of the entrance-hall there are two large and curious bell-metal andirons or fire-dogs, which apparently had belonged to the monasterial owners of the house, and from which Sir William Cordell had removed the original bases, replacing them with new ones, bearing cast on them his cockatrice crest, together with the date on each, of 1559, which is palpably not that of the original parts, which belong to a far earlier era, and are much more worn by time and cleaning than the added bases. It would be an interesting question for antiquaries, with a knowledge of early metal-work, to define what is the date of the upper original portions of these fire-dogs. They are obviously very ancient; and there is a peculiarity in the subjects with which they are embellished, which appears to refer somehow to Abbot Samson. Of the four compartments into which these dogs are each alike divided, the top one represents Samson slaying the lion, and under it is an inscription, now partly illegible; but the word "*Sammsunn*" remains, and under this word are the letters, each separate, "B. D. L. D.," and opposite, "*Leve Peter Sen* . . ."

In the second compartment are two subjects, separated by an oblong projecting boss, which has had something engraved upon it, but is now worn smooth. (There are two of these bosses on each dog.) These figures are David, and *Samson* again, carrying away the gates of Gaza; and over each of them is inscribed, "Davet," "*Samson.*" Next below is our Saviour on the cross, with a female figure on each side, over whom are the names of "Magdelen," "Marie." In the lower space are Adam and Eve, on each side of the tree, from which they are taking the fruit, and their names are over them, "Adam," "Eva." Now, the standard of the Abbey of St. Edmund, in the time of Abbot Samson, bore this very device of Adam and Eve.

It is represented pictorially in miniature as the standard of St. Edmund, in Lydgate the Monk's "Lives and Miracles of the Saints" in the Harleian Collection (2278). He speaks also of the banner thus:—

> Adam b' a serpent banysshed fro paradys,
> Eva also, because she was nat wys,
> Eet off an appyl off fleshly fals pleasance:
> Which thre figures, Edmund, by gret avys,
> Bar in his baner, for a remembrance.

Whether the two bosses on each dog, now worn smooth by age and cleaning, had borne either a mitre or Samson's seal of the Holy Lamb, is only conjectural; but the before-mentioned facts considered together appear to connect these very curious and massive bell-metal andirons or fire-dogs in some manner with Abbot Samson de Botington.

Among the painted glass in the Hall windows are several German coats of arms, with inscriptions from 1608 to 1742; a cloth-mark of A. W. A., dated 1551; a coat of arms of John Winthrop, formerly of Groton, the *first Governor of Massachusetts*, quartering Forth: motto: "Spes vincit thronum, 1630." Winthrop's arms were granted the 24th of June, 1591. The larger subjects are a curious kneeling figure of a man in a furred gown, before an altar or desk, which bears a coat of arms, apparently foreign; behind him stands a bishop robed, wearing his mitre, and bearing a crosier in one hand and holding a ring in the other: the date on this glass is 1551. Also a kneeling figure of a man in a flowered gown, evidently 15th century, with the legend "Sanct: Mark ora pro nobis." There are two fine large coats of arms, one of King Henry VII., with his name on a scroll. The supporters are white greyhounds, having collars of red and white roses; the badges are the red and white quartered rose, crowned; and the portcullis crowned. The other large coat is of his wife, Elizabeth of York, in which the arms are inclosed in a rose, party-coloured red and white, and surmounted by a beautiful large jewelled crown.

Although from various minor data an inference might be drawn that the new house was completed about 1559, there is no certain record of the progress of the building. Some few years, however, after its erection, Queen Elizabeth signified to Sir William Cordell her intention of honouring him with a visit at his new house during her progress through Suffolk and Norfolk. Melford being on the county border, Sir William, now Master of the Rolls, was the first gentleman who entertained her Majesty in Suffolk, and he appears to have given her a sumptuous reception, such as she always delighted in.

In the "Progresses and Public Processions of Queen Elizabeth," edited by John Nichols, there is contained "*Churchyards Discourse on the Queenes Majesties entertaynemente in Suffolke and Norfolke, imprinted at London by Henrie Bynneman, Servante to the Righte Honourable Sir Christopher Hatton, Chamberlayne.*" Churchyard appears not to have been with the royal suite at Melford, but to have joined it subsequently at Norwich. In the original plan of this progress it would seem that it was not intended that the Queen should visit any other place in Suffolk, except Melford, for Lord Burghley wrote thus to the Vice-Chancellor: "Thence [from Audley End] she intended to proceed in her progress to Suffolk, to the house of the Master of the Rolls; and if she went not further, which was not presently concluded upon, then she would *return* by Cambridge."

In August, 1578, Sir William Cordell, with a great retinue, met the Queen at the county border, and escorted her to Melford Hall. Churchyard's quaint account runs as follows :—

"To wright of the receiving of hir Highnesse into Suffolke and Norfolke in everie poynte as matter may move me, woulde conteyne a great time in making a just rehearsall therof: wherfore I will but briefely recite it and committe the circumstance and manner of the same to your dyscretion and judgemente. The trothe is, albeit they hadde but smal warneing certaynely to build upon, of the comming of the Quenes Majestie into both those sheeres, the Gentlemen had made suche ready provision, that all the velvets and silkes were taken up that mighte be layde hande on, and bowght for any money, and soone converted to suche garmentes and sutes of robes, that the show therof might have beautifyed the greatest tryumph that was in Englande these many yeres. As I hearde there were 200 young gentlemen cladde alle in whyte velwet, and 300 of the graver sorte apparrelled in blacke velwet coates and with faire chaines, alle redy at one instante and plaice, with 1500 servyng men all on horsebacke, well and bravelie mountyd, to receive the Queene's Highnesse into Suffolke: a comelie troope and a noble sighte to beholde. Alle thes waited on the Sherriffe, Sir William Spring, and there was in Suffolke suche sumptuous feastinges and bankets as seldome in anie parte of the worlde there hathe been seen afore. The Maister of the Rolles, Sir William Cordell, was the firste that beganne this greate feastinge at his house of Melforde, and did lyght suche a candle to the reste of the shire, that they were gladd bountifullie and francklie to followe the same example, with suche charges and costes as the whole traine were in some sorte pleased therewyth."

Pleasanter, doubtless, for the train of courtiers than for the several entertainers, to whom the great charges and costs of the Queen's visit were probably a heavy tax. On the 5th of August she proceeded on her way, dining at Lawshall Hall.

In a letter from Richard Topclyffe to the Earl of Shrewsbury, dated 30th August, 1578, there occurs the following passage relative to this progress :—

"I did never see her Majestie better receved by two counties in one jorney then Suffolke and Norfolke now: Suffolke of gentillmen, and Norfolke of the meaner sorte: with excedinge joye to themselves and well likinge to her Ma.ᵛ· Great interteignmente at the Mast of the Rowlls: greater at Killinghall, and exceedinge of all sorte at Norwiche."

The royal visit was the last event of importance in Sir William Cordell's life. Three years later he had done with all earthly ambition. Kind and upright gentleman, and honest and zealous public servant as he appears to have been, and distinguished as his name must ever remain in the annals of Melford, the history of his career cannot be closed without a few words of notice. He rose to fame and fortune by his own industry and talents, unaided by any accident of birth ; for in a deed of grant of a messuage of the 29th of Henry VIII., his father is described as "John Cordell of Long Melford, yoman" ; though in a subsequent grant of arms called gentleman.* Sir William's date of

---

* Sir William Cordell's father, John, is said to have married Emma Webbe. Now Sir William Clopton, Knight, of Kentwell, by his will, made 1530, left to *John Cordell, his servant, and Emma his wife*, a legacy of property and money. Sir William's son, John Clopton, in his will of 1541 left a legacy to his *godson*, John Cordell. A John Cordell was churchwarden of Melford with Roger Martyn in 1559, during the Marian return to Popery ; from which it may be inferred that he was a Papist, as were the

birth is uncertain; he was brought up to the bar, and in 1553 became Lent reader at Lincoln's Inn, of which house he was afterwards frequently governor, and in the same year was appointed Solicitor-General. On the 5th November, 1557, he was made Master of the Rolls and a Privy Councillor, with a grant of the privilege of twelve retainers. In 1557 he was also High Steward of Ipswich, with an annual allowance of £4, payable half-yearly. In 1558, being elected knight of the shire for Suffolk in the last Parliament of Queen Mary, Sir William was chosen Speaker of the House of Commons, and was knighted in the interval of the two sessions of which it consisted.

In the first session of this Parliament the Queen's wants and the state of the nation were discussed by a committee of both Houses, the Speaker, with ten other members, having been invited by the Lords for that purpose. This was not altogether the constitutional mode, but it does not appear that Sir William (great lawyer as we are told he was) objected to the proposal; for on the 4th of February a bill was read for the grant of a subsidy of two-fifteenths and tenths, "as agreed upon by the Lords and Commons in Committee," which occasioned some debate, and it appears that the Speaker was desired to see the Queen and ascertain whether a smaller amount would not satisfy her Majesty; for on the 10th of the month Sir William Cordell acquainted the House "that he had opened to the Queen's Majesty his commission touching the grant of the subsidy, which the Queen thankfully took, giving those present hearty thanks, and all the realm." The Speaker had acquitted himself well, for it seems he induced the Queen to accept a subsidy of one fifteenth, which was all that was granted that session. The next session of this Parliament was remarkable for an Act which was intended to put the first restraint upon the liberty of the press, but the further proceeding of the bill, which had come down from the Lords, was stopped by the death of the Queen.

In 156⅔ he was a commissioner sent to Scotland with Sir William Cecil (the great Lord Burghley) and Dr. Wotton, and concluded the treaty of peace called the Treaty of Leith. In Stow (p. 644) is recorded, "the 18th June, Sir Willm Cecill, principall Secretary to the Queene's Maiestie, with Sir William Cordall, and Dr. Wotton, deane of Canterbury and Yorke, came to Barwike: being appointed Commissioners on her

---

Cloptons. And a person of this same name, John Cordell, was buried at Melford 7th January, 1564.

In the Visitation of London of 1568, a John Cordell is named in the Cordell pedigree, as of Enfield, and his son, William Cordell, is therein described as of Fulham, master cook to Queen Elizabeth. This probably refers to another branch of the family, for among the accounts of the queen's new year's gifts presented to her, and given by her in return, there occurs a notice that "William Cordall, maister cooke, gave to the Queene in 1⅖ one Marchpane"; and he received from her at the same time, "in guilte plate, 7 ounces—di—& di—gr." This was several years after Sir William Cordell's death, for he died 1581.

said Maiestie's behalfe to treate of an accord with the Count de Randon and the Bishop of Valence, Commissioners sent for that purpose from the French Kinge and his wife Mary, Q⁰ of Scots. The 16th of June the forenamed Commissioners came to Edenborough, and as Master Secretary and the others passed the English forts and campe, they were saluted with a gallant peale of harquebusiers."

In 1571 Camden records Sir William Cordell as member for Westminster.

In 1578, as already related, he entertained Queen Elizabeth at Melford Hall. Himself a scholar, he was a patron of learned men, and he is supposed to have drawn up the statutes of St. John's College, Oxford, by the desire of the founder, Sir Thomas Whyte, who appointed him visitor thereof, and where his portrait by Cornelius de Zeem still exists.

Through his aid, the first complete English county maps, by Christopher Saxton, were published in the reign of Queen Elizabeth. William Lambarde dedicated to him his "Archaionomia," or system of Saxon laws, in 1568. Abraham Fleming also dedicated to him his translation of the "General Doctrine of Earthquakes." The book called "The Queene Marie's Panoplie of Epistles, or a looking glasse for the unlearned," and the reprint by R. Newberie, in 1576, of "The supplication at the coming of Kinge Philippe into England," likewise bear dedications to "Syr Wᵐ Cordell, Knt., Maister of the Queenes Maiesties Rolles." He was one of the executors of the will of Cardinal Pole, with a bequest of £50; also an executor of the Earl of Dorset; and the Countess of Bath bequeathed to him a ring of the value of five marcs (£3. 6s. 8d.).

In the accounts of the "Oblata Rolls," of the new year's gifts, which it was the fashion of those days to give to the sovereign, who generally gave some present in return, Sir William Cordell's name appears several times. The first entry is in the reign of Queen Mary, before the great lawyer became Master of the Rolls. The gift of Maister Cordall, solicitor, in 155⅞, is described as "*two Poringers worth £7.*" And he received from Queen Mary, in return, "*a guilt cup with cover, weighing 18 ounces and three quarters.*"

In 156¼, "*Newe years gyfts to the Quene by Sʳ W. Cordall, Masʳ of the Rolles, in a whyte satten purse, in Angells,* £10.

"*Dᵒ by the Quene to him, oone guilt Tankered, 21 ounces.*"

In 157¼ it does not mention that he gave any present, but he received from the Queen; "*To Sir William Cordell, Knight, Maister of the Rolls, in guilt plate; 'Brandon,' per oz; 20 oz: 3 qʳˢ di.*" Brandon, here named, appears to have been a court goldsmith, for there are entries in the Queen's accounts, "Item, Bought of Robert Brandon and Hugh Reall, our Goldesmithes, &c."

The last entry is of 157⅜: "*To the Queenes Maiestie at her Highnes* manor of Richmond, by Sir William Cordell, Master of the Rolles, in Golde, £:10." "Given by the Queene to Sir William Cordell, M: of R: a guilt pot: 'Reall:' per oz: 20 oz."

Sir William Cordell married Mary, daughter of Richard Clopton, Esq., of Fore Hall (now Ford Hall farm), Melford, and of Castlyns, in Groton. Her picture is in the Cordell room at Melford Hall, a handsome, dark-haired lady, with a somewhat sad face; perhaps to be accounted for, when it is borne in mind that her two sons and two daughters all died as children, and that she and her husband, at the zenith of their fortunes, were left childless. The eldest son was buried at Melford 12th February, 1567.[*] She outlived her husband three years, and was buried by him and her lost children, 18th March, 1584. By her will she bequeathed "to the making and setting up of the bridge near Melford, called Rodbridge, 40 shillings." The reason for this bequest appears to have been that the parish of Melford had been put to considerable recent expense concerning the bridge; for they had disputed their right to repair, and a short time before the date of Lady Cordell's will, the parish officers had been proceeded against by indictment at the Assizes at Bury in 1579, and had been defeated.

Sir William Cordell was buried at Melford in the chancel of the church, on the 19th June, 1581. His monument has been already described in the history of the church. His portrait, in the Cordell room at Melford Hall, represents him with a somewhat plebeian countenance, but with a shrewd, thoughtful expression of face. He wears a fine ruff, and is dressed in black satin, slashed with red. He has bright red hair, moustache, and beard. (There is another curious portrait of him by Cornelius de Zeem, at St. John's College, Oxford.)

By his will he largely endowed with lands and tithes the Hospital of the Holy Trinity, which he had shortly before his death erected on Melford Green for the support of 12 poor brethren, a warden, and two sisters. As to the rest of his estates, he gave a life interest to his wife, then to his sister Jane, widow of Richard Allington, Esq., for her life, and then entailed them on his brothers Francis and Edward, and their heirs, with remainder to the heirs of his said sister, Jane Allington, and in default, eventually to his cousin, Thomas Cordell, of London, son of Robert Cordell, "beer brewer," deceased, and his heirs. (The portraits of both these last-named are in the Cordell room at Melford Hall.) Francis died, s.p., 1586, before he had livery of the estate, as also Edward in 1594: he was one of the Six Clerks in the ancient Six Clerks' Office. Jane Allington died 4th January, 1602, leaving two daughters, co-heiresses,—Mary, wife of Sir John Savage, Knight, of

---

[*] In this year Sir William Cordell sold his property of Smeeton Hall, near Bulmer, Essex, to Mr. Richard Martyn, of Long Melford.

Clifton, Cheshire, and Cordelia, wife of Sir John Stanhope, Knight, and mother of Philip, first Earl of Chesterfield.

Melford Hall passed to Sir John Savage in right of his wife Mary.

In the year 1613 King James I. granted, by letters patent, to their son, Sir Thomas Savage, and his wife Elizabeth (eldest daughter of the third Lord Darcy, to whom he was married in 1602), 340 acres of park and warren around Melford Hall, with the deer therein, and full rights of chase and warren. This patent is at Melford Hall. As the land in question already formed part of the estate, the object of this patent was apparently to constitute part of the new park as a regular deer-park, in lieu of the old park of Elmsethe (now Old Park farm), which had been recently disparked. As shown by the Manor map of 1613, this new park comprised not only the present park, but also all the Lodge farm, and the fields now called Great Ley, Oxley, Barn Pasture, and Ley Meadow, on High Street farm; the southern and eastern boundaries being the stream; and it must then have been nearly 500 acres in extent. It included a wood, since stubbed up, and now called Great and Little Coppice fields, on the Lodge farm. Part of this park was broken up, converted to tillage, and fields inclosed, and the Lodge farm made early in last century, taking its name from the old keeper's lodge, which stood there; when also seven or eight small plots of land, belonging to various owners, and which ran into the park on the western side, were bought and added to it, and the present Hare-drift road was made for access to the new farm. The remainder of the park was then inclosed as a deer-park, of the size which it now remains; though there are no longer deer in it, the herd having been sold some years since by the late Sir Hyde Parker.

Sir Thomas Savage was created Viscount Savage, of Rocksavage, 6th November, 1626, taking his title from his noble mansion and estate of Rocksavage, at Hurley, in Broxton hundred of the Vale Royal of Cheshire. This stately fabric had been built by Sir Thomas's grand-father. In 1617, Sir Thomas Savage entertained James I. there, and the King, after his repast, killed a buck in the neighbouring Halton Park.[*]

We learn from Howell's published Correspondence, that William Noye was, in his time, steward of Sir Thomas's manor of Melford. At what period he commenced to serve in this capacity does not appear; but he first comes on to the scene at Melford, acting as arbitrator between the owner of Kentwell Hall and the rector of this parish, in a dispute as to some Kentwell tithes, on the 1st of June, 1614.

He must have continued as the steward of this manor till some years subsequent to Howell's visit in 1619, for his signature is attached

---

[*] See King's " History of the Vale Royal of the County Palatine of Chester," published in 1656.

to several of the manor documents (now at Melford Hall), one of which, signed *Wyllᵐ Noye*, is dated 1622.

Noye greatly owed his after-advancement in life to his patron, Lord Savage, and became a person of historical celebrity as a profound lawyer, who, however, made an evil use of his great talents; and also as an author of many learned works. He was made Attorney-General in 1631, and was foremost among those unwise counsellors who first suggested to King Charles I. the imposition of the obnoxious and illegal ship-money tax, which in a great measure hastened the outbreak of the rebellion.

Worn out with drudgery and fatigue, Noye died at Tunbridge Wells, in August, 1634, at the age of 57, and was buried at New Brentford. History records that he was hated by the public, and not even regretted by any of those of his own party; except perhaps by those supporters of false advisers, the King and Archbishop Laud. In Somers's Tracts, reign of Charles I., page 273, there is a curious supposed dialogue between Lord Strafford, Charon, and Noye, in Hades.

James Howell, who, in his quaint letters recorded Noye's office here, among many other matters connected with Melford, and who subsequently became one of the clerks of the Privy Council, was, when a young man, engaged by Lord Savage to travel abroad in charge of his two sons. Howell accordingly joined the family party at Melford, but the proposed arrangement shortly afterwards came to an end, Howell apparently having some scruples about taking charge of young people who were Roman Catholics. Though Lady Savage and the children were of this religion, it seems that Lord Savage did not profess the same; and he had at that time a resident domestic chaplain, who was a Protestant, the office being held by the Rev. John Kidby, who afterwards became Rector of Shenfield, in Essex.

Though Howell did not go on the continental tour, he remained for some time domesticated at Melford Hall; and while there he wrote the following interesting description of this house and grounds, addressed to his friend, Mr. Daniel Caldwell, of Sheriff, in Essex:—

"May 20, 1619.

"To Dan. Caldwell, Esq., from the Lord Savage's house in Long Melford.

"My dear Dan,—

"Though considering my former condition in life I may now be called a countryman, yet you cannot call me a rustic (as you imply in your letter) so long as I live in so civill and noble a family, so long as I lodge in so vertuous and regular a house as any I beleeve in the

2 u 2

land, both for œconomical government and for choice company: for I never saw yet such a dainty race of children in all my life together: I never saw yet such an orderly and punctuall attendance of servants, nor a great house so neatly kept. Here one shall see nor dog nor cat, nor cage, to cause any nastines within the body of the house. The kitchin and gutters and other offices of noise and drudgery are at the fag end:—There is a back gate for the beggars and meaner sort of swains to come in at. The stables butt upon the Park, which for a chearfull rising ground, for groves and browsing ground for the deer, and for rivulets of water may compare with any for its bigness, in the whole land. It is opposite to the front of the great house, whence from the gallery* one may see much of the game when they are a hunting. Now, for the gardening and costly choice flowers, for ponds, for stately large walks, green and gravelly, for orchards, and choice fruits of all sorts, there are few the like in England. There you have your Bon Christien Pear and Bergamott in perfection—your Muscadell grapes in such plentie that there are some bottles of wine sent every year to the king; and one Mr. Daniell, a worthy gentleman hard by,† who hath ben long abroad, makes good store in his vintage. Truly this house of Long Melford, tho' it be not so great, yet it is so well compacted and contrived with such dainty conveniences every way, that if you saw the landskip of it, you would be mightily taken with it, and it would serve for a choice pattern to build and contrive a house by. If you come this summer to your Mannor of Sheriff in Essex, you will not be far off hence, and if your occasions will permit, it will be worth your coming hither.

" Yours,　　　　" JAMES HOWELL."

A few years later the handsome, well-ordered Hall, with its deer-stocked park, as described by Howell, the pretty green, and the quiet village, wore a very different aspect. The early and better Puritan feeling, which had been steadily growing and taking deep root since the days of Elizabeth, and which in its first great struggle for freedom of conscience had in the year following the date of Howell's letter, driven the brave little band of pilgrim fathers in the ship *Mayflower*, across the broad Atlantic, became hardened in its onward progress into a system of narrow-minded and egotistical intolerance, which, on the breaking out of the great Rebellion, bore the evil and bitter fruit of fanatical fury and bigoted persecution; resulting often in such outrages on churches, religious symbols, property and persons, as

---

* The bridge suspended between the towers of the entrance-court; since taken down.
† Of Acton. His family also held property at Bulmer. His arms were, Argent, four fusils in pale, sable.

those which the schismatic mob of over 3,000 of the scum of Colchester and other neighbouring towns perpetrated at Melford.

The chief sufferer here was Elizabeth Viscountess Savage, who became a widow 16th December, 1635, and who, after the death of her father, Earl Rivers, in 1639, was created Countess Rivers for life, by patent of the 21st April, 1641. This lady was possessed of great property: the Rocksavage estates in the Vale Royal of Cheshire, the priory and manor of St. Osyth, Lady Lumley's property around there, Hengrave Hall, and Melford Hall estate. She was, like her father, a stanch Roman Catholic, and at the outbreak of the rebellion supported the Royalists with arms and money, thus becoming even yet more obnoxious to the party of the Parliament than she would have been by her religion alone. The countess, in consequence, suffered very severely by the civil war, and her losses on her various estates perhaps exceeded those of any other person, not excepting even Lord Arundel of Wardour; and her son John, Earl Rivers, was excepted by name out of the indemnity which the Parliament offered in Lord Essex's manifesto. The first step taken against her was the seizure of arms and equipment at Hengrave Hall, under an order of the House of Commons.

In August, 1642, a mob of 2,000 Essex schismatics, composed of the scum of Coggeshall, Bocking, Braintree, Halsted, and Colchester, headed by Captain John Langley, of the Colchester trainband, a grocer of that town, and Henry Barrington, a brewer and alderman of the same, sacked the house of Sir John Lucas, near Colchester, completely wrecked it, tortured his servants, and even broke open his family vault and violated the coffins of his ancestors. Their next plundering expedition was to the Countess of Rivers's house at St. Osyth, a rich prize. There they entered the house, pulled down, cut in pieces, and carried away the costly hangings, beds, couches, chairs, and the whole furniture of her house, and robbed her of her plate and moneys. They tore down the wainscoting, broke the windows, stripped off the lead from the house, and did not leave a door, or so much as the bar of a window, behind them. The countess and her family, forewarned of the intention of the mob, escaped from St. Osyth, and retired to Melford Hall. The fate which had befallen her other goodly mansion was but the prelude of what was to happen here.[*] In a day or two the Essex mob pursued her to Melford, reinforced by further rabble on the way, till it numbered several thousands. The countess, just warned in time, barely escaped with her life, for the ringleaders swore that if they found her they would try what flesh she had; abandoning the Hall,

_____

[*] These accounts are taken from Lord Clarendon's "History of the Rebellion," "The History of Hengrave," "Anglica Ruina," the "Mercurius Rusticus" of 1685, and Peck's "Desiderata Curiosa."

which in a few hours was completely disfurnished of all the rich goods and furniture, which had been for many years with great curiosity collected. The whole house was, like St. Osyth, completely rifled, wrecked, and gutted, and the new deer-park, which Lord Savage had made, was utterly despoiled of all therein. The countess fled to Bury St. Edmund's; but there the Roundheads shut the gates against her; but at length she was suffered to lodge there that night, and next day, with a strong guard, she was conveyed out of the town, and making her way as privately as she could, she escaped to London. Her losses at both her houses were valued at a hundred thousand pounds at least, though some that knew the rich furniture that adorned both, affirmed it to be no less than a hundred and fifty thousand pounds. One of the plunderers of Melford Hall, whose name was Bowyer, was apprehended in London in the very act of selling some of these goods, and was committed to Newgate for the felony; two of the countess's servants entering into recognizance to give evidence against him; but on his petition to the House of Commons, he was ordered to be discharged without paying any fees, and public thanks were given to him for his zeal in the cause, and his prosecutors were fortunate in not being imprisoned in his place. One of these was probably Mr. Bare, the steward of Melford Hall.*

In the "Desiderata Curiosa" is an account given by Mr. Wilson, the historian, then agent for the Earl of Warwick, in connection with the plundering of Melford Hall. He says:—

"The 20th August, 1642, the king having left the Parliament and thereby a loose reine having been put into the mouth of the unruly multitude, many thousands swarmed to the pulling down [i.e. pillage] of Long Melford House, a gallant seat belonging to the Countess of Rivers, and to the endangeringe of her person: she being a recusant, they made that their pretence; but spoile and plunder was their aim. This fury was not only in the rabble but in many of the better sort, so that no man could remaine in his house without fear, nor be abroad with safety.

"A gentleman came posting from the Countess of Rivers to crave the protection of my Lord Warwick, who was then at sea, being Lord High Admiral for the Parliament. Soe I was commanded to take some few men and a coach with six horses to fetch Lady Rivers to

---

* The names of several stewards of Melford Hall are stated in olden documents. The last two in the Abbot's time were Swayne and Antony. In 1570, "Harry at the Hall" was steward, and was succeeded by Mr. Thrower, who filled the office while the estate was in the hands of Lady Cordell, Sir William's widow; then Mr. John Cary; then the above-named Mr. Bare was steward to Lady Rivers till after 1647, and was succeeded by Mr. Hobart, who was also a churchwarden in the year 1662; 1671, Thomas Page; and between 1680 and 1690, George Wymarke.

Leeze;* which I hastened to do, not dreaming of any danger by the way, though I might haply meet some there.

"With difficulty I passed through the little villages of Essex; and but they had some knowledge of me and the coach, I had not passed with safety. My design and pretence was to go for Bury; but to stay in some place near Long Melford, to find out where the Lady Rivers was.

"When I came to Sudbury in Suffolk, within three miles of Long Melford, not a man appeared till we were within the chain,—and then they began to run to their weapons, and before we could get to the Market-place, the streets swarmed with people.

"I came out of the coach as soon as they took the horses by the heads, and desired that I might speak with the mayor, or some of the magistrates, to know the cause of this tumult, for we had offended nobody. The people cried out, This coach belongs to the Lady Rivers, and they are going to her. Indeed the gentleman who came along with me was known to some in the town. Some who pretended to be more wise and knowing than the rest, said that I was the Lord Rivers; and they swarmed about me, and were so kind as to lay holde upon me. But I calmly entreated those many hundreds who encircled me, to hear me speak, which before they had not patience to do, the confusion and noise was so great.

"I told them I was steward to the Earl of Warwick,† now in the Parliament's employment; that I was going to Bury about business of his; and that I had letters in my pocket, if they would let any of the magistrates see them.

"At last the mayor came crowding in with his officers, and I showed him my letters (which, indeed, I had received a little before from my lord, and, fearing the worst, I had thought the bringing of them might be an advantage to my passage). The Mayor's wisdom said he knew not my lord's hand: it might be, and it might not; and away he went, not knowing what to do with me, nor I to say to them.

---

* Leeze or Leese, or, as now spelt, Leigh's Priory, was seven miles north from Chelmsford and four from Braintree. It was a noble seat, built by the Lord Chancellor Rich, soon after the dissolution of the religious houses. In the last century it became the property of Guy's Hospital, and the Governors of that institution pulled down the old mansion and turned the greater part of the park into tillage, and nothing now remains of the fine old building except the massive and handsome gatehouse.

† This Earl of Warwick was the son of that Baron Rich who, in 1619, was created Earl of Warwick. In the receipt-books of the Exchequer there remains the entry that he paid £8,000 for his title. Rich was addicted to piracy, and in 1616 he fitted out two pirate ships, which returned laden with Spanish treasure at a time when we were at peace with Spain. His son, the Lord High Admiral of the Commonwealth, who is here mentioned, followed his example; for in 1618, in conjunction with a Genoese merchant of London, he privately sent two piratical vessels to the East Indies, which attacked a rich junk belonging to our Indian allies, but failed in capturing it, owing to ships of the East-India Company coming just in time to the rescue.

But I found they had an itching desire after the coach horses (the town being to set out horses for the Parliament service) and therefore they were the willinger to believe nothing till Mr. Man, the town clerk (whose father was my lord's servant), saw me at a distance, and came crowding in to be assured, having once seen me, as he said, at Leeze. He told the mayor and the people I was the Earl of Warwick's steward, and his assurance got some credit with them, and so the great cloud vanished.

"But I could get no further to succour the Lady Rivers. For I heard from all hands that there was so great a confusion at Melford, that no man who appeared like a gentleman but was made a prey to that ravenous crew.

"So my lady's gentleman, Mr. Man, and myself, took horse, leaving the coach at Sudbury, and went a bye-way to Sir Robert Crane's [Chilton], a little nearer Melford, to listen after the Countess.

"Sir Robert told us that she had in her own person escaped to Bury, and so was gone to London. But he was forced to retain a trainband in his house, though he was a Parliament man, to secure himself from the fury of that rabble, who threatened him for being assistant to her escape.

"My business being done, my lady's gentleman went towards London; I back to the coach, and returned home!"

With the sack and plunder of Melford Hall, the poor Countess of Rivers's troubles were not yet ended. Having lost an enormous amount by the pillage of her houses, and believing her life to be still in danger, she obtained a pass to go beyond seas; but while she was preparing for her voyage, Mr. Martin, who was called the Roundhead Plunder-Master-General, seized her carriage-horses, in spite of a protection warrant granted by the House of Lords; and though the Countess obtained from the Earl of Essex another warrant for their restoration, Mr. Martin, to overbear all, procured an order from the House of Commons to keep them; and these, besides all her other goods which had been licensed to pass by the Lords, and had been allowed by the Custom House, were, after all, seized, and she never recovered any of them.

Plundered as Lady Rivers had been on all sides, she had yet escaped hitherto some of the legal forfeitures attaching to recusancy. Her case is mentioned in some papers in the British Museum relating to sequestrated estates in Essex, as follows:—

"She is a Papist, and two parts of her estate by the ordinance ought to be sequestered. But she, pretending that, being indebted unto several persons in the sum of £1,600, about three years since, for payment of that debt, assigned over all her lands in Essex unto the Lord Lumley and Isaac Oreme, gent., for divers years, reserving only £800 per annum for maintenance. Upon these pretences she had gotten an order from the Committee of Lords and Commons to discharge her estate in land, and all wood-sales from sequestration."

But the order did not avail her long, for in spite of all her calamities, the commissioners for sequestrating the estates of Roman Catholics finally obliged her to compound for her lands at £16,979. 9s. 10d. Her affairs then became irretrievably embarrassed, and she sold a large part of her Essex estates; and though still the nominal owner of great possessions, so impoverished had she become, that in the early part of 1650 she was arrested for debt, and though pleading her privilege as a peeress, she was imprisoned. The misfortunes of the old countess were now, however, drawing to a close, for she died on the 9th of March, 1650.

Her son John, Earl Rivers, was also shortly before his death a prisoner for debt in the Upper Bench prison in Southwark. He died in 1654.

In consequence of all these family troubles, the Melford Hall estates, which had been previously mortgaged to Sir John Cordell, Knight, a merchant of London, were obliged to be sold. By a deed of sale of the 12th May, 1649, between John, Earl Rivers, and Elizabeth, Countess Rivers, his mother, and Mr. Robert Cordell, the then mortgagee, who was created a baronet in 1660, it appeared that the Rivers's owed him £20,488. 12s.; and for this sum and an additional amount of £8,511. 8s. paid by Robert Cordell to them, they conveyed to him the estate, with all appurtenant rights, and the advowson of Melford Church, and the right of the nomination of the warden and brethren of the Hospital of the Holy Trinity. In addition to this purchase-money of £29,000, there was an annuity charged on the estate to a "Mary Savage" of £100 a year. This continued to be paid to midsummer, 1690.

Another deed to the same effect, and also one of the original mortgage-deeds, were afterwards lost in the great fire of London in 1666. This said mortgage-deed was dated 27th November, 1641, between John, Earl Rivers; Richard, Viscount Lumley; Thomas, Lord Brudenell; Gilbert Gerard, and others; and John Cordell, alderman of London, and Robert Cordell, and comprised Melford Hall, the park, manor, and all the various lands and the advowson of the church, &c., for the sum of £15,000.

Sir Robert Cordell's grandson, Sir John, was killed by a fall from his horse, when the male line and the baronetcy became extinct.

Some of the wills of members of this family are quaint, and may be briefly noticed here as carrying out the family history.

The will of Sir Robert Cordell, of Melford, the first baronet (created in 1660), is dated 18th December, 1679. He left to his eldest son and

2 x

heir, John, half of all his household stuff, plate excepted; all the deer in Melford Park, and the *great sapphire jewel.* To his grandson John (who was the last baronet of his race), son of the above John, his great silver basin and ewer. To his wife, Dame Margaret, half of his household stuff: all other plate and jewels to be divided afterwards between his younger children. To his sons Edmund, Charles, and Chester, certain sums owing to him, and a house in Moorfields, London. To his second son, Robert, certain property in Yorkshire. And he desired to be buried privately in St. Lawrence's Church, London.

Sir Robert's third daughter, Margaret, married John Barnardiston, Esq. Her marriage portion was £2,000.

The will of Sir John Cordell, the second baronet, is dated 26th August, 1690, immediately before his death, for he was buried a fortnight afterwards in Melford chancel, 9th September, 1690. He appointed Dame Elizabeth, his wife, sole executrix, provided for her, and bequeathed to his two daughters, Elizabeth and Margaret (who eventually became, after the death of their brother, co-heiresses of the estate), £1,600 each; and until paid, £50 a year each for their maintenance. To his only son John Cordell his estates, and all his household stuff, tables, stools, forms, carpets, hangings, linen, woollen, pewter, brass, plate and jewels, in or belonging to Melford Hall, save and except only that his wife, Dame Elizabeth (she was a Waldegrave), was to have all the jewels she brought upon her marriage, one bed, and all belonging thereto, and one suit of damask linen, a coach and coach-horses; and to continue to live at Melford Hall till their son was of age or married. He gave to his old servant George Mimarde (or Wymarke), and his heirs, two small cottages in Bull Lane, Melford, upon the side of the inn called "the Bull"; and £5 a year for his life. To Mary French, his wife's maid, £5 to buy mourning.

Lady Cordell's accounts as executrix exist at Melford Hall, and form a parchment roll nine feet long. A few details from them may be amusing. Sir John appears to have been somewhat hampered for money, for, besides owing to many persons, for cash lent to him, £1,767, his debts show various arrears of wages due to his servants, nineteen in number being inserted by name, some of whom had for many years only been paid small sums on account; such as William Cooper, his butler, to whom was due 6¾ years' wages at £12 a year, and 12s. a year for washing; to Thomas Baker, the cook, nine years' wages, at £6 a year; to Mary French, Lady Cordell's maid, 9½ years' wages, at £6 a year. Among tradesmen there was owing to grocers, £212. 18s. 7d.; mercers, £43. 14s. 10d.; tailors (among whom was one of the Dansies of Lavenham, long established there as clothiers), £81. 9s. 10d.; physician, £7. 5s. 11d.; apothecary, £28. 6s.; for a peruke, £2. 16s., and for another one, £1. 5s. The ladies seem to have dealt with a good many milliners, whose bills amounted to £118. 11s. 8d. Among them is noticeable the name of Mrs. Elizabeth Bisbie, of Melford, *for milliners' wares.* She was the wife of Dr. Bisbie, who had been deprived of the living for refusing the oath of allegiance to William III. The wine appears to have circulated freely at the Hall, for there was owing to various vintners £585. 7s. 3d. Among these vintners or wine-merchants are the names of two of the Dansies of Lavenham; and to Francis Drew, of the Bull Inn, Melford, was owing for wine, £90. 9s. 2d. There is one sporting item : to making a setting spaniel by Ralph Adams, £3. 4s. 6d. Under the head of education of the family, there appears due to Mr. Jonathan Moor, writing-master (he was the master of Melford free school), £1. 2s.; and to Mr. Estland, a dancing-master, *for teaching the children to daunce,* £2. 8s. Sir John's funeral and mourning cost the large amount of £225. 11s. 9d. : he was buried in Melford Church. The adjoining county has always been noted for its breed of *Essex calves,* but it would seem that it was equally famous at that time for its *donkeys,* for there is a debt due of the large sum to Esquire Pett, of Sampford, for an ass, £7. A debt of money borrowed is recorded as due by Sir John *to the Governor and Brethren of the Hospital of the Holy and Undivided Trinity in Melford, secured by a Jewel left there in pledge,* £100.

The total sum of Sir John's debts amounted to £8,433. 11s. 6d., and it must be remembered that this represented a far larger amount of the present value.

The will of Mr. Thomas Cordell, merchant, of London, is dated 30th December, 1674. He was third son of the first baronet, was born at Melford and baptized there, 2nd of December, 1650; he made his will before leaving England, as "being designed to go beyond seas." He died at Zante in 1686, aged thirty-six; appoints his mother, the Lady Margaret Cordell (widow), and Mr. Hugh Norden, citizen of London, his executors. He leaves to his mother £20 a year for life; to each of his brothers, Robert, Charles, and Edmund, £250; to his youngest brother, Mr. Chester Cordell, he leaves twelve tenements in Milk Street, Lad Lane, and Cateaton Street, London, valued at £1,700. To his sister, Margaret Cordell, who married John Barnardiston, Esq., £250. To his brother-in-law, Sir William Spring, and his wife, £10 each for mourning, and to their two sons £50 each; and legacies for mourning to his eldest brother, Sir John, and his wife, and others. To the poor of Melford, £10.

Then he proceeds to give an account of where his goods will be found. Apparently his business was in the mercery line. Goods in Leghorn, value £550. In Zante, 850 pair of silk stockings sold; cost £340; profit made thereon, £210; total, £550. In Venice,

goods that cost £200. Ditto, 206 pairs of silk stockings, cost £100;
estimated profit to be made on these goods, £200.

Among his debts, which were to be paid, was one to Mr. Nicholas
Dansie, of Lavenham, of £12. Concerning whom has been already
mentioned the curious fact, that a copper tradesman's token of his,
with the inscription " Nicholas Dansie, woolcomber, of Lavenham,"
coined in 1667, in perfect preservation, was found under the floor of
the old Melford Hall pews in 1858.

Thomas Cordell's will was proved in London, 20th September,
1686.

Will of Mr. Chester Cordell, merchant of Zante, youngest son of
the first baronet. He was born at Melford, 1662; baptized there
8th June, 1662; made his will 26th February, 168⅘, and died unmarried at Zante, 1691, aged twenty-nine. He desires to be buried at
St. John's, the English burial-place of Zante, near his brother Thomas's
tomb (who died there 1686). He gives his property in London, which
was bequeathed to him by his brother Thomas, to his eldest brother,
Sir John Cordell, Bart., and 1,000 dollars between Sir John's two
daughters, Elizabeth and Margaret; 500 dollars between the three
children of his brother-in-law, Sir William Spring, deceased; 50 dollars
for the repair of the English burial-place of St. John's, Zante;
50 dollars to the Hospital at Santa Maria; 50 dollars towards the
building of the church of the Madonna di Santi Angeli. Several
legacies to friends in Zante, and to one, besides money, three small
bars of gold; to another, besides money, 12 silver forks and 12
silver spoons; *500 dollars for the redemption from captivity of the
young Turk named " Mahomet;"* 200 dollars towards the reparation of
the English gardens at Argals. To the poor of his neighbourhood at
Zante, 40 dollars. Various mourning rings, and to one executor a
diamond ring. To his brother, Sir John Cordell, a mare and a colt
(probably Barbs or Arabs), and the colt's furniture, a Turkish embroidered saddle, two Turkish bridles plated with silver and gilt, a
saddle-cloth of silver and gold; a head-stall plated with silver gilt; a
matè of silver gilt, and a waistbelt of silver gilt. This will was offi-
cially verified in Zante, 4th May, 1691, by the consul and four other
persons. Proved in London 24th November, 1691.

Will of Dame Elizabeth Cordell, daughter of Thomas Waldegrave, Esq., of Smalbridge, Bures, and widow of Sir John Cordell, the
second baronet, dated 2nd March, 1692. She was buried in the chancel
of Melford Church, 26th March, 1709. She directs that her body shall
be buried in a leaden coffin in the vault in Melford chancel, near to
the body of her late husband. She recites her husband's will, and
that the sum of £2,000 has been paid to her daughter Elizabeth, wife

of Thomas King, Esq., and provides for her daughter, Margaret Cordell, a similar portion. She bequeaths to her son, Sir John Cordell, the third baronet, the *great jewel of sapphire*, which her husband, who received it from his father, had left to her. Also her plate, linen, and other goods at Melford Hall, her gold medal, her seals, and the pictures she had bought since her husband died; excepting the portraits of her two daughters, which she gives to them respectively. She also leaves to her eldest son her best colt and her *wedding ring*. To her son-in-law, Thomas King, her double "Lowidore," her scrutore (escritoire), her silver filligrim sword, and case, and her second best colt. To her eldest daughter, Elizabeth, a diamond brooch, her father's picture set in gold, and the bed and furniture of the room she now occupies, and half her books. To her younger daughter, Margaret Cordell, her diamond earrings, watch, her mother's (Lady Waldegrave's) picture, the bed and all things belonging thereto, which she brought when she married Sir John Cordell; her olive-wood chest of drawers, the furniture in her closet, her coach, horses, silver teapot, silver spout-pot, six silver salts, and half of her books;—any gold not disposed of, to be divided equally between her daughters. Several small legacies. To the poor of Melford £3, to be given at the church the Sunday after her interment.

In this will occurs the first mention of a legacy of books in this family,—and this lady's children were, like most gentlefolk of that period, very illiterate: the two daughters both wrote and spelled most wretchedly. These ladies, after the death of their only brother, Sir John Cordell, the third baronet, without issue, became co-heiresses. Sir John, who sat in Parliament for the borough of Sudbury, was killed two years and a half after his marriage (with Eleanora, daughter of Joseph Haskin Stiles, merchant, of London), by a fall from his horse, and was buried at Melford 12th May, 1704, in the 27th year of his age. His eldest sister, Elizabeth, married, at about 17 years of age, Mr. Thomas King, of Thurlow, to whom his mother-in-law had left the legacy of a silver filigree-mounted sword,—a gift of ill omen to one who fell by the sword; for he was killed in a duel by Sir Sewster Peyton, of Peyton Hall, Boxford, in 1698, leaving an only son, who died unmarried. The other sister, Margaret, who survived her, inherited under her will, and became the sole owner of the Melford Hall estate. She remained single till she was about 34 years old, when Mr. (afterwards Sir) Charles Firebrace (eldest son of Sir Basil Firebrace, Knight and Baronet), who appears to have been a fast gentleman, and a good deal in debt, married the great heiress, who only survived her marriage about two years. The Earl of Scarsdale, Sir Samuel Barnardiston, and Mr. Baynes, of Acton, were left trustees of their only son, Sir Cordell Firebrace, who succeeded his father in 1727, and who was born 20th February, 17$\frac{11}{12}$ at lodgings in King

Street. Bloomsbury. His godfathers were the Duke of Beaufort and the Earl of Denbigh, and his godmother Lady Gage. He married Bridget, daughter of Philip Bacon, Esq., and widow of Mr. Eure, of Ipswich. They were married by special license, 25th October, 1737, in a room in the house of Severn, an upholsterer, in Jermyn Street, London, between the hours of six and seven in the evening.* Sir Cordell Firebrace dying in 1759, without issue, the estate soon after passed from his family. His widow married Mr. Campbell, of Lyston Hall, Essex.

A tradition has long attached to Melford Hall that at one time during the Rebellion, a company of Parliamentarian soldiers were quartered in what is called the "Long Gallery" of this house. This gallery, which still remains, is 135 feet long. Probably this so termed company of soldiers was in reality only a portion of the Colchester trainband commanded by Captain John Langley; and that this force was quartered at the Hall, and held possession of it until it had been finally stripped by them and their companions, and the rebel mob in Lady Rivers's time.

The traditional ghost which is said to haunt this house, has not reappeared for many years past, and the accounts of her former visits are very vague and conflicting. The ghost has generally been called "Lady Firebrace;" but as she is always described as an old woman, she could not have been Margaret, the wife of Sir Charles Firebrace, for that lady was only about 36 years old when she died. The only other Lady Firebrace of Melford Hall was Bridget, the wife of Sir Cordell Firebrace, who survived him, and married Mr. Campbell, of Lyston Hall, as her third husband. She lived to a good old age, and her life appears to have been quiet, respectable, and uneventful; and as she only died towards the close of last century, her identity must be rejected as being much too modern and uninteresting a ghost. If a ghostly visitor does really sometimes walk the house, it is more satisfactory to presume the shade to be that of the old Countess of Rivers, who, while in this world, saw much trouble, danger, and sorrow at Melford Hall. Anyhow this shadowy supposition is a more romantic one; and the era at which that lady lived, and the history which attaches to her, would make her, as ghosts go, a fairly respectable apparition.

So down to the present day more than three centuries have rolled over the "new house," with which Sir William Cordell replaced the old Hall, toning its once red and florid colour with venerable grey, but dealing lightly with the massive structure. Many strange scenes have been enacted in and around it, and it seems curious to picture to our-

---

* The certificate of marriage was signed by the Rev. Richard Warren, D.D., Rector of Cavendish.

selves how many various comers and goers, long passed away, have looked just as we do, at its picturesque features; or may, like us, have strolled about the surrounding ground, over which in olden time abbots and monks, knights and ladies, courtiers and royalty, have in their day walked or ridden, hunted and hawked.

After the long lapse of years since the maiden queen was entertained here, this century has again brought royal personages under the old roof. In its earlier part the Duke of York was a guest here; and of later years the visits of the Prince and Princess of Wales in 1865, and of Prince Alfred, the Duke of Edinburgh, in the following year, have added yet further links to its long chain of historical interest.

CHAPTER XI.

~~MELFORD HALL AND MANOR~~ *(continued).* †

THE general history of Melford is so identified with the church and the manor, and so many details connected with it have been already adverted to under those heads, that but little further remains to be told.

First, as to another old and distinguished family now passed away from here, but many of whose monuments remain in the church. The Martyns were very early residents in Melford; but whether at their first coming they lived where Melford Place now stands, does not clearly appear. The first of the family who is said to have settled at Melford was Richard Martyn, in the reign of King Richard II. (1377—1399), and who died 1438. He was succeeded by his son Lawrence, who died in 1460, and was buried at Melford, and relative to whom there is in the Abbots' Parchment Register a description of certain copyhold lands here, held by him from Abbot William Curteys, which formerly belonged to William Newman, and subsequently to Walter de Melford, his son, the copy of whose grant in Abbot Henry's chartulary runs thus, with this heading, viz. :—

CHARTA ABBATIS DE BURY, qua concessit xv Acras Terræ, jacentes in villa de Melford, p: redd 6ˢ· 8ᵈ· annuatim solveñd: aulæ de Melford, quas nunc occupat Laurencius Martyn.

(Translation.)

A.D. 1234—1248.

Know all men, &c. &c., that we Henry, D. G. Lord Abbot of St. Edmund's, and the convent of the same, have conceded to Walter de Melford, to hold by his homage and service, that grant which Hugh [*of Northwold*], formerly Abbot of St. Edmund's [1213—1228], made to William le Newman, father of the said Walter de Melford, of those acres of land in Melford, which Amfreda, the aunt of the said William, held after his death, to have and to hold to the said Walter, by a payment of 6s. 8d. annually to our Court of Melford, at four periods of the year; viz., at Easter 20d., at the Feast of St. John the Baptist 20d., at the Feast of St. Michael 20d., and at the Feast of St. Andrew 20d., in lieu of all customary services, except the general aid to us, and any other customs which the freemen owe in the said town, according to the charter which the said William had by the gift of the said Hugh the Abbot, and which he bequeathed to the said Walter, his son.

Witnesses hereto :

Sir HENRY DE HASTYNG.[*]
Master ROBERT DE SHARDELOWE.
ADAM DE PHALESHAM.
THOMAS at the Pond.
GILBERT DE FORNHAM.
WALTER DE BRADEFELD.
THOMAS DE WHEPSTED.
GALFRIDUS DE MELFORD.
BRIAN the Forester.
ANDREW the Gatekeeper.
STEPHEN DE FREUSE, Clerk.
And others.

This Laurence Martyn and his successors were great benefactors towards the rebuilding of Melford Church, as already noticed, and many of them are buried in the Martyn chancel. To one of them, Roger Martyn, who was born in 1526, and lived to the great age of 89, we owe the interesting account of the pre-Reformation church, its ceremonies, vestments, and furniture, all of which have been described in the history of the church. He was a stanch Roman Catholic, and eminently distinguished for piety and generosity. It is recorded of him that at one period, when there was a somewhat bitter persecution of the Catholics, he was obliged for a while to hide himself during the daytime under a hay-rick; but all his neighbours of Melford did everything in their power for his security and protection. He was a person of great learning and strict integrity, and Queen Mary offered to make him a Secretary of State; but in declining this honour his answer to her Majesty was that he felt entirely content and satisfied with the station he enjoyed in private life, and the sufficiency God had bestowed upon him. He died in 1615, without any appearance of pain, taking an affectionate last farewell of his family and friends whilst at dinner. He was a proclaimed recusant; but, probably owing to the respect in which he and his family were held here by all classes, he did not suffer as many mortifications and annoyances as commonly fell to the lot of those who were under the ban of recusancy. Till towards the close of the reign of James I., the laws against recusants

---

[*] In A.D. 1200, the family of this baron held of the Abbey of St. Edmund five knights' fees; viz., three in Lidgate, Blunham, and Harling; and two in Tibenham and Gissing. They had also large estates in Essex and Norfolk. Sir Henry, who was one of the great nobles, died about the year 1250, and was the ancestor of the Barons Hastings, Earls of Pembroke.

were not only in themselves very severe, but they were also constantly strained and abused through private malice. It was by law enacted that a recusant was not to go more than five miles from his dwelling-place, and two-thirds of his property was under forfeiture to the Crown, and he could not legally bequeath his lands; and where the penalty of the law had not been demanded or fully enforced, he was yet at the mercy of a host of informers, often his own neighbours, who were able to extort money from him by threats of further persecution. If a bribe was refused, they took his plate or any other valuables, or goods with impunity, knowing that he could not venture to complain for fear of further spoliation.[*]

In a list of recusants belonging to Melford in 1595, the following names are included :

"Roger Martyn, Esq: and Avys (?) his wyffe.

"Richard Martyn, Gent: and Alice his wyffe, sudjoners with the saide Roger.

"Matthew, a reteyner to the saide Martyn.

"Elizabeth Knapton, single woman, his servante.

"Clemens Payne, single woman, his servante.

"Peter Pattison, a reteyner; a vagrant.

"Richard Howe, yeoman, servante to Mr. Martyn, woorth three or fower skore pounds in goodes; a sudjoner at Stanstead."

There are also named as recusants in the adjoining parish of Acton in 1595 :

"John Danyell, Esq: and Margaret his wyffe.

"Henrye Danyell, Gent: and Margaret his wyffe.

"Also two reteyners with their wyffes."

Many of the Martyns were connected with the cloth trade, which appears to have been considerable and prosperous in Melford in the 15th and 16th centuries; and which probably dates here from the time of Edward III.

Until after the Reformation this family in a measure maintained a chapel, dedicated to St. James the Apostle, on Chapel Green, which was also called the Old Market, opposite their mansion of Melford Place. In the histories of Essex it is stated that the last-mentioned Roger Martyn is believed to have built the chapel dedicated to St. James, *which was attached to the family mansion on Chapel Green.* There appears to be a confusion here between the old pre-Reformation chapel and the chapel subsequently built attached to the house. Among the early mentions of the original St. James's Chapel, are bequests in wills thereto; as in 1464 by Roger Carter; in 1479 by

---

[*] Proceedings of the House of Commons, 1620-1; Statutes of 28 & 35 Elizabeth, and 1 & 3 of James I.

Richard Brightewe, in 1535 by Willam Norman, and in 1538 by James Hewer, Mr. Martyn's priest, who mentions in his will not only St. James's Chapel but also certain furniture therein. As Mr. Roger Martyn was not born till 1526, it is quite clear that these four bequests relate to a chapel which was built long before his time. In like manner, some of the Martyn wills also refer to the older chapel; for Richard Martyn, in June, 1500, makes a bequest to St. James's Chapel; and Roger Martyn, Bencher of Lincoln's Inn, who died 1542, by his will, dated April, 1535, left bequests for masses in St. James's Chapel; also a third part of the reversion of estates to the same; and this will contains this further curious legacy: " Item : · I bequeth to ·the heremytt now lying and being at Saynt Jamys Chapell, in Melford, an Aungell noble of Gold, for to bye hym therwyth a cote, and so to have every yere tene yeres immedyatly after my deth." Roger Martyn, the first of the two recorded " recusants," mentions certain church furniture, which at the time of the Reformation had been removed from St. James's Chapel and brought into his house; and in the Manor map of 1580, St. James's Chapel is shown as still existing, and being on the Green nearly opposite Melford Place. It seems therefore probable that after the Reformation the old chapel was disused and allowed to fall into decay; and the Martyn family (who continued to be Roman Catholics for two centuries afterwards) then erected, as part of their residence, a private chapel, which, like the old one, was dedicated to St. James the Apostle.

Later on, in 1567, Sir Roger Martyn, Knight, a mercer by trade, was Lord Mayor of London. He died 20th of December, 1573, and was buried in St. Antholin's Church, London.

This family was very consistent in its attachment to the Roman Catholic religion, and Sir Roger Martyn, knighted in 1625, who was the grandson of old Roger the recusant, was a recusant also; of whom it is recorded that by letters patent of King Charles I., dated 3rd January, 1627, the statutes against recusancy were in his case in a measure relaxed. He was a Cavalier, and suffered so much in the rebellion, that he afterwards petitioned both houses of Parliament for redress, setting forth in his petition that he and his ancestors had lived quietly among their neighbours in Melford for about 300 years. He died 1657, aged 71. His grandson, Sir Roger Martyn, of Melford, was created a baronet on the 28th March, 1667, at the age of 28, and he died 8th July, 1712, aged 73. His daughter, Tamworth Martyn, married Thomas Rookwood, of Coldham Hall. She was the niece of that Lady Monson on whose portrait over the hall chimney-piece at Coldham are the lines from Hudibras, commencing,

Did not a certain lady whip
Of late her husband's own lordship, &c.

2 Y 2

Sir Roger Martyn, the first baronet, who was buried here, purchased an annuity of 260 French livres for ever, issuing out of the Bank of Paris, and by deed dated 21st March, 1709, directed the same to be paid to some priest of the Roman Catholic Church, for him to distribute one-third part thereof among such poor Roman Catholics as may live in or near the parish of Melford, and the remainder to the support of the said priest, on condition that he reside in or near to Melford, and never fail to remember in the oblations of holy mass the dead and the living of the donor's family, saying before or after mass the *De profundis*, with the proper absolve for their souls, mentioning the last of the deceased, and shall make a more especial memory upon the obiit days respectively of himself, his ancestors, his lady, children, and descendants who shall be heirs of his estate, and Roman Catholics, according to a schedule annexed; but the whole number of souls whose obiits are to be commemorated are never at any time to exceed twenty-four, but the first eleven in the list, and the eight then living to be continued in perpetuity, The priest was to be appointed by the Provincial of the English Dominicans for the time being.

Four more baronets succeeded Sir Roger. The fourth baronet of the name, Sir Mordaunt Martyn, who died in 1815, sold the Melford Place estate, and with his son, Sir Roger, the baronetcy became extinct; and after a tenure of 400 years, the Martyns of "the Place" ceased to reside at Melford.

The old house, which was a timber-and-plaster erection, was pulled down about seventy years ago, when the present house was built a little in advance of the site of the old one. The chapel still, however, remains, but about ten feet have been taken off its length, and its exterior has been modernized to correspond with the new house. In the inside this chapel has been divided in its height to make a bedroom above the ground-floor, but the original waggon-roof, and the panelled ceiling, with cornice and beams carved with rich and bold foliage, remain still perfect, with the bright paint of various colours upon them.

Houses of the 16th and 17th century still exist in Melford, but almost every year decreases their number. Built of timber and wattle, the hand of time is heavy upon them; and as they decay they are pulled down to give place, alas, generally to the unpicturesque brick tea-caddy-shaped cottage-house of the present practical century.

Among old timber houses is that now called "Brook House," but of which the original name was "the Hart," and which was formerly wattled, but is now bricknogged between the timbers. The date on the porch, of 1610, is not that of the house itself, which is probably of older construction, unless it was rebuilt in the early part of the 17th century on the site of the older house. It is first mentioned as the Hart in the Manor map of 1613; but in 1575 one

William Dash lived either in this house or in the former one on the same spot, and he held the Hall Mill and meadow adjoining, and Bulney Moors, and he owned some meadow land of his own, and in the above year he paid tithe to the rector for twelve beasts, 4s. In 1581, one Fosset succeeded him.

In the drawing-room ceiling are large moulded girders and a finely carved diagonal dragon-beam.

The Bull Inn is among the oldest of the houses in the street. In the Manor map of 1580 it is shown as bearing the sign of the bull at that time; and though its exterior has been modernized, its carved and moulded girders, joists, and other portions of its ancient interior construction, remain well preserved.

With the exception of the time of the Rebellion, the names of its landlords in the 17th century are all recorded. In the year 1613 it was kept by William Drew; in 1660, Robert Barker held it; in 1667, Thomas Firmin; 1668, James Munnings; 1669, Thomas Dansy; and in 1672, one of the Drew family again, viz. Francis Drew, who held it till near the close of the century. In 1648, a troubled and unsettled time, its old hall-floor was stained with the blood of a murdered man. Few details of the event are handed down to us; but in the month of July in that year, a substantial yeoman of this place, a member of a family who had for a long time held considerable property in Melford (part of Windmill farm and Chesawick among the rest), by name Richard Evered, was murdered in the hall of the Bull Inn by a man named Roger Greene, who there stabbed him. The cause of the crime does not appear, but the verdict returned against Greene was wilful murder. Evered was buried within Melford Church, the 26th July, 1648.

Besides the Bull, there were the following inns in Melford in the seventeenth century. In the year 1678 there were, in Hall Street, the *White Horse*, kept by James Munnings, who had previously held the Bull; the *White Hart*, kept by John Hempstead; the *Fox*, by Peter Salter; and the *Bell*, by William Corker. On the Green there were the *Black Lion*, kept by Thomas Windle; the *Angel*, by widow Rebecca Gilson; and the *Eight Ringers*, kept by William Turner. This latter house had then recently changed its name, for in 1666 it was called the Great Oak Inn, with the same landlord. The present Falkland House, on the Green, appears to have been also once an inn, for in 1750 it is mentioned as "formerly the White Lion, and at one time the Eight Bells."

Many of the old timber-and-plaster houses, with their over-sailing upper stories, are picturesque specimens of timber architecture, now rapidly disappearing. It seems natural to conclude that "Clay-pits Pond" on the Green, an evidently artificial excavation, formerly supplied the clay for the old wattle-and-daub houses of this place;

and the name of this pond is mentioned in documents 500 years ago, and has remained unaltered to the present time.

As to the pretty village green, how many varied scenes have been enacted on it. We may dreamily fancy the olden weekly market from the far-back days of King John, clustered round the yet remaining base of the stone market-cross, as still so often seen in foreign towns; and also the ancient yearly fair existing from the same remote period, and continuing for more than 670 years down to the present day, gathering into it in bygone times, in the changing costumes of successive centuries, those buyers and sellers from the neighbourhood around, who flocked to this mart to dispose of their produce, or to lay in their annual stock of household wares, clothing, and salt food, the staple winter diet of the greater part of the community. We read of the yearly perambulations and processions; of feastings on the Green; and of the great gatherings for the church ales, which we find brought visitors to them from as far as Braintree and Ipswich.

And when the abbots were at their country seat here, how often they, with their retinues, must have passed over the Green between Melford Hall and the church. Look at this picture of the commencement of the 13th century, dim with age as it is. The bells of the (former) old church are going for daily mass, and there issues forth from Melford Hall gate, taking its way across the Green towards the church, a small group of notable people. A little in advance walks William de Gretingham, the seneschal, followed by a few armed retainers. Then comes the prominent figure, a remarkable-looking man. He is an abbot of St. Edmund's, of the Benedictine order, but little distinguished in dress, though greatly so in appearance, from those members of his abbey who follow him. He wears a black cloak and scapular over the white robe of his order. His tall frame is still upright and active, though time, thought, and care have turned snow-white his once auburn hair and beard. He is a silent man, and never laughs; but a faint smile, half sad, half amused, comes over his strongly-marked dignified features, as he listens to the shallow prattle of the handsome young monk who walks near him. This young man knows few cares in life, and though not overwise, is a favourite with every one, and laughs and jests from morn to night. Perhaps his little joke has been made in French, for he is a Norman by birth, and the Abbot, who has studied in the schools of Paris, well knows this man's native language. But young as he looks for his important post—for he is barely thirty years of age,—this is Herebert, the Prior of St. Edmund's. He is the Abbot's guest at Melford Hall, with some others of his fraternity. Mark the difference between the next two white-robed monks who follow. The one immediately behind the Abbot is an elderly, sedate-looking man, whose clever face, with its expression of intellectual power, is brightened up by a gleam of shrewd, irrepressible humour. His name is Jocelin de Brakelond, the Abbot's close friend, and formerly his chaplain; now the almoner of the Abbey, and its chronicler. Beside him walks a very different man. Look under his cowl. He is coarse and sensual-looking, and his red nose tells the tale of many a debauch, when he is not even amusing, but always a good-for-nothing, wicked old reprobate. It is morning now, and the drink is out of him, and he rolls sulkily along, very unwillingly on his way to church, in the wake of the grave, temperate Abbot, who, in old days, had been his subordinate and sub-sacristan, and who, of all persons in the world, he most hates and envies, and yet fears; perhaps with an instinctive foresight that the time is nigh at hand when he will be deposed by that man from his conventual dignity, and subside into obscurity and enforced temperance. His companion, Jocelin, glances sidelong at him now and then, and seems slily amused at the heavy morose look of his silent, red-nosed companion, who is none other than William the Sacrist, whose surname is Wardell. Then come Walter the Medicus, Manric the Chaplain, and good venerable old monk Dennis, formerly selected as a candidate for the Abbacy.

So they wend their way up the Green, towards the church, pausing for a moment to do reverence to the cross of the market; while every inhabitant they meet bends the knee and doffs the bonnet to the great spiritual and temporal lord, who, though gravely courteous to all, looks most kindly on those of the poorest and neediest among them; for he never forgets how poor he was in his youth, or what privations he underwent, and how sorely he himself needed charity, when, as an obscure monk, he was sent alone, on foot, in disguise, from St. Edmund's Bury, across Europe to Rome and back, begging his bread from door to door; and his rest, after his weary pilgrimage, was in the Abbey prison! Yet this man is Samson, the great and powerful Abbot of St. Edmund's.

And since that far-back time, in the course of centuries, how many cavalcades of knights, nobles, abbots, and even kings and queens, with their armed followings, may have passed over this village green, on the high road to and from the great Abbey and shrine of St. Edmund's Bury.

Later on in peaceful times again in ordinary village life, according to old English customs, until the middle of the 17th century, in addition to the sports of particular seasons, on Sundays generally, service in church being over, the inhabitants gathered on the Green for amusements; such as morris dances, leaping, vaulting, and archery, especially; for every village had its pair of butts, and Sundays and holidays were, by various enactments, the days appointed for men to practise archery, "as valyant Englishemen oughte to doe."* These

* Modern archers would find it difficult to shoot the distances required in former

were considered innocent and lawful Sunday recreations; for the distinction was made, that on that day bear and bull-baitings, interludes, and the game of bowls in public, were by law prohibited.* But in 1642 came the riot of the schismatic Puritan mob; the Green covered with a rabble of the scum of neighbouring towns; the sack and plunder of Melford Hall; the lawless fanatics tearing down the old market-cross, and venting their spite in mischief to the church; and then, under the austere Puritan rule, the Sunday amusements ceased, and the young no longer danced or sported on the Green.

Many personal names, still familiar in Melford, are traceable in different parts of the parish, hundreds of years back; but among those who have died out, interest attaches to an old family who lived in Hall Street (where the late Mrs. Atkins's fancy-work shop was), with whom a very tragical story is connected. The Drews were old residents in Melford, and many of them are buried in the church. Besides the two landlords of the Bull Inn, in the 17th century, a John Drew lived in Hall Street in 1665, and at the same date Edward Drew held property at Rodbridge. In the early part of last century there resided at Melford, in Hall Street, a Mr. Charles John Drew, an attorney in considerable practice, who, besides being possessed of a fair estate of his own, had married a lady of some fortune, by whom he had five daughters and one son, who was considerably younger than his sisters. The father, Charles John Drew, appears to have been a man of very sullen, morose temper, quarrelling with Deborah his wife, and his children; so that some years before his death his wife had separated from him. He then continued to live in what was called the "Upper House," while his wife and children went to reside in the "Lower House," some few hundred yards distant. Although the children visited their father often, yet he would occasionally pass the whole time of their stay without speaking to them; as he did when they dined with him on the day he was murdered. He always, however, after the separation from his wife, refused to speak to her, or even to consent to see her. Their only son, Charles Drew, who was born at Melford in 1714 (as entered in the Register), received but little education, and was brought up in boorish ignorance. He grew up a handsome young man, but he associated only with persons of the lowest class, some of whom were disreputable characters, such as smugglers and poachers. His mode of life being very dissipated, and his father keeping him short of money, he was constantly involved in debt and difficulties, till at last, galled by these embarrassments and by the taunts of his profligate companions,

days, which were for every man over 24 years of age, with the heavy war arrow, up to 220 yards; with the light-flight arrow, not less than that distance was to be shot at all. A bowstave was to be three fingers thick, and squared, and seven feet long.

* Wilkin's "Consilia." James I.'s declaration of 1617, concerning lawful sports to be used on Sundays.

he became so exasperated against his father that he resolved to procure his murder. With this aim, he consulted with one of his companions named Humphreys, a smuggler and a convicted felon, and endeavoured to bribe him to commit the crime. It appears probable that Humphreys consented at first, though at the last moment his heart failed him, and that, though he was an accomplice and witnessed the deed, he took no part in its execution. On the night of Thursday, the 31st of January, 1740, Drew and Humphreys met at the back gate of the Upper House. Drew carried a gun, which he hid in the orchard, while, accompanied by Humphreys, he went to the Lower House, where, in young Drew's room, they drank a bowl of punch together. They then returned for the gun, and Humphreys, now refusing to commit the murder, though he remained a short distance off, about midnight Charles Drew went to his father's house, when, having got the old man to come down to the door, he shot him with three bullets, or slugs, through the body, killing him instantly. No one in the house appears to have noticed the report of the gun, and the body was not found till six o'clock the next morning, when one of the servants came downstairs. Drew and Humphreys, directly after the commission of the act, went towards Liston, Drew hiding the gun in a hollow tree. Very early that morning Humphreys rode up to London, where he remained a few days, awaiting a letter which was to contain a bank-bill for £100 from Drew; but this letter not arriving, he returned to Melford, where he was shortly after apprehended, having in his possession the very gun which Drew had hid, and suspicion against him being strong, and his account of his proceedings unsatisfactory, he was committed to Bury Gaol on the charge of murder. Upon this young Drew became very uneasy, and offered large bail for Humphreys, and supplied him with money while in gaol. Soon afterwards Drew went to London to prove his father's will, and on his return journey, he heard at Sudbury, that the officers were searching for him, to apprehend him on suspicion of being concerned in the murder. He therefore went back to London, and remained there in hiding in a lodging at a cobbler's in Sheer Lane, near Temple Bar, under the assumed name of Thomas Roberts, until he was taken. A curious incident led to his discovery. Humphreys, while in prison, getting short of money, wrote to Drew, asking for £100; but not knowing where he was hidden in London, inclosed the letter to one William Mace, a smuggler, who went by the *alias* of Captain Ratt, begging him to find Drew and give him the letter. Mace, on receipt of this, went to a coffee-house in Holborn, and asked the people of the house if they knew one Mr. Drew: they replied that they knew him very well, and sent for a customer of theirs, who, though not related, happened to bear the same surname—Mr. *Timothy* Drew. Mace, who knew Charles Drew by sight, told him he was not the Mr. Drew he was seeking, and for whom he had a letter; but

Mr. T. Drew offering to assist in its delivery, Mace confided it to his care. It would seem that Mr. T. Drew, knowing the proclamation and reward published concerning the murder, had some suspicions as to this letter; he therefore privately opened and read it, and his conjecture being thus confirmed, after communication with a magistrate, from whom he obtained a warrant for Charles Drew's apprehension, and Mace having been taken into custody, he commenced a search to discover where the murderer was concealed, and eventually succeeded in taking him, under his assumed name of Roberts, at a disreputable house in Leicester Fields, and after examination before a magistrate, had him committed to Newgate. While in prison there, Drew attempted to tamper with one of the turnkeys, named Jonathan Keate, to aid his escape to France; and he executed an agreement, dated 16th March, 1740, promising this man an allowance, during life, of half his yearly fortune, besides a bond securing payment of £1,000. The matter was, however, disclosed to Mr. Akermann, the governor of Newgate, and the night before the escape was to have been effected, he removed Charles Drew into the secure cell called the Old Condemned Hold, in the prison. Though Mr. Akermann, in his evidence, takes credit to himself for this discernment, he altogether omits to state that he had obtained from his prisoner a promissory note for £50, and had retained Drew's seal with his coat of arms; but Drew, in a letter written the day before he was executed, affirmed, as a dying man, that Mr. Akermann had extorted these things from him. This original letter still exists. It is indorsed thus :—

"Mr. Charles Drew's note to me the day before he dyed—wrote in Bury Gaile. "E. HOWARD."

"Mr. Gent had of me £.10 just after my ffathers deth: which he is to account for. I payd Mr. Hart, in London, for ye rings I had made for a Punch ladell, which I gave away, and for ye proveing of ye will, which Probate and receipt Gent has. I dont know what Bonds, mortgages, or notes, he has in his hands. But I believe they will amount to about £: 800 or more. Mr. Purkins and Mr. Gent have each of yᵐ an account of what goods and money Jonathan Keate, Turnkee of Newgate, got from me, and Mr. Akerman has got my seal with my coat of arms, and when he removed me into ye place called ye old Condemned Hole, he made me give him a promissory note for Fifty Pounds, but gave me no consideration for it. I paid Mr. Hilyard half a guinea towards my ffathers shaving before left : and ye like sum to a carpenter of Stanted, but did [? not] pay ye whole bill. I am informed that some think that ye will I had proved was not ye will of ye latest date, I saw or new of. But I do affirm as a dying man it was.

"Mr. Gent told me he paid Mr. Moore five guineas after ye assizes."

As the writer of this letter is said to have been very ignorant and illiterate, he was probably assisted by some one in its composition.

Charles Drew was tried at the assizes at Bury St. Edmund's, the 27th March, 1740, was convicted of the murder of his father, Humphreys being admitted as king's evidence against him, and he was hanged there the 9th April, 1740, at the age of twenty-five.

After his execution his body was brought secretly to Acton church, and buried in the chancel during the night after he was hanged. The advowson of Acton had been part of the estate of his murdered father; and the vicar of Acton, the Rev. Charles Umfreville, was the murderer's brother-in-law, having married his eldest sister, Mary Drew.

Of the other sisters, Hannah married William Cawston, Deborah married Thomas Hickeringill, Ursula married John Hayward, and Bridget married John Gent.

The freehold estates in Melford and Acton, which were considerable, in one document being named as £600, and in another as £900 a year, were forfeited in course of law by the felony, but were restored by letters patent of the 17th of George II. to the five sisters of the murderer. Some forfeited copyholds, however, of which part of Bull Meadows formed a portion, lapsed to the lord of the manor of Melford, and still continue to belong to Melford Hall estate.

Another family name is of interest to us, though it is an uncommon one among Melford names. In 1521, Sir John Milborne, Knight, a draper by trade, who was a son of John Milborne, of this parish, became Lord Mayor of London. By his will, dated 10th of June, 1535, he left 6s. 8d. to each of the marriages of sixty poor maidens of Long Melford; and weekly, every Sunday, during a term of ten years, thirteen penny loaves to thirteen poor people of the same place, to the intent that they should come to the parish church of Long Melford, and there kneel down before the holy sacrament at the high altar, and say a Paternoster, an Ave, and a Credo for his soul. He bequeathed all his lands in Melford to Katharine Smyth, his cousin. He was buried in Crossed Friars' Church, London, but his body was subsequently removed to St. Edmund's, Lombard Street. So within fifty years Melford supplied to London two lord mayors, Sir John Milborne and Sir Roger Martyn. It also claims from among its people a Speaker of the House of Commons, who was Master of the Rolls and Solicitor-General; a Bishop; and an Abbot of Bury.

Near the centre of Hall Street stands the Chapel, with the Melford British Schools attached thereto. About the year 1724 a piece of ground was procured and a building for religious worship was erected on the west side of the street, and in May, 1725, the trustees were admitted to the manor of Melford. Its constitution is "Independent," or "Congregational," holding infant baptism, but admitting open

2 z 2

communion. The funds attached to this chapel and to Glemsford
Meeting are united, and designed for the support of the minister for
the time being of Melford cum Glemsford, who shall hold and teach
the above doctrines. There are some endowments in connection with
it. In 1726 Mrs. Row left £1,000, 3 per cents, of which the interest
is to be paid to the pastor for the time being of the Congregational
Church in Melford, on condition that he preach the Gospel once a
fortnight at Glemsford. About the year 1808 divers sums of money
belonging to the chapel were invested in the purchase of £413. 2s. 6d.
(3 per cent. reduced), the interest of which is paid to the minister of
Melford. The Rev. John Howard also left the sum of £366. 13s. 4d.
(3 per cent. consols), to the intent that the minister of Melford Chapel
should preach the Gospel at Foxearth once a fortnight. The interest
of these endowments amounts to about £55.

The Melford British Schools were built in 1862, at a cost of
about £350.

Although this chapel was not built till the year 1724, there appears
to have been a Nonconformist congregation here since the middle of
the 17th century, for a record of its founder exists as follows :—

"On that memorable day * when 2,000 ministers of the Gospel
left the Established Church of England, the Rev. John Wood was
ejected from that of Long Melford, in Suffolk; and though but little
is said of him in the history of that day, yet it is presumed that his
ministry was not without a blessing, as a number of pious persons,
not many years after, are said to have become a separate people, and
for some time assembled together for religious worship in a barn fitted
for that purpose, and several ministers are known to have laboured
among them occasionally."

There is a difficulty in arriving at a clear understanding as to
who the person was who is named in the detail above quoted; for
from its wording that the clergyman in question was ejected from the
church of Long Melford, the inference would be drawn that the
Rev. John Wood had been a rector of Melford of the Established
Church. Such, however, was not the case, for since the Reformation
there has never been a rector of that name. From October, 1643,
when Dr. Wareyn, after a tenure of twenty-five years, was ejected from
the living at the Rebellion, six Puritan ministers (mentioned in
Chapters III. and VI.) held the benefice till 1660, when Dr. Bisbie
was presented to the living, at the Restoration, and he held it till
1689. Again, Mr. John Wood could scarcely have been a curate of
Melford at the time named, for in 1662 the Rev. John Firmin was the
curate here, and so remained till 1663-4, when he became rector of

* 24th August, 1662, when the Act of Uniformity had passed, and the 2,000
ministers resigned, not choosing to conform to the Thirty-nine Articles.

Stanstead, and the Rev. William Steuckley then succeeded him as curate of Melford. The name, however, of a Rev. John Wood appears in the following records. In "The Humble Petition of the Ministers of the Counties of Suffolke and Essex concerning Church Government, presented to the Right Honourable the House of Peers on Fryday, May 29, 1646" (printed for John Wright, at the King's Head, in the Old Bayley, 1st June, 1646), among other signatures thereto is that of Mr. John Wood, an Essex minister. In November, 1664, a Mr. John Wood, *Clerk*, was appointed Governor of Melford Hospital. In April, 1664, Dr. Bisbie preached a funeral sermon for the wife of this Mr. Wood, - who is entered in the Register as "Minister." She was buried the 30th March, 1664, and in accordance with the custom of that period, when every respectable person of sufficient means bespoke and paid for a funeral sermon, on terms varying according to social degree, from 10s. to £2, Mr. Wood, the Minister, paid the Rector £1 for the funeral sermon. This Mr. John Wood was buried at Melford, the 23rd September, 1671, when 10s. were paid for his funeral sermon.

The few following little jottings concerning Old Melford possess a certain amusing quaintness. The first is an account of the culture, on a large scale, of a crop of saffron, grown by Henry Waddington, the tenant, on Cranfield farm, 1676–7, which was evidently regarded here as an important experiment, and purporting to be a lucrative one, as it was tithed by composition, as though the crop had been wheat. Whether it proved a good speculation we are not informed, but the inference is against it, as there is no record of any repetition of this crop; and we are told that it was an expensive one to grow, requiring much labour, tillage, and manure. In olden days saffron was much used, and greatly esteemed, as well for a dye and a drug as for cooking purposes. Between the years 1515 and 1557 saffron was cultivated in Cambridgeshire to a considerable extent; and small quantities were then also grown in parts of Suffolk; but as the following description from a tithe-book is the first entry of it as a titheable crop grown at Melford, we may presume that it was an unusual experiment here; but on Ford Hall farm there was a field called in 1580 the "Saffron Pane," now corrupted into "Seven Penn." The account runs as follows:

"In 1676–7 there were 40 acres or more of arable land in the farm called Cranfield sown with safflower [saffron], the flowers gathered and tithed as though the crop were corn, also the hop-ground at the same place was sown with the same. This was described as the manured bastard saffron, thus: It hath sundrie leaves next ye ground, without any pricks, or with very few white ones at ye corners of ye leaves and divisions, among wh. riseth a strong hard round stalke, three or four feet high, branching itselfe up to ye top, and at their ends

a great scaley open head, out of which thrusteth forthe marygold
yellow threds of a most orient and shineing colour, wh. being gathered
in a dry, warm time, will abide in the same delicate colour for a very
long time.   It flowers in the end of July or beginninge of August, and
the seed is ripe about the end thereof.   It is put into broths and meats
to give them a yellow collour, and used for dyeinge of silk into a kind
of carnation colour, and yts seed used in physick for purgation.".

Cranfield farm was then valued by the poll bill at £90 a year, and
contained 150 acres of arable, besides meadow land, and two acres of
hop-ground.
  At about the above-named time hops were grown in various parts
of the parish; for in 1662 we find mention of hop-gardens as above,
and also near the church; two near Westgate Lane; one at the back
of the houses on Melford Green; at Kentwell Hall; Melford Hall; and
Melford Place; at which latter the quantity is named as one acre; and
the price of the hops grown here was then estimated at tenpence per
pound.   The hop-ground at Melford Hall, 1a. 1r. 3p., existed before the
year 1580.   Hops were first introduced into this country from Flanders,
in 1524.
  Another crop, now unknown here, must have been grown in the
sixteenth century, and some fields in the parish still bear the name of
"Hemplands."   An Act of the 24th Henry VIII. enacted that every
person occupying land for tillage, for every sixty acres under plough,
should sow one quarter of an acre in flax or hemp; so that there
would have been about fifteen acres of this crop in Melford.   Bishop
Latimer, referring to this in one of his sermons, says, " the quantity, if
doubled, would be far too little to grow the hemp required to hang all
the thieves that be in England."
  Although, from very early times there are records of perambulations
of the bounds of the parish, some of which are minute in their detail,
there is no mention of the Gospel Oak which stands at the boundary of
the parishes of Melford, Lavenham, and Acton, being called by that
name till about 1650.   The trees, known in many places by this same
designation, appear to have derived their name from the fact that they
stood in some marked situation, where the perambulating procession
used to halt, and some short appropriate sentences or prayers from the
Gospels were in former times read or said; thanks for the fruits of the
earth were offered to God, and the curse for removal of neighbours'
bounds or doles was repeated; and very commonly the ciii. psalm was
sung.
  The following are only a few selections of some of the more quaint
or interesting entries from the parish registers of baptisms, marriages,
and burials.   They are thus headed :—

The REGISTER of alle the CHRISTNINGS, BURIALS, and MARIAGES, which have bene at Millford since the first yeere of the Rayne of our most gratious Queene Elizabeth, by the grace of God, of England, France, and Ireland, Queene: which was the 17th daye of November, Anno Domini 1559.

Memorand : that ther is noe mencion in the ould Regester Booke of any that were Baptized before the month of January, 1559.

REGISTER OF CHRISTNINGS.

The word baptized was not generally used till after 1583.

1559, January 1.—Anne, daughter of Robert Jue [*first entry*].

1561, June 15.—Thomas, son of Thomas Kerington.

A family long settled here.

1562, and after.—There are many entries of the Martyn family.

1665, March.— Fourteen persons, six bastards, were all baptized at riper years.

Some of the entries are very circumstantially minute in their details, as,

1668, November 24.—Rebecca, daughter to Edw⁴ Haynes, Gent, and Rebecca his wife, borne the 13th day, half an hour past 9 o'clock at night, being Wednesday; baptized yᵉ 24th.

1706, January 19.—John Betts baptized. Parents unknown.

1708, March 23.—Elizabeth, who was left at John Kemp's door. Parents unknown.

1714, October 6 —Charles, son to Charles John Drew and Debora his wife.

The infant here baptized murdered his father in 1740, and was hanged at Bury.

1717, January.—John, base child of Lucy Martin. Reputed father, Sir Roger Martyn.

1717, October 4.—Sarah, daughter of John Moore, Esq. [of Kentwell Hall] and Maria his wife, born September 18th, at about one o'clock in ye morning.

1720, May 13.—John [son of the same], born 21 April, at about 10 in ye morning.

1722, October 28.—John, base son of Alice Barker. Reputed father, Sir Roger Martyn.

The following child has a fine lot of names :—

1743, November 11.—Philip George Rex Tomson, son of Philip and Susan Boreham.

1767, September 15.—Richard, son of Richard and Mary Phillips.

This child was privately baptized by the name of Richard ; but when he was received into the Church, his sponsors gave the name of William.

In the register of marriages (as in those of baptisms and burials) there occur numerous entries of names connected with the principal families formerly resident here, and of others connected with Melford; but to record many of them in detail would be tedious. In the marriage register there is a hiatus without entries, between February, 1652, and October, 1660. The first entry of marriage appears to be on the 13th September, 1570, between William Grigge and Anne Phywale.

The following are extracts from the burial register, some of which are quaint, and serve to throw additional light on the domestic history of Melford.

REGISTER OF BURIALS.

Motto thereto in the heading: "Calcanda semel via Leti." ("The way of death must once be trodden."—*Horace.*)

1559, October 5.—John, sonn to Richard Milson [*the first entry*].
1560, February 30.—Ould mother Margrett.
1560, May 22.—Audrey Dyster.
1560, September 30.—John and Joan Matin.
1561, August 24.—Townsend Clopton.
1562, August 17.—William Clopton, Esq.
1564, January 7.—John Cordall.
1564, April 12.—John Dyster.
1567, February 12.—Thomas, sonn to Sir William Cordwell.
1578, April 16.—Margaret, wife of Roger Martin, Esq.
1582, December 8.—Roger Martin.
1590, May 26.—Lawrens Martin.

In 1593 this parish suffered from a visitation of the plague, which in that year doubled the mortality, 23 persons dying in the month of August.

1593, August 8.—Elizabeth Doe, of ye plauge.
1593, August 17.—Margery Doe, of ye plaugue.
1593, August 18.—Fortune Doe, of ye plaugue.
1593, September.—Four members of a family named David. [Several other families lost two or three of a household.]
1594, June 13.—Mrs. Anne Allington.
1596, July 20.—Robert Allington.
1598, June 8.—John Road, drowned at the Hall Milne.
1598, December 11.—Goodwen, a prentice with Thos: Ambrose.

In 1600 an entire family was swept away in a few days.

1600, March.—A whole household buried this month.
    March 2.—John Heble (or Hibble).
     ,,   4.—William Heble.
     ,,   7.—Mary Heble.
     ,,   9.—Elizabeth Heble.

1600, March 12.—Sarah Heble.

    „   15.—Clement Heble [the father of the family].

    „   16.—Alice Heble [the mother].

1600, June 25.—Stephen Cheap, a Master of Arte, and somtymes scholemaster of this towne.

1600, August 29.—William Dash, Innkeeper of the Harte in this towne.

This is now Brook House, and W. Dash lived there in 1575, when he also held the Hall mill.

1601, February 8.—Thomas Mountaine, a stranger.

1602, March 16.—A childe founde dead in the Hall Mill damme.

1603, May 1.—Dorrathee Doughty.

    „   16.—Tobias Doughty.

In the year 1604 the plague ravaged many parts of England, and in London there died of it in that year 30,578 persons. Melford was swept by this visitation, which, in five months, carried off a fearfully large proportion of the inhabitants. In this dreadful plague, which in July was at its height, Mr. Gilbert, the rector, lost four children; and the mortality in the parish rose to 148, out of which number, 119 died of plague in five months.

1604, May.—The Plauge begunn : 15 buried this month.

    June.—14 persons buried of the Plauge.

    July.—Widow Sander, *a searcher;* Margery, daughter of Mr. William Gilbert, minister, and 53 others, were buried of Plauge.

    August.—Ann, daughter to Mr. Gilbert; Prudence, daughter to Mr. Gilbert; and 34 others were buried of the Plauge.

    September.—Jerrom, sonn to Mr. William Gilbert.

This Plauge lasted fro ye beginninge of May to ye ende of September, in which 5 monthse the tottall that dyed and are her regystred, were juste one hundred and nineteene men, women, and children.

Heavy as the mortality was in this village, carrying off about one-seventh of its inhabitants, this epidemic was light as compared with the fearful loss in the village of Eyam during the great plague of 1664, when the almost incredible number of 267 persons were swept away out of a population of only 350, as recorded by Mompesson, the rector, who survived. Melford appears to have escaped the visitation of this latter plague, which was spread from London over England, for there are no entries of death from plague at that date.

1606, June 11.—Agnes, daughter to Mr. William Gilbert.

1607, October 21.—Robert, whose parents wer not knowne.

1607, November 8.—Thomas, sonn to Mr. William Gilbert.

1610, March 4.—Jane, a Recusant [no surname is given].

1610, December 15.—John Coe, the elder.

1610,   „   21.—John Coe his sonne, a blind man, teacher in the arte of musique.

1611, July 27.—John, a strange boy, killed with a carte.

1611, September.—Margery, daughter to Mr. William Gilbert.

1612, February.—Henry Lacy, a scholler, and one of the brethren in the Hospitall.

1612, July 4.—Anne Jones, widow to Mr. Dr. Jones, somtimes minister of this parishe.

1612, September 11.—Mr. Robert Darcye, brother unto the R^t Honble Lord Darcye of Chich, allso St. Outsiddes [St. Osyth], of Essex.

1613, July 7.—John Hogg, a passenger fro St. Edmond Bury.

1615, May 16.—John, sonn to Michell Kinge, minister.

1615, August 7.—The wife of Michell Kinge.

1615, August 7.—Mr. Roger Martin, Esquier.

1616, February.—The Lady wiffe of Sir Wm Clopton, K^t.

1617, August 30.—Ales [Alice] Wyat, daughter to Richard Wyat, borne at Sudbury, and late servant to Mr. Thomas Johnson at Pentlowe, was drownd by accident at Hunn Mill, Melford, the 28th of August.

Hunn Mill was on the site of the late paper-mill, and appears to have been a dangerous spot, for there are other entries of persons being drowned there.

The next is an extraordinary record.

1618, April 26.—Rose, the wiffe of William Sheap, was delyvered of a childe with 2 faces, 4 armes, and 4 legges.

1618, August 7.—Mr. William Gilbert, Minister of the parishe.

1621, September 17.—James Flower dyed of the fallinge of his horse.

1621, December 2.—Mr. Lawrence Martin.

1624, August.—Sir James Croft, K^t.

1625, August 8.—Mr. William Mayor, Minister and Curate of this towne.

The family of Mayor, long settled here, owned Proudes farm, now in Melford Place.

1627, July 29.—Jonathan, sonn to Theophilus Gee, was drownd at the Bridge in the Hart Lane, and after the Crowners Quest had sate on him he was buryed.

1627, November 30.—Elizabeth, wife of Mr. William Gilbert, minister.

This is the last entry of the Gilbert family.

1629, April 28.—Mr. Lowell, Curate under Mr. Doctor Wareyn.

1631, April 9.—Thomas Dike, a straunger, which dwelte at Bury.

1632, May 13.—Thomas Lees, an anciente Batchelor.

1632, November 28.—A childe borne by a travellinge woman in Kentwell barne.

1634, February 18.—A childe of William Swannes was drowned nere to the Parsonage, on whom the Crowners queste sate.

This was at the old Parsonage near Cranmoor.

1634, June 20.—William Page, a London prentice borne in this towne, comminge fro London, was drowned in the fflogin pit, on whom the Crowners queste sate.

Query: What place is here meant?

1634, April 21.—Richard Loxton, master of Musique and servant to the Right Worrshipful Sir Roger Martin, K^t.

1634, August 7.—William Aggas, an anciente Batchelor.

1634, December 7.—William Chapman, who was drowned in the ffloggin pit, on whom the Crowners quest sate.

1638, August 22.—Edward Drew and Mary his wife, having been married 43 years, laye both sicke and dyed: and wer both buryed in one grave in the Churche.

1639, May 26.—William Malkin, of Ballington, falling from his horse and so dyeing, the 25th being Satterday: on whom the Crowner sate with his jury.

The following entry requires interpretation.

1642, January 19.—Alice Spencer, who was ript in the churchyarde, and found to dye of a timpany.

There are very few entries in this Register for 1643, only two for 1644, and none from April 1644 to April 1646; part of the unsettled time of the Rebellion.

1646, September 11.—Thomas Wood, a souldier.

1648, February 25.—Thomas Smith, the butcher.

1648, February 28.—Roger Garrold, which was killed with an empty carte overthrowinge uppon him, as hee was fetchinge of a loade of wood home for his master, was founde smuthered under the carte whele with the wane on his backe: on whom the Crowner sate.

1648, July 26.—Richard Evered, who was stabbed by one Roger Greene standinge in the Bull hall: on whome the Crowner satt, and was founde willfull murther, and was buryed within Melford Churche.

The Evereds were a family of substantial yeomen, who owned considerable property here.

1648, September 13.—Richard Phipps, a Corperall under Captaine Puckle, was marcheing from the seege of Colchester, and fell sicke and was buryed.

1649, May 28.—William Mendham, who was killed falleing off a carte loaden with timber and the wheele wente over his head and so forwarde to his thigh: on whome the Crowner satt.

1651, February 7.—Edmond Rule founde dead in the strete as he was running home, and judged to dye in a swoone by the Crowners quest.

1653, January 2.—Mr. Samuel Bordman, Rector.

In another handwriting is written over this entry the word "Intruder." Mr. Bordman was the second of the Puritan ministers here during the Rebellion, having succeeded Mr. Seth Wood in 1648.

1656, October 5.—Sir Roger Martin.

There are very few entries for the years 1656, 1657, 1658, 1659, and none until October in 1660.

1661, July 9.—Robert Warren [Wareyn], Doctor of Divinitie. Buryed at Borley.

Dr. Wareyn was deprived of this living during the Rebellion, but reinstated at the Restoration. He was a very old man.

1661, June 1.—The Honored Lady Sisilla, wife to Sir Thomas Darcy, Knight and Barronett.

1663, June 20.—Maudlin Chaplaine drowned at Hun mill.

1664, January 24.—Robert Cole, gentleman and Sergeante at Law.

1664, March 30.—The wife of Mr. [John] Wood, minister.

1676, February 21.—Robert Green.

He was married a few days before his death.

1682, August 1.—John Foster, executed at Chelmsford.

His body was buried here.

1683, August 2.—Sir Thomas Robinson, Bart., buryed in the Temple Churche, London.

He was killed by jumping out of a window during a fire.

1684, June 6.—Sir Lumley Robinson, Bart. [son of the above], dyed in the parishe of Saint Margaret, Westminster, and was buryed in the Abbey Church, Westminster.

The Robinsons were the then owners of Kentwell Hall.

1684, August 3.—Mr. Thomas Witham, Rector of Chilton.

1689, September 26.—Charlotte, daughter to Doctor Nathaniel Bisbie, and Elizabeth his wife.

1693, October 10.—Henry Palmer, a souldier.

1695, May 16.—Nathaniel Bisbie, D.D.

He was for many years rector of Melford, but was deprived of the living in 1689, for refusing to take the oath of allegiance to King William III.

1695, August.—Mary Barker, a towne childe.

A pauper: they were generally farmed out, to be supported by some person in the parish.

1706, March 24.—Roger Albourn, a Jew.

1712, May 21.—Mrs. Margaret Firebrace.

1714, June 16.—A traveller founde dead in the parishe: his name unknowne.

1716, April 23.—Thomas Smith, the butcher.

1717, April 18.—John, base son to Lucy Martin: the reputed father Sir Roger Martin.

This child had been born in January of the same year.

1718, November 17.—A travellinge woman at the George Inne, whose name is unknowne.

1729, September.—Dearmont Smallbones, a traveller.

1736, February 28.—William Smith, a husbandman.

1736, March 23.—Mrs. Mary Bisbie.

Query: Was she a daughter of Dr. Bisbie, who died 1695?

1738, February 20.—Dame Elizabeth Barnardiston, widow to Sir Robert Barnardiston, Bart.

1740, February 3.—Mr. Charles John Drew.

He was murdered by his only son on the 31st January, 1740, who was hanged in the April following.

1741, September 8.—Mr. Nathaniel Bisbie, son of the Rev⁴ Nath. Bisbie, D.D., formerly Rector of this parish.

1748, August 14.—Martha, daughter of the Rev⁴ Nath. Bisbie, D.D.

1765, October.—Mrs. Mary Armstrong, a stranger from the kingdom of Ireland, who desired to be buried at 5 in the morning. What clothes she had on when she died was never taken from her body, and was buried therein.

1767, August 29.—Tollemach Bacon, Attorney at Law.

1793, May 14.—Mrs. Anne Johnson, relict of the Rev⁴ Mr. James Johnson, late Rector of this parish.

1812, January.—Sir Harry Parker, Bart., aged 77.

1830, April.—Sir William Parker, Bart., aged 61.

1856, March.—Sir Hyde Parker, Bart., aged 71.

Parish surveyors or waywardens may like to read a few notes of their predecessors' expenditure here, more than 300 years ago.

There are many such accounts existing in the parish archives, of which the following may serve for an example:—

Surveyor's Account for the year 1554.

Payde to Newman for mendyng of Hall Myll Brydge, and
makyng of a worlegyg   .   .   .   .   .   .   22ᵈ.

This Hall-mill bridge was probably a foot-bridge, where the present foot-bridge now is; for there was no bridge for horses or carriages over the ford in the road till 1762, and since then the original narrow bridge appears to have been widened. In 1778 there is a bill for the repairs of the pales of the *small bridge*, and somewhat later a tender for building a new bridge there (probably the present one) for sixty guineas. The whirlegig was a turnstile to prevent horsemen riding over the foot-bridge.

Payde to Wayd for mendyng the Brydge entryng uppon the Grene, and for tymber for ye same, and the worlegygg . . . . 2ˢ·

Query: Where was this foot-bridge? Was it at the side of the road near the present Hall lodge, where a ditch ran down the side of the Green, and so into the moat?

To ye Smethe for yerne worke of ye sam worlegygg . . 14ᵈ·
To Fletcher for castyng of ye dytch by ye grene . . 4ᵈ·

Probably by the side of the road where the iron rails now are.

To Codde for 1 dayes worke, mete and drynke, abowte the Brygges at Hall Myll . . . . . . 6ᵈ·

Here we see the wages of that day, inclusive of food and beer, 6d. a day here; in 1670, more than a century later, the Churchwardens' books show the wages of a master carpenter as 22d. a day, his journeyman 20d. a day, his apprentice 12d. a day; and bricks were then 12s. a load.

Payde for ditchyng, and sett for ye same dytche, at Prowde's Brygge for the savyng of ye comon footpathe 5ˢ· 6ᵈ·

At the Water Lane, opposite Melford Place.

For a plancke for ye brygge . . . . . . 2ᵈ·
For ye myddle worlegygg and ye Poste and Yerne . . 21ᵈ·
For xxi lodes of stones gatheryd . . . . . 3ˢ· 6ᵈ·
For mendyng of hye wayes beyond the Hye Crosse at one tyme . . . . 14ᵈ·
For carrying xliii lodes of gravel unto ye same Hye-wayes 12ˢ· 10ᵈ·
For xxii lodes . . . . 6ˢ· 6ᵈ·
For xxx lodes . . . . 8ˢ· 9ᵈ·

Melford must have been in advance of its day in road-making, even though it was only a small portion of the highway that was repaired, for road-metalling was almost unknown then, the common plan being, when a hole in the mud road became very bad, to throw into it a few faggots, and some earth or a little gravel on the top. This continued till near the end of last century. Arthur Young, in his journey through Suffolk, describes the state of the roads in his day, and the miseries of travelling, even so late as that time. In some of the more ancient deeds there are in various instances reservations of right to *cut woods*, in order to mend the roads adjacent thereto. Horace Walpole, Lord Orford, mentions that in 1755 the road into Ipswich was so bad that his chaise was overturned in the mire at the entrance of the town.

Total expended this year, 1554, on the Hye wayes and Brygges of Melford, ye summe of . . . . £:2: 9ˢ·:4ᵈ·

In 1555 the roads appear to have lain fallow.

Expended in 1556 . . . . £:2: 6ˢ·: 0ᵈ·
Expended in 1557 . . . . £:2: 0ˢ·: 0ᵈ·

Again the following years,

1575 expended	£ : 1 :	7ˢ· :	4ᵈ·
1577 ,,	1 :	14 :	9
1578 ,,	2 :	3 :	6
1580 ,,	2 :	8 :	10

Now (in 1871) the length of roads in Melford (inclusive of former turnpike) is seventeen miles, and the expense of their maintenance by the Highway Board, £126.

Truly Melford has mended some of its ways since olden days.

As to old church fees, in 1662 the following fees appear to have been the customary dues to the parson :—

For everie Buryal in ye Churchyarde there is sixpence due to ye parson.

For Funeralle sermons preached, 10ˢ· per sermon.

Churcheings of Women, fourpence for everie woman.

Marriage dues (when the Banns are published), for everie couple 2s. 6d.

Publishyng ye Banns in order to their marriage, 1s.

If a buryal happen to be in ye Churche, or in any of ye Chancells, the Parson hath for his due 2s. 6d. But if within yᵉ Cordell's Vault or the Cloptons Chappell, never less than 10 shillings.

In the account of the Manor many examples have been given of old rents. The following rentals of land on the Melford Hall estate may be interesting for comparison. Taking the year 1613 as an example throughout, the rents were thus :—

Ford Hall Farm was let at the rate of 9s. 4d. per acre, and to supply yearly to Melford Hall one seam (8 bushels) of peas.

Wash Farm, which, until 1580 was called Hundens, and after that Holpotts, and Howlpits, was let at 10s. per acre, and four seams of oats a year.

High Street Farm, formerly called Martyns, was let at 6s. 3d. per acre, two seams of peas a year, and to do for the landlord three days' carting.

Lodge Farm was at that day all in Melford Hall Park, and was not made into a farm till 1734.

Old Park Farm was let at 9s. 3d. per acre. This had been then recently converted to tillage from being a deer-park.

Duntons Farm, formerly De Dontons, was let at 6s. 4d. per acre, and two seams of peas a year.

Slough Farm, formerly called Lavenham farm, was let at 6s. 10d. per acre, and ten seams of oats a year.

Ralsdon Hall Farm at 5s. 10d. per acre.

Valley Farm, formerly called Harolds Well, was let at 5s. 7d. per acre, and four seams of oats a year.

Stoneylands, Masons, and part of *Nether Bulney* were let at 14s. per acre.

Part of Bulneymoors was let at 11s. per acre.

Bull Lane Farm and *the Burtons* were divided, and parts belonged to other owners, so that their rents cannot well be ascertained. But a large portion (161 acres) of Bull Lane farm, formerly called *Garnetts,* was let at 7s. 6d. per acre, and twenty seams (160 bushels) of barley, one seam of peas (8 bushels), four loads of straw, and four days' carting to Melford Hall.

Parts of what is now Mr. Westropp's land, then called *Prowdes,* eighty-seven acres, were let at about 12s. 9d. per acre, but with also the following curious additions in kind ; viz., *one bushel of oysters, two couple of Habberden* (small-barrelled cod-fish), *two couple of green fish* (? fresh-water fish, as pike), and four days' labour of a man. This land formerly belonged to Melford Hall, but was sold in 1710.

Part of Mr. Mill's farm at Rodbridge (then belonging to Melford Hall) was let at about 5s. 6d. per acre. Some of this was low meadow.

Roughedge Farm (then also belonging to this estate, afterwards sold to Kentwell), at this time containing 308 acres, was let at a trifle less than 7s. per acre.

Part of *Clapstile Farm,* 104 acres, then also belonging to Melford Hall, was let at 7s. 8d. per acre, and two seams of oats.

Cuckoo Tye Farm, now Mr. O. Brand's trustees (also part of Melford Hall, but sold away in 1710), was let for 7s. 1d. per acre, and four seams (32 bushels) of oats, one load of straw, and two days' carting.

The farm at Stallhouse Tye, now Brand's trustees, with part of *Clark's and Highlanders,* was let for 4s. an acre, *one flitch of bacon,* and two days' carting.

The Hall Mill, then held by one William Crismas, was rented at £18 a year.

Wissendale Mill was out of lease and has no rental named. It then belonged to Melford Hall.

The total extent of the land let in 1613 was 2,960 acres, at a rental of £1,196. 2s. 8d., or an average of 8s. per acre, various houses and cottages included.

The total rental of the estate was £1,236 a year, besides 739 acres of park, woods, and lands in hand, to which no rental was estimated; and which would have raised the value of the estate to about £1,500 a year.

Comparing then roughly the rental value of Melford land for three periods, each about 300 years apart, we find the following curious results. Thus, in the year 1287, arable land was let at about five pence per acre; pasture land somewhat higher. Again, in 1613, land produced a rent of about eight shillings per acre. Now, in 1872, the gross estimated value of the land of the parish for poor rates, which may approach somewhat near, but below the rental value, shows an average of about £1. 8s. 6d. per acre.

The area of Melford parish is computed at 5,185 acres, of which 87¼ are waste; such as rivers, roads, &c.: these roads and lanes extend over 17½ miles; and 54 acres are occupied by the Great Eastern Railway lines within the parish. Of the total amount of acreage, 3,512 acres are arable land; 1,083 acres grass land; and 374 acres woodland. The gross estimated rental of the parish is £15,012, and its rateable value is £11,389.

Since the commencement of the present century this place has increased very considerably not only in prosperity but also in size and population. In 1813 it contained about 550 houses and cottages, and its population was 2,200. Now (1872) the dwelling-places have increased to 661, and by the census of the last three decades the population has been raised as follows:—In 1851 the number of inhabitants was 2,587; in 1861 it amounted to 2,870; and the census of 1871 has brought the population up to 3,046; showing an increase of 846 persons in less than sixty years.

It is almost a vain endeavour to make any close comparison in statistics of births, deaths, and marriages at former dates with the present time; because, although we can find in the Church Registers the numbers of baptisms, burials, and marriages, these are not always complete records; and further, we have no accurate knowledge of what the population of Melford was before the present century, to form a basis of comparison of the several rates. The following is only given as a matter of curiosity and speculation, so far as the figures may be contrasted.

	Burials.		Baptisms.			Marriages.
Year 1560	. . 56	.	. 42	.	.	(A.D. 1571) 8
1561	. . 29	.	. 43	.	.	(A.D. 1572) 8
1562	. . 41	.	. 36			

If the present birth-rate might be taken as any comparative guide to the population, the number of inhabitants of Melford at the period of the years 1560 to 1570 would have been about 1,140 persons; and this rate appears to have remained unaltered in the year 1590, when, however, the death-rate was swollen to 81 burials, owing to an

3 B

epidemic of plague ; and again in 1604 the like pestilence swept over Melford, and 148 persons, or nearly one-seventh of the whole population, were buried that year.

Between the years 1660 to 1680 the average rates were,

Burials.	Baptisms.	Marriages.
40	48	18

On a similar calculation to the above, the population of Melford at that period would have been 1,370 inhabitants.

Between the years 1760 to 1770 the average rates were, burials 45, baptisms 53 ; making the population in those years amount to 1,509 persons.

Recapitulating, we thus arrive at the following apparent results ; viz., that in the year 1560 the population of Melford numbered 1,140 inhabitants ; in the year 1660, 1,370 ; in the year 1760, 1,510 ; in the year 1813, 2,200 ; in the year 1861, 2,870 ; in the year 1871, 3,046 ; and the last year's registers show the rates of burials 47, births 107, marriages 20.

The number of inmates to a dwelling now averages more than in 1813, and additional cottage accommodation is much needed to meet the requirements of the increasing population, as well as the demands of sanitary improvement. Notwithstanding the overcrowding of the poor, the place is a healthy one, and the death-rate here shows on an average a very small mortality : in 1872 only sixteen per thousand ; and the birth-rate of the last year was considerably more than double the death-rate. The oldest person belonging to this parish is now in the union house. She is a single woman, named Susan Debenham, who has attained the great age of at least 104 years, having been baptized in Melford Church on the 15th June, 1768. She is, notwithstanding her extreme age, still active and in good health.* In common with most country places, education was until recently at a low ebb here. There were two small dame-schools supported by old charities, and a day-school was held in the Lady Chapel of the church. This desecration has happily now ceased, for in 1860 handsome and adequate National Schools, with masters' and mistresses' houses attached, were erected at a cost of £2,118 ; and another school and mistress's house was built privately (by Sir W. Parker), in 1862, to supply the want of the detached hamlet at Bridge Street.

This record of Old Melford draws to a close. Those who have patiently waded through these details of the far past, will have seen

---

* Since the above was written, Susan Debenham, commonly known as Old Sally, has died of sheer old age, the 17th March, 1873, having lived to near the extraordinary age of 105, if she did not quite attain it, though it is probable she did, as she was *baptized* in June, 1768.

that, from various favouring causes, besides its natural pleasantness and fertility, this place has always been of more importance than an ordinary country village.

The lords of the greater part of its soil, ever since the Conquest, have been persons of rank and importance, some of whom have left their mark in the two great halls, as well as in the noble church and the charitable hospital.

The fostering care of the powerful Abbey of St. Edmund shielded Melford and its inhabitants in old times of trouble and violence; for, prior to the Reformation, men feared to injure the property of the Church, or those immediately under its protection. The religious houses seem to have been easy landlords, too, and their vassals and tenants throve and dwelt in safety; though in the narrow groove of the feudal system social advance was slow. When the Reformation revolutionized society, the old restrictive barriers broke down, and with increased civil and religious freedom, trade flowed in; and here, as elsewhere, the traders gradually enriched themselves, and took their stand as a prominent and important class. Many proofs are left to us that the old fathers of this parish dearly loved, and were proud of their birth-place; with yet more reason those of the present day should be grateful that their lot has been cast in such a pleasant place and in times of advanced civilization. Our village, as we still humbly style it, though its older folk called it a town, and in America it would be a "city," seems inclined to hold its own in the onward course; for, with its junction lines of railroads, gasworks, foundry, factories of various kinds, good schools, advanced husbandry, increasing trade and prosperity, and many other advantages and improvements, Melford steadily progresses; and though much still remains to be done for the amelioration of its working classes, and for the completion of its moral and social education, yet Melford past need not be ashamed of the child of its old age,—Melford present.

INDEX.

A

ABBEY of Bury receives grant of a tithe from Melford, 5; its relation to St. Saviour's Hospital, ib.; chartulary of Melford property and manor, ib.; various chartularies, 256; its protection to Melford, 371.

Abbots of Bury: Anselm (1119–1148), 5; Leofstan, second abbot (1044–1065), 31; Sampson, tenth abbot, 7; Sampson de Botington (1182–1211), ib.; Abbot William Codenham, 25.

Acton (see Aketune).

Aelmus [Anselm?] Ernoldhug, his dues to the Abbey of St. Edmund, 2.

Aketune [Acton], mentioned in original grant of Melford, 2.

Album Registrum of the Abbey of Bury, 7.

Album Registrum, sive Vetus Registrum, of the Abbey of Bury, 7.

Aleyn, alias Carver, Thomas, rector of Melford, 34.

Alfric, Earl, first patron of Melford Church, 30; his grant of the manor of Melford to the Abbey of St. Edmund, 1; his possessions in Suffolk and Essex, ib.

Allington, Mistress Jane, sister of Sir William Cordell, patron of Melford Church, 31.

Almack, Mr., superintends restoration of windows in Melford Church, 47.

Amyot, Simon, feoffee in lands under Colet's Charity, 188.

Anchorites and anchoresses, singular extract from John Clopton's will relative to them, 175.

Ancient extinct bequests, 212.

Anselm, Abbot of Bury (1119–1148), receives a grant from Pope Eugenius III., 5; grant to from Melford, ib.

B

BABBER, or Babergh, the letes of the hundred of, 2.

Babergh (see Babber) hundred, its description in Domesday Book, 3.

Babwell, original name of the Hospital of St. Saviour, 7.

Bacon, Sir Robert, possessor of the Album Registrum of the Abbey of Bury, 7.

Bailey, Charles, his facsimiles of portraits in Melford Church, 69.

Barker, John, his charity, 201.

Barker, Margaret, wife of John Barker, 87.

Barnsley, Thomas, priest, rector of Melford, 33.

Barrell's charity, 199.

Benedict the Jew, advances money for the repairs of the Abbey of St. Edmund, 11.

Bequests, ancient extinct, 212.

Berde, John, his bequest, 219.

Bisbie, Nathaniel, M.A., rector of Melford, 36; his account of Melford Church in 1688, 38; of the window inscriptions, 47; of the ancient plate, furniture, vestments, and utensils, 76; his rectorship, 158; his published works, 165.

Bonard, Richard de, Juliana his wife, Adelina and Juliana, their daughters, 17.

Bordman, Samuel, puritan minister of Melford, 157.

Brasses and monuments in Melford church, 124.

Bretyner, Sir William, his bequest, 224.
Brideoak, Ralph, puritan minister of Melford, 157.
Brightewe, Richard, his bequest, 215.
Bungetown, demesne tithes of, to the Hospital of St. Saviour, 9.
Bury, the hospital of St. Saviour at, 5, et al.
Butts, Robert, rector of Melford, 36.

C

CARTER, Roger, his bequest, 214.
Cavendish (see Cawndish).
Cawger, John, his bequest, 226.
Cawndish (or Cavendish), John, his bequest, 225.
Cawston, Robert, warden of the church of Melford, 77.
Celestine III., pope, bull of, relative to St. Saviour's, 14 ; his bull approving of the charter of St. Saviour's Hospital, 7.
Chaplyn, William, his charity, 194.
Charities of Melford, 187.
Chelsworth, demesne tithes of, to the hospital of St. Saviour, 9.
Church house, the, of Melford, 153 (see Melford Church).
Clopton Chantry in Melford church, 128.
Clopton family : John, his wife and children, fresco portraits of, in Melford church, 127 ; memorial of, in Melford Church, described in Bisbie's MS., 39 ; inscription to, 43 ; his will, ib. ; sent under arrest to the Tower, 44 ; his character, ib. ; lease of lands belonging to St. Saviour's, 25 ; memorial of, in Melford Church, 43 ; inscription to, in window of Melford Church, 54, 55 ; brass in Melford Church, 126 ; monumental stone slabs to, 127 ; allusions to, 56, et al. ; quaint wills, 174.
Cobbold, Edward, rector of Melford, 36.
Cobbold, John, Esq., patron of Melford, 32 ; son of John Cobbold, Esq., patron of Melford, ib. ; Chevalier, M.P., patron of Melford, ib.
Cokefelde, demesne tithes of, to hospital of St. Saviour, 9.
Colet, Robert, his charity, 187.
Colet's Charity, 188.
College, or Parish Priest's house, 151.
Colman, Simon, his bequest, 226.
Congregational Chapel at Melford, 355.
Cordell Family : Margaret (wife of Sir Chas. Firebrace), patron of Melford, 31 ; Sir

Robert, Bart., patron of Melford, ib. ; Sir John (son of Sir Robert), patron of Melford, ib. ; Sir John (son of Sir Robert, second of same name), patron of Melford, ib.; Sir William, Knt., patron of Melford, ib. ; tomb of, in the chancel of Melford Church, 136 ; his history, 326.
Cordell wills, 337.
Corder, John, his charity, 195.
Coxe, William, B.A., rector of Melford, 34.
Cradock, Mr., of Rickinghall, Suffolk, his possession of the Nigro Registro de Vestiario, 12 ; of the Register of Walter Pinchbeck, ib.
Crameworth, Thomas, priest, rector of Melford, 34.
Crane window in Melford Church, 57.
Culford, demesne tithes of, to the Hospital of St. Saviour, 9.
Curson window in Melford Church, 58.

D

DANSIE, Nicholas, incident relative to, 75.
Danvers (see Dame Annes Fray).
Darcy, name of, in epitaph of Sir William Clopton, 126 ; Sir Thomas, Bart., of Kentwell, 129 ; Dame Sissellia, his wife, ib. ; Alice, 43, 174.
De Botington, Sampson, Abbot of Bury, his character, 10 ; his death, 12.
De Cavendish, William Wygor, rector of Melford, 33.
De Chedworth, Thomas, rector of Melford, 32.
De Clayber (Simon, priest), rector of Melford, 32.
De Cornwall, Sir Edmond, his connection with Kentwell, 168.
De Draughton, Simon, rector of Melford, 32.
De Ely, Allanus, priest, rector of Melford, 32.
De Gray, John, Archdeacon of Cleveland, 17.
De Gretingham, William, Steward of St. Edmund's, 10.
De Grynesby (or Grymesby), Thomas, rector of Melford, 33.
De Harlinge, Richard, rector of Melford, 32.
De Neville, Hugo, signatary to King John's Charter to St. Saviour's, 16.
De Norwold, John, Abbot, his chartulary, 1, 230.
De Otlauia, Theodorus, rector of Melford, 32.
De Stanton, Henry, rector of Melford, 32.
De Stuteville, William, signatary of King John's Charter to St. Saviour's, 16.

De Tottiugtune, otherwise Sampson de Botington, *q.v.*

De Turnham, Robert, signitary of King John's Charter to St. Saviour's, 16.

De Valence, holder of the manor of Kentwell, 5, 169; his descent, *ib.*; death, and burial in Westminster Abbey, *ib.*

De Welborne, rector of Melford, 32.

Denston portrait in Melford Church, 58.

Dent, Giles, or Ægidius, rector of Melford, 34; memorial of in Melford Church, 41; window in Melford Church, 59.

Dispute of 1199-1200, between St. Saviour's and the vicar of Melford, 17.

Dister, John, memorial of, in Melford Church, 42.

Domesday book, reference to Melford in the, 1, *et al.*

Dowe, John, feoffee in lands under Colet's Charity, 188.

Dowsing, William, his works of demolition, 59; his diary, 60.

Drew, the family of, 352; murder of Charles John, *ib.*

Dyer, *alias* Turnour, Henry, *q.v.*, 214.

Dynham, John, Lord, inscription to, in window of Melford Church, 54.

E

EDWARD THE SIXTH, king of England, resigns his patronage of the living of Melford to his sister Queen Mary, 31; his grant, 194.

Elizabeth, queen of England, presents to the living of Melford, 31; visit to Sir William Cordell, 325.

Elmeswell, demesne tithes of, to the Hospital of St. Saviour, 9.

Elmsethe, anecdote of, 311.

Elveden, demesne tithes of, to the Hospital of St. Saviour, 9.

Elys, Thomas, manorial free tenant, 42; his lands, *ib.*

Emma, Queen, possessor of the liberty of St. Edmund, 1.

Enachdunensis, Johannes, rector of Melford, 33.

Enachdun, or Enaghdun, now Annadown, John, Bishop of, 34.

Eugenius III., Pope (1145-1153), Bull granting to the Abbey of Bury a tithe from Melford, 5.

Extinct bequests, 212.

F

FAIR and market at Melford, 246.

Farman, John, his bequest, 219.

Felton, Henry, LL.D., rector of Melford, 36.

Firebrace, Lady (wife of Sir Cordell Firebrace), patron of Melford, 31; Sir Cordell, Bart., patron of Melford, *ib.*; Sir Charles, Bart., 341.

Firmin of Sudbury, his demolitions, 60.

Foote (*see* Fote).

Fote, Gafferye, his charity, 200.

Francis, Bransby, rector of Melford, 36.

Fray, Dame Annes, portrait of, in Melford Church, 56.

Frewer, Miss, her charity, 197.

Frodo, his connection with the manor of Kentwell, 5.

Fyska, John, his bequest, 222.

G

GALEUS, grant from his land to Abbot Anselm, 5.

Gente, John, his bequest, 215.

Germayn, Thomas, his bequest, 215.

Germon, Rosa, her bequest, 215.

Gilbert, Claudius Salmasius, Puritan minister of Melford, 157; Rev. Wm., presented to Melford by Queen Elizabeth, 31; son of Paganus, his dues to the Abbot of St. Edmund, 2; William, clerk, rector of Melford, 35.

Goscelinus, almoner of St. Edmund's, 10, 311.

Groome, Nicholas, his bequest, 215.

Gualterus, tenant of the Abbot of St. Edmund, 3.

Guilds, ancient, at Melford, 78.

H

HAGIOSCOPE, or squint, in Melford Church, 129.

Hall and Manor of Melford, 228; plunder of, 333.

Hall, Symond, his charity, 202.

Hannibald, William, rector of Melford, 34.

Hanus, his holding mentioned in original grant of Melford, 2.

Harset, Robert, inscription to, in window of Melford Church, 52; his bequest, 217.

Hede, Thomas, bequest of his wife, Margaret
    Heede, 215.
Heede, Margaret, her bequest, 215.
Hengham, Abbot Richard, window in Mel-
    ford Church, 59.
Henry VIII., king of England, patron of
    Melford, 31.
Herebert, his signature as prior of St. Ed-
    mund's, 9; the contest for the office of
    prior, ib.; his character according to
    Jocelin de Brakelond, 10, 350.
Hermeus, sub-prior of St. Edmund's, 9.
Herringswell, demesne tithes of, to the hos-
    pital of St. Saviour, 9.
Hervey de Clerbec, his holding mentioned in
    original grant of Melford, 2.
Hervey, Master, vicar of Melford, 17, 18;
    Walter, vicar of Melford, 32.
Hewes, James, his bequest, 224.
Hill, Christopherus, rector of Melford, 35.
Hill, John, his charity, 189.
Holy Trinity, the hospital of the, 206.
Hoo (see Howe, Roger).
Hoore, Sir Thomas, his bequest, 225.
Horningsherd, demesne tithes of, to the
    hospital of St. Saviour, 9.
Horset (see Harset).
Hospital of the Holy Trinity, 206.
Howard, Elizabeth, portrait of, in Melford
    Church, 55; William, portrait of, in
    Melford Church, ib.
Howe, Roger, window inscription to, in
    Melford Church, 51; his bequest, 216.
Howell, James, clerk of the Privy Council,
    331; his description of Melford House
    and grounds, ib.
Howes, John, his bequest, 221.
Hubert [Walter], archbishop of Canterbury,
    14; his confirmation of the endowment
    of St. Saviour's, 7.
Hugh the clerk, rector of Melford, 32.
Humphry, Edmund, rector of Melford, 35.
Hungerford, Lady, her window in Melford
    Church, 56.
Hyacinthus Bubo, Cardinal (see Celestine
    III.).
Hyll, or Hill, John, inscription in Melford
    Church, 42; his charity, 189.

I

Icklingham, grant from, to the hospital of
    St. Saviour, 9.
Ickworth, Sir Richard, witness to the charter
    of St. Saviour's, 10.

J

Jocelin de Brakelond's Chronicle, descrip-
    tion of the character of Herebert, 10;
    of Sampson de Botington, ib.; his own,
    311.
John, bishop of Norwich, his confirmation of
    the charter of St. Saviour's Hospital, 7;
    diocesan of Melford, 12; his confirma-
    tion of the endowment of St. Saviour's,
    Bury, 13.
John of Oxford, Dean of Salisbury and
    chaplain to Henry II., 12.
John, king of England, sanctions the
    charter of St. Saviour's Hospital, 7, 12;
    terms of other charters, 15.
Johnson, James, rector of Melford, 36.
Jones, Ralph, rector of Melford, 35.
Joslin, Ralph, window in Melford Church,
    56, 57.
Juliana, wife of Richard de Bonard, 17.

K

Kertz, John, his bequest, 216.
Kentwell Chapel, in Melford Church, 128;
    manor of, held by De Valence, 5, 169;
    its connection with the manor of the
    Monks, 23; in possession of Frodo, 167;
    extract from Domesday Book relative
    thereto, ib.; comes into possession of the
    Clopton family, 170; the monks and
    Manor-house, 172; successive possessors
    of, 174; Hall, description of, 183;
    painted glass coats of arms therein, 184.

L.

Lady Chapel of Melford Church, 43, 141.
Le Bigod, Hugh, son of Roger le Bigod,
    16.
Le Bigod, Robert, [supposed] son of Roger le
    Bigod, 16.
Le Bigod, Roger, Earl of Norfolk, 16.
Leofstan, abbot of Bury, 1; second abbot
    (1044-1065), patron of Melford, 31.
Leprosy common in the Middle Ages, 8;
    persons afflicted with it excluded from
    St. Saviour's Hospital, ib.
Leroo, the Rev. John, patron of Melford, 31;
    rector of Melford, 36, 151.
Lewysham, Thomas, rector of Melford, 34.
Leynam, Dame Margaret, window in Melford
    Church, 56.

Longespée, William (*see* William, Earl of Salisbury), 16.
Loveday, Richard, memorial of, in Melford Church, 44.
Lucius II., Pope, allusion to, in grant to the Abbey of Bury, 5.
Lutons, ancient name of Kentwell, 25, 170.

M

MALLET, Henry, chaplain of Queen Mary, 31.
Mallett, Henry, rector of Melford, 35.
Maltby, Johannes, rector of Melford, 35.
Manor of the Rectory of Long Melford, 145; survey of, 1287, *ib.*; remains of the Rectory manor-house, 150; new building of, 1832-3, 151.
Manor of the Monks in Melford: originally belongs to the Hospital of St. Saviour, 23; early lease of it to a tenant, *ib.*; the " rectory " of Melford included in it, *ib.*; deed of 1372-3, 24; of 1501, 25; to Sir William Clopton, *ib.*; to Richard Hoo (1516), 28; to Robert Coleman, *ib.*; to Robt. Simon and James Coleman, *ib.*; dissolution of the abbey, 29.
Mansel, Nicholaus, priest, rector of Melford, 33.
Maps of Melford: Amyce's, of 1580, 39; Pearse's, of 1613, *ib.*
Maresc, William, Earl of Pembroke, 16.
Martyn aisle of Long Melford Church, 124.
Martyn, Charles John, the Rev., M.A., patron of Melford, 32; rector of Melford, 37, 144.
Martyn, Lawrence, of Melford Place, 41; inscription in the Martyn Chapel, 42; and his wives, tomb of, 124; feoffee in lands under Colet's Charity, 188; his bequest, 221; his will, 125; grant to him, 344.
Martyn, Marion, wife of Lawrence Martin, 124.
Martyn, Richard, co-conveyancer in Colet's Charity, 188; his bequest, 220; his will, 124; memorial of in Melford Church, 42.
Martyn, Roger, bencher of Lincoln's Inn, 124; his will, *ib.*; his bequest, 222, 347.
Martyn, William, tavern held by, 41.
Mary, Queen of England, patron of Melford Church, 31.
Mayor, Dr. John, his charity, 195.
Mayor family, 88.

Melford, ancient houses in, 348; charities, 187; tithe from, to the Abbey of Bury, 5; its contribution to the use of St. Saviour's, 7; register of christenings, burials, and marriages, 359; its area, 369; examples of ancient rentals, 367; births, marriages, deaths, and population, *ib.*; charter of King John relative thereto, 15; demesne tithes of, to St. Saviour's Hospital, 15; derivation of the name, 1; fair and market, 246; Hall and manor, 228; inns, 349; royal visit to, 325, 343; list of the rectors of, 32; population of, A.D. 1250-1300, 37, 369; village green, 350.
Melford Church, original endowment of, 30; the ancient fabric, *ib.*; the Lady Chapel, *ib.*; dedication, *ib.*; architecture, *ib.*; patrons of the church and living, *ib.*; rectors of, 37; restoration of in the 15th century, 38; description of, by the Rev. N. Bisbie (1688), 38; gutted for restoration in 1867-8, 39; inscriptions in, according to Bisbie's account, *ib.*; designer of the present fabric, 45; appearance of the ancient church, *ib.*; the Martyn Chapel, *ib.*; the painted glass, 47; restoration of the east and west windows, *ib.*; window inscriptions, *ib.*; the east window described, 62; the west windows, 64; Mr. Roger Martyn's description of, 70; its gradual decadence, 74; ancient plate, furniture, vestments, and utensils, 76; rebuilding of the tower (1711), 123; monuments and brasses, 124; Martyn aisle, *ib.*; the Kentwell Chapel, or Clopton Chantry, 128; the hagioscope or squint, 129; the chancel, 136; dispute as to the seating, 164; the Lady Chapel, 141; its conversion into a public school, 142; condition of the church in the present century, 143; the rectory pew dispute with Sir Robert Cordell, 163; restoration of the church, 144.
Meryell, Richard, his bequest, 213.
Milborne, the family of, and its connection with Melford, 355.
Mildenhall, charter of Richard I. relative thereto, 15.
Monks, the manor of, in Melford, 5; Manor-house, 172.
Montgomery, Sir Thomas, portrait of, in Melford Church, 55; window in Melford Church, 57.
Monuments in Melford Church, 124.

Moore's Charity (1700 ?), 196.
Moore, John, his charity, 195.
Moore, Robert, his bequest, 226.
Moryell, Roger, memorial of, in Melford Church, 40 (see also Meryell).
Mydwell, John, rector of Melford, 34.

N

NELL, Isabella, conveyance from. for Colet's Charity, 187.
Nelys lands (so-called), bequeathed to the parish, 41 ; the Colet Charity, 187.
Newton, demesne tithes of to the Hospital of St. Saviour, 9.
Newton, William, rector of Melford, 31, 35.
Nigro Registro de Vestiaria, and the charter of Abbot Sampson, 12.
Nigrum Registrum of the Abbey of Bury, mention in, of bull ratifying grant to Abbot Sampson, 9.
Nonconformist chapel in Melford, 356.
Norman, William, his bequest, 222.
Norton window in Melford Church, 59.
Noye, William, Attorney-General, 331.

O

OAKES, Abraham, LL.D., rector of Melford, 36.
Ogard window in Melford Church, 57.
Oliver, Mrs. Harriett, her charity, 195.
Original grant of the manor of Melford, 1.
Ormingesalen, mentioned by clerical error in King John's Charter to St. Saviour's, 17.
Osmund's Charity lands, 197.

P

PAKENHAM, demesne tithes of, to the Hospital of St. Saviour, 9.
Parish Priest's house, or the College, 151.
Parker, Capt. Hyde, R.N., mural monument of in Melford Church, 136.
Personal names in ancient records connected with Melford, 352.
Peyton window in Melford Church, 58.
Plandon, Richard, his bequest, 216.
Puritan ministers of Melford, 157.
Pygot, Richard, portrait of in Melford Church, 55.
Pykenham, William, rector of Hadleigh, 177.

R

RADULPHUS DE HODEBOVILLE, his holding mentioned in original grant of Melford, 2.
Rectors of Melford, 32.
Rectory Manor in 1287, its contents, 4, 145 (see Manor) ; pew, dispute as to, with Sir Robt. Cordell, 163.
Redgrave, tithes of, to Hospital of St. Saviour, 9.
Register Pinchbeck, quotation of Bull of Eugenius III. in, 5.
Richard I., king of England, charter of, relative to Mildenhall, 15.
Richards, Roger, his bequest, 213.
Rickinghall, tithes of, to the Hospital of St. Saviour, 9.
Rivers, the second Earl, son of Sir Thomas Savage, patron of Melford Church, 31 ; Countess of, 333.
Rookwood window in Melford Church, 58.

S

SAHAM, demesne tithes of, to the Hospital of St. Saviour, 9.
Sampson, tenth Abbot of Bury (1182-1211), commences to build the Hospital of St. Saviour, 7 ; his foundation charter of St. Saviour's, 8 ; his character, as described by Jocelin de Brakelond, 10, 350.
Sainthill, Peter, Puritan minister of Melford, 157.
Savage, Sir Thomas (Viscount Savage of Rocksavage), patron of Melford Church, 31.
Shawe, Gyles, his bequest, 227.
Skone, otherwise Skyrne, q.v.
Skern or Skeyne, William, rector of Melford, 35.
Skerne (see Skyrn).
Skyrn, or Skene's Charity, 193.
Smith, Richard, his charity, 194.
Smyth, John, and another Smyth, hold lands in Melford in 1442, 41.
Sparrow, Robert, his family, 40 ; his bequest, 214. [Robd. Spar'we and Marion his wife, ancient inscription in Melford Church, 40.]
Spurdens, the Rev. William Tylney, patron of Melford, 32 ; his possession of the Bisbie MS., 38.
Stanton, Henry de, rector of Melford, 32.
Story, John, clerk, rector of Melford, 34.

Stourton, Robert, rector of Melford, 35.

St. Edmund, the liberty of, acquires the manor of Melford, 1 ; the carta de libera warenna (charter of free warren), 251.

St. James's Chapel on Chapel Green, 73, 346.

St. Saviour's Hospital at Bury : its history, 5 ; bull of Pope Eugenius III., granting a tithe from Melford, ib. ; its foundation, 7 ; grants and confirmations of its endowments, ib. ; the Album Registrum, ib. ; intention of its foundation, 8 ; Abbot Sampson's charter, 9 ; its abbots, ib. ; Abbot Sampson's character, 10 ; confirmation of the original endowment by the diocesan of Melford, 12 ; bull of Pope Celestine III., 14 ; charter of King John, 15 ; dispute between the Hospital and the vicar, ib. ; its manor becomes known as the Manor of the Monks in Melford, 23 ; dissolution of the abbey, 29.

Story window in Melford Church, 58.

Suit of 1199–1200 relative to lands in Melford, near Cranmoor, 17.

Surveys of Melford Hall and Manor, 299.

Swyfte, Thomas, his bequest, 214.

T

Tendrixg, Lady, relict of Sir Thos. Clopton, 173 ; her bequests, ib.

Thetford, tithes of, to the Hospital of St. Saviour, 9.

Thresher, Clemente, bequests, 86, 99, 221.

Tiversall, demesne tithes to the Hospital of St. Saviour, 9.

Trainband of Melford (circa 1683), 121.

Turnour (alias Dyer), Henry, his bequest, 214.

Turret, or Tirret, priest, 80.

Tyleneye, demesne tithes of, to the Hospital of St. Saviour, 9.

Tymworth's, Abbot, Chartulary of 1386, 238.

Tyrell window in Melford Church, 57.

W

Walgrave, Elizabeth, window in Melford Church, 56.

Wallis, William, M.A., rector of Melford, 37.

Walter, sacrist of St. Edmund's, 9.

Warden, Thomas, rector of Melford, 34 ; window inscription to, 48.

Wareyn, Robert, M.A., D.D., rector of Melford, 35 ; sequestered from his benefice, 155 ; succeeds to it on the Restoration, 157 ; burial, 364.

Wareyn, Rose, her bequest, 214.

Waryn, John, co-conveyancer in Colet's Charity, 188 ; his bequest, 213.

Waryn, Richard, window inscription to, in Melford Church, 51.

Wellen, S., Archdeacon of Wells, 17.

Wentworth, Peter, clerk, rector of Melford, 35.

William, Earl of Salisbury, 16.

Wilton, Stephanus, rector of Melford, 33.

Widgar (see Withgar).

Wirlingworth, demesne tithes of, to the Hospital of St. Saviour, 9.

Wirlingwood, mentioned, vice Wirlingworth, in King John's charter of St. Saviour's, 17.

Wisgar (see Withgar).

Withgar, or Wisgar, otherwise Widgar, custodian of the liberty of St. Edmund's, 1.

Wood, Seth, Puritan minister of Melford, 157.

WYMAN AND SONS, PRINTERS, GREAT QUEEN STREET, LINCOLN'S-INN FIELDS, W.

CPSIA information can be obtained at www.ICGtesting.com
Printed in the USA
BVOW02s1114041114

373599BV00023B/834/P

9 781295 807536